H•O•T Credits

lynda.com Director of Publications: Tanya Staples

Editor: Karyn Johnson

Production Coordinator: Myrna Vladic

Compositors: Rick Gordon, David Van Ness

Copyeditor: Darren Meiss

Beta Testers: Christy Bond, Paul Jordan

Proofreader: Evan Pricco

Interior Design: Hot Studio, San Francisco

Cover Design: Don Barnett, Owen Wolfson

Cover Illustration: Bruce Heavin (bruce@stink.com)

Indexer: Julie Bess, JBIndexing Inc.

Video Editors and Testers: Auriga Bork, Charles Ramirez, Charles Ward, Eric Geoffroy

H•O•T Colophon

The text in *Final Cut Pro 5 H·O·T* was set in Avenir from Adobe Systems Incorporated. The cover illustation was painted in Adobe Photoshop and Adobe Illustrator.

This book was created using QuarkXPress and Microsoft Office on an Apple Macintosh using Mac OS X. It was printed on 60 lb. Influence Matte at Courier.

About the Author

Larry Jordan is a post-production consultant and Apple-Certified Trainer in Digital Media with over 30 years experience as an award-winning producer, director, and editor with network, local, and corporate production credits. Based in Los Angeles, he's a member of both the Directors Guild of America and Producers Guild of America. Visit his Web site at **www.larryjordan.biz**.

Acknowledgments

This book would not be possible without the generous support and encouragement of Lynda Weinman, of Lynda.com. Thank you, Lynda, for giving me this opportunity.

This book grew out of my production and teaching experience where I discovered my students had a good understanding of a piece of the process, but were weak on how all the different pieces fit together. The goal of this book is to provide both the detail and the greater context of where post-production fits in the grand scheme of storytelling. And this, I think, is what makes my book different from the other Final Cut books that are available. This is more than a "tools" book, it's a book on using Final Cut in post-production. Anyone can teach you how to use a hammer, this book goes further and helps you understand how to use that hammer to build a house.

I also want to thank Karyn Johnson at Peachpit Press for shepherding this book through production, Tanya Staples of Lynda.com, for her kindness and understanding, and two amazing beta testers, Paul Jordan and Christy Bond, for making sure my exercises and explanations were accurate. Thanks, too, to Michael Cooper for the great illustrations, Darren Meiss for his copyediting, and Nathan Dugi-Turner for some killer original music.

Finally, I want to thank Mike Hatchett, Waide Hoyt, and Tim Manning at Standard Films (**www.standardfilms.com**) for providing absolutely stunning snowboarding footage, as well as the still image of Fred Kalbermatten (photographed by Sullivan). Joel Suttles at CNN ImageSource (**www.cnnimagesource.com**) for the hurricane footage. And Brian Greene, of GreeneHD Productions (**www.greenehdtv.com**) for the spectacular *Moscow on Ice* footage. Brian, this just goes to show that chance meetings at NAB can actually amount to something. Thanks!

Lynda Weinman's | **Hands-On Training**

Final Cut Pro 5

Includes Exercise Files and Demo Movies

lynda.com

By Larry Jordan

Final Cut Pro 5 Hands-On Training

By Larry Jordan

lynda.com/books | Peachpit Press
1249 Eighth Street • Berkeley, CA • 94710
800.283.9444 • 510.524.2178 •
510.524.2221(fax)
http://www.lynda.com/books
http://www.peachpit.com

lynda.com/books is published
in association with Peachpit Press,
a division of Pearson Education
Copyright ©2006 by lynda.com

ISBN: 0-321-37571-8

0 9 8 7 6 5 4 3 2 1

Printed and bound in the
United States of America

Dedication

To my parents, Dean and Lee Jordan.

Table of Contents

Introduction

Welcome to the newest edition of *Hands-On Training* for Final Cut Pro 5! I'm really glad you decided to buy this book, because I think you'll find it an exciting, interesting, and engaging way to learn Final Cut Pro 5.

At least, I hope so. That's been my goal.

What Is Final Cut Pro 5?

Final Cut is a delightfully powerful tool to help you create, organize, craft, and output the ideas you have in your mind, and in your camera, so that you can share them with the rest of the world.

And "tool" is the most important word in that paragraph. Because Final Cut is not just software—it's a tool to help you with your story-telling. Stories are at the heart of all compelling video; whether a feature film, documentary, corporate training, or wedding video. The goal of this book is not to teach you the definition of each menu, but, rather, how Final Cut fits into the whole picture of editing. Not just the "what" but the "when" and the "why."

Remember, even with an incredibly powerful tool like Final Cut, *your* creative vision is still in charge. Final Cut simply helps you give that vision life.

Which brings me to my first important point: There is nothing you can do in Final Cut that will damage your computer, or the media files you have stored on your hard disk. So feel free to experiment. Choose a menu, or click a button and watch what happens. It may not always look good. It may not be what you want or expect. But, you won't hurt anything. You can always undo your changes. Remember, many a famous filmmaker owes a part of their reputation to blind dumb luck at the right moment.

Voltaire once wrote: "The perfect is the enemy of the good." In editing, this means spending so much time to create the perfect effect that you run out of time to finish the show on deadline.

There is no such thing as the "perfect" way to edit. Final Cut doesn't care if you like the keyboard or the mouse—it allows you to edit either way. Final Cut doesn't care if you are a slow or fast editor—your program plays back at the same speed regardless of how fast you edit.

Final Cut does not giggle. Final Cut does not smirk. Final Cut does not call its friends after you've finished working for the day, exclaiming, "did you see that bizarre edit he did today?" Final Cut does not evaluate your worth as an editor and give you a report card at the end of your project.

So, don't get hung up in the search to edit "perfectly." This book is filled with tips and techniques that will make you a more efficient and proficient editor. Make you faster. Make you more comfortable. Make you more effective. But neither this book, nor Final Cut, can help you be more creative—or improve the quality of your story. That comes from within you.

And telling your story is why you are editing in the first place.

What's New in Final Cut Pro 5?

Here's the big news in FCP 5:

- Multicamera editing (Chapter 7)
- Dynamic RT (Chapter 11)
- Native HDV editing (Chapter 3)
- Multiple audio channels in and out (Chapter 3)
- Improved motion effects, like scaling and rotation (Chapter 11)

Since Final Cut Pro 5 builds on the foundation of Final Cut Pro HD, not everything in this version is new. Still, there *are* a host of small improvements throughout the program. So, to help you find all this new stuff, both big and small, I'll use the symbol **NEW ▶** so you can quickly spot what's new.

Who Is This Book For?

This book is for anyone who wants to improve their understanding and skills using Final Cut Pro 5. I've written it for the beginning and intermediate editor, especially someone who is self-taught, to round out your understanding of the program and give you a solid foundation you can build on for the future.

This book assumes you are using some form of Digital Video (MiniDV, DVCAM, or DVCPRO-25), although higher-end users can also learn from the techniques in this book.

This book also assumes you are not a computer geek, nor particularly interested in becoming one.

This is OK. Final Cut does not require you *understand* a computer in order to *use* a computer.

A recent survey showed that Final Cut was being used to cut documentaries, corporate presentations, broadcast programs, weddings, training, commercials… in short, Final Cut is being used everywhere in all kinds of video production.

This book is focused on the process of editing. Its goal is to help you tell your story—whether you are creating a 30-second commercial or a 2-hour documentary—and to make that process fun along the way.

How to Use This Book

At the core of this book are dozens of hands-on tutorials so you can *learn* Final Cut by *using* Final Cut. I believe that the best way to learn is to do—though my students would probably tell you that I also have strong opinions on which ways are better than others. And throughout this book, I'll share those opinions with you as if you were in one of my Final Cut classes.

As you will learn in the next chapter, there is a flow in editing from initial planning to final output and archiving. This book walks you through every step of this process and shows you what you need to know.

All the examples in this book use NTSC video, running at 30 frames per second. If you are a PAL or film editor working with different image sizes or frame rates, you can still benefit from this book, because the techniques are the same, regardless of the media you are editing. This consistent interface is one of the great strengths of Final Cut.

(Also, on a technical note for readers outside North America, you can edit the NTSC video included in this book on your computer with no problems. The only issue is that you can't display NTSC video to an external PAL monitor.)

Final Cut has over 600 keyboard commands. (No, don't panic, you don't need to know all of them to use Final Cut. In fact, you can edit quite happily using only the mouse. The keyboard just makes you faster.)

But, the last time I checked, my keyboard did not have 600 keys on it. In fact, it has 104. I just counted them. So, in order to access all 600 keyboard shortcuts, you need to use "modifier keys." These are keys you press and hold while typing other keys. There are, specifically, four:

- Shift
- Control
- Option
- Command

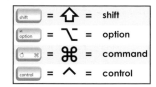

(And here's a note about this Command key. Some people, and I won't name names, call it an "Apple" key. I'm sorry, I don't "Apple" my computer. I "Command" my computer. Now, this may say more about me than it does about my computer, but for the rest of this book, I'll refer to this key as the Command key. That's because I'm in charge of my computer—at least, I want to *think* I'm in charge. You'll see these keyboard commands abbreviated like this: **Cmd+S**.)

Andrew Balis once suggested a good way to think of the Option key is that it is the "opposite" key. If you are using a tool to perform some action, holding down the Option key will often, but not always, perform the opposite action. You'll learn more about this throughout the book. (For instance, clicking in the Timeline with the Zoom tool zooms into the Timeline, Option+clicking with the Zoom tool zooms out.)

At the end of each chapter, I list helpful keyboard shortcuts that were either mentioned during that chapter or are relevant to the material covered in that chapter. I've found these lists to be handy in the books I read, and I wanted to provide the same service to you.

Finally, Final Cut has a hidden treasure trove of shortcuts that you can find only with the mouse. They are called **contextual menus**, and you access them by either holding down the **Control** key and clicking, or, if you have a two-button mouse, clicking with the right mouse button.

In this book, I will always refer to these using the term **Ctrl+click**. All Macintosh computers ship with a single-button mouse. This means that if

you learn how to use the Ctrl+click to access a contextual menu, you can use Final Cut with any mouse; which is why I teach it this way. If you have a two-button mouse, you can either Ctrl+click or right-mouse-click. It's the same result, just a different procedure.

NEW▶ System Requirements for Final Cut Pro 5

The system specifications for FCP 5 are significantly greater than with FCP HD. In fact, they've almost doubled. So, if your computer is on the lower end of the scale, especially if it's a single processor CPU, FCP 5 may run slower than FCP HD.

Apple's Web site states the minimum computer requirements for Final Cut Pro 5:

- Macintosh computer PowerPC G5, or G4 (500 MHz or faster). HD video requires 1 GHz single or dual processors.

- 512 MB RAM, though HD video requires 1 GB of RAM. Final Cut does not use more than 4 GB of RAM, even if it is installed on your computer.

- Mac OS X v10.3.9 or later. Final Cut works the same whether you are running on 10.3.9 or 10.4 (Tiger).

- QuickTime 7.0 or later.

- AGP graphics card.

- Monitor capable of displaying 1024 × 768 resolution or higher; 1280 × 1024 is recommended.

- Storage requirements range from a minimum of 11 GB for just Final Cut, to over 35 GB for the full Final Cut Pro Studio.

- DVD drive for installation.

"Starter" System Configuration

Your editing system is more than just your computer. And, in fact, there are a number of other pieces you need in order to successfully launch yourself on the road to editing glory… or, um, well, at least to get started.

Apple's list provides a basic computer system— here's what else you need to get started:

- More RAM. Try to give your computer between 1.5 GB and 2.5 GB of RAM. FCP will work faster.

- A second hard drive to store media (more on this in a moment).

- A DV camera to transfer your media into the computer.

- Final Cut Pro 5.

- A copy of this book.

NOTE:

NEW▶ Additional Tech Notes

There is no way to display HDV back out to your camera or monitor. So, to view HDV video, use your computer monitor in Digital Cinema Desktop Preview mode (see Chapter 4, "Build Your Story"). Also, editing HDV really stresses your computer. So, get the fastest computer you can afford for smooth HDV editing. Finally, FCP 5 allows you to change the gamma (grayscale) settings on your computer monitor to more closely resemble a video monitor. This is dependent on your graphics card. See Apple's Web site for more information.

Why a Second Hard Drive?

Although it is technically possible to edit using only one hard drive, it is not a wise idea to do so. This is because your hard drive has many, many, many calls on its attentions: the operating system, Final Cut, any background applications, all background processes, then, finally, and dead last in priority is playing your media.

Yet, unless your media plays smoothly, without any fits and starts, the rest of your editing system is useless.

By adding a second drive, you not only provide a whole lot more storage space for your media, you significantly improve the performance of your system by allowing your boot disk (that is, the one that contains the operating system and applications) to concentrate on serving the needs of the operating system and Final Cut, while the second disk concentrates on playing all media.

For editing DV (by which, I mean MiniDV, DVCAM, or DVCPRO-25), an internal drive will be faster than an external FireWire drive. If you are editing larger file formats, such as DigiBetacam, an external RAID (**R**edundant **A**rray of **I**nexpensive **D**isks) will be faster. It is beyond the scope of this book to detail all the different hardware options you have for storage, however:

- RAIDs are the fastest, largest, and best storage devices; however, they are also the most expensive. The fastest RAIDs connect using either Fibre Channel or SCSI. There are some new, less expensive FireWire and SATA RAIDs, which can be effective when you are editing DV.

- Internal hard disks are faster and generally cheaper than external FireWire drives, but are not portable. Be sure to get one that spins at least at 7200 RPM.

- FireWire drives are portable and will generally meet the needs of editing DV, provided you get a FireWire drive that has *at least* a 7200 RPM spin, 8 MB cache, and an Oxford 911 chip for FireWire 400 or an Oxford 922 chip for FireWire 800.

- If speed is as important as price, the new SATA RAIDs offer much better performance than FireWire on a G-5. I use one on my system and am very impressed with it.

- Brand names are not always good guides to drive performance, so be sure your hard drive meets or exceeds these specs.

In the Appendix, "*Additional Resources,*" you'll find Web sites and other resources you can use in selecting and maintaining your system.

Suggested Accessories

The following accessories will make your editing environment more efficient and productive. However, not everyone needs all these, so consider this a wish list for future purchases. (In my project studio, I use all of these.)

DV deck: Very useful because it reduces wear and tear on your camera, plus you can wire the deck into your computer and monitors, which means you can stop plugging and unplugging cables whenever you want to switch between shooting and editing.

NTSC (for North America) or PAL (for everywhere else) monitor: Notice that I said "monitor," not "TV set." A monitor allows you to watch your productions as video, rather than on the computer, which has several advantages:

- The color display is accurate. Computers don't display video colors accurately.

- Interlacing is displayed properly. These are the horizontal "forked" lines that appear on your computer monitor when you watch video with fast action.

- You see your project as your audience will see it.

- Also, bigger is not better for video monitors. The best monitor sizes are 14- to 19-inches.

Audio speakers: The tiny speaker on your computer is inadequate for anything, much less working with audio. Again, you can choose among a wide variety of speakers; my recommendation is to spend a couple hundred dollars and buy studio monitor speakers. mAudio, Tannoy, Event, Mackie, and JBL are all good brands. (I use mAudio in my studio.) Also, avoid subwoofers for mixing unless you *know* that subwoofers will be how your audience watches your project. Otherwise, subwoofers just distort the mix.

Audio mixer: This is really useful for monitoring audio from your computer as well as plugging in a mic to record narration or voice-overs. There are lots of mixers to choose from; my favorite, above all others, is the Mackie 1402 for DV or 1604 for multichannel DigiBetacam.

NEW ▶ Audio control surface: New with FCP 5 is support for audio control surfaces. This is a mixing console that controls Final Cut's faders and transport. It isn't a mixer, it's simply a control for the faders and settings inside the software. FCP 5 supports the Mackie Control Protocol.

Final Cut keyboard: This is a standard computer keyboard with the normal keycaps replaced by brightly colored ones that show which keys to press to select a particular tool, task, or effect. (Final Cut ships with little stickers that you can put on your keyboard as reminders. Although useful, I find them annoying because they keep peeling off.) The FCP keyboard is available at a variety of retail and mail-order outlets.

UPS (uninterruptible power supply): This protects your computer from surges, lightning strikes, and power failures.

RAID: This high-capacity, high-performance storage system is exceedingly useful when you have hours and hours and hours of documentary footage to edit, or you need the ultimate in performance. Not needed for DV, but necessary for all other formats.

Software, plug-ins, and other stuff: Your editing system is, in the end, as individual as you are. Depending on what you are doing, you can add

- Sound effects libraries

- Music libraries

- Graphics software

- Video effects software

- Audio production software

- Effects and transition plug-ins for Final Cut

- Two-button mice

- Shuttle controllers

- And dozens of other accessories

The purpose of all this customization is to give you the creative tools you need for your productions. However, don't feel you need to buy everything at once. Start editing and see what you need—where you are spending your time and what needs speeding up. I can assure you that you will *always* think of something else you "absolutely have to buy."

Sigh …

What's on the HOT DVD-ROM?

Bound into the back of this book you will find a DVD-ROM containing the following:

- Project lessons and media files for this book

- QuickTime movies that illustrate key concepts that are hard to convey in print, but easy to follow in video

The text file **Readme.rtf** on the DVD-ROM gives you a list of the movies available.

Thoughts on Final Cut and Multiple Users

One of the strengths of Final Cut is that it takes advantage of the multiple-user capabilities built into OS X.

For instance, if you have several people who will be using this computer, assign each one of them a separate login and user account (using **System Preferences > My Account**). Final Cut stores each user's preferences separately, so that when Paul finishes editing and Julia logs in and starts, all of Paul's customization and preferences are safely stored and replaced by Julia's so that to each user, Final Cut appears exactly as he or she left it.

Another example is that if you are using Final Cut at home, create a separate user account for your editing. That way, all your editing files and preferences are safely stored when someone else is using your computer.

Installing the Project and Media Files onto Your Local Hard Disk

1 Insert the **Final Cut Pro 5 HOT DVD** into your computer. You must copy the files from the DVD to your local hard disk. The DVD player is too slow to run the files directly from the DVD itself.

FCP Projects

2 Create a new folder on your boot disk called **FCP Projects**.

The boot disk—the drive that contains the **Applications** folder—is generally displayed in the upper-right corner of your computer screen and is often named **Macintosh HD**.

FCP 5 Hot Files

3 Copy the entire **FCP 5 HOT Files** folder from the **Final Cut Pro 5 HOT DVD** into the **FCP Projects** folder. All the lessons and media for this book are contained inside the **FCP 5 HOT Files** folder.

The nice thing about using the **FCP Projects** folder is that as you create new projects in the future, not just for this book, but during your real-life editing, you can store them in the **FCP Projects** folder. You'll learn more about how to use this organizational structure in Chapter 1.

(After my long rant about the need for two hard drives to edit, why am I telling you to copy all these book files to one drive? Because I've specifically designed these files for this DVD. For these tutorials, you can get away with using a single drive. In real life, you'll need two.)

4 The **Movies** folder you can copy or leave on the **Final Cut Pro 5 HOT DVD**, whichever you prefer.

NOTE:

How to Open Lesson Files

All lesson files require FCP 5 to open. An error message will appear if you try to open these files with an earlier version of Final Cut.

The lesson and media files you just installed are used throughout this book. There are two ways to open lesson files:

Method 1

1. Open Final Cut Pro 5.

2. Choose **File > Open** (or press **Cmd+O**).

3. Open the boot disk (often called **Macintosh HD**, but not always).

4. Open the **FCP Projects** folder.

5. Open the **FCP 5 HOT Files** folder.

6. Open the **Lessons** folder.

7. Select the project file you want to open; for example: **Chapter 02 Lesson**.

8. Click **Open**.

Method 2

1. From the **Finder**, open the boot disk (often called **Macintosh HD**, but not always).

2. Locate and open the **FCP Projects** folder.

3. Open the **FCP 5 HOT Files** folder.

4. Open the **Lessons** folder.

5. Double-click the project file you want to open; for example: **Chapter 02 Lesson**.

You can select whichever of these two methods is most convenient for you.

After you've opened a lesson file, you can easily find it again inside Final Cut by choosing **File > Open Recent** and selecting the file you want to reopen.

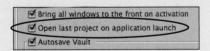

Also, the next time you start Final Cut, it will automatically open the last project you were working on, unless you have unchecked **Open last project on application launch**, which is part of **Final Cut Pro > User Preferences** on the **General** tab.

If you want to go back to the original project as it was before you started making changes (or go back to the last time you saved the project), choose **File > Revert**. Click **OK** to agree to losing all changes.

Summary

I find editing to be exciting, frustrating, challenging, and intensely involving. I love telling stories, and Final Cut makes it possible. This book will show you how. We welcome your comments at **fcp5hot@lynda.com**. The support url for this book is **http://www.lynda.com/info/books/fcp5/**.

1

Get Organized

In this chapter, you'll learn a system of organizing your computer and editing projects so you can concentrate on being creative without worrying where all the pieces are stored.

You'll also learn an editing workflow within Final Cut that will help you concentrate on accomplishing tasks in the right order, without wasting a lot of time. In editing, there is so much to do and so little time. Unless you stay focused and concentrate on working through the steps of your project in the right order, you can easily lose time working on the wrong things.

For instance, spending time creating the perfect transition between two shots before you've even figured out whether either of those shots will be in the final version of your project is simply a waste of time and creative effort.

What Is Editing?

A few months ago, I saw the following anonymous sign taped on the wall of an edit bay at KTLA-TV, Los Angeles:

"What is Editing?

Editing is the process that transforms a miscellaneous collection of badly focused, poorly exposed, and horribly framed shots containing reversed screen direction, unmatched action, disappearing props, flair, and hair in the aperture (but not containing any close-ups, cut-ins, or cut-aways) into a smooth, coherent, and effective visual statement of the original script... for which the director gets the credit."

Final Cut Pro won't make you a great editor. But using Final Cut can help you do great editing.

Regardless of whether your story is a feature film, corporate training, or home movies of Jennifer's first birthday, the essence of all video and film production is storytellling.

Compelling media, meaning programs that you want to watch, all have a solid story—with a beginning, middle, and an end—at their core. Now, this story doesn't have to be fictional. Maybe it's a biography of someone you respect, or training for a new piece of equipment, or a news report, or a documentary.

What makes a story compelling is that it stays focused on its mission. It doesn't wander about, highlight irrelevant material, or meander through meaningless backwaters. A good storyteller knows what's essential for telling his or her story, tells it, then stops.

Editing is essential to storytelling. Editing is the process of getting rid of everything that isn't relevant to the telling of your story, arranging the pieces for the greatest impact, then tweaking the timing until it flows smoothly. Only after you have it organized can you "fancy your story up."

In short, editing is a process that requires both logic and creativity to be successful.

A Few Key Terms

A complete glossary of digital video terms would fill an entire book, but here are some key terms you need to know to get started with Final Cut Pro 5. You'll work with all these terms throughout the rest of the book.

Final Cut Pro 5, Final Cut Pro, Final Cut, and FCP: These are all different ways of describing the same great editing package—Final Cut Pro 5. (And, as you'll discover, I use all of them interchangeably.)

Project (or project file): A Final Cut Pro project file stores pointers, or references, to all the different elements that make up your production. Video, audio, graphics, sound effects, text—everything that is in your final edit is stored in the project file. All editing is done in the project file.

Generally, when you are done with a project, you archive this file for permanent storage.

Media: I use this to mean the timecode-based video and audio files stored on your hard disk and referenced by your Final Cut Pro project. Although others might also include graphics files, sound effects. and other elements, when I use the term "media," I'm generally referring to material initially stored on a videotape. Generally, when you are done with a project, you trash all timecode-based media to save disk storage space.

DV: This is a generic term that includes three different media formats: MiniDV, DVCAM, and DVCPRO-25. Although each format writes data to the tape differently, they all have the same basic image compression and quality. For this reason, I describe all three formats using the generic term, "DV."

SD: This refers to professional-grade video, though what constitutes "professional" is increasingly up for debate. The "SD" refers to standard definition video, which we watch on our TV sets every evening. The dimensions of SD images are different from DV images.

HDV: This is a new intermediate HD format, combining the file size of DV with the image quality of HD. It uses a different form of video compression than DV, which makes it difficult to edit on slower computers. The dimensions of HDV images are larger than DV or SD.

HD: High definition video. There are a variety of standards and image sizes in HD; however, they all have greater picture resolution than either SD or DV. They also create much bigger files with heftier system requirements. And, as you've come to expect, HD images have different dimensions than HDV, SD, or DV.

Clips: These are the individual shots or elements stored inside your Final Cut project file that get edited into your finished project. A clip is anything that is stored in the Browser or located on the Timeline. (You'll learn more about these terms in Chapter 2, "*Understanding the Final Cut Pro Interface.*") Clips are the basic building blocks you use to create your program.

Pointers: Final Cut Pro uses references inside a project file to "point" to the actual media files stored on your hard disk. Using pointers, rather than the actual media, in your Final Cut project helps keep the project file size small. Also, when you make changes to an edit in Final Cut, these changes affect only the pointers, not the actual media files stored on your hard disk, which enables you to easily undo your changes, without damaging quality. You don't actually see these pointers; rather, the clips you see inside Final Cut use pointers to reference the actual media files stored on your hard disk.

Timeline: The Timeline is that part of a Final Cut Pro project that allows you to assemble all the different elements of your program from beginning to end. If clips are building blocks, the Timeline is the table that allows you to lay them all out and get them organized in the order you want to best tell your story.

The Editing Workflow of Final Cut Pro 5

Final Cut doesn't force you to work in any particular order. However, what I've learned during years of editing and working with Final Cut is that I can be more productive, which means I have more time for creativity, if I break down each project into individual steps and focus on completing each step before moving on to the next.

There are ten basic steps to editing any project:

- Planning and organization
- Gathering media
- Building your story
- Organizing your story
- Trimming your clips
- Adding additional audio
- Adding transitions
- Adding text, graphics, and effects
- Outputting the project
- Archiving the project

The outline of this book follows these same steps, though I've added a few extra chapters to avoid cramming too much information into one chapter.

Planning and Organization

By spending a little time getting your project organized at the very beginning, you can save huge amounts of anguish at the end. Hundreds of different elements go into even a medium-sized project. Planning upfront about how files are named, where they are stored, what format they should be in, and what you want to keep (or trash) after the project is over can make the difference between getting a job done by deadline or frantically floundering at the finish.

Planning is covered in this chapter.

Gathering Media

Bringing audio and video elements into a Final Cut project is the subject of Chapter 3, "*Gather Your Media.*" Although you can bring elements into your project lots of ways, there are basically two broad categories: "capturing" elements that need to be converted from videotape into a format the computer can read, and "importing" elements that are already digitized and simply need to be brought into a project file. Chapter 3 covers both.

Building Your Story

Once you've assembled the components that make up your story, you need to start putting them together. Chapter 4, "*Build Your Story,*" teaches you how to create a new project, view your clips, set Ins and Outs, and edit them together into the Timeline. From a purely editing point of view, Chapter 4 is probably the most important chapter in the book—you'll use its tips the most. (At least, they're the ones I use the most.)

Organizing Your Story

In Chapter 5, "*Organize Your Story,*" you'll learn techniques to easily delete and rearrange clips in the Timeline.

Trimming Your Clips

After you have all your clips organized in the Timeline, it's time to start trimming the fat. Chapter 6, "*Trim Your Story,*" teaches you the different trimming tools built into Final Cut. Also, you'll spend time learning when to use a particular tool, along with the effect it has on the rest of your Timeline. One of the key features of Final Cut is that there are multiple ways to do the same thing. My goal is to teach you many different approaches so you can pick the ones that work best for you.

NEW▶ Multiclip Techniques

Multiclips, the ability to edit multiple camera angles at the same time, are new to Final Cut Pro 5, and even though it isn't part of the 10-step workflow, it is a major new addition to the program. So it gets its own chapter, Chapter 7, "*Multiclips—Many Views of the Same Thing.*"

NEW▶ Adding Audio

Chapter 8, "*Audio—The Secret to a Great Picture,*" brings sound into your project. Great sound makes even mediocre pictures seem interesting. Final Cut gives you some serious audio tools, and Chapter 8 shows you how to put them to work.

Adding Transitions

Purists would argue that a cut is a transition—and they are right—but I haven't seen many people get excited about how sexy a cut is. However, I have seen them wax eloquent describing the wipes in Star Wars or diss a page peel because it is "so 1990's." Chapter 9, "*Transitions—Making Change Beautiful,*" will teach you everything you need to know to hold your own in these discussions, plus a few tricks that will shut up that know-it-all in the second row.

Adding Text, Graphics, and Effects

This could easily fill an entire book, but here you'll do it in only three chapters. Chapter 10, "*Text, Titles, and Graphics*," covers a variety of different ways to put text on the screen. Chapter 11, "*Motion Effects*," discusses how you can get your pictures to move. And Chapter 12, "*Filters and Keying*," presents a variety of ways you can give your images a unique look.

Outputting Your Project

Whether you want to show your work on the Web or on prime-time network television, you'll need to get your project out of Final Cut. Chapter 13, "*Output Your Project*," teaches you the best way to get your projects out of FCP for the Web, CD, DVD, and videotape.

Archiving Your Project

Finally, when everything is over, all the dust has settled, and the client's check has cleared the bank, it's time to back up essential information and trash the rest. Chapter 14, "*Archiving Your Project*," shows you how.

Chapter 14 also includes a section on media management. This is the process of tracking, moving, copying, adding, deleting, or changing just about every file that Final Cut Pro uses. Not every project needs to use this. So, I saved it for the end. You'll either really need to know this, or you'll never use it. After you read this, you can decide for yourself.

Appendix

There's one more section, an appendix, that provides troubleshooting help and additional resources to keep you current on this frequently changing application.

Organize Your Life

Well, OK, maybe not your *whole* life, but certainly that part of your life that involves editing. Planning your project is critical, so I want to spend the rest of this chapter making sure you start off on the right foot.

There are three stages to getting organized:

- System-wide naming conventions
- Organizing your computer
- Organizing Final Cut Pro

Naming Conventions

I realize that nothing empties a room faster than some intensely earnest person saying, "We need to have a meeting to discuss naming conventions." Most people would rather watch paint dry. But naming conventions are important—especially when it's 11 o'clock at night, and you can't find that one graphics file that has the closing animation

to the project you've been working on for the last six weeks, because you forgot how it was named or where you stored it.

Perhaps spending a little time thinking about filenames isn't such a bad idea after all.

Here's why developing a system for consistent filenames is important. A typical Final Cut project contains hundreds of files:

- Video files
- Audio files
- Music files
- Sound effects files
- Graphics files
- Project files
- And narration, animation, backups, alternate versions, and, well, you get the picture

If you already have a naming system in place, great! You can skip to the next section. If not, I can save you the meeting—here's the naming system I use. You can use my system until you think up a better one. Believe me, using *something* is *much* better than using nothing!

Let's create a fictitious client named "Just-a-Moment Productions." In my system with every new client, I create a two-letter code that represents that client, in this case, "JM." Next, when Shannon at Just-a-Moment calls me with a new job, I assign a job number and create a new, four-digit job code: "JM04," which means the fourth job from client JM.

Now, whenever I create a new file for this project (except media files, which I'll talk about next), the filename *always* starts with "JM04." That way, if a file gets lost, or wanders away, I can easily figure out where it belongs.

On small- to medium-sized projects, starting with a job code followed by a brief description is enough to keep track of most files. For instance, in the illustration below, "JM04_open.mov" tells you that this is the file for the opening animation.

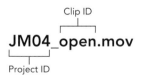

On larger projects, involving thousands of files, I use a more highly formatted name, such as "JM04_anim_a2_intro_v2.mov," which stands for "Just-a-Moment Productions, Job 4, Animation for the Introduction to Act 2, version 2." Remember, filenames can't be longer than 31 characters, and you'll find that FCP displays shorter filenames more easily than longer ones in the Browser.

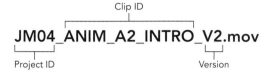

I carry this one step further and label camera master videotapes as "JM04_01," "JM04_02," "JM04_03," and so on, meaning the first, second, or third tape shot for the fourth job for Just-a-Moment Productions.

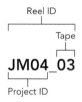

I am a *huge* believer in uniquely labeling all your videotapes as soon as they are shot, and I'll talk about this more in Chapter 3, "*Gather Your Media*." (I also keep a database of all my videotapes so that I can find a shot or location when I need it later, long after the project is over.)

The nice thing about this structured file-naming system is that files automatically sort by project, file type (animation, image, sound effect, music), act (or location in the project), location within the act, and version. This makes finding a file and understanding where it goes simple, easy, and fast.

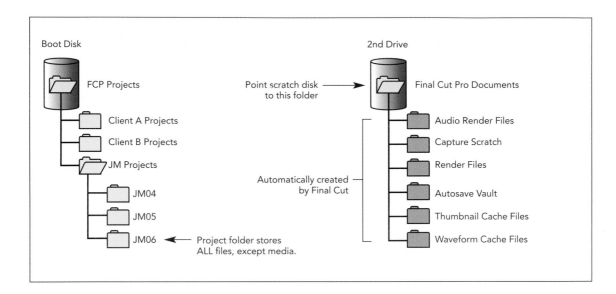

Organize Your Computer

As you read in the Introduction, editing video is at least a two-hard-drive proposition—initially because using two hard drives improves performance, but more importantly, because it simplifies organization.

In the next two exercises, you are going to set up your system so that, when you are finished running the tutorials in this book, your system will be ready to edit in the real world.

1 | Create a Folder System That Works

In this exercise, you'll learn a method to organize your files that you'll use for the rest of this book. However, the real power of this system is that if you use this same system to organize your real-life projects, you'll never need to wonder where project files are stored, or where to find a file, or how to back-up your data.

---

1 In the boot drive (the drive that holds the **Applications** folder), create a folder called **FCP Projects**, if you haven't already done so. You can use this folder for the rest of the exercises in this book, as well as storing later, real-life projects.

Inside that folder, in addition to storing the files from this book, create a folder for every client, and inside each client folder, create a folder for every project from that client. Although your folders will be different than mine, inside that project folder put **every** file you create that relates to that specific project: Final Cut project files, memos, budgets and spreadsheets, audio files, LiveType and Soundtrack Pro projects, graphics files, and so on, everything **except** timecode-based media. ("Timecode-based media" is a fancy term that means all the stuff you capture from videotape.) You'll store this media on the second hard drive.

---

2 On the second drive, create a folder named **Final Cut Pro Documents**, which FCP uses to store media for every project. You'll learn in Exercise 3 how to tell Final Cut to store all time-code-based media in this folder (called a **scratch disk**) on your second drive. If you have more media than will fit on a single hard disk, create a **Final Cut Pro Documents** folder on *every* hard disk you plan to use to store media.

Make Archiving Easy

Media files are *huge*. An hour of DV footage takes 13 GB of hard disk space to store. And, even though hard disks are getting bigger, they are not designed for long-term archiving. Even a 100 GB drive holds only about eight hours of footage, and that's without including the space needed for render files. You just can't afford to keep your media permanently on your drives. This means you need to trash all your captured media when a project is over, and not use your hard disks for long-term storage.

(Here's another reason: think of any piece of computer equipment you purchased seven years ago that you can still connect to your current computer. Right, me neither. My garage is full of computer gear that I can no longer use. Computer technology changes at a dizzying pace—exactly what you DON'T need for media you want to archive for years.)

Nope. The best place for long-term storage of your media is on videotape.

Here's why I differentiate between timecode-based media and other files: timecode-based media is most often stored on videotapes. Because this tape has timecode, which uniquely identifies each frame of video, it's simple to capture or recapture this media from tape back into your computer whenever you need it. And this is done using Final Cut's Batch Capture, which you'll learn about in Chapter 3, "*Gather Your Media.*"

The benefit to this organizational system is that when a project is complete, all your essential project files are stored neatly in the project folder, and all expendable media is stored in the scratch disk. To make a permanent backup of your project files, simply drag the project folder from within the **FCP Projects** folder to a CD (or DVD) for storage. With your project files backed up, you can now safely trash your media.

That's why your project file is so important—it keeps track of all the media you use, so you can easily recapture it in the future.

NOTE:

Storing Videotape

Nothing lasts forever, including CDs, DVDs, and videotapes.

You should always store your videotapes on edge, not flat, and wound all the way to the end (or beginning). Following these simple storage guidelines minimizes the effect of magnetic print-through on the tape, gravity, and the earth's magnetic field. Oh, and try to keep your tapes from getting too hot, too cold, or too exposed to harsh sunlight. In other words, treat them like the valuable records they are.

The lifespan of a videotape stored in a normal environment (not too hot, too cold, too wet, or too dusty) is 20 to 25 years. VHS tapes don't last quite as long; premium tapes somewhat longer. To be safe, assume 20 years. After that, the magnetic oxide that stores all your precious images starts to flake and fall off.

Although there is increasing debate about the life expectancy of CDs and DVDs due to what's called *CD rot*, generally, if you store your discs on edge, away from heat, direct sunlight, and humidity, and don't bang them around too much, they should last at least as long as videotapes and probably longer.

If keeping your media safe for long periods of time is important, be sure to write the date you put the tape, or disc, into service so you'll know when to make dubs to whatever storage media is current at the time.

Setting Preferences—
Getting Final Cut Ready

When you first install Final Cut Pro, the installer puts it into your **Applications** folder. In this exercise, you'll move the FCP icon into the Dock to make it easier to access, then start Final Cut and configure some initial preferences to get it ready to run.

---

1 In the **Finder**, open the **Applications** folder (press **Shift+Cmd+A**) and locate Final Cut Pro.

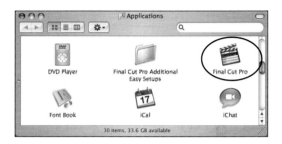

---

2 Click once on the **Final Cut Pro 5** icon and drag it into the **Dock**. Put it anywhere you like, except into the **Trash**, which would erase the program!

---

3 To move the **Final Cut Pro 5** icon elsewhere in the **Dock**, simply grab it with the mouse and move it to its new home. Notice how the other icons scuttle out of the way?

NOTE:

Organizing Final Cut Pro

There are hundreds of different preferences within Final Cut Pro. Rather than spend dozens of pages creating a laundry list of all possible variations, this book divides preferences into three main sections, spread across three chapters:

- Getting Final Cut Pro set up and organized (Chapter 1)

- Understanding the Final Cut Pro interface (Chapter 2)

- Getting Final Cut Pro ready to capture video (Chapter 3)

And even with these three large categories, there are still a variety of preferences targeted at the professional user that won't be covered in this book; that is, after all, why Apple printed a 1,868-page manual!

4 While you're there, move the **Dock** so it doesn't get in the way. Click the **Blue Apple** and choose **Dock**. Choose **Turn Magnification Off** and **Turn Hiding On**. Then position the **Dock** to the right, or left, side of the screen. You can change this again at any time.

I prefer the **Dock** on the left side of my screen and hidden, to keep it out of my way. (By the way, a neat keyboard shortcut is **Option+Cmd+D**, which hides, or reveals, the **Dock**.)

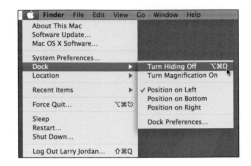

5 Start Final Cut by clicking its icon once in the **Dock**. (You can also start it by double-clicking its icon in the **Applications** folder, but the **Dock** is faster.)

6 **NEW ▶** If Final Cut is loading for the first time, this dialog appears. The top pop-up menu sets the video format. For the exercises in this book, use **DV – NTSC**. The bottom pop-up menu sets the scratch disks, which will be discussed in detail in Exercise 3. For now, change the bottom menu to point to your second hard drive. Then click **OK**.

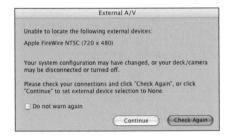

7 This dialog will appear next if you don't have a DV, or other video, device connected and turned on. Because you are simply setting up Final Cut for the first time, turning on your camera or deck is not necessary, so click **Continue** and let Final Cut finish loading. (If you want to turn your camera or deck on at this point, do so, then click **Check Again**, so that Final Cut will look for and connect to it.)

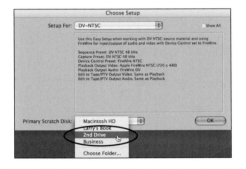

8 Chapter 2, "*Understanding the Final Cut Pro Interface,*" discusses in much more detail the Final Cut interface that now appears. For this moment, however, concern yourself just with setting some initial preference files. Choose **Final Cut Pro > Easy Setup**.

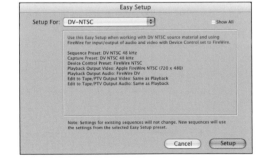

The **Easy Setup** dialog is your one-stop shop to setting virtually every audio and video preference within Final Cut. If you are capturing and editing DV footage, make sure your menu choices match those shown in the previous screenshot. (If you are outside the U.S., you would normally select **DV-PAL** from the top pop-up menu; however, for the exercises in this book, please select **DV-NTSC**.)

This table illustrates some of the more popular video formats and the **Easy Setup** selection to use for each. Clicking the **Show All** check box provides a listing of over 50 video formats to choose from.

Video Format Settings

Video Format	Menu Choice (Codec)
MiniDV, DVCAM, DVCPRO-25 (NTSC)	DV-NTSC
MiniDV, DVCAM (PAL)	DV-PAL
DVCPRO-25 (PAL)	DVCPRO-PAL
DVCPRO-HD (1080 interlaced) (PAL)	DVCPRO HD – 1080i/50
DVCPRO-HD (1080 interlaced) (NTSC)	DVCPRO HD – 1080i60
DVCPRO-HD (720 progressive 24 frames/sec)	DVCPRO HD – 720p24
DVCPRO-HD (720 progressive 30 frames/sec)	DVCPRO HD – 720p30
DVCPRO-HD (720 progressive 60 fields/sec)	DVCPRO HD – 720p60
HDV 1080 interlaced (PAL)	HDV – 1080i/50
HDV 1080 interlaced (NTSC)	HDV – 1080i/60
HDV 720 progressive 30 frames/sec (NTSC)	HDV – 720p/30
Betacam SX (NTSC)	8-Bit Uncompressed NTSC
Betacam SP (NTSC)	8-bit Uncompressed NTSC
Betacam SP (PAL)	8-Bit Uncompressed PAL
DigiBetacam (NTSC)	10-bit Uncompressed NTSC
DigiBetacam (PAL)	10-bit Uncompressed PAL

3 | Setting Scratch Disks

My opinions about naming scratch disks have changed since the last edition of this book. By default, FCP 5 looks for a folder called "Final Cut Pro Documents" as the default scratch disk. You created this in Exercise 2. My feelings now are to go with the flow. Using this folder name minimizes the possibility of creating multiple scratch disks by accident. (Remember, you want to have only one scratch disk folder per hard disk.) As well, I've found it best to always create scratch disks at the highest level of a hard disk, rather than burying them inside multiple levels of folders. This exercise shows you how to set up your scratch disks.

---

1 Choose **Final Cut Pro > System Settings (Shift+Q)**.

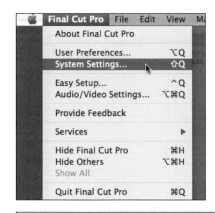

This screen allows you to set scratch disks. (Note the Scratch Disks tab at the top of the screen.)

NOTE:

Scratch Disks

A scratch disk is where Final Cut Pro stores all the media you capture from videotape, along with the variety of other files FCP creates during the editing process. Because scratch disks are so important, Final Cut won't even start until you tell it where at least one scratch disk is located. As I mentioned earlier, I strongly recommend that you store all your timecode-based media (that is, the material you captured from videotape) to a second hard drive.

Final Cut Pro 5 allows you to have up to 12 scratch disks. However, you generally won't use anywhere close to that number because hard disks are getting bigger, allowing storage of far more media than even a year ago. And, the more FireWire drives you add, the slower they go. The general limit for efficient FireWire use on a G5 is five to seven drives, due to the nature of how FireWire communicates between devices. If you need more hard drive space than that, move up to a RAID.

A RAID (**R**edundant **A**rray of **I**nexpensive **D**isks) is a very high-performance, high-capacity storage system for video editing. It's also the most expensive. For DV footage, unless you have hours and hours and hours of material, a RAID is not necessary. For other video formats, however, RAIDs are often essential.

2 To set your scratch disk, click the top **Set** button, and navigate to the **Final Cut Pro Documents** folder you created earlier on your second hard drive. In this example, I have the scratch disk pointing to the **Final Cut Pro Documents** folder on my second hard drive. Select the folder you want to use as a scratch disk (**not** the files in it), then click **Choose**. Never point to the individual folders *inside* **Final Cut Pro Documents**.

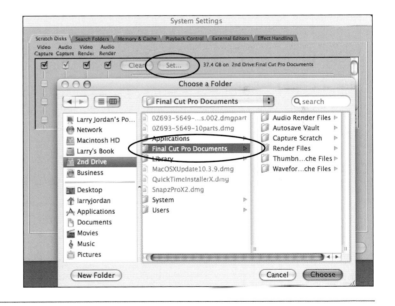

3 If you have multiple hard disks, create a scratch disk on each one of them by moving down to the next line in the **Scratch Disk** window that doesn't have a hard disk assigned to it. Click the **Set** button, navigate to the **Final Cut Pro Documents** folder you created on each disk, select it, and click **Choose**.

4 Be sure each line has all four columns checked. (It's normal for the **Audio Capture** check box to be dimmed). If you are using DV video, it is perfectly OK for all four file types to be stored on one disk. There is virtually no reason to ever check the **Capture Audio and Video to Separate Files** check box unless you are in an HD environment, and even then, check with your capture card manufacturer. Capturing audio and video to separate files causes far more problems than it is worth.

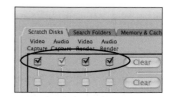

5 You can leave the **Waveform Cache**, **Thumbnail Cache**, and **Autosave Vault** set to their default locations, but I generally set them to match my first scratch disk. Although these files are rarely large and can easily be stored on any hard disk, I like having them all together in one spot.

6 However, you **do** want to change the default setting of **Minimum Allowable Free Space on Scratch Disks** from its default setting of **2048 MB**. Hard disks hold only a certain amount of data. Once they are full, they can't hold any more, obviously. What isn't obvious is that a hard disk gets full sooner than you expect.

Essentially, you never want to fill a hard disk any fuller than about 90 percent of its capacity. One reason is that some types of hard disks slow down as they get fuller. Also, when a hard disk is reading or writing information, it creates invisible, temporary files. If there isn't sufficient room to create these temporary files, the hard disk just plain refuses to work.

So, to prevent the calamity of your hard disk locking up, set **Minimum Allowable Free Space on Scratch Disks** to be 5 percent of the size of the largest hard disk that **isn't** your boot disk. A fast way to determine the size of your hard disk is to select it in the **Finder**, then choose **File > Get Info**. The **Get Info** window will show you the total capacity of your hard disk, how much space is available, and how much is used.

For instance, let's say you have three hard disks:

- Boot disk (internal): 160 GB

- Internal hard disk #2: 120 GB

- External hard disk: 250 GB

You would then set **Minimum Allowable Free Space on Scratch Disks** to **12500 MB** (12.5 GB), which is 5 percent of the size of the largest hard disk (250 GB) that isn't the boot disk. (Technical purists will gleefully point out that a gigabyte is actually 1,024 megabytes. And, although they are correct, for the purposes of this dialog, using 1000 megabytes to equal a gigabyte works just fine.)

7 You can leave the **Limit Capture/Export File Segment Size To** box unchecked. This box is useful if you need to make movie file sizes compatible with OS 9 and some versions of Windows. If you work exclusively with OS X, you won't need to use this. If you send movies to OS 9 or Windows, turn this on.

8 Check the **Limit Capture Now To** box with a default setting of **30 minutes**. I'll explain more about this in Chapter 3, "*Gather Your Media.*"

---

9 That ends this initial exercise for setting preferences in Final Cut. To save your preferences, click **OK** in the bottom-right corner of the **System Settings** dialog. If you are done working with Final Cut, choose **File > Quit** or press **Cmd+Q**.

Helpful Keyboard Shortcuts

Shortcut	Action
Shift+Cmd+A	Opens Applications folder (from Finder only)
Shift+Cmd+U	Opens Utility folder (from Finder, in OS 10.3 or later)
Option+Cmd+D	Hides, or reveals, the Dock (all applications)
Ctrl+Q	Opens Easy Setup preference window
Shift+Q	Opens System Settings preference window
Tab	Moves forward between settings in a dialog
Shift+Tab	Moves backward between settings in a dialog
Escape	Exits a dialog without saving any changes
Enter (on keypad)	Closes a dialog and saves all changes
Cmd+Q	Quits Final Cut Pro

Summary

This chapter focused on getting you, your computer, your projects, and Final Cut Pro organized—from filenames to scratch disks. Now it's time to fire up Final Cut and get your hands dirty exploring the interface.

2

Understanding the Final Cut Pro Interface

In this chapter, you finally come face-to-face with the Final Cut Pro interface.

The good news is that you really only need to read this chapter once. The bad news is that until you read it, you won't be able to take advantage of all the power and flexibility in Final Cut.

So, grab an extra large cup of coffee and snuggle up next to your computer—by the time you're done with this chapter, you'll know everything there is to know about the FCP interface: how to navigate in it, how to customize it, and the best keyboard shortcuts to use to run it.

The Final Cut Pro Interface

The good news about Final Cut 5 is that Apple didn't change the interface, much, from FCP HD. This means that if you are upgrading, there won't be a lot of new stuff to learn. So you might want to just skim this chapter for what's new.

However, if you are new to Final Cut, this chapter is essential. There are four main windows in Final Cut Pro. This chapter presents their purpose and use, then follows with a series of exercises to help you explore the interface further.

During this initial presentation, I use the files that you'll be editing in Chapter 4, *"Build Your Story."*

Four main windows and two small palettes make up the principal interface of Final Cut Pro:

- Browser
- Viewer
- Canvas
- Timeline

The principal interface also includes two floating palettes:

- Tool palette
- Audio meters

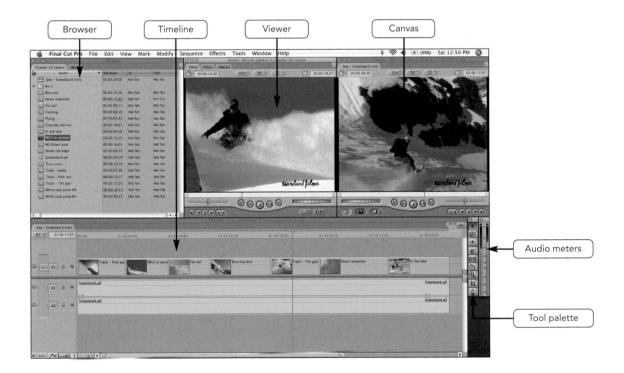

DVD MOVIE: | **interface.mov**
If you want to see the Final Cut Pro interface in action, be sure to watch the **interface.mov** located inside the **movies** folder on the **Final Cut Pro 5 HOT DVD**.

All windows float, meaning you can drag them anywhere on your computer screen, resize them, park them on the Dock, even make them disappear—though it is very tough to edit your project when some windows are missing.

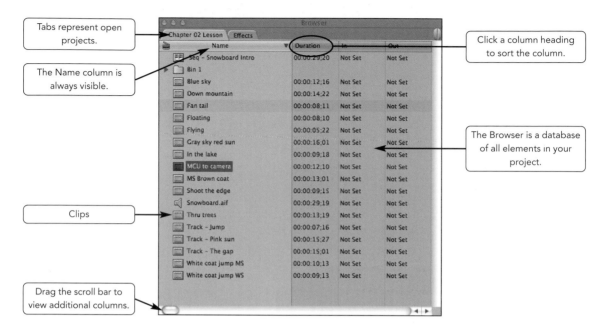

Tabs represent open projects.

The Name column is always visible.

Click a column heading to sort the column.

The Browser is a database of all elements in your project.

Clips

Drag the scroll bar to view additional columns.

The **Browser** is a list of all the elements you can access for your project. Think of this as a database, showing you everything you need to know about all the different clips, graphics, music files, and sequences in your project. (The files in this example are the ones you'll be using in Chapter 4, "*Build Your Story.*")

NOTE:

Definitions

Project: This is the master file that Final Cut Pro creates to store all the information needed to edit your video—*except* the actual media itself.

Media files: These are the actual audio and video elements, most often recorded on videotape, that get transferred to your computer's hard disk for editing and output. All media files created by Final Cut are stored as QuickTime movies.

Clips: References stored within Final Cut to the actual media files stored on your hard disk. Clips stored in Final Cut are simply pointers that "point" to the media files. Although it seems like you are editing your actual media files, in fact, you are simply arranging these small pointer files. The benefit to this approach is that your project files remain small, allowing you to edit huge projects easily.

Sequence: When you edit in Final Cut, you are editing a sequence of clips that start at the beginning and go to the end. Some projects have only one sequence; others have dozens. There is no real limit to the number of sequences you can store in Final Cut.

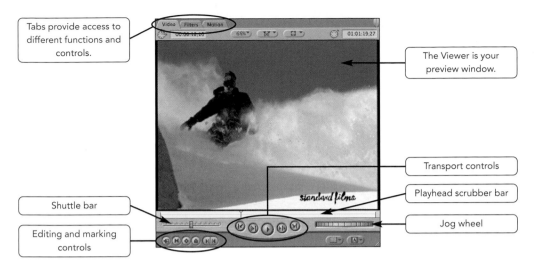

Tabs provide access to different functions and controls.

The Viewer is your preview window.

Transport controls

Playhead scrubber bar

Shuttle bar

Jog wheel

Editing and marking controls

The **Viewer** window is where you preview and modify your clips, transitions, filters, and effects. It has the following sections, starting at the top:

- Window tabs to select specific window functions
- Timecode and window display controls
- Video frame or audio waveform display
- Playhead scrubber bar
- Playback controls
- Editing and marking controls (left side)
- Recent clips and Generator pop-up menus (right side)

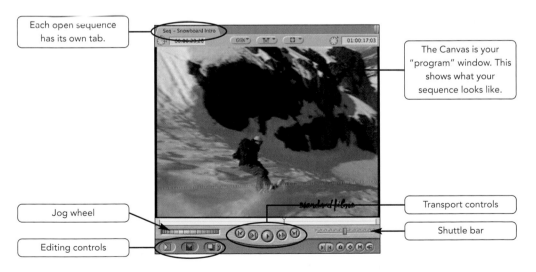

Each open sequence has its own tab.

The Canvas is your "program" window. This shows what your sequence looks like.

Jog wheel

Transport controls

Shuttle bar

Editing controls

The **Canvas** window displays your final program. Its layout is almost identical to the Viewer window, but its function is different. The Viewer helps you decide how to edit your clips or create your effects. The Canvas shows you the final results. In fact, the Canvas window works in tandem with the Timeline to show two different views of a sequence. The Canvas shows how the sequence looks, the Timeline shows its organization.

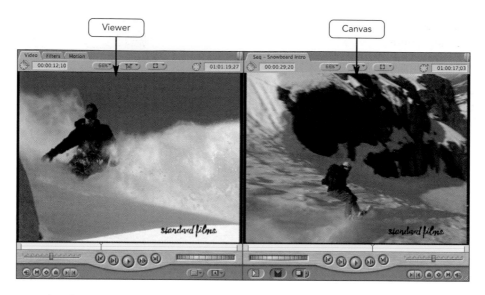

The Canvas window layout is almost identical to the Viewer's, except for the names of the tabs at the top and the controls in the bottom corners of each window. The great benefit to this is that once you know how to operate one window, you know how to operate both. And, in fact, it's even better than that, because there are several other specialized windows that also involve video control—Log & Capture, Trim Edit, and Edit to Tape—that look and act just like the Canvas and Viewer. This consistency of interface is one of the great strengths of Final Cut and helps make learning it a lot easier.

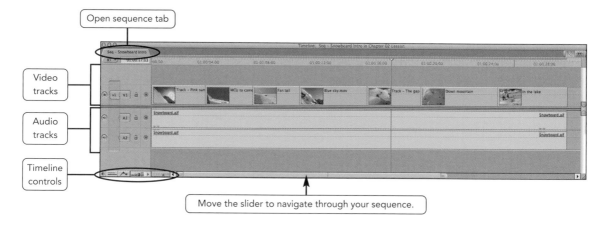

The **Timeline** window is where you assemble all your clips into a final program. Clips are laid out from left to right, with the start of your program beginning on the left. The Timeline has four major sections:

- Video tracks, on top, in blue

- Audio tracks, on the bottom, in green

- Track controls, on the left side

- Timeline controls, on the bottom

In addition to these four main windows, two floating palettes have a principal role in Final Cut. The first is the **Tool palette**, which contains the editing, sizing, and trimming tools. You'll start working with this in Chapter 5, *"Organize Your Story."*

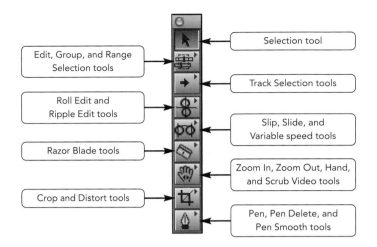

Edit, Group, and Range Selection tools

Roll Edit and Ripple Edit tools

Razor Blade tools

Crop and Distort tools

Selection tool

Track Selection tools

Slip, Slide, and Variable speed tools

Zoom In, Zoom Out, Hand, and Scrub Video tools

Pen, Pen Delete, and Pen Smooth tools

The other floating palette holds the **audio meters**. You'll learn more about these in Chapter 8, *"Audio—The Secret to a Great Picture."*

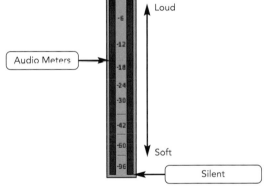

Clipping lights (audio is too loud)

Loud

Audio Meters

Soft

Silent

Now that you've been introduced to the interface, it's time to take a closer look at each of these windows. Since you'll be spending a lot of time with them, you might as well be friends.

Editing Flow in Final Cut Pro

There's a basic system to how Final Cut encourages you to edit:

1. Load a clip from the Browser into the Viewer.

2. Set the In and the Out points for the clip.

3. Edit the clip from the Viewer into the Timeline.

4. View the finished result in the Canvas.

Although there are lots of different ways you can accomplish each step, these four steps lie

at the core of all your editing. You'll perform them dozens, even hundreds, of times in each project.

You may recognize these steps as a subset of the 10-step editing workflow you learned about in Chapter 1. That's because even though many shows may not need any special effects or animation, they each need their clips strung together in the correct order, then viewed to make sure everything looks right.

1 | Explore the Browser

In this exercise, you'll learn what the Browser is, how to organize column headings, how to create a new storage bin, and how to use clip labels.

NOTE:

How to Open Lesson Files

The lesson and media files you installed in the Introduction are used throughout this book.

There are two ways to open lesson files:

Method 1

1. Open Final Cut Pro.

2. Choose **File > Open** (or press **Cmd+O**).

3. Open the boot disk (the one in the upper-right corner of your Mac's screen—often called **Macintosh HD**, but not always).

4. Open the **FCP Projects** folder.

5. Open the **FCP 5 Hot Files** folder.

6. Open the **Lessons** folder.

7. Select the project file you want to open, for example **Chapter 02 Lesson**.

8. Click **Open**.

Method 2

1. From the **Finder**, open the boot disk.

2. Locate and open the **FCP Projects** folder.

3. Open the **FCP 5 HOT Files** folder.

4. Open the **Lessons** folder.

5. Double-click the project file you want to open, for example **Chapter 02 Lesson**.

You can select whichever of these two methods is most convenient for you to use.

After you've opened a lesson file, you can easily find it again by choosing **File > Open Recent** from within Final Cut and selecting the file you want to reopen.

If you want to go back to the original project before you started making changes (or go back to the last time you saved the project), choose **File > Revert**. Click **OK** to agree to losing all changes.

1 Open **Chapter 02 Lesson**.

If you already have this project open, choose **File > Revert** (and click **Yes** to agree to lose all changes) to reopen the project to the condition it was in the last time it was saved.

This is the Browser. (Notice that the window is labeled at the top in its title bar.) The Browser acts like a database tracking all the elements of your project. It contains 65 columns of information (called **metadata**, or data about data) on each of the items loaded into it. Thirty-seven columns are initially visible in the Browser, the other 28 are hidden, but accessible if you know where to look.

On the left side of the Browser are icons that indicate the form of each element stored in the Browser.

The eight Browser icons indicate the following:

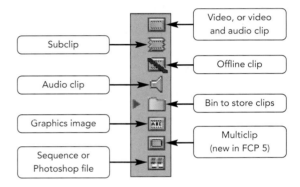

- A video clip, which can be video-only or video and audio (see Chapter 3, "*Gather Your Media*")

- A subclip, which is a special form of a normal clip (see Chapter 6, "*Trim Your Story*")

- An offline clip (see Chapter 3, "*Gather Your Media*")

- An audio clip with audio only (such as a sound effect or music file) (see Chapter 8, "*Audio—The Secret to a Great Picture*")

- A bin (or storage folder) (see Chapter 4, "*Build Your Story*")

- Imported graphics file, such as a scanned image (see Chapter 10, "*Text, Titles, and Graphics*")

- Multiclip, containing multiple camera angles all linked together (see Chapter 7, "*Multiclips—Many Views of the Same Thing.*")

- Timeline sequence (see Chapter 4, "*Build Your Story*") or Photoshop PSD file (see Chapter 10, "*Text, Titles, and Graphics.*"

You'll work with all of these during this book.

---

2 For now, grab the window sizing tab in the lower-right corner of the **Browser** and drag it down and to the right to make the **Browser** bigger. (If other windows also shift, move the cursor until it looks like an arrow.)

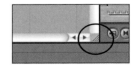

Notice, as you do so, all the additional columns of information that appear. Scroll around them using the horizontal scroll bar at the bottom of the Browser.

Revealing the Hidden Secrets of the Browser

There are 37 columns of information displayed by default in the Browser, with another 28 columns of less-used information initially hidden. To display a hidden column, **Ctrl+click** any Browser column heading *except* the Name column, and choose one of the columns in the shortcut menu to display it.

To hide a column, **Ctrl+click** any column heading *except* the Name column and choose **Hide Column**. However, even though the column is hidden, Final Cut still keeps track of the information it contains.

---

3 Reorder the columns in the **Browser** by clicking a column header and dragging it to a new location. In this case, use the horizontal scroll bars and scroll right until you find the **Reel** column, about two-thirds across the **Browser**.

Click and drag column header to move it.

---

4 Click and drag the **Reel** column to the left, until it is next to the **Name** column.

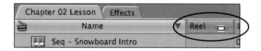

NOTE:

Reel Names and Numbers

As you will learn, reel numbers are essential to harnessing the power of Final Cut because they allow you to find and recapture clips if you ever need to re-edit a project in the future. For this reason, I always move the Reel column from the far right where it's buried in the Browser, all the way to the left, next to the clip name column, so I can easily see it.

Chapter 3, *"Gather Your Media,"* covers working with reel names in more detail.

5 Click the column header to alphabetically sort a column. (Notice the downward-pointing arrow.)

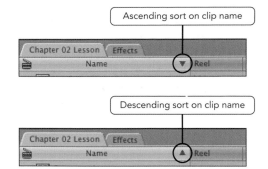

To do a reverse sort, click the header again. (Notice that the arrow direction now points up.)

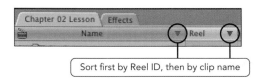

6 It is often useful to sort on two columns at once. To do this, click the first column header (the primary sort), then hold the **Shift** key and click the second column (the secondary sort). For instance, click first on the **Reel** column to sort all clips by reel name, then **Shift+click** the **Name** column to sort clips alphabetically by reel.

To switch from sorting on two columns to sorting using only one column, click any column head that isn't one of the sorting columns. For instance, if you are primarily sorting on Reel, and secondarily on Name, clicking the Name header will toggle between ascending and descending sorts by clip name. Clicking the Duration column header (or any header that isn't the Reel or Name column) will re-sort the Browser by only that column.

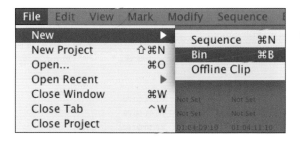

7 Bins in the **Browser** are used just like folders in the **Finder**: to help you organize, store, and locate clips. There are three ways to create a new bin in the **Browser**:

- Choose **File > New > Bin**.

- **Ctrl+click** in the light-gray area of the **Name** column and choose **New Bin** from the shortcut menu.

- Click in the **Browser** to make it active, then press **Cmd+B**.

Note | How to Tell if a Window Is Selected

You can tell if a window is selected by looking at the color of the title bar at the top of a window.

Selected

Selected windows have a light-gray title bar with a subtle, rounded, 3-D look.

Not selected

Unselected windows have a dark-gray title bar, with a flat look.

NEW▶ Here's another new FCP 5 goodie. You could always move a window by dragging on its title bar. Now, you can move a window by holding down **Option+Cmd** and clicking anywhere on a window to move it.

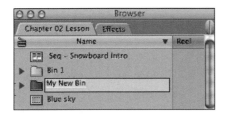

8 Change the name of any bin or clip by double-clicking it, then typing in a new name.

WARNING:

Clip Names and Media Files

Changing a clip name in the Browser does *not* change the name of the media file to which that clip points. If you plan to recapture the media for a project, for instance to convert from a low-resolution offline edit to a high-resolution online edit, try not to change your clip names. Keeping file names consistent minimizes confusion in matching clips.

However, if you are working at your final resolution (such as DV) and don't plan to recapture media, renaming clips in the Browser will not cause any problems.

Tips on Naming Bins

I use bins to keep similar things together: music files, sound effects, all answers from one interview guest, all B-roll, and so on. Generally, I try to keep the top level of the Browser pretty well organized and not have hundreds of files to scroll through.

For most projects, I find myself creating a similar series of bins:

- Interviews

- B-roll

- Music

- Graphics

- Sound effects

NEW▶ Final Cut 5 allows you to nest bins (meaning a bin stored in a bin stored in a bin, and so on) at least 16 levels deep. However, I've found that FCP sometimes has trouble if you get more than five or six bin levels deep. Since there is no limit to the number of bins you can create at a single level, and you can store hundreds of clips in a single bin, I've not found this five- to six-level bin-inside-a-bin-inside-a-bin restriction a significant limit.

9 You can also use labels to help organize your bins and clips. To apply a label, **Ctrl+click** a clip in the **Browser**, choose **Label**, then slide across and choose one of the five label choices. (There's also a label column in the **Browser** you can use, but this is faster.) Notice how, when you label a clip, it changes color. You'll learn later in this chapter how you can change the text of a label, but not the color. Sigh…

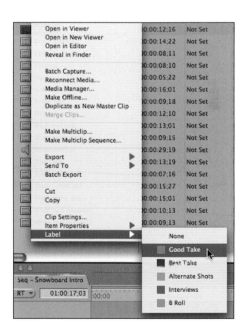

10 NEW► Here is a new feature in FCP 5: The ability to change the size of the text in the **Browser**. Yay, finally! To change font size, **Ctrl+click** in the gray area of the Name column in the **Browser** and choose **Text Size > Medium**, which changes the font size for the current project. (Step 11 shows you an alternate way to do this.)

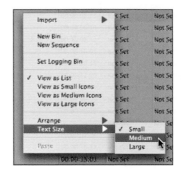

11 NEW► Or, you can choose **Final Cut Pro > User Preferences** and click the **General** tab. Choose the **Browser Text Size** you want to make the default setting for Final Cut. This changes the default text size for all future projects. (By the way, this text change applies in both the **Browser** and **Timeline**.)

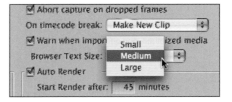

12 If you are done exploring for the moment, choose **File > Close Project** and don't save changes. Otherwise, leave Final Cut open to take a look around the **Viewer**.

2 | Explore the Viewer

In this exercise, you will learn what the Viewer is, how it works, and how to navigate around in it.

The Viewer is your preview window. In it, you'll set Ins and Outs, modify transitions, adjust filters and effects, enter type, and create animations. Not, however, all in this lesson! Still, the Viewer is a highly flexible device that gives you plenty of control over your program.

NOTE:

Larry's First Interface Rule of Final Cut Pro

Thinking about the Viewer brings to mind the first of my two interface rules for Final Cut Pro:

Select something, then do something to it.

Although this may not be as deep as "I think, therefore I am," it *is* the underlying method Final Cut uses to determine what you want to do. You select a clip and edit it to the Timeline. You select a clip and delete it. You select an edit point and add a transition. You select an audio clip and apply a filter. And so on.

NOTE:

The Great "Mouse vs. Keyboard" Debate

I will confess right here near the beginning that I am a huge keyboard shortcuts fan; which is why you'll find a summary of relevant keyboard shortcuts at the end of each chapter.

On the other hand, I work with a very talented editor who does everything with the mouse. In fact, Ed does everything he can to avoid touching the keyboard.

Fortunately, Final Cut is not so partisan. It doesn't particularly care if you edit using just the keyboard, just the mouse, or some combination of both. There are over 600 menu commands in Final Cut Pro. You can access them using menus, program them into keyboard shortcuts, or create individual mouse button shortcuts (which you'll learn later in this chapter).

My goal is to show you the options, then let you pick the one that works best for you.

Clip duration — 00:00:12;10

Timecode position of playhead — 01:01:19;27

Playhead

Start of clip

End of clip

This is the Viewer window, with the Video tab selected. Although there's a lot of depth here, for right now, you'll concentrate on general layout and navigation.

1 Start by opening **Chapter 02 Lesson**, if it isn't already open.

If you already have it open, choose **File > Revert** (and click **OK** to accept losing all changes) to reopen the project to the condition it was in the last time it was saved.

2 Look for the **MCU to camera** clip in the **Browser**. Load it into the **Viewer** by double-clicking it.

NOTE:

Three Ways to Load a Clip into the Viewer

In order to view a clip or set Ins and Outs, you need to load it into the Viewer. Because loading clips is something you'll do hundreds of times in a project, Final Cut makes it easy by providing three ways to load a clip into the Viewer:

- Double-click the clip icon in the **Browser**.

- Select the clip in the **Browser**, then press **Return**.

- Drag the clip icon from the **Browser** to the image section of the **Viewer**.

I've used all three, but I tend to be a double-clicker.

Larry's Second Interface Rule of Final Cut Pro

Loading a clip into the Viewer reminds me of my second interface rule for Final Cut:

Double-click something to load it into the Viewer.

As you've just seen, double-clicking a clip loads it from the Browser into the Viewer. Double-clicking also can do the following:

- Load clips from the Timeline into the Viewer (see Chapter 4, "*Build Your Story*")

- Load edit points into the Trim Edit window (see Chapter 6, "*Trim Your Story*")

- Load transitions into the Transition Editor (see Chapter 9, "*Transitions—Making Change Beautiful*")

The Viewer is where you make changes to a clip. Whether you're doing something as simple as setting an In or an Out, or as complex as modifying a filter, you first load a clip into the Viewer and then make changes.

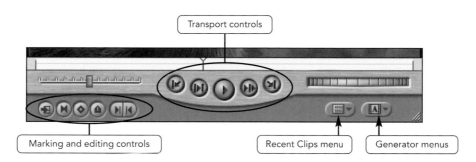

The lower portion of the Viewer window contains the playback controls for a clip, which consist of the following:

Playhead: The vertical black line with the yellow triangle on top is called the playhead, and it represents the width of a single frame. The frame the playhead is parked on, or playing over, or scrolling across, is shown

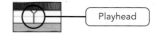

in the image section of the Viewer. By sliding the playhead back and forth in the white horizontal scrubber bar at the bottom of the clip (remember, clips can be video, audio, or both), you can quickly view the entire contents of the clip.

The look and operation of the playhead is identical in the Viewer, the Canvas, and the Timeline. The key point is that the vertical black line represents the frame displayed in the window.

Media limits: The thin black vertical line at the left and right edges of the playhead scrubber bar represent the absolute beginning and end of the clip loaded into the Viewer. These are called the clip's **media limits**. You'll discover the importance of these in Chapter 6, "*Trim Your Story*," and Chapter 9, "*Transitions— Making Change Beautiful*."

Shuttle bar: The shuttle bar allows you to quickly scroll back and forth in your clip. The farther you move the bar from the center, the faster you go in that direction.

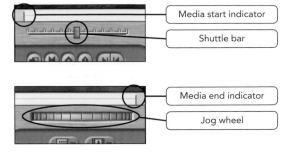

Jog wheel: The jog wheel allows you to slowly move the playhead through a clip. You move it by dragging it left or right.

Playback buttons: The playback buttons provide a series of specialized button shortcuts for playing the clip in the Viewer. The center button plays a clip from the location of the playhead. When a clip is playing, this button converts to a Stop button. You can also play a clip by pressing the spacebar. When a clip is playing, the spacebar also stops it. The other buttons will be discussed more in Chapter 4, "*Build Your Story.*"

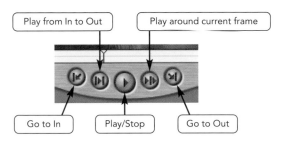

---

3 Experiment with moving around in a clip:

- Press the spacebar to play and stop the clip.

- Grab the playhead with the mouse and drag it around.

- Slide the shuttle bar to the left (rewind) or right (fast forward) to move through a clip.

- Turn the jog wheel to learn how to move a clip in slow motion.

---

4 Experiment with the five buttons just below the image of the clip to see what they do:

- Click the center button (the right-pointing arrow) to play a clip.

- Click it again to stop the playback.

- Click the leftmost button to jump to the beginning of a clip.

- Click the rightmost button to jump to the end of a clip.

- Click the second button from the left to play a clip from beginning to end. (You will learn about a more powerful function of this button in Chapter 4, "*Build Your Story,*" when you see it also allows you to play a clip from the In to the Out.)

- Click the second button from the right to play a clip starting a few seconds before the playhead and ending a few seconds after the playhead. (You'll learn how to change the length of this pre-roll and post-roll in Chapter 4.)

But there are even more powerful tools you can use to play clips, as described in the following sidebar.

NOTE:

Note | Power Playback: The J, K, and L Keys

In addition to the buttons and controls built in to the Viewer, there are three power keys that I use all the time: the J, K, and L keys. They have a variety of functions, depending upon how many times you press each key, as the following table illustrates:

J, K, and L Playback Control Keys

Press	What Happens
L	The clip plays forward from the location of the playhead.
K	The clip stops.
J	The clip plays backward from the location of the playhead.
L+L (press L twice)	The clip plays forward at double speed from the playhead.
L+L+L	The clip plays forward at 4x speed from the playhead.
J+J	The clip plays backward at double speed from the playhead.
J+J+J	The clip plays backward at 4x speed from the playhead.
K+L (hold down both)	The clip plays forward at about one-third normal speed from the playhead.
K+J (hold down both)	The clip plays backward at about one-third normal speed from the playhead.

I use the J, K, and L keys all the time. In fact, I almost never use the shuttle bar or jog wheel. Between the mouse and the J, K, and L keys, I have all the speed and control I need.

Duration of clip

Timecode

Notice the two boxes at the top-left and top-right corners of the Viewer window. These are placed to display and enter timecode. The left box displays the duration of the clip loaded in the Viewer. The right box displays the location of the playhead in timecode. You'll work with these boxes extensively in Chapter 4, "*Build Your Story.*"

---

5 Grab the playhead and slide it around. Notice how the timecode in the upper-right display changes as you move the playhead.

---

6 Put the playhead in the middle of the clip.

---

7 Type **–30** (minus 30) and press **Enter**.

See how the playhead jumped backward a full second?

---

8 Type **+45** and press **Enter**.

See how the playhead jumped forward a second and a half? (If it didn't jump, press the **Shift** key and type **+**, then **45** and press **Enter**, or just use the keypad.)

You can move around in a clip this way because Final Cut uses timecode to keep track of every frame of video. I call it moving using a timecode "offset." And you'll learn about timecode next.

---

9 That's it for the moment. If you want to stop, choose **File > Close Project** and *don't* save your changes. Otherwise, leave everything right where it is and go on to the next section.

What Is Timecode?

Timecode is one of the core concepts at the foundation of all professional video editing. In this section, you'll learn what timecode is, how to read it, and how to use it in Final Cut.

Timecode is a label that uniquely identifies each frame of video in your project. In fact, when you record a video tape, you are actually recording more than just audio and video. You are also recording timecode. Each frame of video, and its corresponding audio, is assigned a unique, sequential timecode label.

Final Cut reads that timecode and uses it to make sure all your clips and edits are exactly where you want them.

Timecode consists of eight numbers, grouped in pairs and separated by colons or semicolons. The first pair of numbers (01) represents the hour—in this example, hour 1. There are 24 hours of timecode, starting at hour 00 and ending at hour 23. In a DV environment, all recordings start at hour 00. In a professional environment, timecode can be preset to any number. One of the tricks professional camerapeople often use is to change the timecode hour to reflect the number of tapes being shot. Thus, the first tape would be set to hour 1, the second to hour 2, and so on. This helps keep track of tapes and shots during the editing process.

The second pair of numbers (23) represents minutes. There are 60 minutes of timecode, starting at 00 and ending with 59. When the 60th minute arrives, the minutes reset to 0 and the hours increase by 1.

The third pair of numbers (15) represents seconds. There are 60 seconds of timecode, starting at 00 and running through 59. When the 60th second arrives, the seconds reset to 0, and the minutes increase by 1.

The fourth pair of numbers (08) represents frames. There are three principal frame rates: 24, 25, and 30 frames per second. Frames are displayed from 0 to 23, or 24, or 29, depending upon frame rate. Then the frame number resets to 0.

Final Cut can edit any of these three frame rates. However, only one frame rate can be selected per sequence. You need to create different sequences for each frame rate you want to edit. A project can contain multiple sequences, each with different frame rates, as needed.

Who Uses What Frame Rate?	
Frame Rate	**Used Where**
30 frames per second	NTSC video—North and Central America, Japan, Philippines, Taiwan, S. Korea
25 frames per second	PAL video—Virtually the rest of the world
24 frames per second	Film, most high-definition video, a few DV cameras

The Power of Timecode

The power of timecode is that, since every frame has its own unique identifying number, every frame can be precisely located and displayed. This makes it possible to do frame-accurate edits.

In Final Cut, a clip is identified by both its reel name and its timecode, which is why keeping the reel names accurate is so important.

Timecode is a label that identifies each frame (the way that "Fred" and "Ginger" uniquely identify two dancers). There are two types of timecode: **drop-frame** and **non-drop-frame**. The difference between the two is that drop-frame timecode is used when you want to represent real-time, whereas non-drop-frame timecode gives every frame a perfectly sequential number.

All DV footage uses drop-frame timecode; professional formats can select between the two. Final Cut also has the capability to select between the two. Which should you choose? If you are shooting DV footage, stay with drop-frame timecode.

In a professional environment, non-drop-frame time code is used in film, commercial, DVD, and animation work. Drop-frame timecode is used in any program that will be broadcast or cablecast, or any situation where knowing exactly how long a sequence runs in real time is important.

Because timecode is a number, Final Cut uses it to make calculations regarding clip location, duration, playhead placement, and edit points. That's why you are able to move the playhead by simply typing an "offset timecode." What you are saying to Final Cut is, "Please move the playhead forward (+) or backward (–) the number of frames I type next."

In the example at the end of the preceding exercise, we moved the playhead back 30 frames and forward 45 frames. Remember, there are 30 frames of video in every second of time for NTSC video.

3 | Explore the Timeline

In this exercise, you'll learn the basic operation of the Timeline and how clips are laid out in the Timeline, and you'll discover the similarities between how the Viewer and Timeline play back clips.

The Timeline and the Canvas are, essentially, two views of the same thing. The Timeline allows you to organize your clips from start to finish, whereas the Canvas displays the video under the Timeline playhead. You need both to be able to edit and view your program.

NEW▶ The maximum length of a sequence in the Timeline changed in FCP 5. You can now build sequences that are up to 12 hours long using 48K audio, or 6 hours long using 96K audio.

---

1 Open **Chapter 02 Lesson**, if it isn't already open.

If you already have it open, choose **File > Revert** (and click **OK** to agree to lose all changes) to reopen the project to the condition it was in the last time it was saved.

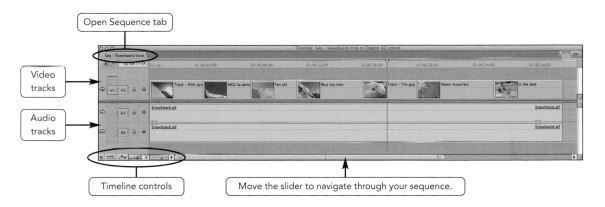

Open Sequence tab

Video tracks

Audio tracks

Timeline controls

Move the slider to navigate through your sequence.

Notice that when you open this project, a sequence automatically opens into the Timeline. The Timeline is the window that contains sequences of edited clips. You can have as many sequences open as you like—in all cases, though, they are displayed in the Timeline.

NOTE:

Sequences Take Memory

Although Final Cut allows you to open as many sequences into the Timeline as you want, the more sequences you open, the more memory they will take. For this reason, I make it a habit to keep the number of open sequences to a minimum. Sequences in the Browser take almost no memory, but memory *is* allocated when they are opened in the Timeline.

The Timeline is divided into four main sections: video tracks and audio tracks that contain clips, track controls, and Timeline controls.

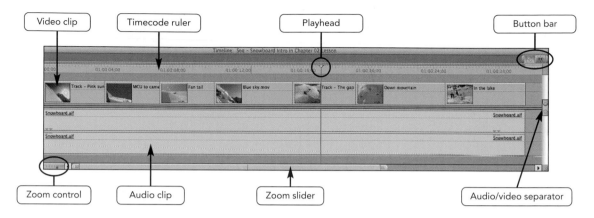

The audio and video clips section of the Timeline is divided into two halves, separated by the double-gray line in the center: the top half contains video clips, displayed in blue, and the bottom half displays audio clips, displayed in green.

Each horizontal line of clips is called a **track**. Final Cut allows you to create sequences containing up to 99 tracks of video and 99 tracks of audio. In general, you stack clips vertically when you want more than one image (or sound) on the screen at one time. You lay out clips horizontally when you want one shot followed by another. The shot on the left goes first.

NOTE:

Turn Off Audio Waveforms for Better Performance

The Timeline in this exercise shows audio waveforms off, which provides the fastest editing performance. However, when you are editing audio, you may want to turn on waveforms to better see where to make your edits. But, when waveforms are on, the computer allocates CPU resources to calculate them. Especially if you are using a slower computer, turning off waveforms will make a big difference in how quickly Final Cut responds.

To turn off waveforms, press **Option+Cmd+W**, or click the small right-pointing arrow in the lower-left section of the **Timeline**, then uncheck **Show Audio Waveforms**.

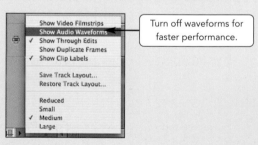

Notice that the playhead in the Timeline is similar to, but much bigger than, the playhead in the Viewer. However, its function is identical. The thin, black, vertical line stretching down from the yellow triangle of the playhead represents the frame currently displayed in the Canvas.

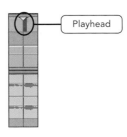

Playhead

2 To play the playhead, press the **spacebar**. To stop, press the **spacebar** again. The **J**, **K**, and **L** keys also work. Everything you learned about how to play clips in the Viewer also applies here in the Timeline!

However, there's a new way to move between clips that applies more to the Timeline than the Viewer or Canvas. Press the **Home** and **End** keys. Notice that you jump to the beginning and end of the sequence. Now, type the **up** and **down arrow** keys. Notice that you jump from the beginning of one clip to the beginning of another. I use the arrow keys a **lot**, so I want to make sure you know about them.

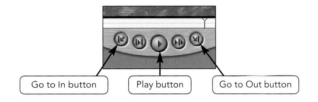

Go to In button   Play button   Go to Out button

Since the Canvas and Timeline are two different views of the same sequence, you can also use the buttons on the Canvas to control the playhead in the Timeline.

3 Click the **Play** button in the lower center of the **Canvas**. Watch what happens to the playhead in the Timeline.

4 Click the **Go to In** button and watch what happens. The playhead jumps to the beginning of your sequence.

5 Click the **Go to Out** button and watch what happens. The playhead jumps to the end of your sequence.

6 Click the second button from the right (**Play Around Current Frame**) and watch what happens. The playhead jumps back a few seconds, plays, then stops a few seconds after the point where playback started. Again, just like the buttons in the Viewer.

You'll learn ways to use the **Play In to Out** button (second from left) in Chapter 4, "*Build Your Story.*"

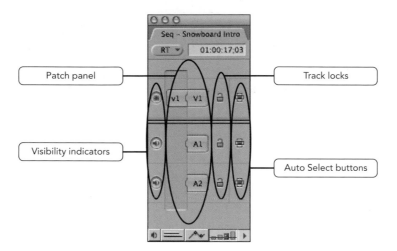

Patch panel

Track locks

Visibility indicators

Auto Select buttons

On the left side of the Timeline are the track controls. The green visibility indicators are all lit by default. Turning *off* the visibility indicator for a track makes a video track invisible or an audio track inaudible. You'll work with these more in Chapter 8, "*Audio—The Secret to a Great Picture,*" and Chapter 11, "*Motion Effects.*"

---

7 Put your playhead in the middle of a clip. Click the green **visibility indicator** next to the **V1** patch panel. Notice that your **Canvas** has gone black because all your video clips on the **V1** track are now invisible.

---

8 Turn off the green **visibility indicators** for all audio tracks and play a portion of your sequence. Notice that all the audio has now become silent.

---

9 Turn on all **visibility indicators** by clicking them so they glow green.

The patch panel controls how audio is routed from the Viewer to the Timeline. You will learn more about this in Chapter 8, "*Audio—The Secret to a Great Picture.*"

The track locks are off by default. Turning a lock *on* makes it impossible to make changes to a track, including repositioning a clip. You'll learn more about them in Chapter 6, "*Trim Your Story.*"

The Auto Select buttons are on by default. Turning them off, or on, controls track and range selection, as well as copy and paste. You'll learn more about them in Chapter 5, "*Organize Your Story.*"

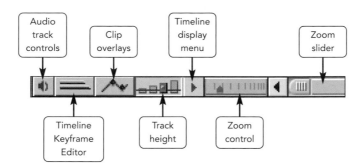

10 At the bottom left of the **Timeline** are the **Timeline** controls. Click one of the four bars in the "bar chart" and notice how the height of the tracks changes.

---

11 Click the small right-pointing triangle to display the pop-up menu for the **Timeline**. You've already used this to turn off, or on, the display of audio waveforms. Turn on, or off, the other four options in the top section of the menu and watch what happens.

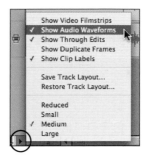

---

12 Click one of the bottom four choices (**Reduced**, **Small**, **Medium**, or **Large**). Notice that choosing one of these is exactly the same as clicking the blue/gray bar chart icons immediately to the left of this menu.

---

13 Next, grab the **Zoom control** and slide it back and forth. Notice how the horizontal scale of the **Timeline** changes.

---

14 Now, grab either end of the **Zoom slider** (I tend to call this the "mad popsicle stick") and drag it to change the scale of the **Timeline**. As you do so, the size of the **Zoom slider** also changes. However, I've found the **Zoom control** to be both faster and more predictable, so I suggest you use that.

---

15 If you want to stop, choose **File > Close Project** and don't save your changes. If you are ready to tackle the next stage, leave the project file open.

Which Should You Use: Zoom Control or Zoom Slider?

By dragging the middle of the Zoom slider from left to right and back again, you can easily get from one side of a large sequence to another. It can also be used to quickly change the scale of the Timeline, by grabbing one of the tabs at either end and dragging. However, zooming using the Zoom slider changes the scale of the Timeline without any respect to the playhead.

This means you can zoom in such a fashion that the play-head will totally disappear off the edge of the screen. When this happens, look in the Zoom slider track and you'll see a small, thin, almost invisible purple line. Click it and the Timeline will automatically jump to the current location of the playhead.

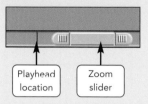

Playhead location

Zoom slider

Zoom control

Zooming by using the Zoom control, however, automatically centers the playhead in the Timeline, then changes the scale of the Timeline. For me, using the Zoom control, rather than the Zoom slider, helps keep me from losing the playhead (which is the principal reason I call the Zoom slider the "mad popsicle stick").

Still, I do love keyboard shortcuts. So, when I want to zoom in or out on the Timeline, I *could* press **Cmd+ +** (that's the Cmd key and the plus key) to zoom in, or **Cmd+ −** (Cmd and the hyphen key) to zoom out. The more you type, the more you zoom.

But, uh, if you demand absolute honesty, I don't really use any of these. I use the Zoom tool. I wasn't going to mention this until later, but, well, you force me to reveal another secret.

To access the **Zoom** tool, either click the **magnifying glass** in the **Tool** palette and select the **Zoom** tool with a plus (**+**) sign in it, or press the letter **Z** once. To zoom out, select the second **Zoom** tool, the one with a minus (**−**) sign in it, or press the letter **Z** twice. Then, drag the **Zoom** tool around the portion of the **Timeline** you want to enlarge (or shrink).

Zoom In tool

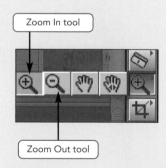

Zoom Out tool

Even faster, press the letter **Z** once, to select the **Zoom In** tool, then hold down the **Option** key to switch to the **Zoom Out** tool.

Like I said, Final Cut has lots and lots of different ways to do the same thing.

4 | Explore the Canvas

By now, you know almost everything you need to know to get started using the Canvas. (Not, however, everything about the Canvas there is to know.) In this exercise, you'll review what you've learned about playing video in the Viewer, then you'll explore the Fit to Window, Sync, and View pop-up menus.

Remember, the Canvas is simply another view of the Timeline. The Timeline shows the organization of your program on a clip-by-clip basis. The Canvas provides you a way to view it.

---

1 Open **Chapter 02 Lesson**, if it isn't already open.

If you already have it open, choose **File > Revert** (and click **OK** to agree to lose all changes) to reopen the project to the condition it was in the last time it was saved.

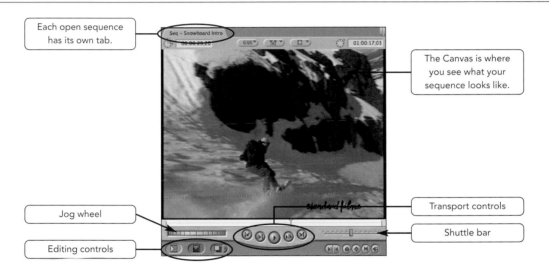

Each open sequence has its own tab.

The Canvas is where you see what your sequence looks like.

Jog wheel

Editing controls

Transport controls

Shuttle bar

---

2 Notice that the **Canvas** window looks pretty darn near identical to the **Viewer** window. Spend a minute reassuring yourself that the spacebar, J, K, and L keys, arrow keys, shuttle bar, and jog wheel work exactly the same as in the **Viewer**. Because they do.

---

3 Drag the **playhead** in the **Canvas** and notice that the Timeline playhead moves exactly in sync with the Canvas. Move the **playhead** in the **Timeline**. Notice that the playhead moves in the Canvas. As I said, these are two views of the same thing—your sequence.

Can't find the playhead? Remember, it's the thin vertical black line with the yellow triangle on top that you first met when you explored the Viewer and the Timeline.

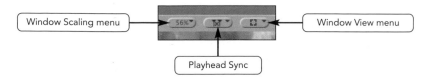

Window Scaling menu

Playhead Sync

Window View menu

Now, time to move on to something new. At the top of both the Canvas and Viewer windows are three small pop-up menus, which are identical for both windows.

The Window Scaling pop-up menu controls the scaling (or size) of the image inside the Canvas window. (Remember, this same menu also appears in the Viewer, so everything you learn here applies to the Viewer, too.)

4 Experiment by selecting different zoom sizes and watch what happens to the picture. Be sure to always leave **Show as Sq. Pixels** checked.

When editing, the best practice is to always display your images using the Fit to Window option. The additional scaling options in this menu are very useful when you are creating effects and animation, so you'll revisit these concepts in Chapter 11, "*Motion Effects.*"

NOTE:

Pay Attention to This Sneaky Trick

If you, in a fit of wild enthusiasm, zoom into your image so that vertical or horizontal scroll bars appear, and then you try to play your movie, Final Cut will attempt to display your video to the computer monitor in real time in this zoomed-in mode. However, what FCP will not do is display your video to an external NTSC monitor or FireWire device. So, if you are busily editing and all of a sudden your external monitor stops working, it's probably because you zoomed into either the Canvas or Viewer windows.

Which brings me to my second favorite keyboard shortcut, one that solves this problem: **Shift+Z**. It's called **Fit to Window**, and it automatically scales the video in the Canvas, or the Viewer, or the clips in the Timeline to fit into whatever the active window is. I use this keyboard shortcut constantly.

NEW▶ The second pop-up menu, in the middle, adjusts playhead sync. This provides some very handy power features that changed with FCP 5. This will be explained in Chapter 6, "*Trim Your Story,*" and Chapter 7, "*Multiclips—Many Views of the Same Thing.*" However, for normal editing, set it to **Sync Off**.

The third menu, all the way to the right, is the Window View pop-up menu. This controls how images in the window are displayed. For editing, using the defaults is the best choice. (The defaults have the first line in each of the four menu sections checked.) You'll learn more about using this menu throughout the rest of this book, especially in Chapters 10, 11, and 12.

5 If you want to stop, choose **File > Close Project** and don't save your changes. If you are ready to plunge forward, leave the project file open.

Power Tools—Specialized Windows You'll Learn About Later

Although the windows discussed in this chapter are the principal windows in Final Cut, there are a whole variety of other windows you'll learn about later, as shown in the following table:

Other Windows in Final Cut Pro

Window Name	Function	Chapter Discussed
Audio meters	Measures audio levels	Chapter 8
Audio Mixer	Combines and controls audio tracks	Chapter 8
Frame Viewer	Simultaneously compares frames	Chapter 12
Log & Capture	Controls and captures clips	Chapter 3
Media Manager	Copies, moves, and converts clips	Appendix
QuickView	Views effects without rendering	Chapter 11
Storyboard editing	Edits clips using thumbnails	Chapter 4
Tool palette	Contains trimming and editing tools	Chapter 6
Transition Editor	Modifies transitions	Chapter 9
Trim Edit	Allows precision, on-the-fly editing	Chapter 6
Video Scopes	Checks color and video levels	Chapter 3
Voice Over tool	Records narration directly into FCP	Chapter 8

5 | Customize Final Cut Pro

In this exercise, you'll learn how to customize Final Cut Pro. The best tools, I've discovered, disappear as you learn how to use them. Thus, with practice, you stop worrying about how to hold the hammer, and instead concentrate on hitting the nail.

This is also true for Final Cut Pro. As you get familiar with how it works, you'll pay less attention to the software and more to bringing the ideas in your mind out into your project. One of the ways Final Cut makes this possible is through some truly extensive customization. This exercise explains how it works.

DVD MOVIE: **customize.mov**

If you want to learn more about how to customize the Final Cut Pro interface, be sure to watch the **customize.mov** located inside the **movies** folder on the **Final Cut Pro 5 HOT DVD**.

---

1 Open **Chapter 02 Lesson**, if it isn't already open.

If you already have it open, choose **File > Revert** (and click **OK** to agree to lose all changes) to reopen the project to the condition it was in the last time it was saved.

---

2 Click the **Browser** to make it active.

---

3 Change the size of the window (or any active window) by grabbing the resize tab in the lower-right corner of any window and dragging the window to whatever size you want.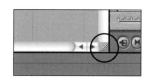

---

4 However, it's more efficient, and a lot more fun, to put your cursor on the black dividing line between any two (or three) windows (notice the shape of your cursor) and drag them all as a group.

---

5 Best of all, once you have a window layout you like, store it by holding down the **Option** key and choosing **Window > Arrange > Set Custom Layout 1** (or **Set Custom Layout 2**). These layouts are stored in your Preferences files. It's easy to change them by creating a new layout, then using this same procedure to save the new layout in place of the old.

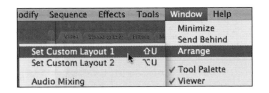

This brings me to my third favorite keyboard shortcut: **Ctrl+U**. This shortcut automatically resets all your windows to a default layout—something I find very useful because I constantly rearrange windows when I'm editing.

Even better, when you save a window layout using this Option key method, you can toggle between the default layout and your new custom layout by pressing **Ctrl+U** and **Shift+U**.

---

6 To save a window layout permanently to disk, arrange the windows to your liking, then choose **Window > Arrange > Save Window Layout**.

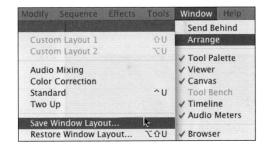

---

7 In the **Save** dialog box that appears, give your layout a name and save it. By using the default location, Final Cut will display the first five of your saved layout files in the **Window > Arrange** menu.

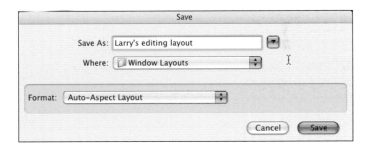

Auto-Aspect Layout means that if you move that layout to a different monitor, using a different screen resolution, the layout will automatically scale to fit the new monitor size. The default is **Fixed Aspect Layout**.

---

8 Earlier you learned how to customize the **Browser** by changing the size of its text, or dragging columns to different locations. You can also resize column widths. Try it now. Grab the divider between two **Browser** column headings and slide it from left to right to change the width of a column.

9 Two default column layouts are built into the Browser: **Standard Columns** and **Logging Columns**. Toggle between them by **Ctrl+clicking** any column header, except **Name**, and choosing the layout you want to use.

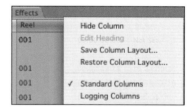

10 You can also hide columns you don't want, or show columns you do, by **Ctrl+clicking** any column heading, except **Name**, and choosing either **Hide Column** or the name of the column you want to show.

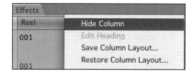

NOTE:

A Fast Way to Move Columns

A trick to quickly move a column is to hide it where it is, then **Ctrl+click** the column header where you want it to move to. Your new column will appear to the **left** of the column you Ctrl+clicked.

11 Again, Final Cut will remember your columns just the way you left them. However, to make your layouts permanent, save them by **Ctrl+clicking** any column header, except, you know, the **Name** column, and choose **Save Custom Layout**.

---

12 To recall a saved layout, **Ctrl+click** any header and choose **Restore Column Layout**. Notice that saved layouts automatically appear in this contextual pop-up menu.

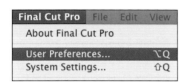

13 Remember, a while back, when you applied a label to a clip, I mentioned that you can customize the text for the label? To do so, choose **Final Cut Pro > User Preferences**.

14 In the **User Preferences** dialog box, click the **Labels** tab.

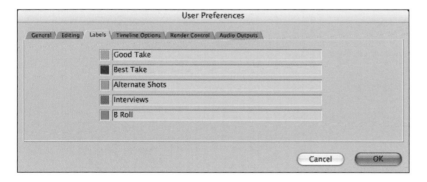

15 In the **Labels** window, you can't change the ugly colors. But you can change the label text to anything you want, by simply selecting the text in the field you want to change and typing in your new label text. Click **OK** to save your changes.

You can even customize the Timeline in terms of track height and a series of attributes. You've already learned how to use the small bar graph to set the track height for all tracks.

There Are FOUR Ways to Apply Labels to a Clip (Whew!)

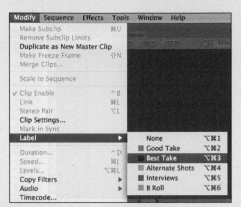

Method 1

Select a clip. Choose **Modify > Label** and choose the label you want to apply to a clip. This is the only method that works on clips in both the **Browser** and the **Timeline**.

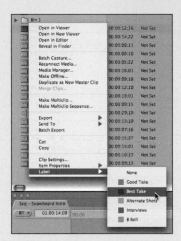

Method 2

Ctrl+click a clip in the **Browser**. Choose the label from the shortcut menu.

Method 3

Ctrl+click in the **Label** column in the **Browser** on the line for the clip you want to change.

Method 4

Use the keyboard shortcuts—**Option+Cmd+1** (the first label, **None**) through **Option+Cmd+6** (the last label, **B Roll**).

16 You can adjust the height of individual tracks by clicking the small gray line between tracks on the far left side of the Timeline. Hold the **Option** key and drag to adjust the height of all audio or all video tracks. Hold the **Shift** key and drag to adjust the height of all tracks.

17 Click the small right-pointing arrow next to the track height bar chart, and a pop-up menu appears where you can choose Timeline attributes. The bottom four menu choices duplicate the gray bar chart to adjust track height. The purpose of the top five choices is illustrated in the following table:

Timeline Attributes

Attribute	What It Does
Show Video Filmstrips	Toggles between displaying video clips as picture and file name, and a series of pictures.
Show Audio Waveforms	Toggles audio waveform display on or off.
Show Through Edits	Indicates when you've made an edit where there is no change in video, audio, or timecode. In other words, it's a cut invisible to the viewer. This is often done to start or end an effect.
Show Duplicate Frames	Used when editing film to indicate if you've used the same shot more than once.
Show Clip Labels	After all the work you've done to create custom labels, this prevents them from being displayed on the Timeline. (Labels are always displayed in the Browser.) Labels are often used to minimize confusion when editing a complex project.
Save... Restore	Saves and restores Timeline layouts to disk.
Reduced... Large	Duplicates the function of the track height bar graph.

18 Choose **Save Track Layout** to save your **Timeline** settings. Previously saved layouts also appear on this menu. Choose **Restore Track Layout** to load a previously saved layout back into the **Timeline**.

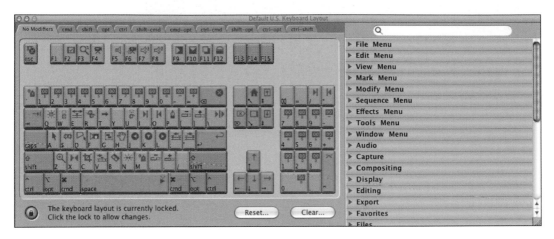

One of the most powerful customization features of Final Cut is the capability to modify the keyboard layout. Your layout may not look exactly like this, because the layout changes depending on which keyboard you are using.

19 Choose **Tools > Keyboard Layout > Customize** to display the **Default Keyboard Layout**.

20 In this case, you will learn to map one of my favorite keyboard shortcuts (**Fit to Window**) to a different key combination, **Ctrl+0** (zero). To do this, first click the **Lock** icon in the lower-left corner to unlock the keyboard; this allows you to make changes.

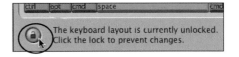

21 Next, type **fit** in the data entry box in the upper-right corner. (Or, if you know the menu it is located in, twirl down the menu list on the right hand side of this dialog box to display the menu choice you want to map to a particular keystroke.)

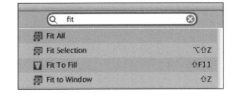

Notice that every menu command containing the letters "fit" is now displayed. There are four of them.

22 Click the **ctrl** modifier key tab to assign this particular command to a specific combination of modifier and keyboard keys. Clicking the tab itself brings it to the front and makes it active. Again, in our case, we want to map the **Fit to Window** command to **Ctrl+0** (zero).

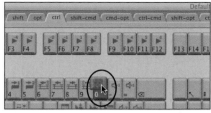

23 Now, grab the **Fit to Window** command from the right side of the window, and drag it on top of the number **0** on the keyboard display.

Ta-DA! That's it. You have now mapped the **Fit to Window** command to a new key combination. Notice that both the old and new keystrokes are listed in the command list on the right of the name of the command.

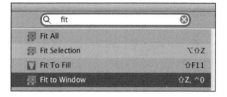

---

24 To delete a command from a key combination, be sure the keyboard is unlocked (remember that lock icon in the lower-left corner?), then drag the icon for the command you want to remove off the key.

Poof! It's gone.

---

25 You can save multiple keyboard layouts, or export one to use on another computer, by choosing **Tools > Keyboard Layout > Save Keyboard Layout**. To change your layout from the default to something else, choose **Tools > Keyboard Layout > Load Keyboard Layout**. Layouts are normally stored in the FCP Preferences folder.

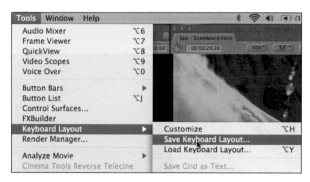

An excellent editor who I work with hates using the keyboard. He does everything with the mouse. So, Ed was rather put out with all the keyboard customization—until I showed him how to create mouse button bars, which converts menu commands into buttons.

NEW▶ New in FCP 5 is the ability to quickly switch between multiple button bars by using **Tools > Button Bars**.

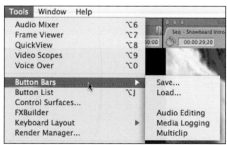

---

26 To convert menu commands to buttons, choose **Tools > Button List (Option + J)**.

---

27 Then, just as you did in finding a command to customize into a keyboard shortcut, type the first few letters of the command you want to convert into a button. (*Secret tip:* You can also type a keyboard shortcut, and FCP will find the menu that matches it.)

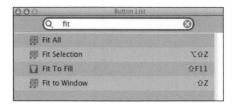

To convert a command to a button, drag it from the button list into a button bar. Button bars are located in the upper-right corner of each of the four main windows. You can reorganize buttons in the bar by dragging them to their new locations.

---

28 Drag the command **Fit To Window** into the button bar at the upper-right corner of the **Timeline**. Voilà! Instant button shortcut.

In fact, all four windows have button bars that expand to fill the dark gray area at the top of each window. If you fill the entire space with buttons, the button bar prevents you from adding more buttons.

---

29 And here's my favorite part. If you want to delete a button, simply grab it and drag it out of the bar. Poof! It disappears in a puff of smoke. (Ah, I love that part!)

---

30 If you **Ctrl+click** a button in any button bar, you can color it, add a spacer, save the button bar to a disk file, or load a different button bar from disk. What you can't do with buttons is rename them, or add something that isn't a menu (like a clip or favorite transition) to the button bar. My suggestion is that if you use buttons, save your layout to disk—just in case.

---

31 It's time to end this chapter. Choose **File > Close Project** and don't save changes. If you are done using Final Cut for a while, choose **Final Cut Pro > Quit Final Cut Pro**. Otherwise, go on to Chapter 3, "*Gather Your Media.*"

Helpful Keyboard Shortcuts

Shortcut	Action
Option+Cmd+D	Shows, or hides, the Dock
Cmd+O	Opens a Final Cut project file
Cmd+1	Shows, or hides, the Viewer
Cmd+2	Shows, or hides, the Canvas
Cmd+3	Shows, or hides, the Timeline
Cmd+4	Shows, or hides, the Browser
Option+Cmd+W	Shows, or hides, audio waveforms in the Timeline
Double-click a clip name	Loads a clip from the Browser (or Timeline) into the Viewer
Type a letter	Selects clip name starting with that letter in the Browser
Option+Cmd+1	Removes a label from a clip in the Browser or Timeline
Option+Cmd+2 through 6	Assigns a label to a clip in the Browser or Timeline
Spacebar	Plays, or stops, a clip in the Viewer, Canvas, or Timeline
J, JJ, JJJ	Plays a clip in reverse at normal, 2x, and 4x speed
K	Stops clip playback
L, LL, LLL	Plays a clip forward in normal, 2x, and 4x speed
K+L (hold down both)	Plays a clip forward at about one-third normal speed
K+J (hold down both)	Plays a clip backward at about one-third normal speed
A	Selects the Selection tool (the Arrow) from the Tool palette
Z	Selects the Zoom In tool from the Tool palette
ZZ	Selects the Zoom Out tool from the Tool palette, or press **Option** and click the Zoom In tool to convert it to the Zoom Out tool
Shift+Z	Fits to Window
Ctrl+U	Resets all windows to their default size and position
Shift+U	Resets all windows to the layout you saved as Custom Layout 1
Option+drag gray bar	Changes height of all audio or all video tracks
Shift+drag gray bar	Changes height of all tracks
Option+Cmd+drag	Moves any window

Summary

This chapter covered a lot of territory in providing an overview of the Final Cut interface, along with ways you can customize it to make it more efficient. During the rest of this book, you'll discover additional depths in this interface, along with more shortcuts and power tools.

3

Gather Your Media

In this chapter, you will learn how to capture media into Final Cut Pro 5.

Capturing is the process of converting the information stored on your videotapes into something the computer can read. And, whether you are capturing DV, VHS, Betacam SP, or high definition, the process of capturing media using Final Cut is exactly the same. (Well, mostly the same. Capturing HDV video is a bit different, so I've written a separate exercise just for HDV.)

And, as usual, Final Cut gives you a variety of ways to capture media. This chapter shows you the options.

The Capture Process

This chapter is an exercise in using your imagination. Why? Because the video you capture from your projects on your system won't match the illustrations in this book. So it's hard to write a step-by-step tutorial unless I ship you the same videotape I'm using to create this chapter.

Sadly, I can't ship a videotape with each copy of the book, because it doesn't fit in the binding. So, I'll just show you how to capture and make sure you understand how the whole process works.

Here are the basic steps:

1. Get organized.

2. Set up Final Cut to capture your media.

3. Determine what you want to capture.

4. Capture it.

Chapter 1, *"Get Organized,"* got you and your system set up and ready to go.

Chapter 2, *"Understanding the Final Cut Pro Interface,"* gave you an orientation to the Final Cut interface.

Now, the next step is to get Final Cut ready to capture media. The good news is that Final Cut is automatically configured during installation to work with DV video. So, if DV is your medium, you don't need to do a lot more to prepare.

About Video Formats

I tend to be persnickety about terminology because, goodness knows, there's a lot of it, both in computers and video. So, if you're going to impress people with your ability to talk in jargon, at least use it correctly! Nothing makes me feel like I'm talking to a flake faster than hearing them spout off using words totally out of context.

So, to improve your status in life, here are some key terms you need to understand:

Capturing: The process of converting the information stored on your video tapes into a QuickTime file that Final Cut can read. This "information" includes the video, audio, timecode, and metadata (the data that describes your media) that is recorded on your tapes.

Importing: Bringing information that is already in digital form into Final Cut. For example, all the files I included on the DVD have already been captured, so if you want to bring them into one of your projects, you would only need to import them. The difference between capturing and importing is that a captured file needs to be converted before Final Cut can use it.

FireWire: FireWire is a communications protocol; it is not a video format. FireWire is simply how two devices, such as a computer and hard disk, or computer and video camera, communicate. It's like two people deciding they will both speak French so they can communicate. If one were speaking English and the other German, they would not be able to understand each other. FireWire is a high-speed protocol for communication.

DV, or digital video: As I use it, DV means the collection of all video formats that include MiniDV, DVCPRO-25, and DVCAM. Technical purists will argue that Betacam SX and DigiBeta are also digital formats and, although that is true, for the purposes of this book I'm going to use the term "DV" to mean these three video formats.

The reason for lumping MiniDV, DVCAM, and DVCPRO-25 together is that, given the same camera, lens, lighting, and subject matter, the image quality and data rate of all three are the same. They just record their data to tape differently.

Video images in DV are significantly compressed in order to keep their file sizes and data rates small, but the video image quality remains high. The data rate for DV is about 3.75 megabytes per second (MB/s).

SD, or standard definition: As I use it, SD is a higher-quality video signal than DV. Generally, SD video comes from DVCPRO-50, Betacam SX, Betacam SP, and DigiBetacam. In order to capture SD video, you generally need to use a capture card, which is a device to convert this higher-quality video into a format Final Cut can read.

The quality of SD images is, generally, better than DV, and the data rate for SD ranges from 7.5 MB/s all the way to 27 MB/s.

HD, or high definition: HD is the new darling of video production. Its images are spectacular, but so are its file sizes. HD video comes from a variety of sources, but fits into one of several file types: DVCPRO HD (DVCPRO-100), 1080p, 1080i, 720p, or 720i.

HD video file sizes range from roughly the size of DV to 40 times larger than DV. In fact, the largest HD image file has a data rate of almost 150 MB/s!

HDV: HDV is a new format combining DV file sizes and data rates, with HD image quality. HDV is captured using FireWire; HD requires you to use a capture card. HDV is envisioned as a transition format to allow DV filmmakers to step up to HD. The only downside is that it requires a very fast computer to edit. HDV data rates range from 2.5 to 3.75 MB/s, which gives you an idea of how much it is compressed!

Frame rate: The speed, measured in frames per second, that your video plays back. There are, essentially, three playback rates: 24 fps, 25 fps, and 30 fps. And, in general, film and some HD use 24, PAL uses 25, and NTSC and other HD formats use 30. (Purists would argue that there are additional frame rates, such as 29.97 and 23.98. They are correct, but for now I'm ignoring them.)

Reel: A name or number given to each reel of videotape to uniquely identify it to Final Cut Pro. I am passionate about using Reel IDs and will explain why later in this chapter.

Data Rates and File Sizes

Video Format	Approx. Data Rate (MB/s)	Approx. Size 1 Hr. Video
DV (MiniDV, DVCAM, DVCPRO-25) and HDV	3.75	13.5 GB
DVCPRO-50	7.5	27 GB
DVCPRO-HD	15	54 GB
8-bit uncompressed (Betacam SP)	20.2	72 GB
10-bit uncompressed (DigiBetacam)	26.7	97 GB
HD (1080p, 30 fps)	150	540 GB

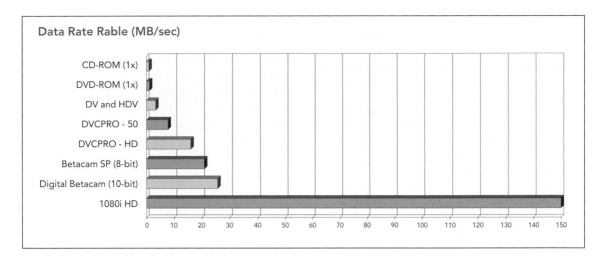

Data Rate Rable (MB/sec)

Format	
CD-ROM (1x)	
DVD-ROM (1x)	
DV and HDV	
DVCPRO - 50	
DVCPRO - HD	
Betacam SP (8-bit)	
Digital Betacam (10-bit)	
1080i HD	

A single, external hard disk is fast enough to capture and play back video for DV and DVCPRO-50. However, for all other video, a RAID provides faster performance and greater storage.

The key point behind these specs is that even though the video formats change, Final Cut remains the same. So, whether you are cutting DV footage or a major motion picture, the process of capturing, editing, and outputting remains the same.

1 | Getting Ready to Capture

How you capture your video determines your project's organization and technical quality. Although you can always change where files are stored or change their file names, it's a *whole* lot easier to spend a few extra minutes at the beginning of a project getting your system set up properly, rather than spending days later in your project trying to convert everything into the proper format.

In this exercise, you'll learn how to set key Final Cut preferences.

---

1 Open Final Cut Pro. Close any open projects (**File > Close Project**). Choose **File > New Project**.

Final Cut instantly creates a new project and displays an **Untitled Project 1** tab in the Browser. Get in the habit of *immediately* saving all new projects. Choose **File > Save Project**.

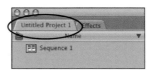

Saving a new project (that is, giving it a name) allows Final Cut to store all media for that project in the same folder. This makes capturing, file management, and, ultimately, archiving a whole lot easier. So remember to immediately save all new projects. I won't remind you again. (And, did you notice I saved it in the **FCP Projects** folder? I *told* you this folder would be useful!)

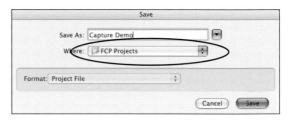

Now that we have a new project to work with, let's get FCP ready to capture. Final Cut has four main preference screens:

- Easy Setup
- Audio/Video Settings
- System Settings
- User Preferences

Let's take a quick look through all of them, to make sure your system is ready.

---

2 Choose **Final Cut Pro > Easy Setup**.

The Easy Setup dialog gives you a single, simple location to set all your audio and video preferences for DV or any other format.

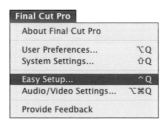

---

3 Click the **Setup For** menu. Choose the video format you want to use for this project. If you are in North America, choose **DV-NTSC**; elsewhere, the **DV-PAL** option is the best choice. (Keep in mind that all the exercises in this book are DV-NTSC.)

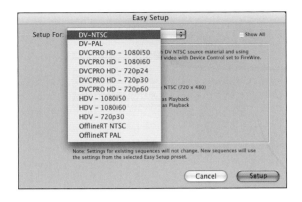

However, Final Cut can handle a whole lot more video formats than just these twelve. If you want to be impressed, click the **Show All** check box, then reselect the **Setup For** menu. Fifty-one different video formats are available, and capture card vendors provide even more. Whew!

Generally, my recommendation is to match the setup for your project with the video format of your camera.

When you select an Easy Setup, Final Cut uses that choice to set a vast range of technical preference settings, which affect sequences, media capture, video deck control, and video and audio playback. Let's take a closer look.

---

4 Choose **Final Cut Pro > Audio/Video Settings**.

The Audio/Video Settings dialog illustrates the benefit of using Easy Setup. Easy Setup sets all these options with one menu. Or, you can use the Audio/Video Settings dialog to set each area individually. If you use only one video format, you'll set these once, then leave them alone.

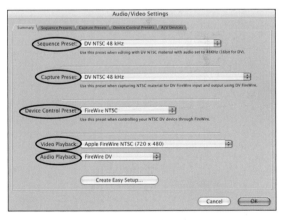

---

5 Click the **Video Playback** menu. (Your list may be different.) This controls where you see the video playback from Final Cut. If you intend to have your camera or deck connected to the computer, set this to **Apple FireWire NTSC** or **Apple FireWire PAL** (depending on your video format).

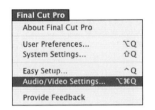

If you don't intend to have a deck or camera connected, set this to **None**, or to a new feature I find quite helpful: **Digital Cinema Desktop Preview**. (**None** means you are watching video only in Final Cut's windows.)

6 Click the **Audio Playback** menu. (Again, your list may be different.) This controls where you hear the audio playback from Final Cut. If you have your speakers connected to your camera or deck, set this to **FireWire DV**; otherwise, set it to **Built-in Audio**.

NOTE:

Monitoring Audio and Video

It is important to monitor your audio and video from the same source. If you are watching your video on your computer screen, set your audio playback to **Built-in Audio**. If you are watching your video on a monitor connected to your camera or deck, set audio playback to **FireWire DV**.

If you listen to your audio on the computer and watch it on a monitor connected to your camera or deck (or vice versa), the audio and video will be four to eight frames out of sync. (That is, their lips are moving earlier or later than when you hear the sound.)

To minimize your headaches, leave audio playback set to **Audio Follows Video**.

As an additional note, if you change your video playback settings, or connect a new device, choose **View > Refresh A/V Devices** (or press **Option+F12**) so that FCP will recognize the new device. You don't need to restart FCP when you connect, or turn on, your camera.

7 In the **Audio/Video Settings** window, click the **Sequence Presets** tab. This illustrates the large number of presets and settings that Final Cut uses to make your video look great.

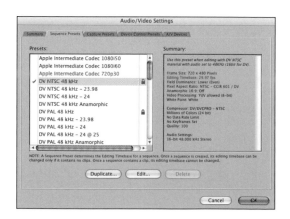

8 Click **Cancel** to close the **Audio/Video Settings** window without saving any changes.

9 Choose **Final Cut Pro > System Settings**. We talked about this dialog in Chapter 1, *"Get Organized."* However, before the start of every project, I always open it to make sure my settings are correct. This is a good habit for you to start as well.

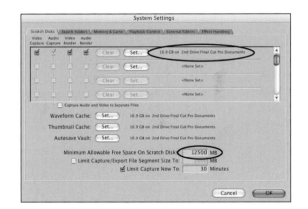

10 Verify that your scratch disk points to the **Final Cut Pro Documents** folder on your second hard drive. Make sure you have at least five per-cent of your hard drive's total space reserved as **Minimum Allowable Free Space On Scratch Disks**.

NEW ▶ New in FCP 5 is the **Search Folders** tab. FCP uses the folders set in this tab to search for media when reconnecting files, which you'll learn about later in this chapter. This significantly speeds up locating missing files, instead of searching an entire hard disk.

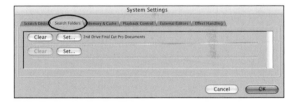

11 Here's a power-user tip: Click the **Memory & Cache** tab. If you intend to use a lot of still images in your projects *and* you have more than 1 GB of RAM in your computer, increase the **Still Cache** so that it is at least 120 MB. Assigning more memory improves how FCP handles still images. Also, set-ting **Application** memory to **90%** will improve performance of background processes.

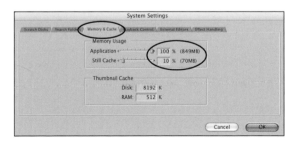

12 Click **OK** to accept the changes you made to **System Settings**.

13 Choose **Final Cut Pro > User Preferences**.

This **General** screen changed, again, in Final Cut Pro 5. A few more options have been added. The settings shown here are how I set up my system, which is changed somewhat from the defaults.

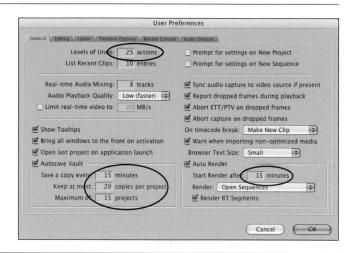

14 **NEW►** If you are looking for a quick tip, change your settings to match mine in the screen above.

New in FCP 5 is **Browser Text Size**, yay!, which you learned about in Chapter 2, and **Limit real-time video to**. This allows you to "tune" FCP to the data rate supported by your hard disk. This will help eliminate the dreaded "Dropped Frames" warning. To set this, either measure the data rate of your media drive or, when you get the dropped frames warning, set this 2 MB/s lower until either a red render bar appears or until the clip plays smoothly. On an external FireWire 400 drive, I set this to 16 MB/s.

Increasing the **Levels of Undo** makes sense only if you have more than 1 GB of RAM. The maximum is 99. I like 25. Too many levels of undo soaks up too much memory.

The **Autosave Vault** is an automatic backup system built into Final Cut to help make sure you don't accidentally lose a project due to a crash. You should still save your project files, as you would do normally. This is an insurance policy to protect against disaster, not a means for you to avoid saving your projects.

Save a copy every is a timer, which saves a copy of your project at that moment in time and stores it in the **Autosave Vault** folder inside the **Final Cut Pro Documents** folder on your second hard drive. Fifteen minutes is, for me, a nice balance between safety and the interruption for saving my project. (You change the location where the Autosave Vault saves files using the **System Settings > Scratch Disks** dialog.)

Keep at Most tells Final Cut how many backup copies of your project you want to keep. In this case, when the twenty-first version is saved, the first version is erased. This makes sure your hard disk doesn't fill up with backup project files.

Maximum Of tells Final Cut how many projects should be backed up. I don't work on that many projects at one time, so, in this case, when the sixteenth project is backed up, all the backup files from the oldest project are erased. If you are editing lots of projects at once, you should increase this number.

The **Auto Render** settings tell Final Cut that when the application is idle, in this case, for 15 minutes, to go ahead and render all open sequences. Notice, I said when the "application" is idle, not the computer. This is significant. You'll learn more about rendering in Chapter 9, "Transitions—Making Change Beautiful."

This preference screen also contains the menu setting for what to do on a time-code break. Timecode breaks are the bane of our existence. In the past, when Final Cut Pro tripped over a timecode break, it would just stop the capture and stand there, pouting. Now, instead, Final Cut gives you three choices:

Make New Clip: FCP closes the current clip it is recording to disk, creates a new file, gives it a new reel number (by incrementing the old reel number by one), creates a new file name (by incrementing the old file name by one), recues the tape as close to the timecode break as possible, and starts capturing the new clip, starting about 3 seconds after the break. Best of all, this is all done automatically. I recommend this setting.

Abort Capture: Here, Final Cut stops immediately after it senses a break and waits for instructions from you. Nothing gets recorded to the disk.

Warn After Capture: Final Cut captures the clip with the bad timecode, then warns you after it's finished recording the clip that the captured clip will probably be unusable. I can't think of a single reason why using this is a good choice—unless you have bad timecode recorded on your tape, but the video is good. Use this option, then replace the timecode once the clip is in Final Cut.

15 Click the **Editing** tab. Again, as long as we are here, change your settings to match mine. You'll learn more about what these settings do in Chapter 4, *"Build Your Story."*

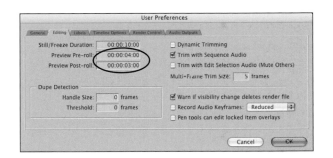

16 Click **OK** when you are done making changes.

One last point. There are two options in the **File** menu that relate to the User Preferences dialog: **Revert Project** and **Restore Project**.

Revert Project cancels your current project, though giving you the ability to save your changes, and loads the last version of the project that you saved to disk.

Restore Project cancels your current project, though giving you the ability to save your changes, and opens a dialog listing all the different versions of the project saved in the Autosave Vault, sorted from most recent at the top to oldest at the bottom.

17 You are now done with this exercise. If you are done using Final Cut, choose **Final Cut Pro > Quit**; otherwise, choose **File > Close Project** and don't save changes.

2 | Exploring the Log and Capture Screen

I probably get more questions from my students about capturing than any other two subjects in Final Cut Pro. In this exercise and demo, you'll explore the Log and Capture screen, discover how Final Cut captures audio, and hear my final rant on reel numbers.

First, though, a definition of "logging." **Logging** is the process of describing each shot you plan to capture. Generally, this involves recording the timecode for the start and end of a shot, the reel it is on, a description of what is in the shot, and whether it is any good or not. Final Cut simplifies this process, but logging is just about everyone's least favorite editing activity.

Sadly, it is also indispensable. You need to know what you have before you can edit it.

---

1 Open Final Cut Pro. Then, choose **File > New Project** to create a new empty project. Choose **File > Save Project** and give it a name—**Capture Demo 2**.

---

2 Choose **File > Log and Capture (Cmd+8)**.

The **Log and Capture** window is divided into two sections:

* The left side contains a preview window, timecode entry boxes, and machine controls.

* The right side contains three tabs, the first of which contains the data entry fields for logging a clip.

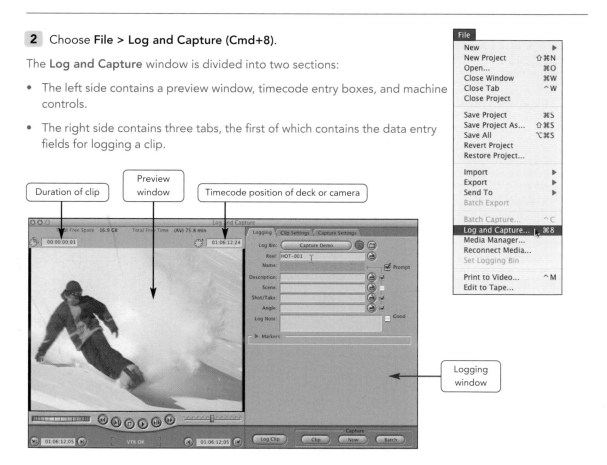

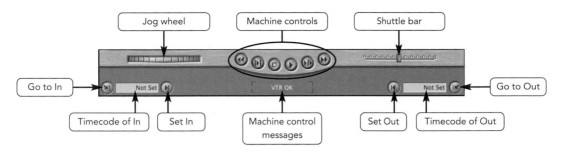

This is the bottom of the image preview window. The machine controls are exactly like those in the Viewer and Canvas, which you learned how to use in Chapter 2, *"Understanding the Final Cut Pro Interface."* The machine control message panel in the lower center of the screen, here showing **VTR OK**, indicates whether Final Cut can communicate with your camera or deck.

The timecode boxes in each of the four corners are discussed later in this exercise.

Machine Control Messages

Message	Meaning
VTR OK	This means that Final Cut is able to control your deck or camera. Generally, when you are using FireWire, this message also means that FCP is also able to see audio, video, and timecode. When using RS-422 signals to communicate with your deck, which is very common in SD and HD editing, this message means that Final Cut has machine control. You should not assume that Final Cut can also see audio or video.
VTR in Local	You need to set your Local/Remote switch on the deck to Remote for Final Cut to control the deck or camera.
Not threaded	There's no videotape in your deck.
No communication	Final Cut is not able to communicate with the deck for deck control. This message is always displayed when using Capture Now to capture from a noncontrollable device, such as a VHS or DVD deck.

NOTE:

Log and Capture Window Secret Tip

Don't tell anyone, but here's something new. The Log and Capture windows opens with the Preview window set to the same size as the Viewer. So, if you want the Log and Capture window to open bigger, or smaller, change the size of the Viewer before opening Log and Capture. Choose **Window > Arrange > Two Up**, then open Log and Capture. Wow!

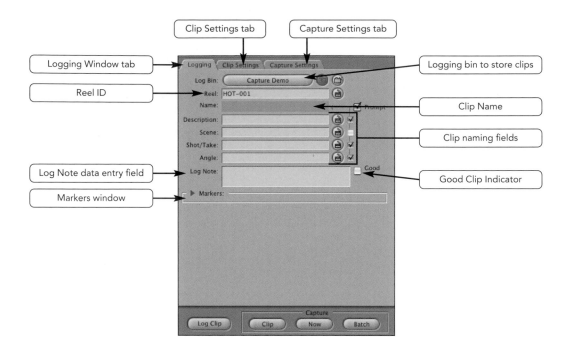

The right side of the Log and Capture window is where you log clips (the top half) or capture clips (the bottom panel).

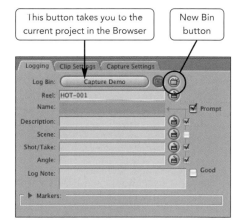

Clicking the long oval, here labeled **Capture Demo**, automatically takes you to the **Browser**. The name in the oval is the name of the currently active project. Final Cut stores all newly logged or captured clips in the active project. An active project is indicated by its tab being frontmost in the Browser. To make a project active, click its Browser tab.

Clicking the **New Bin** button creates a new bin in the Browser for you to store your clips.

Just below the **Log Bin** button is the **Name** section, where you enter the **Reel** name or number, along with naming the clip.

The check box next to **Prompt** means that Final Cut will ask you to confirm the clip name before it saves it to the Browser.

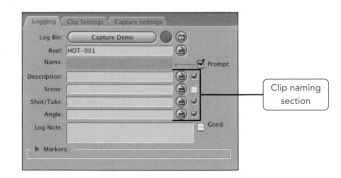

NOTE:

Set Logging Bin

Unless you tell Final Cut otherwise, all your newly logged clips go into the Browser at the top level, that is, outside any bins.

If you want FCP to automatically store all your newly logged clips into a specific bin, select the bin (here, I used Bin 3) and choose **File > Set Logging Bin**.

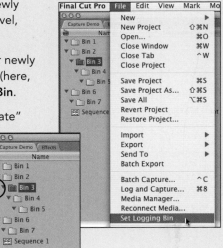

Notice when you do that the little "logging slate" icon moves from the upper-left corner of the Browser, down next to the bin you selected as your logging bin. This slate icon indicates where all newly logged clips are stored: either the default setting of the Browser at large, or next to a specific bin.

NOTE:

A Rant on Reel Numbers and Names

If you never, ever, not even once, plan to reuse any of your projects or media, you can skip to the next section. On the other hand, if you are like the rest of us, you're always reusing projects, in which case, this rant is important.

When you log a clip, Final Cut records the reel number along with the rest of the logging information. When you capture a clip, Final Cut records the reel number into the media file itself, which is stored on your hard disk, and into the clip information tracked by the Browser. This means that if you ever use the same clip in more than one project, the reel information follows right along with it.

Why is this important? Because when it comes time to recapture a project, either because you want to convert it to higher quality, or you want to reedit an old project, Final Cut uses the reel numbers to locate the source reels of your clips.

If all your reel numbers start with "001," the default for Final Cut, how will you, or Final Cut, know which tape a piece of media came from? Right. You won't. And Final Cut won't. Which means you'll need to go through every one of your tapes to find the one you need.

And that is just plain stupid. Whenever you put a new tape into your deck to capture into Final Cut, enter its reel number into the Reel data field and let Final Cut track it, automatically.

By the way, reel numbers can contain letters, numbers, spaces, and underscores. Avoid punctuation. Keep them short.

Whew. OK—I'm done now.

The **Description**, **Scene**, and **Shot/Take** fields are simply text fields you use to name your clip. Final Cut combines what you enter here to form the clip name, based on the check boxes to the right of each field.

NEW▶ New in FCP 5 is **Angle**, which allows you to enter the camera angle, which is helpful when creating a multicam clip. See Chapter 7, *"Multiclips—Many Views of the Same Thing."*

For instance, in the left screen shot, all four check boxes are checked, so the **Name** field combines all four fields into one name, with each field separated by an underscore.

In the center screen shot, the first and third check boxes are checked, so the **Name** combines only the first and third fields.

In the right screen shot, only the first check box is checked, so the **Name** uses only the contents of the first field.

This automation helps make naming clips easier.

Good is simply a check box that means anything you want it to mean.

And **Log Note** is a text entry box that is useful for adding a description about the clip. Later, you'll learn how you can search in the Browser for data in this field.

The **Capture** controls, at the bottom of the right side, are explained a little later in this chapter, during the capture demo.

NEW▶ The **Clip Settings** tab totally changed in FCP 5. The big addition is the ability to capture more than two channels of audio at once. (More on that in a second.)

The **Video** checkmark means you are capturing video. (The default is checked.) The **Audio** checkmark means you are capturing audio. (The default is checked.)

When you are capturing DV, none of the video or audio control settings are active, because DV is a purely digital transfer from deck to computer. These controls become active only when you are using a capture card to bring in analog video (such as VHS, live camera, DVD player, or Betacam SP).

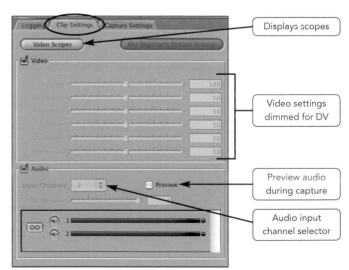

Displays scopes

Video settings dimmed for DV

Preview audio during capture

Audio input channel selector

NEW▶ Final Cut Finally Captures Multiple Audio Channels

Granted, if you shoot only DV, the ability to capture more than two audio channels isn't that impressive because DV uses only two audio channels. However, a lot of my work is with professional formats, and this feature is "Huge!" as Michael Horton, Head-Cutter of the L.A. Final Cut Pro User Group would say.

If you are capturing DV, all these settings are dimmed. If you are capturing in other formats, the Audio Input Channels pop-up lights up. Select the number of audio channels you wish to import. Note that they are always imported in pairs.

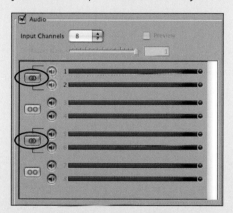

I selected 8 channels to import; then, I clicked on the small icon to the left of the first and third pairs to toggle them from their default of dual-mono to a stereo pair. Notice that each channel has its own audio meter to help assure your input levels are correct prior to capture.

Plus, in the upper-right corner is a small Preview button. When that's checked, you are able to hear the audio that Final Cut is capturing during the capture.

Also new in FCP 5 is the ability to capture and edit 24-bit, 96 kHz audio files.

All in all, these are some wonderful audio enhancements, which you'll learn more about in Chapter 8, *"Audio—The Secret to a Great Picture."*

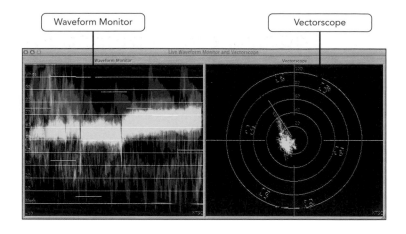

Waveform Monitor

Vectorscope

There's one other section on this tab to look at—Video Scopes; specifically, the **Waveform Monitor** and **Vectorscope**.

The **Waveform Monitor** (left picture) shows the grayscale shading in your picture from black, at the bottom, to white, at the top.

The **Vectorscope** (right picture) shows the color in your picture, from all shades of gray at the center, to highly saturated colors radiating out toward the edges.

If you are capturing DV, you can ignore the scopes during capture, because DV is simply transferring the digital signal from the tape to your computer. All video adjustment settings are turned off.

If you are capturing analog tape, scopes are important in properly setting up your images. Chapter 10, *"Text, Titles, and Graphics,"* covers scopes in more detail.

The third tab, **Capture Settings**, allows you to change device control, capture settings, and scratch disks. These are simply shortcuts to preference windows you've already learned; it's just that Apple has provided you a quick way to access them from the Log and Capture window.

Generally, when capturing DV, once you have these set, you won't need to change them.

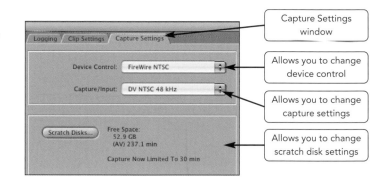

Capture Settings window

Allows you to change device control

Allows you to change capture settings

Allows you to change scratch disk settings

---

3 Close the **Log and Capture** window. This exercise is done. If you are done using Final Cut for now, choose **Final Cut Pro > Quit**; otherwise, choose **File > Close Project** and don't save changes.

DVD MOVIE: | **capture.mov**

If you want to watch capturing in action, check out **capture.mov** in the **movies** folder of the **Final Cut Pro 5 HOT DVD** bound into the back of this book.

3 | Logging and Capturing Media

In this exercise and demo, you'll learn how to mark clips, name clips, determine the best way to capture them, and then capture the media. Capturing media changed slightly in FCP 5 in that capturing HDV is different from what we are used to. For this reason, Exercise 4 discusses how to capture HDV media.

Keep in mind that since you and I are working with different tapes, our screens won't match. However, the process of capturing is identical, regardless of the content.

For the media in this exercise, I am working with snowboarding footage shot by Standard Films, Lake Tahoe, Nevada. The footage was first shot on Super 16 film, telecined to Betacam SP, then converted to DVCAM for use in this book (**www.standardfilms.com**).

---

1 Open Final Cut Pro. Create a new project by choosing **File > New Project**, then save it by choosing **File > Save Project**. Call it **Capture Demo 3**.

---

2 Open the **Log and Capture** window (**Cmd+8**).

---

3 Put a tape in your deck or camera. (OK, stop laughing. You must admit, it is pretty hard to capture a tape when you forgot to put it in your deck.)

NOTE: **Deck vs. Camera**

I tend to use the term "deck" because that's what I work with most often. If you are serious about your editing, and can afford it, a videotape deck makes a great deal of sense. It decreases wear and tear on your camera, it has a more rugged tape transport, it allows you to permanently connect your video monitor and speakers to something that doesn't keep moving around all the time, and it frees up your camera for shooting.

So, from here on out, I'll use the term "deck" to include both camera and deck.

Notice that when you put the tape in your deck, the message at the bottom of the **Log and Capture** window changes from **Not Threaded** to **VTR OK**.

---

4 Enter the reel number for that tape in the **Reel** field. (After all the preaching I've done on this point, don't let me down.)

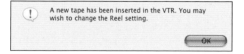

NOTE:

Definitions

Scrub a clip	To view a clip in Log and Capture, Viewer, or Canvas by dragging the playhead.
Marking a clip	To view a clip to set an In (where it starts) and an Out (where it ends) using timecode.
Logging a clip	Giving a clip that you've marked a name and storing it in the Browser.
Capture Now	Capturing a clip immediately, without first assigning an In or an Out.
Log and Capture	Capturing a clip after you first assigned a name and given it an In and an Out.
Talking head	The audio and video of the person being interviewed.
B-roll	Pictures of what the person being interviewed is talking about, used for illustration.
SOT	Sound on tape. Video with audio, generally meaning a person talking.
Natural sound	Sounds from the environment, not from someone being interviewed, such as the sound of machinery being used, an audience applauding, or animals in the field, which are included with B-roll video to provide a greater sense of realism.

NOTE:

Log and Capture vs. Capture Now

There's a lot of heated debate about which is better, Log and Capture or Capture Now. Each has its benefits, and as usual, Final Cut supports both. You get to pick.

Log and Capture: The benefit to Log and Capture is that you look at all your tape before you capture it and make decisions on what you want to capture. This means that you don't waste disk space, or time, capturing footage you won't use; for example, the 20-minute shot of the cameraman's foot as he walks from one location to another when he forgot to turn off the Record button.

The logging side of the Log and Capture window is specifically designed to make logging as painless as possible.

The disadvantage to Log and Capture is that you have to look at all your tape and start making decisions before you capture anything. This takes a lot of time and thought.

I am a huge fan of Log and Capture, but I will confess I hate to log my tapes. It takes time, and it forces me to start making editing decisions very early in the process.

Capture Now: The benefit to Capture Now is that you click one button, **Capture Now**, and Final Cut starts immediately recording whatever you play from your deck

continues on next page

NOTE:

Log and Capture vs. Capture Now *continued*

onto your hard drive. This means that you can capture huge quantities of media, without having to watch them first.

Capture Now is a favorite of assistant editors in Hollywood whose job description is to capture material so that the editors can decide what they want to cut.

It is also a favorite of people who shoot DV material, because of the capability of Final Cut to flag the start of each scene where the Record button was pressed, which can be a great help in figuring out what you want to edit. (This process of marking DV Starts and Stops is discussed later in this chapter.)

The disadvantage to Capture Now is that you are capturing *huge* data files, most of which you won't use. If disk space is at a premium, this is not an ideal way to work.

Personally, I am not a fan of Capture Now. My recommendation, if you want to capture long clips, is to set an In at the beginning of the tape and an Out at the end, then capture using Capture Clip. I've found this to be the most reliable way to capture long clips.

This first example shows you how to capture a clip using logging techniques. Later in this exercise, you'll learn how to capture a clip using Capture Now.

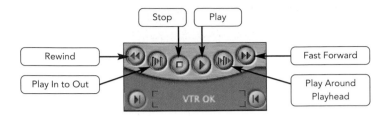

There are six machine control buttons (from left to right):

- Rewind

- Play In to Out

- Stop

- Play

- Play Around Playhead, which plays from a few seconds before the current playhead location to a few seconds afterward. (You set this timing in the Editing tab of **User Preferences**.)

- Fast Forward

---

5 In the **Log and Capture** window, use the machine controls, or the navigation controls you learned in Chapter 2, *"Understanding the Final Cut Pro Interface"* (the J, K, and L keys, spacebar, jog wheel, or shuttle bar), to play your tape until you find the beginning of the shot you want to use.

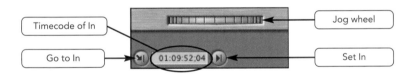

6 Press the **I** key to set an **In**, or click the **Set In** button in the lower-left corner of the window. The timecode for your **In** now appears in the **In** field.

---

7 Play your tape until you find the end of the shot.

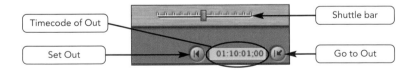

8 Press the **O** key to set an **Out**, or click the **Set Out** button in the lower-right corner of the window. The timecode for your **Out** now appears in the **Out** field.

Duration of clip

Timecode position of deck

Notice that Final Cut automatically calculates the duration of your clip and displays it in the upper-left corner of the window; the box in the upper-right corner displays the current timecode location of the deck.

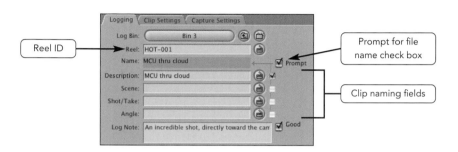

Reel ID

Prompt for file name check box

Clip naming fields

9 Give your clip a name by entering it into the **Name** fields you learned about in the last exercise. (I just used the **Description** field with a **Reel** ID of **HOT-001**.)

Generally, when I am editing an interview with B-roll, I start all interview clip names with the last name of the person being interviewed, and all B-roll shots with the letter "B." This makes it easer for me to find the shots I need later.

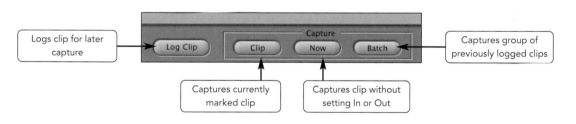

Logs clip for later capture

Captures group of previously logged clips

Captures currently marked clip

Captures clip without setting In or Out

10 In the **Capture** box, click **Clip**. Final Cut cues up the deck to the proper spot and captures the clip. Once the clip is captured, Final Cut gives it the name you assigned in the logging window and displays it in the Browser. This is the easiest way to capture a clip when all you need is one clip.

11 Ta-DA! You've captured your very first clip . (Well, at least, the very first clip using this book .) Double-click the clip in the **Browser** to load it into the **Viewer**, then scrub it to see how great it looks!

Although it is not a good idea to leave the **Log and Capture** window open while you are editing, for now you can leave the window open to view this clip in the **Viewer**.

12 When you are done viewing the clip, click once on the **Log and Capture** window to bring it to the front. Notice, when you do that the clip name in the logging section of the **Capture** window has a number after it, or, if it ended with a number, that number has been increased by one. This is Final Cut's way to help you name your clips.

NOTE:

Clip Names Must Be Unique

The name you give a clip is used in two places: one is the Browser, the other is the name of the actual media file recorded on your hard disk. For this reason, all of your clip names *must* be unique and not contain any characters prohibited by the operating system—such as colons, semicolons, question marks, exclamation points, and other punctuation.

Because file names must be unique, Final Cut adds, or increments, a number at the end of a name after capture. It wants to make sure that all clip and media file names are unique.

13 Repeat Steps 5 through 9 to mark and log a second clip.

14 This time, click the **Log Clip** button.

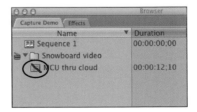

15 A dialog pops up (if the **Prompt** check box is checked on the main logging screen) asking you to confirm the clip **Name** and allowing you to modify the **Log Note** or check box indicating if the clip is any good. All of this information is also displayed in various columns in the **Browser**.

If the **Prompt** check box is not checked, the clip is recorded directly to the **Browser** using the name you entered in the **Name** field. The confirmation dialog is not displayed.

Remember, the name you give a clip is the name of the media file stored on your hard disk, as well as the clip name in the **Browser**. Also, the reel ID is permanently recorded into the media file. So, be sure to take a minute to make sure both of these are correct.

Notice that the **Browser** clip has a red line through the icon. This indicates that the **Browser** has all the information it needs to capture the clip, but the media file itself either doesn't exist or needs to be reconnected. You'll learn about reconnection in Exercise 5. You'll learn about how to capture this clip in a few steps.

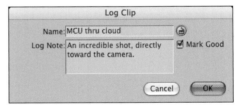

16 Repeat Steps 5 through 9 to select another clip, then click **Log Clip** to load it into the **Browser**. Do this again until you have a series of clips that are ready to capture . (A clip is ready to capture if it is listed in the **Browser** with a red line through its icon.)

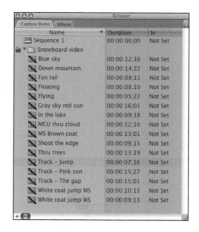

17 Select all the clips you want to capture (all the clips with red lines through them). Then, choose **File > Batch Capture**.

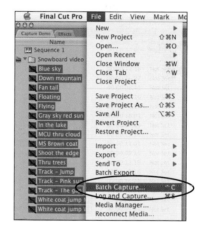

18 In the **Batch Capture** screen, I strongly recommend checking **Add Handles**.

Handles are extra video before the In and after the Out, which you use a lot during editing. You'll find handles extremely helpful in trimming shots, adding transitions and just giving you room to change your mind as you put your show together. Generally, I put 3-second handles on all clips I capture.

Notice how Final Cut prompts you to make sure the right tape is in the deck. If you had selected clips from more than one tape, Final Cut will group them by tape, then prompt you to put in each tape as Final Cut needs it for capture.

This is one reason I am such a firm believer in using reel IDs.

19 Once you verify the tape in the deck is correct, click **Continue**.

Sigh…this is my favorite part of editing. Final Cut now goes off and captures every clip you've selected, while you put your feet up and sip a cup of tea. You can monitor progress by viewing the **Capture** window.

---

20 When Final Cut is done capturing, up pops another screen reporting completion, or requesting a new tape. Click **Finished**.

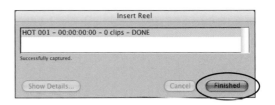

Final Cut removes the red lines from each icon, meaning that each clip in the **Browser** is linked to its media file on your hard disk.

You've now captured individual clips, using the **Clip** button, and a range of clips by logging them first, then capturing them all as a batch.

There is no limit to the number of clips you can capture at one time in batch mode. You can capture clips from multiple reels during the same batch capture. And once a clip is in the **Browser**, you can drag it into whatever bin you want to help keep your clips organized.

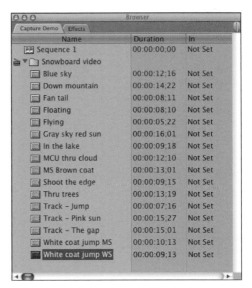

---

21 There is no reason to save this project. If you are done using Final Cut, for now, choose **Final Cut Pro > Quit**; otherwise, choose **File > Close Project**. You don't need to save changes.

---

4 | Using Capture Now

In this exercise, you'll learn how to capture clips using Capture Now, discover clip markers, and use the automated tools in Final Cut to indicate the start of scenes on DV tapes. In many ways, Capture Now is easier than logging, because you don't need to make as many decisions at the outset.

NEW▶ One of the complaints with Capture Now is that it often took the computer a long time to get ready to record (in other words, the "Spinning Beachball of Death" would appear and hang around too long). With the release of QuickTime 7, the processing time has been vastly reduced.

---

1 Open Final Cut Pro, if it isn't already open. Choose **File > New Project**. Save the project and call it **Capture Demo 4**.

---

2 Open the **Log and Capture** window.

---

3 Insert a tape into your deck for capture. Be sure to enter its reel number into the **Reel** field. A dialog pops up to remind you. (Feel VERY guilty if you don't enter a unique reel ID for each tape you capture!)

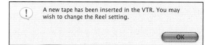

---

4 Using either the controls on your deck, or the navigation controls in the **Log and Capture** window, cue the tape so you are a few seconds before the shot you want to capture.

---

5 Click the **Capture Now** button.

---

6 The **Capture Now** screen appears. Press the **Play** button on your deck to start capturing.

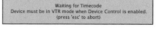

After a brief pause, the **Capture** screen appears, showing the clip you are capturing.

---

7 When you reach the end of the clip you want to capture, press the **Esc** key.

---

8 Notice that once you are done capturing, the clip appears in the **Browser** with a name already assigned. If there is no name in the **Name** field of the **Log and Capture** window, it will be named **Untitled**; otherwise, FCP gives the clip the name entered in the **Name** field.

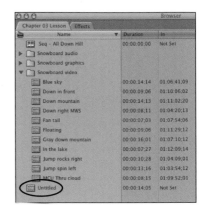

NOTE:

Wow! Why Not Use Capture Now All the Time?

Well, you can.

Log and Capture is more precise, Capture Now is easier. However, you can't use Batch Capture with Capture Now. That means that you need to stay at your computer to capture every clip.

Also, there's sometimes a problem with Capture Now capturing long clips (say, longer than 15 minutes). To prevent this, set an In at the beginning of the tape you want to capture and set an Out at the end. Then, capture it using either Batch Capture, if you have a lot of shots to capture, or Capture Clip, if you only need one shot. Even if you are capturing long passages, capturing using Ins and Outs keeps your clips in sync.

Capture Now is best used with video sources that don't have timecode—for instance, a VHS deck, DVD deck, live camera, or other noncontrollable device. My recommendation is to always capture clips using Capture Clip, using timecode, and using Capture Now only when absolutely necessary.

WARNING:

Renaming Clips

Generally, if you are using Capture Now, you will probably want to rename the clips in the Browser after they've been captured to change the default names to something you'd rather use.

Be careful here. Renaming a clip in the Browser does *not* rename the media file on your hard disk. This means that even though you name the clip "WS My House" in the Browser, the media file on your hard disk retains its original name, which might be something like "Untitled 23."

This is another reason I like Log and Capture versus Capture Now.

NOTE:

DV Start/Stop Detection Is a Great Benefit

One of the great benefits to shooting DV footage is using Start/Stop Detection. When you shoot DV footage, every time you press the Record button, an indicator gets recorded invisibly on the tape, saying that the Record button was pressed here.

Once you capture a clip, you can use Final Cut's **DV Start/Stop Detect** to locate those record points.

Select the clip you want to mark for record points. Choose **Mark > DV Start/Stop Detect**.

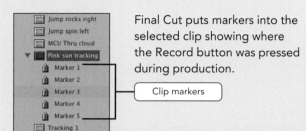

Final Cut puts markers into the selected clip showing where the Record button was pressed during production.

Clip markers

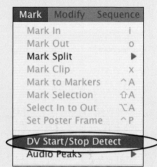

If you double-click the clip icon to load it into the Viewer, you'll see these markers in the white bar along with the playhead. A clip marker is pink, until the playhead is parked on top of it, when it turns yellow.

continues on next page

NOTE: DV Start/Stop Detection Is a Great Benefit *continued*

Yellow = selected marker

Pink = not selected

Clip markers have two colors: yellow for selected markers and pink for unselected markers. The name of the marker is displayed at the bottom of the screen. To change the name of a marker, place the **playhead** on top of a marker, so it changes color, and press **M**.

The **Edit Marker** dialog appears, allowing you to change the name of a marker, add a comment, or change its attributes. You'll learn much more about markers and DV Start/Stop Detection in Exercises 6 and 7 of Chapter 5, *"Organize Your Story."*

9 This concludes the exercise on using **Capture Now**. Choose **File > Close Project**. You don't need to save changes. If you are done using Final Cut for now, choose **Final Cut Pro 5 > Quit**.

5 | Demo—Capturing HDV Media

NEW▶ HDV support is brand-new in FCP 5 and provides a lot of exciting opportunities, especially for independent filmmakers who have been working exclusively in DV media up until now.

I've mentioned earlier that HDV media is different than other video media. For one thing, it is significantly compressed using a process called "long-GOP encoding," which is similar to the way the video for DVDs is compressed. Another difference is that Apple changed the Log and Capture window when capturing HDV.

(Thanks go to Eric Blum, of Eric Blum Productions (**www.ebproductions.com**) for the use of his brand-new HDV camera. Honest, Eric, I *won't* drop it!) If you have an HDV camera, feel free to follow along. Otherwise, skip ahead to the next section.

---

1 Open Final Cut Pro, if it isn't already. Choose **File > New Project**. Save the project and call it **Capture HDV**.

---

2 Make sure your camera is connected via FireWire, turned on, and tape loaded.

---

3 Choose **Final Cut Pro > Easy Setup** and choose the HDV format you want to capture.

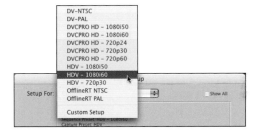

---

4 Notice how all the settings have changed in **Final Cut Pro > Audio Video Settings**. You can set them here instead of using **Easy Setup**, but **Easy Setup** is faster.

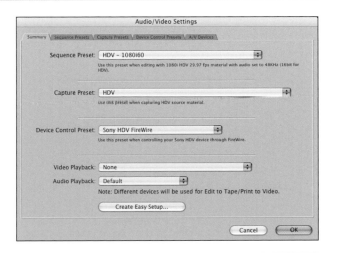

5 Open **Log and Capture**. Notice that with one exception, although the screen looks significantly different, all the functions are the same.

That one different function is a combined shuttle bar and jog wheel in the lower-right corner.

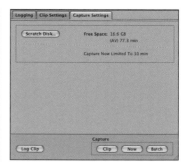

The **Logging**, **Clip Settings**, and **Capture Settings** screens all look different, but work the same. Notice that HDV captures two channels of audio in, and they default to a stereo pair.

---

6 That ends this demo on capturing HDV. Choose **File > Close Project**. You don't need to save changes. If you are done using Final Cut for now, choose **Final Cut Pro 5 > Quit**.

NEW ▶ HDV Isn't DV

One thing I noticed while researching this section on HDV is that HDV playback from the camera is not as responsive as DV when trying to find precise In and Out points. With DV, I could move the deck easily frame-to-frame. With HDV, I tended to give myself more leeway by capturing extra footage at the top and tail of a clip.

Apple's Web site says that due to the nature of HDV, it needs to read entire image blocks before they can be decompressed. So, expect to see different images in the camera monitor and FCP capture window.

In fact, HDV is a significantly different video format from DV, with a variety of quirks all its own. Here's a quick list of things to watch for:

- HDV needs serious CPU power. I strongly recommend a G-5.

- You can't control HDV during capture as precisely as with DV. Editing, however, is very precise.

- You can't monitor HDV on an external video monitor using FireWire, you can only watch HDV on your computer monitor.

- You can only output to tape using Print to Video, not Edit to Tape.

- You must export HDV as a self-contained QuickTime movie to compress the file into MPEG-2. (This reconforms the GOP structure.)

- You don't need to compress HDV using Compressor when going to a DVD because it is already compressed.

- Native HDV resolution is 1440 × 1080.

- There is no HD-SDI deck for high-resolution work.

- HDV converts its native resolution to either 1920 × 1080i or 1280 × 720p.

- HDV has timecode and frame-rate issues; in other words, they are not completely accurate.

- HDV supports only two channels of audio in or out.

You can convert HDV into Apple's Intermediate Codec, which converts HDV from MPEG into a frame-based video format slower computers can edit. This has several benefits and a few disadvantages:

- You can monitor HDV converted into the Intermediate Codec on an external video monitor using FireWire.

- Intermediate Codec is better for slower computers.

- Intermediate Codec file size is four times bigger than HDV.

- Intermediate Codec has quality issues.

- Converting between HDV and the Intermediate Codec is not lossless. There will be a drop in quality.

Demo—Reconnecting Media

NEW▶ Reconnecting media has also changed in this version of FCP, much for the better, I might add. In this exercise, you'll learn why media needs to be reconnected and discover how to reconnect it.

Final Cut stores the path name—the name of every folder between the name of your computer down to each individual media file—for each clip in the Browser. This means that Final Cut knows *exactly* where every file is stored. The problem with this approach is that if you move a media file or, more commonly, rename any of the folders in which those media clips are stored, Final Cut loses track of the file.

Reconnecting is not necessary most of the time. But, if media is missing, this is the only option that puts things back in order.

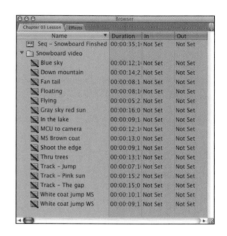

Here, for instance, I moved a lesson file to a new hard disk, and Final Cut can't find the source media. So, it puts a red line through the clip name in the Browser, saying, "Help, I can't find the file."

This is where the organizing you did in Chapter 1, "*Get Organized,*" starts to pay off.

Remember the **Final Cut Pro Documents** folder you created in Chapter 1? Well, when you pointed your scratch disk to that folder, Final Cut created either three or six folders inside it, depending on how you set the rest of your preferences.

All captured media is stored inside the **Capture Scratch** folder. Here, for instance, are media from six different projects.

In the **Capture Scratch** folder, you'll see that Final Cut has created folders for every project you've created. (Again, your folders will be different from mine.) To see all the video I captured for this chapter of the book, I just have to look inside the **Chapter 03 Lesson** folder.

Using this system of setting your scratch disk to **Final Cut Pro Documents** keeps everything clean and organized—provided that you name and save your projects *before* you start capturing media.

Now that you know where Final Cut stores media files (inside the folders named after project files and stored inside **Capture Scratch**), reconnecting lost files is easy.

DVD MOVIE:

NEW▶ archive.mov

Reconnecting media has been improved in FCP 5. If you want to see an example of how to reconnect media, play **archive.mov** in the **movies** folder of the **Final Cut Pro 5 HOT DVD.**

1 When you have missing media, the next time you open a Final Cut project an **Offline Files** dialog appears, asking your help in locating these missing files. Click **Continue** if you don't want to find the missing files, or **Reconnect** if you do.

If you want FCP to ignore the missing files, and never ask you again, check the appropriate box next to either **Media Files** (to ignore missing media) or **Render Files** (to ignore missing render files). As a matter of practice, I never reconnect missing render files, I've found it easier just to re-render. You'll learn more about rendering in Chapter 9, *"Transitions—Making Change Beautiful."*

2 You can also reconnect offline media (that's what FCP clips are called when they are disconnected from the media files stored on your hard disk) by selecting the clips you want to reconnect in the **Browser**, then choosing **File > Reconnect Media**.

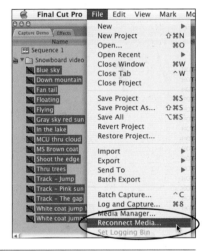

3 In the **Reconnect Files** window that appears, the top box indicates the missing clips. The bottom box shows clips that have been found.

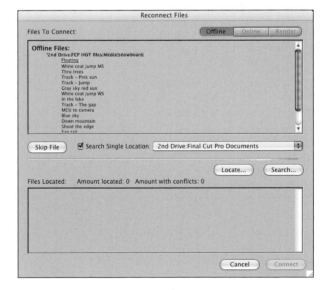

4 This pop-up menu is new and is a huge timesaver. You can search an entire hard disk or, if you know in which folder the files are stored, you can select just a single search location. This significantly speeds file searches. You created a search folder in the **Search Folders** tab of **System Settings** earlier in this chapter.

5 Click the **Search** button. The **Reconnect** window appears. Final Cut attempts to find the missing file by looking for the name of a missing media file on your hard disk that matches the name of the file in the **Browser** (as long as the **Matched Name Only** check box is checked). If it finds the file, it high-lights it in the upper-right side of the dialog.

If you also check **Reconnect All Files in Relative Path**, Final Cut will reconnect all other missing files it finds in the same folder. This can be a huge timesaver when multiple files are stored together.

6 However, in this case, I have a bigger problem. The reel numbers in the **Browser** clip don't match the reel numbers on the hard disk. (This dialog flags only attributes that don't match between media files and **Browser** clips.) Clicking **Try Again** restarts the search which, in this case, won't work. Clicking **Continue** tells Final Cut that you are willing to work with the problem it found, so please connect the files.

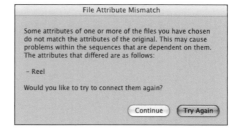

7 This dialog lists all the files it found. Clicking **Connect** relinks them. Clicking **Cancel** exits the dialog and doesn't relink any files.

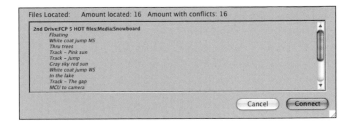

When you're done, all the unlinked files are linked back to the media files on your hard disk, and all the red lines are gone.

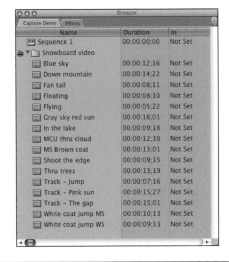

NOTE:

Reconnecting Multiclips

An offline multiclip is the same as a regular clip, except a multiclip contains multiple camera angles all in the same clip. If a multiclip goes offline, or if any angle in it gets unlinked, the entire multiclip is flagged as offline. You reconnect a multiclip the same way as any other clip. If you batch capture a multiclip, FCP captures the media files for all angles.

If you don't know what a multiclip is, don't worry. You'll learn about them in Chapter 7, "Multiclips—Many Views of the Same Thing."

7 | Importing Media

Not all the media you'll use in your project needs to be captured. For instance, scans, graphics, music, sound effects, animation…anything that is already digital doesn't have to be captured. All you need to do to load it into the Browser is import it.

In this exercise, you'll learn how to import video clips, graphics, and audio files into Final Cut. The good news about importing is that all you need to do is find the file. Final Cut figures out what kind of file it is automatically, which makes importing a breeze.

---

1 Start Final Cut Pro if it isn't running already. If you have an open project, choose **File > Close Project**. You don't need to save changes.

---

2 Create a new project by choosing **File > New Project**. You will only use this project for this exercise, so you don't need to save it.

---

3 Start by importing just one file. Choose **File > Import > Files (Cmd+I)**. Navigate to the **FCP 5 HOT Files > Media > Snowboard** folder.

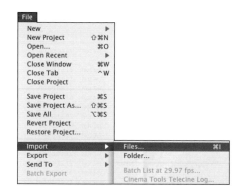

---

4 Select **Thru trees** and click **Choose**. Notice that the file, which had already been captured, is now listed in the **Browser**.

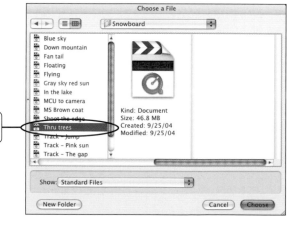

Click to select a single clip

---

5 Choose **File > Import > Files**. Navigate to the **FCP 5 HOT Files > Media > Snowboard** folder and select **Floating**. Then, hold down the **Shift** key and click **Thru trees**. Notice how all files between these two files are also selected. Click **Choose**, and all selected files now appear in the **Browser**.

Shift+clicking selects a range of clips

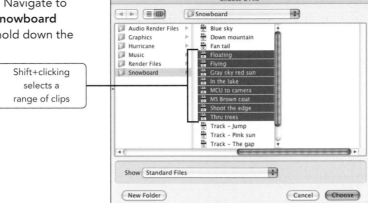

6 Choose **File > Import > Files**, or press **Cmd+I**. Navigate to the **FCP 5 HOT Files > Media > Snowboard** folder and select **Floating**. Hold down the **Cmd** key and click **Gray sky red sun**. Then, while still holding down the **Cmd** key, click **Thru trees**. Notice how only the files you **Cmd+clicked** are selected. Click **Choose**, and all selected files now appear in the **Browser**.

Cmd+clicking selects a discontinuous group of clips

In fact, even though these clips point to the same media file on your hard disk, Final Cut treats each like an entirely separate file, so you see multiple copies of **Gray sky red sun** and **Thru trees**, for example, in the **Browser**.

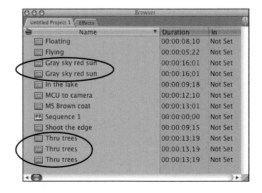

7 However, there's a better way to bring in a lot of files. Choose **File > Import > Folder**. Navigate to the **FCP 5 HOT Files > Media > Snowboard** folder and select it.

8 Now, all the files in that folder are imported and put into a bin in the **Browser** with the same name as the folder. This is a great way to mimic inside Final Cut the way you have your files organized in your computer.

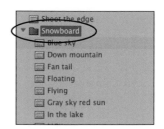

Chapter 10, *"Text, Titles, and Graphics,"* goes into the details of creating video graphics. For now, you just need to know how to import them. There are two types of graphics: single-layer images (such as scans) and multilayer images (such as Photoshop PSD files).

---

9 With either type of graphics, though, the process is the same. Choose **File > Import > Files** and navigate to **FCP 5 HOT Files > Media > Graphics > Canoe.tif**. Click **Choose**.

(By the way, TIFF is an excellent format to use for single-layer graphics. Final Cut supports others, but I've never had a problem with TIFF.)

This hundred-year-old photograph is from a series on turn-of-the-last-century clothing. Notice that it has a default duration of 10:00.

---

10 The default duration for imported graphics is **10:00**. You can change this to whatever length you want by choosing **Final Cut Pro > User Preferences** and clicking the **Editing** tab. Set the **Still/Freeze Duration** to whatever length you'd like; I have mine set to **10:00**.

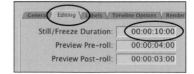

11 Importing a layered Photoshop document is the same, but the results are different. Again, choose **File > Import > Files**, navigate to **FCP 5 HOT Files > Media > Graphics > Snowboard Title.psd**, and click **Choose**.

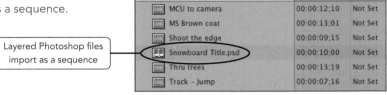

Scans display a graphics icon

Notice that it came in, not as a graphic file, as **Canoe.tif** did, but, instead, as a sequence.

Layered Photoshop files import as a sequence

The great benefit to importing a layered Photoshop file is that all the layers are maintained, along with their alpha channels (transparency information).

In summary, whether you are importing video, audio, graphics, or anything else, it all works exactly the same way—**File > Import > Files** or **File > Import > Folder**.

12 That ends this exercise. Choose **Final Cut Pro > Quit** and don't save changes.

NOTE:

Cheap Importing Tricks

It wouldn't be Final Cut if there weren't some tricks you can use. Here are two tips to speed up importing:

- **Ctrl+click** in the gray area of the **Name** column in the **Browser** and choose **Import > Files.**

- Move some windows around within Final Cut so you can see the **Desktop** underneath FCP. Locate a file or folder that has something you want to import and drag it directly from the **Finder** into the **Browser**.

Both of these tricks making importing faster and easier. Keep in mind, and this is *really* important, that you are *not* importing any *media* into Final Cut. You are only creating a record inside Final Cut that *points* to where this media is stored on your computer. If you move this media file, you'll need to reconnect it. If you delete it from the hard disk, it's gone.

Changing Reel Numbers

Here is a power tip on how to change reel numbers after you've captured a file.

During the first three chapters, I've made a big deal about properly recording reel numbers. However, sometimes, the wrong reel number gets entered into a clip. Sigh...accidents happen. Often, this is due to Final Cut using a default reel ID of 001. If you don't make a point of changing the reel when you put in a new tape, you'll end up with the Browser showing a whole lot of clips—all from reel 001.

Fortunately, Final Cut provides three different ways to change reel numbers.

Remember, back in Chapter 2, *"Understanding the Final Cut Pro Interface,"* when you learned how to rearrange Browser columns by dragging the

column header? Well, one of the clips I captured has the wrong reel number. (I, um, forgot to change it.) So, for convenience, go to the **Browser**, scroll way over to the far-right column, locate the **Reel** column, and drag the **Reel** column header left, next to the **Name** column.

One way to change the reel number is to double-click the reel number. It highlights and allows you to change it. This is the only way to enter a totally new reel number.

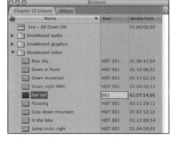

The second way to change a reel number is to **Ctrl+click** it. The shortcut menu that appears allows you to choose from a list of all the dif-

ferent reel numbers currently in use in your project.

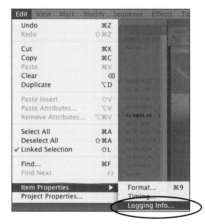

The third way to change a reel number is to use **Edit > Item Properties > Logging Info**. However, the first two ways are faster.

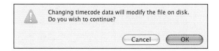

Whichever way you choose, this dialog appears, warning you that you are about to change the actual media file on your hard disk. Why? Because the reel number is stored in the **Browser** *and* the media file. Click **OK**, and the reel number is permanently changed.

Helpful Keyboard Shortcuts

Shortcut	Action
Cmd+8	Opens the Log and Capture window
I	Sets an In
O	Sets an Out
F2	Opens the Log Clip window (use after setting an In and Out)
Shift+I	Shuttles the video tape deck to the In (Log and Capture window)
Shift+O	Shuttles the video tape deck to the Out (Log and Capture window)
M	Places a Marker in a clip in the Viewer
Shift+M	Goes to the next downstream marker
Option+M	Goes to the next upstream marker
Ctrl+Q	Opens the Easy Setup preference window
Option+Cmd+Q	Opens the Audio/Video Preferences window
Shift+Q	Opens the System Settings window
Option+Q	Opens the User Preferences window
Esc	Cancels any open dialog, as well as Capture Now
Option+F12	Reconnects FCP with the audio/video device (camera or deck)
Enter (keypad)	Accepts the default (glowing blue) button in any dialog

Summary

This chapter has covered everything you need to know about capturing media, whether you are using Capture Now, or Log and Capture. And, I can say with relief, that all the hard organizational work is over. Starting with the next chapter, you'll dive right into editing.

And you'll start by creating a 30-second snowboarding commercial.

4

Build Your Story

Any program worth watching has a story at its core. Whether your video is corporate training, a wedding, a commercial, or a documentary, telling your story effectively is essential to keeping the attention of your audience.

The good news about Final Cut is that whether you are editing DV, HDV, SD, or HD, they all edit the same way. So these next five chapters present the heart and soul of editing in Final Cut Pro. The first three cover editing techniques, followed by a chapter devoted to multicam, with the fifth focused on (amplifying?) audio.

I really wanted to call this chapter, "The Ins and Outs of Ins and Outs," because it is. This chapter teaches you how to create and save a new project file, select and view clips in the Viewer, set Ins and Outs, and edit these clips into the Timeline.

Your mantra is, "Editing is the process of getting rid of everything that isn't relevant to telling your story." Sometimes that selection process is easy. Sometimes it's painful. In all cases, it's necessary.

It's now time to put Final Cut to work and start editing.

1 | Creating and Saving a New Project

In this exercise, you'll learn how to create and save a new project, create a new sequence, and learn tips on protecting your projects from disaster.

---

1 Start by opening Final Cut, if it isn't already running. If it is running, close any open projects by choosing **File > Close Project**. (Saving changes is not necessary.)

---

2 Choose **File > New Project**, or press **Shift+Cmd+N**.

---

3 Final Cut automatically creates an empty project and puts a new sequence into the **Browser** and opens it into the **Timeline**.

NOTE: | **Sequence**

A **sequence** is where you edit your clips. A program can consist of a single sequence, or many sequences. Just as the Browser holds clips, the Timeline holds sequences—sometimes just one, other times, lots and lots. Because the Timeline can hold more than one sequence, Final Cut makes it easy to copy clips from one sequence to another.

---

4 Now, before you do anything else— *save* your new project. Choose **File > Save Project As**. In the **Save** dialog, navigate to the **FCP Projects** folder you created during setup at the beginning of this book.

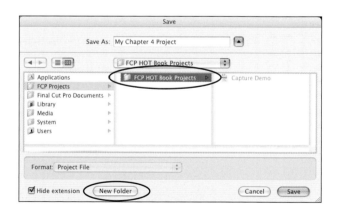

5 Click **New Folder**, in the lower-left corner, and create a folder called **FCP HOT Book Projects**, inside the **FCP Projects** folder. You'll use this folder for all the projects you create in this book.

---

6 Name your project **My Chapter 4 Project**, and click **Save**.

---

7 Create a new bin for your project by choosing **File > New > Bin** (**Cmd+B**). The new bin appears in your **Browser**.

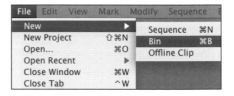

8 Double-click the words **Bin 1**, and type **Video Clips** as the new name. Press **Return**, or click somewhere else to deselect the name.

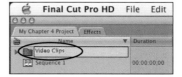

9 As practice in creating a new sequence, create a second sequence for your project by choosing **File > New > Sequence** (**Cmd+N**). Leave it named **Sequence 2**.

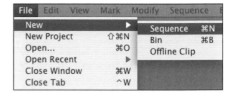

10 Next, make a copy of this sequence by **Ctrl+clicking** the sequence name in the **Browser** and choosing **Duplicate** from the shortcut menu, or press **Option+D**.

Duplicating a sequence is very useful if you have an edited sequence that you like, but want to continue experimenting to see if you can improve it. Duplicating makes an exact copy of the sequence, which you can then change, while still leaving the original sequence intact, in case your great new idea doesn't pan out.

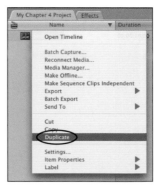

11 In this case, you don't need these sequences, so select both **Sequence 2** and **Sequence 2 Copy** by dragging a rectangle around them, then delete both of them by pressing the **Delete** key.

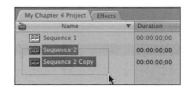

12 Save your project by choosing **File > Save** (**Cmd+S**). Then, close this project (**File > Close Project**)— you won't need it for the next exercise. If you are done working for the moment, choose **Final Cut Pro > Quit**; otherwise, leave FCP running.

N O T E :

Protecting Your Projects

Once you've started working on your project, it's a good idea to protect it from disasters. Here's a tip I recommend to my clients:

If I'm working on a project that will take longer than a day or two to edit, at the end of every couple of days, I choose **File > Save Project As** (or press **Shift+Cmd+S**) and save it under a new name. Most of the time, I just add a new version number at the end, such as "My Project v2," "My Project v3," and so on. However, if I'm still capturing media, I'll rename the old file and keep the new file named the same. Keeping the project name the same means all my captured clips end up in the same folder.

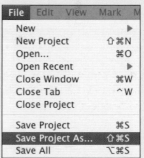

The reason for using **Save As**, instead of duplicating the project in the **Finder**, is that during the **Save As** process, Final Cut straightens out any potential technical problems that may exist with the file. This tends to make project files open and close faster, and have fewer errors during editing. Then, the next time I edit the project, I make sure to open the new version.

2 | Viewing and Marking Clips

In this exercise, you'll learn how to view thumbnails in the Browser, open clips in the Viewer, and set Ins and Outs for your clips.

Why are setting Ins and Outs so important? Because you always capture more footage than you need. Setting an In and Out allows you to select exactly the portion of the clip that best meets the need of your story at that point in time.

In other words, this is all about giving you the control you need to precisely tell your story.

NOTE:

Marking Terms

Media Start: The first frame of the media file stored on your hard disk.

Media End: The last frame of the media file stored on your hard disk.

In: The timecode location where a shot starts. If no In is set, the Media Start becomes the In.

Out: The timecode location where a shot ends. If no Out is set, the Media End becomes the Out.

Marking: Opening a clip in the Viewer and setting the In and/or Out prior to editing it into the Timeline. Marking is generally done in the Viewer, though it can also be done in the Timeline.

Trimming: The process of adjusting the In and Out of a clip, or series of clips, to improve the flow of an edited sequence. Trimming is generally done in the Timeline.

---

1 Open Final Cut, if it isn't already running. Notice, when you do, that it automatically opens the project you were working on when you last quit. If it opens a project file, choose **File > Close Project** to close it.

---

2 Choose **File > Open** and open **Chapter 04 Lesson start**. It's in the **FCP Projects > FCP 5 HOT Files > Lessons** folder you created at the beginning of this book.

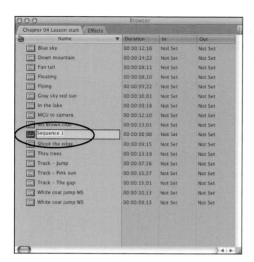
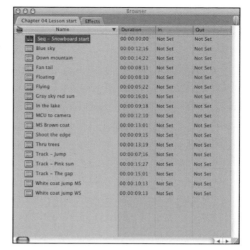

3 Double-click **Sequence 1** and rename it to " **Seq – Snowboard Start**," with a space as the first character, preceding the name. Because the Browser automatically sorts clips and sequences by file name, starting all your sequences with a space means they appear at the top of the **Browser**, making them very easy to find.

What you are about to create is a 30-second commercial for a snowboard company, called **Board Feet**. So, the first thing you need to do in starting a new project is to save it and give it a name.

4 Choose **File > Save Project As**.

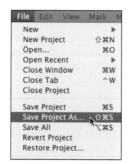

5 Save this in your **FCP HOT Book Projects** folder with the name of **Board Feet**.

Now that you've saved your project, start looking for your opening shot.

The **Browser** provides a handy way to view and play thumbnails of all your clips.

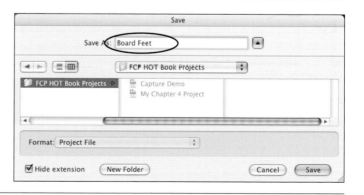

6 Click the **Browser**, **Ctrl+click** the **Duration** column header, and choose **Show Thumbnail** from the shortcut menu.

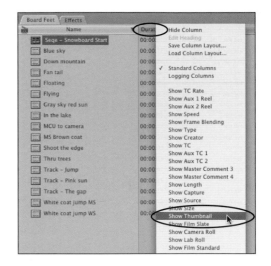

7 Thumbnails of all your clips appear to the left of the **Duration** column. Put your mouse in the middle of the **Floating** thumbnail. Click and drag inside the thumbnail from left to right. Watch, as you do, how the clip plays in the thumbnail.

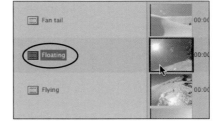

8 The still image you see as a thumbnail is called the clip's **poster frame** (the still image that represents the clip). It defaults to the first frame of the clip, but you can reset it by dragging the thumbnail to the frame you want to set as the new poster frame, then hold down the **Ctrl** key and let go of the mouse.

9 To hide thumbnails, **Ctrl+click** the **Thumbnail** column header and choose **Hide Column** from the shortcut menu.

10 In order to set the **In** and **Out** for a clip, you need to move it to the **Viewer**. There are three ways you can do this:

• Grab a clip in the **Browser** and drag it into the **Viewer**.

• Double-click the icon of a clip in the **Browser** to load it into the **Viewer**.

• Type the first few letters of a clip name to highlight in the **Browser** and press **Return**.

Pick a favorite method (I, personally, am a big fan of double-clicking) and load the clip named **Track – Pink sun** into the **Viewer**.

11 When the clip first loads, the sprocket holes on the left side of the image indicate you are at the start of the media for that clip. (If the sprocket holes are not showing, press the **Home** key.) Press the **End** key to jump to the end of the clip. The sprocket holes on the right indicate you are at the end of the clip.

12 In Chapter 2, "*Understanding the Final Cut Pro Interface*," you learned how to navigate a clip using the spacebar to start and stop, or the J, K, and L keys, or grabbing the playhead with the mouse and dragging it, or using the shuttle bar, or moving the jog wheel. So many choices!

Scrub through this clip using each of these techniques until you are comfortable moving around in a clip.

If you look in the upper-left corner of the **Viewer**, you'll see that the duration of this shot is **15:27** (15 seconds and 27 frames). This is too long for the opening shot, so you need to set a different starting point. This starting point is called the **In**.

13 To set the **In**, move the **playhead** forward a few seconds until the fan of snow behind the board starts to appear. This is at timecode **1:02:13:21**.

14 Now, click the **Mark In** button (or press the letter **I**) to set the **In**.

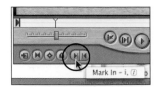

Notice the **In** indicator in the upper-left corner of the screen? Also, a smaller version of the same indicator, called the **In** marker, is now located next to the playhead. This **In** tells Final Cut where you want your shot to start.

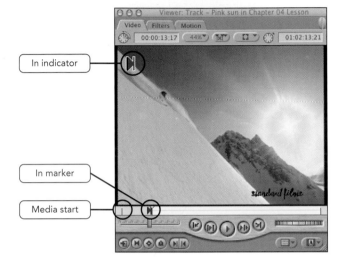

15 If you don't see the **In** indicator in the image, be sure that **Show Overlays** is turned on from the **View** pop-up menu at the top of the **Viewer**.

16 If you want to change the **In**, simply grab it with the arrow cursor and move it. As you do, the picture in the **Viewer** changes as the **In** moves to reflect the change in the starting point. When you are happy with its new position, stop dragging.

Now you need to determine where the shot ends, which is called the **Out**. Make the duration long enough so you can add opening titles when graphics are discussed later, in Chapter 10, *"Text, Titles, and Graphics."*

---

17 Move forward a few seconds until the snowboarder seems swallowed by the cloud of snow. This is around timecode **1:02:19:23**.

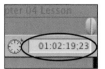

In marker

Playhead

Out indicator

Out marker

Media end

Mark Out – o.

---

18 Click the **Mark Out** button (or press the letter **O**). Notice the **Out** indicator appears in the upper-right corner of the image.

---

19 As well, Final Cut automatically calculated the duration of your shot as **6:03** (6 seconds and 3 frames). And, the **Out** marker moved right next to the **playhead**.

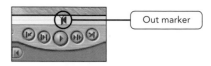
Out marker

---

20 Finally, you can watch your newly marked shot by clicking the **Play In to Out** button (or press **Shift+**) to make sure it looks OK.

Congratulations! You've loaded and marked your first clip!

I spent a lot of time covering this procedure because setting Ins and Outs is essential to editing. You'll do it hundreds of times in a project. And the two Notes that follow provide even more shortcuts you can use to make this whole process even faster and easier.

---

21 Since this is the last step in this exercise, choose **File > Save** (or press **Cmd+S**). It's a good habit to save your work frequently.

NOTE:

Changing Your Mind

If you decide you don't like your In or Out, use these keyboard shortcuts to get rid of them:

Option+I   Clears the In

Option+O   Clears the Out

Option+X   Clears both the In and the Out

NOTE:

Using Timecode to Mark Clips

Because marking clips is so essential, Final Cut allows you to use timecode to help set your Out. Say you want to create a shot that's a specific length (for instance, 3:15). Set your In as you would normally.

Then, double-click the **duration** field at the upper left of the **Viewer** window to select it and enter the duration of your shot (type **315**; FCP inserts the colon automatically). Final Cut sets the Out point exactly 3:15 from the In.

I use this technique a lot, especially for titles, stills, and shots that need to hit a fixed musical beat.

3 | Building the Timeline

In this exercise, you'll start building your first sequence of clips to create your commercial. You'll continue practicing loading clips into the Viewer and marking them. Then, you'll learn ten different ways to edit your clips to the Timeline—and a couple of ways to avoid!

1 If the last exercise is still open, great. If not, open **Board Feet** from your **FCP HOT Book Projects** folder.

2 Load **Track – Pink sun** into the **Viewer** and set the **In** and **Out** as described in the previous lesson. Your clip should have a duration of **6:03**, as shown in the upper-left corner of the **Viewer**.

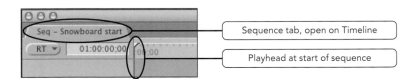

Sequence tab, open on Timeline

Playhead at start of sequence

3 In the **Browser**, double-click the **Seq – Snowboard Start** sequence to open it in the **Timeline**. You know it's open because a tab containing the name of the sequence appears in the upper-left corner of the **Timeline**. Be sure the **playhead** is at the beginning of the sequence. You can move it there quickly by pressing the **Home** key.

Overlay menu

4 Click in the center of the **Viewer** and drag the clip over to the **Canvas** window. As you drag near the right edge of the **Canvas**, a pop-up overlay menu appears. Drag your clip on top of the pink **Overwrite** rectangle and let go.

Your clip has now been edited to the **Timeline** at the location of the **playhead**. Since there is no sound with this clip, only the video has been added to the **Timeline**. You'll start working with audio in Chapter 8, "Audio—The Secret to a Great Picture."

Notice that the playhead automatically moved to the end of the clip. When there is no **In** or **Out** set in the **Timeline** (something you'll learn about in Exercise 4, later in this chapter), the **Timeline** playhead acts as the **In**. All clips edited from the **Viewer** are automatically placed at the position of the playhead in the **Timeline**.

5 Now select and mark a second clip by loading **Blue sky** into the **Viewer**. Move the **playhead** and set the **In** at **1:00:03:11**—just before he slides off the cliff. Then, move the **playhead** and set the **Out** at **1:00:07:10**. If your **duration** is **4:00**, you've done this correctly.

Shot duration   Playhead location

6 This time, click the red **Overwrite** button at the lower left of the **Canvas**. (The **Overwrite** button does the exact same thing as the **Overwrite** overlay you used for the last clip. It's a different interface—a button—but the same result.) Your clip has been edited to the **Timeline** at the location of the **playhead**. And, again, the **playhead** moves to the end of the clip to get ready to position the next edit.

7 Time to add a third clip. Load **Track – The gap** into the **Viewer**. Set the **In** about 5 seconds in, where his legs are covered in a cloud of snow. The timecode is **01:02:33:03**. Set the **duration** to **3:26**.

8 Now, drag the clip from the **Viewer** and place it on top of the red **Overwrite** button in the lower-left corner of the **Canvas**. Again, the clip is edited to the **Timeline**, and the **playhead** moves position.

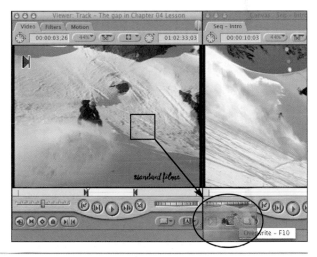

9 Load the fourth clip, **Down mountain**, into the **Viewer** and drag the **playhead** a few seconds in, to where he straightens out to head downhill. (The **In** is **1:00:15:03** with a **duration** of **10:13**.)

Here's the fourth way to edit a clip to the **Timeline**: Press the **F10** key.

If Your Screen Suddenly Goes Crazy...

It's not your fault. When Apple released OS X 10.3, they created a new feature called **Exposé**. Exposé is a very useful tool in that, when your screen is covered with lots of different windows from different applications, Exposé will scale and move all these windows so that you can see them all and pick the one you want. I use it a lot. The problem is that FCP and Exposé use the same keystrokes. Since I use the F10 key combination all the time in FCP (because, for me, it's the fastest way to edit), I've changed my Exposé settings so they don't interfere with Final Cut.

Here's how:

Click the **Blue Apple** at the upper-left corner of your Mac, drag down, and choose **System Preferences**.

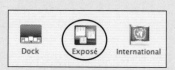

Click the **Exposé** icon. The icon shown on the left is from OS X 10.3. The icon shown on the right is from OS X 10.4 (Tiger).

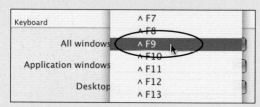
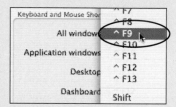

While holding down the **Control** key, click the **All Windows** pop-up menu and choose **^F9**. This changes the Exposé keystroke from **F9** to **Ctrl+F9**.

Do the same for **Application windows** (**^F10**) and **Desktop** (**^F11**). If you are running Tiger, do the same for **Dashboard** (**^F12**).

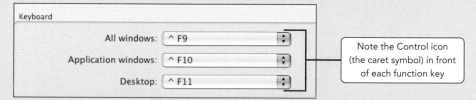

Note the Control icon (the caret symbol) in front of each function key

When you've made these changes, quit System Preferences.

Now, your screen will no longer go crazy when you try to edit a clip to the Timeline using the function keys.

10 Finally, let's add a last shot as payoff to the commercial. Load **In the Lake** into the **Viewer**. Set the **In** where he is just about to take off from the jump. Set the **Out** to where he's trying to keep from drowning. (The **In** is **01:01:06:18** with a **duration** of **6:23**.)

11 This time, drag the clip from the **Viewer** to the end of the clips in the **Timeline**. Watch for the cursor to turn to a downward-pointing arrow, then let go. The clip is added to the end of the **Timeline**.

Five Ways to Edit to the Timeline

You've now learned five ways to edit a clip to the Timeline, four of them automated:

- Drag the clip from the **Viewer** to the overlay window in the **Canvas**.

- Drag the clip from the **Viewer** to the red **Overwrite** button in the **Canvas**.

- Click the red **Overwrite** button.

- Press the **F10** key.

- Drag the clip from the **Viewer** to the **Timeline**. When the cursor turns to a *downward*-pointing arrow, let go.

The first four automatically put the clip at the location of the Timeline playhead. I find that using these automated tools, especially while building my main story track, makes my editing faster and more accurate.

However, I find that using the "drag-to-the-Timeline" approach works well when I am spotting in sound effects or creating composites. In other words, I use dragging to the Timeline only in special situations.

Hmm...there's a problem. I just realized that the beginning of the sequence has two wide shots in a row. This would look better if you put in a different angle between the first and second shots.

12 To do this, load **Fan tail** into the **Viewer**. Set the **In** to **1:00:28:11** and the **duration** to **4:05**.

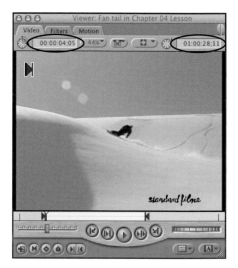

13 Move the **playhead** to the end of the first clip. The fastest way to do this is to use the **up** and **down** arrow keys on your keyboard, but you can also drag the **playhead** with your mouse until it seems to "lock" into position between the two clips.

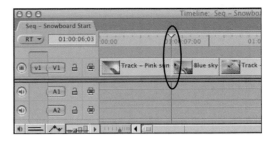

14 Drag the clip from the **Viewer** over to the yellow overlay rectangle in the **Canvas** labeled **Insert**. Notice how the clip is placed where the **playhead** was located, and all the clips, starting with **Blue sky**, were shoved further down the **Timeline**. This new clip was "inserted" into the middle of the sequence.

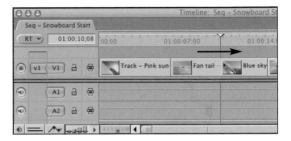

15 Keep this project open. You'll come right back to it in the next exercise. Save your work by pressing **Cmd+S**.

NOTE:

Defining Overwrite Edits vs. Insert Edits

You've just spent a fair amount of time learning how to create an Overwrite edit. An Overwrite edit drops a clip to the Timeline and replaces any video it lands upon.

There is a second kind of edit, called an **Insert** edit. This takes the clip on the Viewer, edits it to the Timeline at the point of the playhead, and pushes all the clips from that location downstream, or later in the Timeline.

An Insert edit is very useful when you want to sandwich a shot between two shots that are already on the Timeline, as you'll see next.

Five Ways to Do an Insert Edit

Just as there are five ways to perform an Overwrite edit, there are also five ways to create an Insert edit. In all cases, you start by setting the In and the Out for the clip in the Viewer.

- Drag the clip from the **Viewer** to the **Insert** option of the overlay window in the **Canvas**.

- Drag the clip from the **Viewer** to the yellow **Insert** button in the lower-left corner of the **Canvas**.

- Click the yellow **Insert** button in the lower-left corner of the **Canvas**.

- Press the **F9** key.

- Drag the clip from the **Viewer** to the **Timeline**. When the cursor turns into a *right*-pointing arrow, let go.

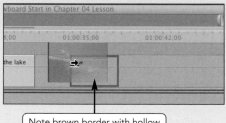

Note brown border with hollow inside icon for Insert edit.

Note solid icon for Overwrite edit.

What determines if the cursor is a down-pointing or right-pointing arrow when you drag to the Timeline? The thin, light gray horizontal line in the middle of the video track. If the cursor is above the line, the arrow points right and creates an Insert edit. If the cursor is below the gray line, the arrow points down and creates an Overwrite edit.

---

editing.mov

If you want to see these ten editing techniques in action, watch the movie named **editing.mov** inside the **movies** folder on the **Final Cut Pro 5 HOT DVD**. This movie illustrates how to mark clips, explains the differences between Overwrite and Insert edits, and shows all the different ways to move a clip from the Viewer to the Timeline.

Don't Drag Clips from the Browser

Although this may seem tempting, it is generally not a good idea to drag a clip directly from the Browser to the Timeline. There are four reasons for this:

- You can't set an In or Out on the clip. Ins or Outs are only set in the Viewer or Timeline.

- You can't use the automated tools to control clip placement, such as using the F10 key or the Overwrite overlay to send a clip to the exact position of the playhead.

- Moving a clip manually means once you move it to the Timeline, you still need to trim it, which creates potential Timeline gaps and positioning errors.

- You can't easily view a clip in the Browser to make sure it's the right one. Yes, you can use thumbnails, but those are often far too small to see what's actually in the shot.

It is faster, more accurate, and easier to get into the habit of loading a clip into the Viewer, setting the In and Out, and using your favorite automated technique to drop the clip exactly where you want it to go on the Timeline.

4 | Three-Point Editing

The techniques you learned in the last exercise assumed that you only needed to set the In or the Out on the clip in the Viewer. However, there are times where setting an In or Out on the Timeline can bail you out of a tough situation.

In point of fact, in order to make an edit, Final Cut needs to know three of four timecode coordinates—the In or Out of the clip in the Viewer and the In or Out of the Timeline—which is why this technique is called **three-point editing**. (If no In or Out is set in the Viewer, Final Cut uses the start of the media for the In and the end of media for the Out. If no In or Out is set in the Timeline, FCP uses the position of the playhead.)

Normally, you would set the In and Out for the clip in the Viewer as the first two points, and use the Timeline playhead for the third reference. However, there are times when you need more precision on the Timeline than that.

---

1 If the project from the last exercise is not open, open **Board Feet** from your **FCP HOT Book Projects** folder.

---

2 Start with a simple example. Create a new sequence and call it " **Seq – 3-point**." (Note there is a leading space in the name.) Double-click it to load it into the **Timeline**. Notice you now have two sequence tabs open in the **Timeline**.

It's OK to have more than one sequence open in the **Timeline** at once. However, if you have less than 1 GB of RAM in your computer, performance improves if you limit the number of opened sequences in the **Timeline**. Sequences in the **Browser** use far less memory, so you can store as many sequences there as you want.

This is why I had you leave the sequence from the last exercise open. It's time now to learn how to close a sequence that's open in the **Timeline**.

---

3 **Ctrl+click** the tab of the sequence you wish to close and choose **Close Tab** from the shortcut menu. The sequence is removed from the **Timeline** but still accessible from the **Browser**. Double-click it to open it back into the **Timeline**.

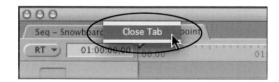

4 Load the clip **Track – The gap** into the **Viewer**. Set an **In** 2 seconds after the start of the clip. Set the **duration** to **5:00** (**In: 1:02:29:08, duration: 5:00**).

5 Now, move the **playhead** in the **Timeline** to **1:00:02:00**. The fastest way to do this is to double-click in the timecode box in the upper-left corner of the **Timeline** and type in the numbers. (Note you don't need to use any periods or commas—more on this later.)

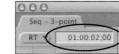

See how the playhead immediately jumped to the timecode you entered?

6 Now, press **I** to set an **In**. Next, move the **playhead** 3 seconds later in the **Timeline**. The easiest way to do this is to press the **+** key on the keypad or keyboard, then type **300** and press **Return**.

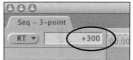

See how the playhead jumped to the new location? You combine + or – with the timecode you entered to move the playhead—in the **Timeline**, **Viewer**, or **Canvas**.

7 Press **O** to set an **Out**.

8 Finally, just to make this challenging, slide the **playhead** so it's before the **In**; the exact amount doesn't matter.

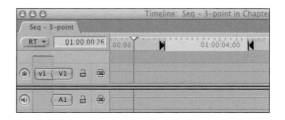

Here's what you've done. You marked a 5-second clip in the **Viewer**. Then, you set a 3-second duration in the **Timeline**. Finally, you moved the **playhead** to a location outside the **In** and **Out** on the **Timeline**.

When you perform this edit, what do you think will happen? Will the edit start at the **playhead** or at the **Timeline In**? Will the edit duration be 3 seconds or 5 seconds?

9 To find out, drag the clip from the **Viewer** onto the **Overwrite** overlay in the **Canvas**.

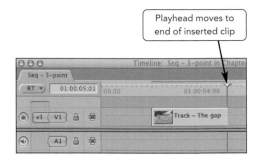

Playhead moves to end of inserted clip

Ah-HA! The clip started at the **Timeline In** and ended at the **Timeline Out**. In other words:

- Setting an **In** on the **Timeline** overrides the position of the **playhead** in determining where a clip starts when edited from the Viewer.

- Setting a duration on the **Timeline** overrides the duration set in the **Viewer**.

Now that you know how Final Cut uses the **Ins** and the **Outs** on the **Timeline**, here's another interesting technique you can use to backtime a clip.

Backtiming means you determine where you want to a clip to end, and Final Cut calculates where it needs to start. Here's an example.

---

10 Again, using **Seq – 3-point**, load the **Thru trees** clip into the **Viewer**. Go to timecode **1:02:01:16** and set an **Out**. (Right, I said set an **Out**.)

---

11 Now, press the minus (–) key on the keypad or keyboard, then type **400**, and press **Return**. The **playhead** in the **Viewer** moves back 4 seconds. Set an **In** (**01:12:03:12**). You should have a clip **duration** of **4:01**.

---

12 On the **Timeline**, move your **playhead** to **1:00:10:00**, either by entering the number into the timecode box or sliding the **playhead**. Set an **Out**. Don't set an **In** on the **Timeline**.

13 Now, drag the clip from the **Viewer** on top of the red **Overwrite** button in the lower-left corner of the **Canvas** and watch what happens.

The 4-second clip in the **Viewer** was moved to the **Timeline** so that the **Out** of the clip in the **Viewer** matched the **Out** set in the **Timeline**.

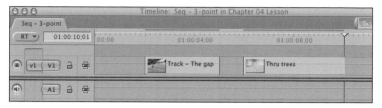

I use this technique frequently when I want to have the end of a video clip match a sound cue or when I need more control over where a clip ends on the **Timeline** than where it begins.

---

14 Save your work, but keep this project open. You'll need it once more before this chapter is done.

NOTE:

Timecode Shortcuts

This last exercise illustrated how you can use timecode to move the playhead in the Viewer and Timeline (and Canvas, too, for that matter). In fact, Final Cut bends over backwards to make it easy to enter timecode.

For instance, the following numbers on each row are equivalent for NTSC video:

1:00:00:00	1000000	1...	
3:00	300	3.	90
1:00:02:15	1000215	1..2.15	1...75

Here's the translation:

- You can substitute a period in place of two zeros for minutes, seconds, or frames.

- Colons are optional; you can leave them out.

- Type a one- or two-digit number, and Final Cut assumes you mean frames. So 15 = 15 frames, 30 = 1:00, 45 = 1:15, and 75 = 2:15.

- Type a three- or four-digit number, and Final Cut assumes you mean seconds and frames. So, 115 = 1:15, 1200 = 12:00, 2445 = 25:15 (that was tricky), and 9999 = 1:42:09. (OK, I haven't really used that last one, but I was curious, so I checked.)

- Type a five- or six-digit number and Final Cut assumes you mean minutes, seconds, and frames.

You can use these techniques to set durations, move the playhead, or, as you'll see later, move clips and even edit points.

Timecode is very cool; it makes video editing much faster and more precise. (For PAL video, the concept is the same, but the numbers are slightly different, because PAL plays 25 frames per second, whereas NTSC plays 30.)

5 | Browser Power Tips

One more quick exercise, this one on harnessing the built-in database power of the Browser to find clips.

---

1 If the project from the last exercise is not open, open **Board Feet** from your **FCP HOT Book Projects** folder.

The easiest way to think of the **Browser** is that it is a database, listing all the elements you can access in your project. Sometimes, though, a project has so many elements, it's hard to find the one you are looking for.

That's where the **Find** command comes in.

---

2 Click once in the **Browser** to select it. Choose **Edit > Find (Cmd+F)**.

---

3 In the **Find** dialog box, type **Flying** in the data entry box and click **Find Next**.

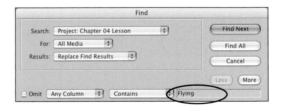

---

4 The **Flying** clip is highlighted in the **Browser**. You can find clips based on an entry in any column or a specific column. If there was another clip in the Browser that contained the word "flying," you would press **Cmd+G** to find another clip that meets the same criteria.

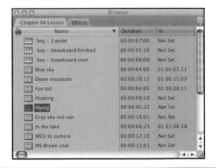

5 But it gets better. This time, choose **Edit > Find**, type **track** into the data entry box, then click **Find All**.

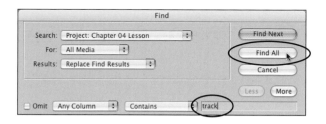

6 This time, every clip, or sequence, that meets your search criteria is displayed in the **Find Results** dialog box. That's why *the two* sequences are included, they *contain* clips whose name includes "track."

Lists all clips or sequences containing the word "track"

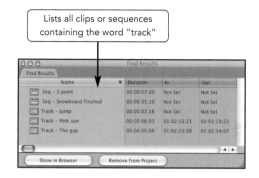

7 Click a clip name in the **Find Results** dialog box to display that clip in the **Browser**.

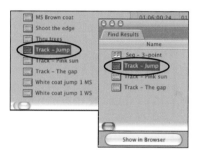

This next tip is one of my personal favorites.

8 Select **Seq – Snowboard Start**. Choose **Edit > Find**.

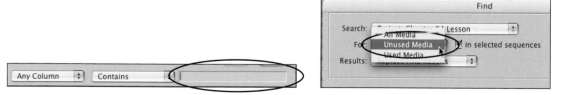

9 Delete any text in the data entry box in the lower-right corner, then choose **Unused Media** from the **For** pop-up menu, and click **Find All**.

Every clip in the Browser that is not in your selected sequence (or sequences) is displayed in the **Find Results** dialog box. Finding unused media is a great help when you are desperate to find a shot you haven't used yet.

A word of caution, however. If you have a clip that runs, say, 30 minutes, and you use 5 seconds of it, the entire clip is flagged as used. For me, this is another great reason to log your clips and capture them in shorter pieces, rather than capturing an entire tape to disk.

All clips that are *not* used in selected sequence

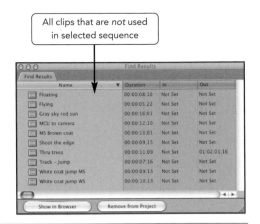

10 NEW▶ Here's a cool technique new to FCP 5. Select a clip in the **Browser**, say, **Down mountain**. Choose **View > Reveal in Finder**. Final Cut locates the source media clip and displays a **Finder** window on top of FCP. This is a huge timesaver, for instance, when you need to rename a media file.

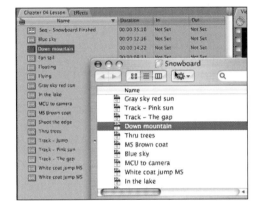

11 Well, that's it for this chapter. Save your work and quit Final Cut if you are going to take a break for a while.

NOTE:

NEW▶ Final Cut Pro 5 Performance Improvements

I guess this is as good a spot as any to mention some of the performance improvements in this version of Final Cut. (If you are new to the program, just nod your head and look impressed.)

- FCP 5 allows sequence durations to be up to twelve hours long.

- FCP 5 has significantly improved performance and stability for large projects, involving hundreds or thousands of clips.

- Audio waveforms draw on screen much faster.

- Zooming into and out of the Timeline is much faster.

- And, best of all, the dreaded Preparing Video for Display dialog is much, much faster. FCP opens and prepares projects for editing much, *much* more quickly.

Helpful Keyboard Shortcuts

Shortcut	Action
Shift+Cmd+N	Creates a new project
Cmd+N	Creates a new sequence in the Browser
Cmd+B	Creates a new bin in the Browser
Cmd+S	Saves the current project
Shift+Cmd+S	Saves the current project using a different name
Option+Cmd+S	Saves all open projects
I	Sets an In
Shift+I	Moves the playhead to the In
Option+I	Clears the In
O	Sets an Out
Shift+O	Moves the playhead to the Out
Option+O	Clears the Out
X	Sets an In and Out simultaneously for the clip the playhead is parked in
Option+X	Clears both the In and the Out
Up arrow	Moves playhead to the In of the preceding clip
Down arrow	Moves playhead to the In of the following clip
\	Plays a few seconds before and after the playhead
Shift+\	Plays from the marked In to the marked Out
Cmd+F	Opens the Find dialog box
Cmd+G	Finds the next clip that meets your search criteria

Summary

You've just learned the technical core of editing with Final Cut. Although there's lots still to learn about how you can make your productions fancier, the techniques you've learned here are the bread-and-butter of every production you will ever edit.

And, although the clips you've been working with are video-only, every technique in this chapter works the same whether you are editing video, audio, or both.

5

Organize Your Story

Repeat after me: "Editing is the process of getting rid of everything that isn't relevant to my story." Make this your editing mantra because it is the heart of all editing.

In Chapter 3, *"Gather Your Media,"* you got rid of all the footage that wasn't worth digitizing. In Chapter 4, *"Build Your Story,"* you got rid of all the footage that wasn't worth putting into the sequence. In this chapter, you'll learn techniques to select, move, and delete the clips in your sequence that aren't worth keeping. Finally, in Chapter 6, *"Trim Your Story,"* you'll learn how to trim your edit points—to get rid of all the frames that make your edits less than perfect.

1 | Navigating the Timeline and Selecting Clips

The number one interface rule for Final Cut is, "select something, then do something to it." Since there is a lot you can do to your clips, it makes sense to spend a few minutes now to learn all the different ways to select them.

---

1 If Final Cut is not running, start it and open **Chapter 05 Lesson**. It's in the **FCP Projects > FCP 5 HOT Files** folder you created at the beginning of this book. Double-click **Seq - Snowboard Start** to open it. This is a modified version of the commercial you started to create in Chapter 4, *"Build Your Story."* I added four shots to the end of it, so the running time is now 59:17, well over the ultimate limit of 30 seconds.

---

2 Save this project as **Board Feet v2** in your **FCP HOT Book Projects** folder. Why "v2?" We could, after all, just create a new sequence in the same project, and that's what I'd probably do in real life. However, for the purposes of training, this gives you practice in creating new projects.

---

3 Take a minute to play the sequence to get familiar with the new shots on it.

So, how did you play the sequence? Did you use the spacebar? The J, K, and L keys? Scroll using the playhead? Everything you learned in the last chapter about navigating a clip in the Viewer also applies to the Timeline.

Plus, in the Timeline you have even more navigation options. With the **Timeline** window selected, press the **up** and **down** arrow keys. See how the **playhead** jumps from clip to clip? This is a very fast way to move precisely through the **Timeline**.

Final Cut is an "inclusive" editor, which means that the **playhead** always shows the frame it is parked on. Here, I've zoomed in on the **Timeline**. See the dark bar starting at the **playhead** and spreading to the right in the screen shot? This dark bar represents the frame currently displayed in the Canvas. It occupies a certain amount of time on the **Timeline** because each video frame is one-thirtieth of a second long in NTSC.

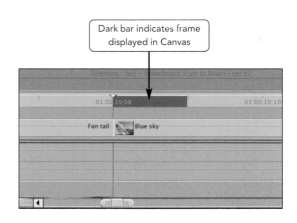

Dark bar indicates frame displayed in Canvas

It is also important to note that when you use the **up** and **down** arrow keys, FCP *always* moves the **playhead** to the **In** of the previous or next clip, never the **Out**. You'll work with this more in Chapter 6, *"Trim Your Story."*

---

4 There are two other keyboard navigation techniques you'll find yourself using frequently:

- Press the **left** or **right** arrow keys to move earlier or later one frame at a time.

- Hold down the **Shift** key and press the **left** or **right** arrows to move earlier or later one second at a time.

Now that you are a wizard at navigation, it is time to learn how to select clips so you can get your Timeline organized.

---

5 In the **Tool** palette, click the **Selection** tool or, what I find much faster, press the **A** key.

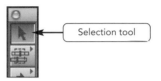

Selection tool

---

6 Click the **Blue sky** clip.

Instant selection. Darn, that was easy! Naturally, this barely scratches the surface.

---

7 Here's a fast way to select a range of clips: using the **Selection** tool, drag a rectangle around the clips. For instance, drag a rectangle around the first three clips in this sequence. (You can also select a range by clicking on the first clip, then **Shift+clicking** on the last clip, but I find drawing rectangles to be much faster.)

Selection rectangle

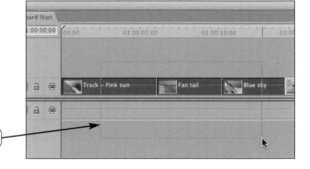

---

8 To deselect a clip, or range of clips, click in the dark gray area above your video tracks but below the timecode bar; or below the last audio track and above the scroll bar. You will find yourself continuously selecting and deselecting clips within Final Cut. (**Cmd+A** to *select* all clips, **Shift+Cmd+A** to *deselect* all clips.)

Click in gray area to deselect.

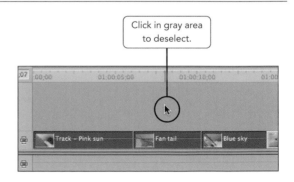

---

9 However, my favorite way to select clips (and most other things in Final Cut) is to use the **Command** key. **Cmd+click** on different clips and notice that only the clips you click are selected. This is called "discontiguous selection," and I use it extensively in every project.

---

10 There are also three selection tools that can help you select clips:

 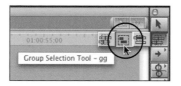 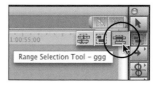

- **Edit Selection** tool (selects edit points across multiple tracks—see Chapter 11, "*Motion Effects*")
- **Group Selection** tool (essentially mimics the Selection tool)
- **Range Selection** tool

In this case, select the third tool: the **Range Selection** tool, or press **GGG**.

---

11 Using the **Range Selection** tool, drag from the end of **Down Mountain** into **In the Lake**. The precise coordinates don't matter. Notice that you've selected portions of two different clips.

You'll learn how to apply these selection techniques next.

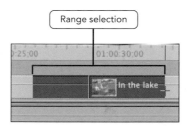

---

12 With that, we end this exercise in selecting clips. Next you'll see how you can use these selection techniques to determine which clips to delete. If you want to take a break, quit Final Cut. Don't save any changes.

Otherwise, leave everything open for the next exercise.

Deleting Clips

In this exercise, you will learn a variety of ways to delete clips and gaps from the Timeline. Remember, "you select something, then you do something to it."

---

1 Open **Chapter 05 Lesson**, if it isn't already open. Load **Seq – Snowboard start** into the **Timeline**.

---

2 Click **Blue sky** to select it. Press the **Delete** key. Poof.

Remember, the **Delete** key is the one that says "Delete" just above the **Return** key, not "del" next to the **End** key. The two keys don't work the same. PowerBooks, and some small keyboards, have only one Delete key. That's, um, the one you should use.

---

3 OK. Maybe that was too easy. Get the clip back by pressing **Cmd+Z** to undo the deletion. But deleting dozens of clips is the same as deleting one: Select what you want to delete, and press the **Delete** key.

---

4 Again, select the first three clips by dragging a rectangle around them, then press the **Delete** key. (You could choose **Sequence > Lift**, but…why? Life is too short.)

Notice the gap that removing these clips has left? Sometimes you want the gap. Sometimes you don't. Removing clips and leaving a gap is called a **lift**. Removing clips and pulling up all downstream clips so that there is no gap is called a **ripple delete**, because its effect "ripples" through the rest of the sequence.

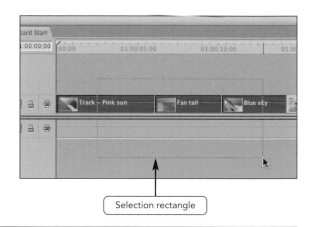

Selection rectangle

---

5 Again, press **Cmd+Z** (or choose **Edit > Undo**) to bring those three clips back.

To perform a ripple delete, select a clip in the middle of the sequence; for instance, **Down mountain**, and press **Shift+Delete**. (Again, you could choose **Sequence > Ripple Delete**, but, really, do you actually have that much time?)

Instead of pressing **Shift+Delete**, you could also press the **del** key, next to the **End** key.

---

6 There are three more selection techniques to illustrate. Select the **Range Selection** tool you learned about in the last exercise, select the end of **White coat jump WS**, and select the beginning of **White coat jump MS**. Then, press the **Delete** key.

Notice that the selected area disappears and leaves a gap.

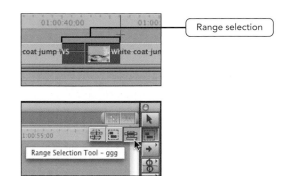

Range selection

Range Selection Tool – ggg

---

7 Press **Cmd+Z** (or choose **Edit > Undo**) to undo that last deletion. This time, press **Shift+Delete** and watch how the selected area disappears, along with the gap.

This gap-closing technique is very helpful in quickly trimming between clips.

The following is another technique that, although I rarely use it for deleting clips, I use a lot with the power editing techniques I will show you in Exercise 4.

---

8 Choose **File > Revert** to load the last saved version back from disk.

When you revert a file, you lose all the changes you've made since you last saved the project. However, sometimes, I make so many changes to a sequence that just don't work out, it is faster to revert back to a saved version than to try to restore everything using undo.

In this case, reverting makes it easy to get all the original clips back that were deleted earlier in this exercise.

By continuing, you will lose all changes made to this project since it was last saved. Are you sure you want to do this?

Cancel   OK

---

9 Now, position the **playhead** in the **Timeline** to timecode **01:00:23:00** and press **I** to set an **In**.

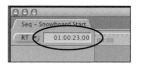

10 Notice that, just as in the **Viewer**, an **In** appears on the **Timeline**. And, unlike in the **Viewer**, the **Timeline** highlights to show which clips are affected by the **In**.

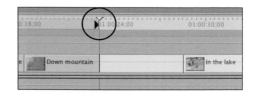

11 Next, drag the **playhead** forward to **01:00:26:00**, and press **O** to set an **Out**.

You could, if you prefer, use the marking tools in the Canvas to set the In and Out, because the Canvas is just another view of the Timeline. The same tools work in both places. However, you can't use the marking tools in the Viewer, because those tools have no effect on clips in the Timeline, only clips in the Viewer.

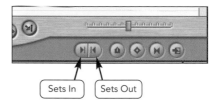

Regardless of how you set the In and Out, when you are done your Timeline now has a highlighted section marked by an In and Out.

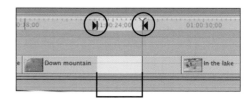

Look up to the upper-left corner of the Canvas. The duration of this Timeline shot is 3:01. Why the extra frame? Because, as you learned in the last exercise, Final Cut is an inclusive editor, which means that it *always* includes the frame the playhead is parked on. From 23:00 to 26:00 is 3 seconds and 1 frame:

- 23:00 – 23:29   (30 frames = one second)

- 24:00 – 24:29   (30 frames = one second)

- 25:00 – 25:29   (30 frames = one second)

- 26:00   (the extra frame)

12 Now, after all this effort setting the **In** and **Out**, press the **Delete** key, and the section bounded by the **In** and **Out** disappears. This is called a **lift delete**. Or, press **Shift+Delete** to make the highlighted section disappear *and* close the gap. This is called a **ripple delete**.

There's one more deletion technique to cover—finding and deleting gaps in the Timeline.

Gaps creep into the Timeline when clips are dragged down from the Viewer, or the playhead is in the wrong position when you apply an automated tool. A **gap** is defined as a horizontal space between *all* tracks in the Timeline.

13 For instance, scroll down the **Timeline** and look immediately after the **In the lake** clip. There's a small gap in the **Timeline** between these two clips.

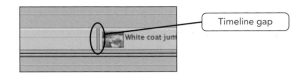

Timeline gap

14 Such a small gap. Wouldn't it be nice to see it more easily? Well, you can—with the **Zoom** tool. Select the first **Zoom** tool in the **Tool** palette (or press the letter **Z**).

Zoom In Tool – z

15 Starting on the left, drag horizontally across the area you want to enlarge and let go of the mouse.

Drag

The **Timeline** zooms in so you can see the gap a whole lot better.

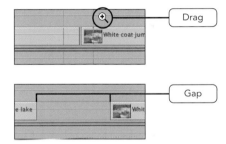

Gap

16 If you zoomed in too far, you can zoom out by selecting the **Zoom Out** tool, or by pressing **ZZ**, or, what's easiest for me, **Option+clicking** where you want to zoom out using the **Zoom In** tool.

17 In any case, click once in the gap to highlight it, then press the **Delete** key, and the gap is closed.

Selected gap

18 Final Cut can help you find gaps in your **Timeline**. Choose **Mark > Next > Gap (Shift+G)** or **Mark > Previous > Gap (Option+G)**.

This jumps the playhead to the next (or previous) gap in the Timeline.

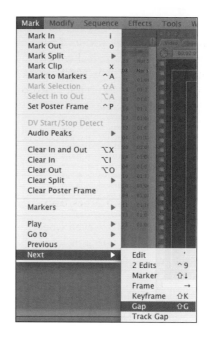

19 Another way to delete a gap is to put the **playhead** anywhere in the gap…

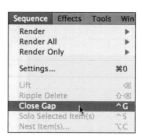

…then choose **Sequence > Close Gap**, or press **Ctrl+G**.

However, not all gaps are across all tracks. Sometimes a gap in a video (or audio) track is covered by other video or audio clips on other tracks. This gap in a single track is called a **track gap**.

There's a special command in Final Cut you can use to find these gaps.

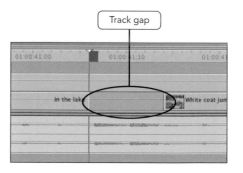

20 For this command to work, select a track by **Option+clicking** its **Auto Select** button. This selects a specific track by turning off all other **Auto Select** buttons except the one for the track you want to select. (You'll learn more about **Auto Select** buttons in the next exercise.)

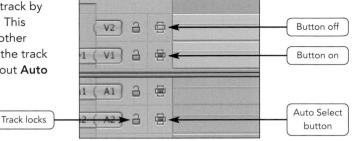

Button off

Button on

Auto Select button

Track locks

21 Next, choose **Mark > Next > Track Gap**.

This technique finds gaps in tracks, even when they are covered by other video or audio clips. Once you've found a gap, you can then decide whether you want to delete it or adjust the clips around it.

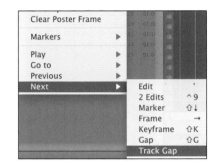

NOTE:

When Deleting Gaps Doesn't Work

If you are trying to close a track gap in a video track, but the audio is continuous underneath, Final Cut will not delete the video gap because, in most cases, this would throw the audio out of sync with the video.

You can solve this problem by locking all your audio tracks by clicking the little padlock icons at the far left of each track (or pressing **Shift+F5**). Once all your audio tracks are locked, you can easily delete the video gap. (This process also works in reverse for deleting audio gaps, by locking all video tracks [**Shift+F4**].)

You'll learn more about locking tracks in Chapter 8, "Audio—The Secret to a Great Picture."

---

22 Well, that ends this exercise on deletion. Next, you'll learn how to harness selecting and deleting clips, along with some new techniques to get your Timeline into shape for final trimming.

If you are done for a while, quit Final Cut and *don't* save changes. If you are going immediately into the next exercise, choose **File > Revert** to revert this lesson back to the last saved version on disk.

3 | Moving Clips

In this exercise, you'll learn techniques to move clips around on the Timeline, as well as an explanation of how to use cut and paste.

---

1 To get started, open **Board Feet v2**, if it isn't open already.

In looking at this sequence again, I realized it would look better if the clip **MCU to camera** moved up to be shot number three in the sequence. Also, the first shot, **Track – red sun**, needs to be deleted and replaced with **Gray sky red sun**.

There are several ways to move clips, but one of the easiest is to create multiple tracks and shuffle clips around until you are happy.

---

2 There are at least four ways to create new tracks in a sequence. Here's the first: choose **Sequence > Insert Tracks**.

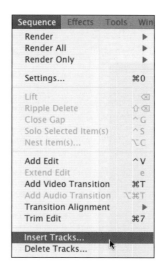

3 From the dialog that appears, indicate how many tracks you want to add. In this case, add one video track and click **OK**. A new video track appears in the sequence, labeled **V2**.

The benefit to this technique is that it easily adds any number of audio and/or video tracks at the same time.

---

4 Here's a second, and faster, approach. **Ctrl+click** in the gray area above the video tracks, and below the timecode bar, and choose **Add Track** from the shortcut menu to add a new video track. Or, **Ctrl+click** below the audio tracks and above the zoom bar at the bottom, and choose **Add Track** from the shortcut menu to add a new audio track. Either way, a new track appears in the **Timeline**.

---

5 This technique, though, is my favorite. Simply drag a clip, in this case **MCU to camera**, where you want the track to appear, and Final Cut creates a track to hold the clip. (I use this technique a lot!)

Drag clip where you want new track.

---

6 However you decide to create an additional video (or audio) track, move the clip **MCU to camera** onto **V2** and slide it left so it starts at the same time as the current third clip in the sequence, **Blue sky**.

---

7 Now, click **Blue sky** to select it. Then, hold down the **Shift** key and click **White coat jump MS** to select the range of clips that needs to move to make room for the new clip.

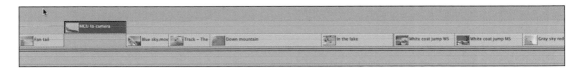

---

8 Grab all the selected clips and drag them right until they fill the hole on the far right of the **Timeline**. Deselect them.

---

9 Grab the **MCU to camera** clip on **V2** and drag it down into its new position. Or, as I prefer to do, hold the **Option** key and press the **down** arrow to move a clip down a track. (Oh, yes. **Option+up** arrow moves a clip *up* a track. Using the **Option+up/down** arrow technique is the fourth way to create a new track.)

NOTE: | **Clip Collisions**

If you get an error message saying, "Clip collision on...," it means that the action you want to take is blocked by another clip. In the case of moving a clip using **Option+down** arrow, it means that the gap you are trying to move the clip into is smaller than the clip itself. Zoom closer and make sure that there's enough room in the gap for your clip to fit.

Final Cut works hard to prevent you from accidentally erasing media.

However, there's a much easier way to move clips. Apple calls it a **swap edit**. I prefer to call it a **move edit**, because nothing actually "swaps."

---

10 **File > Revert** this sequence to go back to the beginning.

---

11 Click **MCU to camera** to select it. Then, grab it with the mouse and start dragging it, still on **V1**, toward its new position. Notice the cursor looks like a downward-pointing arrow.

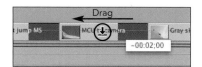

---

12 While still dragging the clip (and this is important), hold down the **Option** key. Notice the cursor has changed shape to a curved downward-pointing arrow.

---

13 Drag the clip until the **In** is where you want the clip to start, then, in this order, let go of the mouse, then let go of the **Option** key.

Everything reshuffles. The clip is in its new position, all other clips move down, and the gap left by the clip you moved is filled. All at the same time.

(If you have snapping turned *on*, it is easier to align the clip by its edit points. If snapping is *off*, it is easier to drop the clip into the middle of another clip. If you don't know what snapping is, you'll learn about it in the next chapter.)

This technique works in both directions, though if you are moving a clip to the right, remember to drag the clip until the In lines up with where you want the clip to start.

There's one more technique still to cover for moving clips: copy and paste. Apple has received a lot of complaints about how this works—mainly because they change it with each iteration of the program. It worked one way in FCP 4.0.x. Then, it changed with FCP 4.1.x. And it changed, again, in FCP HD.

Sigh. Here's how it works in Final Cut Pro 5...at least, for now.

---

14 Select the clip **Gray sky red sun** at the end of the **Timeline**. You are going to move it to the front of the sequence.

15 Choose **Edit > Cut**, or press **Cmd+X**, to cut it to the clipboard and remove it from the **Timeline**.

16 Press the **Home** key to move the **playhead** to the beginning of the sequence. Then, press **Cmd+V** (or choose **Edit > Paste**). The clip appears at the location of the **play-head** as an **Overwrite** edit.

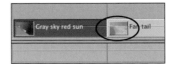

Hmmm…this **Overwrite** edit chops into the second shot. Bad idea. Undo this edit (**Cmd+Z** or **Edit > Undo**).

NOTE:

Setting Undo Levels

The default number of undo levels in Final Cut Pro is 10. However, you can easily change this in **Final Cut Pro > User Preferences**.

When the **User Preferences** window opens, change the **Levels of Undo** to suit your style. I set mine to **25**. You can pick any number from 1 to 99; however, higher undo levels require significant additional RAM in your computer.

---

17 With the **playhead** still at the start of the sequence, choose **Edit > Paste Insert**, or press **Shift+V**.

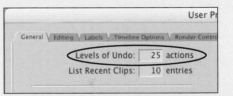

Now the clip appears at the playhead as an Insert edit, pushing everything else down. Much better.

---

18 Click **Track – Pink sun** to select it and press **Shift+Delete** to remove the clip and close the gap.

---

19 And that wraps up this exercise. Save your work. Quit Final Cut if you want to stop. Otherwise, leave everything open for the next exercise.

Copy, Paste, and Auto Select

That copy/paste example wasn't particularly painful, but then again, you were only working on one track. By default, FCP pastes a clip to the same track as the one from which it was copied. Here's the logic behind how Final Cut does a copy/paste.

If you copy a clip from any track, it will paste to the same track, at the location of the playhead, *unless* you click an Auto Select button *after* moving a clip to the clipboard. In that case, FCP will paste the clip to the lowest numbered track whose Auto Select button is lit.

See? Simple.

The Auto Select buttons determine if a track is "selected," or active. If the button is lit (dark), as it is for V1, the track is active. If the button is off (hollow center), as it is for V2, the track is inactive.

If all your video is on one track, this won't be a problem. However, if you start doing multitrack composites, you'll need to pay attention to the Auto Select buttons.

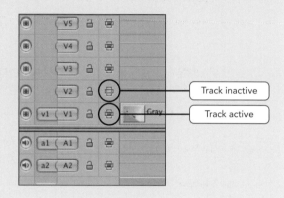

Track inactive

Track active

4 | Power Editing Techniques

In this exercise, you'll learn three power techniques to help you get your Timeline organized: finding the match frame of a shot on the Timeline, doing a Replace edit, and changing the speed of a clip using a Fit to Fill edit. Although you may not use these techniques frequently, knowing they exist can bail you out of some tight editing situations.

---

1 If it isn't open already, open **Board Feet v2**.

The **match frame** technique allows you to find the original clip of a shot in the Timeline.

---

2 Put the **playhead** in the middle of **MCU to camera**. It should be the third shot in the **Timeline**, around **1:00:14:00**.

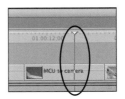

---

3 Choose **View > Match Frame > Master Clip** (or press the letter **F**).

Viewer   Canvas

Notice that Final Cut immediately loaded the source clip from the Browser into the Viewer, matched the In and Out from the clip on the Timeline, and positioned the playhead in the Viewer to exactly match the location of the playhead in the Timeline.

This is because clips in the Timeline are **affiliate clips** to the **master clip** located in the Browser. Although there is only one master for each clip, there can be many affiliate clips to that master.

Recognizing a Browser Clip from a Timeline Clip

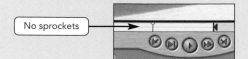

No sprockets

Sprockets

How can you tell if a clip was loaded into the Viewer from the Timeline or the Browser? By looking in the white bar of the Viewer, called the **playhead scrubber bar**, that contains the playhead. Clips that are loaded from the Browser have a clear white bar; clips that load from the Timeline have small "sprocket holes" in the bar. Test it for yourself.

How is this match frame technique useful? Well, for instance, if you make an edit that is video-only, then later discover that you need to add the audio from the shot, using match frame makes this easy. One keystroke and you have the source clip loaded and marked in the Viewer, ready to edit.

4 If you want to find the source clip in the **Browser**, rather than load it into the **Viewer**, choose **View > Reveal Master Clip** (or press **Shift+F**).

NEW▶ There was a bug in FCP HD that prevented **Reveal Master Clip** from working reliably when a clip was nested inside a folder. The bug has been fixed in FCP 5.

Final Cut highlights the name of the source clip in the Browser.

Master clip in Browser

5 NEW▶ To find a match frame of a clip on a video track other than **V1**, select the clip you want to find, and type **F**. The key is to first select the clip. An alternate method is to turn off the **Auto Select** buttons for all tracks *except* the track you want, put your **playhead** in the clip, and press **F**.

6 NEW▶ Also new in FCP 5 is the ability to select a clip in the Browser, then show its Media file in the Finder. This is a great technique to use if you need to locate, or rename, the master media file. To do this, **Ctrl+click** a clip in the **Browser** and choose **Reveal in Finder**. A **Finder** window will open on top of FCP, displaying the media file on your hard disk.

Finding a Shot in the Timeline

Recently, I discovered a way to use match frame in reverse to find a specific shot in the Timeline by using a clip from the Browser as a reference. Here's how it works.

1. Open a clip from the **Browser** into the **Viewer**.

2. Move the **playhead** in the **Viewer** until you find the specific frame you want to find in the **Timeline**.

3. Press the **F** key.

If that frame exists in the currently selected sequence in the Timeline, the Timeline playhead will jump immediately to that frame and display it in the Canvas. If you haven't used that specific frame in the Timeline, the computer will beep, and the Timeline playhead won't move.

This procedure is a fast way to see if you've used a specific shot.

The **Replace edit** technique enables you to replace one clip with another. What makes this tip special is that you don't need to set an In or an Out. This technique works best when you are trying to line up shots based on a frame in the middle of a clip, rather than at either end.

---

7 Put your Timeline **playhead** in the middle of **Blue sky**, where the snowboarder is in midflight (timecode: **1:00:18:00**).

What you are going to do is replace the wide shot of this jump with a closer shot. But, to keep the overall pacing consistent, you need to match where he is in midair, rather than from the start of the clip. You can only do this with a Replace edit.

8 Click the **Browser** and open **MS brown coat** into the
Viewer. Scroll until you see him start his jump (timecode:
1:01:33:04). You don't need to set any **Ins** or **Outs** in the
Viewer. The **Replace** edit doesn't need them.

9 Now, drag the clip
from the **Viewer** to the
Canvas and drop it on top
of the **Replace** overlay
(or press **F11**).

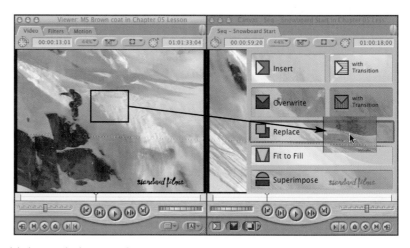

Final Cut instantly replaces the old shot with the new shot—
keeping the same duration and Timeline location—and puts the
frame under the playhead in the Viewer (where the boarder was
just starting his jump) under the playhead in the Timeline.

10 Play this new section of the sequence.

I use Replace edits whenever I need to match action in the middle of the shot. The basic rule is the Replace
edit ignores Ins and Outs in the Viewer and lines up the edit based on the position of the playhead.

NOTE: | **Using Ins and Outs in the Timeline for a Replace Edit**

The Replace edit works a little differently if you set an In or an Out on the Timeline. Although it ignores Ins and Outs in the Viewer, a Timeline In means the Replace edit will replace from the Timeline In rather than the start of the clip. Setting an Out on the Timeline means the Replace edit will replace up to the Out, rather than to the end of the clip. In other words, you can use an In and an Out on the Timeline to restrict how much of a clip the Replace edit will replace.

There's one more technique in this exercise: the **Fit to Fill** edit. This specialized edit changes the speed of an incoming clip to match the duration set by the In and Out on the Timeline.

---

11 Go to the second clip, **Fan tail**, and put the **playhead** anywhere in the middle of the clip. Press **X** to set an **In** and an **Out** for the clip.

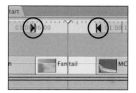

This, in itself, is a really fast way to mark a clip on the Timeline.

Notice that the duration of the Timeline edit is 4:01. What you are going to do is replace this shot with a longer clip, which you will speed up to emphasize just how fast these snowboarders are going. (It will work nicely contrasted with the slow motion of the opening clip.)

---

12 Open **Shoot the edge** and find the spot just after he lands from a short jump. Set the **In** (timecode: **1:01:42:26**). Set the **Out** just after he disappears (duration: **6:09**). Again, notice that this shot is about 50 percent longer than the duration of the edit on the **Timeline**.

13 Drag the clip from the **Viewer** to the **Fit to Fill** overlay in the **Canvas** and drop it (**Shift+F11**).

14 Notice that **Shoot the edge** is edited to the **Timeline** with a green render bar over it. Play the clip and see that it is, indeed, faster than normal speed. The green bar indicates that an effect has been applied to the clip, which Final Cut is able to play in real time. If the bar was red, you would first need to render it. (More on rendering in Chapter 9, "*Transitions—Making Change Beautiful,*" and Chapter 12, "*Filters and Keying.*")

15 That wraps up this exercise. Save your changes, and leave Final Cut open for the next exercise.

5 | Storyboard Editing

When I first saw this next technique, I thought it was pretty silly—until I showed it to some wedding photographers who told me it was an incredible timesaver for the kinds of projects they do. Their opinion has since been reinforced by other editors I've spoken with, which simply goes to show that everyone learns from everyone else—including me.

Final Cut has an additional way you can edit clips in the Browser: the **storyboard edit**. Here's how it works.

---

1 Open **Chapter 05 Lesson** or **Board Feet v2**, whichever is easier, and create a new sequence. Name it " **Seq – Storyboard**". (Notice the initial space.) Double-click it to load it into the **Timeline** as an empty sequence.

---

2 **Ctrl+click** in the gray area of the **Name** column and choose **View as Large Icons** from the shortcut menu.

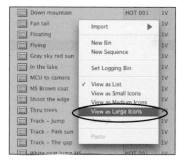

The Browser converts into a digital "light table," allowing you to view all your clips at once. This is a great way to lay out photo montages, animated storyboards, or any other sequence of shots where seeing multiple clips at once is helpful.

NEW▶ New in FCP 5, the duration of the clip is now displayed at the bottom of each thumbnail.

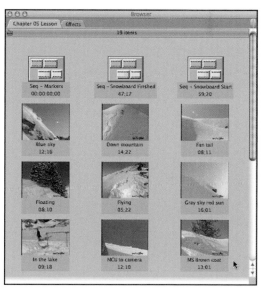

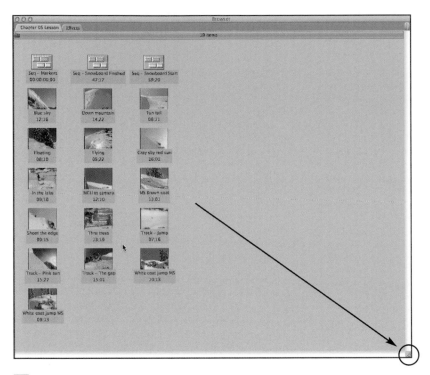

3 Grab the size tab in the lower-right corner of the **Browser** and drag to make the **Browser** bigger. You'll be moving clips into the blank area on the right.

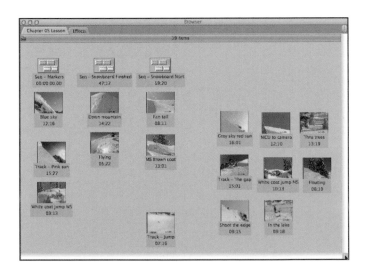

4 Using the **Selection** tool, grab clips and lay them into a grid. The upper-leftmost image will be the first in the sequence, then going across the row, then down until the last shot is reached. Reorganize your shots as much as you wish.

5 To play the thumbnail, select the second **Hand** tool (press **HH**) from the **Tool** palette and drag it over the thumbnail you want to view. (If the **Browser** is active, pressing **HH** doesn't select the **Hand** tool; instead, it jumps down to the next clip that starts with the letter H. To select the **Hand** tool with the keyboard, click the **Timeline** to make it active, then press **HH**. Once the **Hand** tool is selected, you can use it in the **Browser** with no problems.)

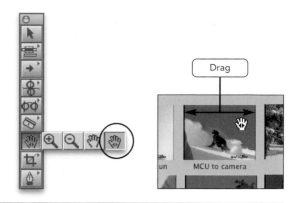

6 If you want to see a shot in the **Viewer** to set a specific **In** or **Out**, double-click it.

7 When you are happy with the order of your clips, use the **Selection** tool and move all the clips you want to edit to the **Timeline** by dragging a rectangle around them.

Final Cut selects the clips starting in the upper-left corner, moving right along the top row, then down to the next row, and the next, until it reaches the end at the lower right.

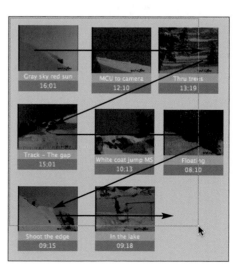

8 Drag the selected clips to the **Overwrite** overlay in the **Canvas**.

Poof! All your clips are edited into the Timeline, in the order selected without any gaps—an instantly completed sequence. (Though we haven't talked about transitions yet, if you drag your clips from the Browser to the **Overwrite with Transition** overlay, they will be edited to the Timeline using the default transition between all clips. You'll learn about transitions in Chapter 9, "*Transitions—Making Change Beautiful*.")

---

9 You are done with this exercise. You can close this project and save your changes. Quit Final Cut if you want to take a break. However, there are two more exercises to go through before the end of this chapter.

---

6 | More on Markers

In this exercise, you will learn more about **markers**. Markers were first introduced in Chapter 3, *"Gather Your Media."* In this exercise, you will learn that there are two types of markers: **clip** and **Timeline**. Plus, you'll learn how to use markers to indicate music beats, create subclips, add DVD chapter markers and, oh, golly, all kinds of neat stuff.

First, though, a quick note. A marker is like the "yellow sticky note" of Final Cut Pro. In and of itself, it doesn't do anything. It just sits there, like a sticky note, reminding you of something you don't want to forget.

---

1 Open **Seq – Markers** in the **Chapter 05 Lesson** project. Then, double-click **Track – Pink sun** to load it into the **Viewer**.

---

2 Move the **playhead** to **01:02:13:04**. Then, with the playhead stopped, press the **M** key to create a marker—the yellow object that appears beneath the **playhead**.

The name of the marker appears at the bottom of the Viewer window. This type of marker is called a clip marker because it is located inside a clip.

---

3 To change the name of the marker, be sure the **playhead** is parked on top of it, and press **M** again. The **Edit Marker** dialog appears.

---

4 Click once in the **Name** field and change the name of the marker to **Skier and Sun**, then click **OK**. See how the new name appears in the **Viewer** window?

---

5 Set two more markers in this clip, one at **01:02:17:00** and the other at **01:02:22:28**. (There's no magic in these numbers, so feel free to set your markers anywhere in this clip.)

Notice, when the playhead is on top of a marker, the marker color is yellow. The normal color of a clip marker is pink.

---

6 To move between markers, press **Option+M** to go to the previous marker and **Shift+M** to go to the next marker. I use this very handy keyboard shortcut a lot. You can also choose **Mark > Previous > Marker** or **Mark > Next > Marker**, but there never seems to be enough time to use the menu.

---

7 Using the **Shift** and **Option** keys, go to the last marker in the clip. To delete a marker, press **M** and click the **Delete** button in the **Edit Marker** dialog or choose **Mark > Markers > Delete**, or press **Cmd+`**. (The ` key is immediately above the **Tab** key.) The **playhead** must always be positioned on top of a marker to edit or delete it. Delete the second marker, so that there is only one marker in the clip—the first one, which you named **Skier and Sun**.

Clip markers are very useful when you want to mark, say, the beat of a music clip, or the location of a sound effect or explosion. The best part about using clip markers is that they travel with the clip.

---

8 With **Seq – Markers** open in the **Timeline** and the **play-head** positioned at the beginning of the sequence, edit the clip **Track – Pink sun** into the **Timeline**.

9 Grab the clip and drag it.

Notice that as you move the clip, the marker moves with it. And, the shape of the marker sprouts a long, thin line out the top, allowing you to align the marker more easily with other elements in the Timeline.

10 Leaving this clip selected, move the **playhead** so that it is not on the marker and press **Option+M** or **Shift+M**.

Just as in the Viewer, the playhead moves to the location of the marker; however, clip marker names show up in the Viewer only when a clip is loaded into the Viewer and the playhead is parked directly on the marker.

11 You can also set clip markers in the **Timeline**. With the clip still selected, move the **playhead** to a location where there isn't a marker and press **M**. Again, a new marker appears in the clip at the location of the **playhead**.

Important note: In order to set a clip marker, the clip must be selected and the playhead must be at the location you want the marker to appear.

12 Deselect this clip. Now press **Option+M** and **Shift+M**. The **playhead** doesn't move.

This illustrates the biggest weakness of a clip marker. Unless the clip is selected, the playhead doesn't know where the marker is. Consequently, although I use clip markers, I don't use them a lot—only to flag the start of a sound or visual effect that I want to remember later. The markers I use all the time are similar to clip markers, but they're located in the Timeline itself. I call them, appropriately, Timeline markers.

13 To set a **Timeline** marker, be sure nothing is selected in the **Timeline**, then move the **playhead** to, say, **01:00:04:00** in the **Timeline**. Press **M** to set the marker and **M** again to open the **Edit Marker** dialog.

You set, edit, delete, and move to a Timeline marker exactly the way you do with a clip marker. The big advantage to using Timeline markers is that you don't have to select a clip first to be able to move to the markers.

14 Set three more markers, one at **01:00:08:00**, **01:00:12:00**, and one at the end of the clip, **01:00:15:27**. (Again, you can set markers anywhere—that's one of their great strengths.) Practice using **Shift+M** and **Option+M** to move between markers.

15 You can remove one marker, or you can remove all markers, but you can't select and remove a group of markers. To remove all the markers in a clip, double-click the clip to load it into the **Viewer**, and choose **Mark > Markers > Delete All**, or press **Ctrl+`**.

16 Move to the first marker in the **Timeline**. Press **M** to open the **Edit Marker** dialog, then change the name to **My Marker 1** and add **This is my first Timeline marker** to the **Description**. Notice that both the name and description are now visible in the **Canvas**.

17 If the marker name and description are not visible, be sure that **Show Overlays** is turned on in the **View** pop-up menu of the **Canvas**. If marker names don't show up in the **Viewer**, be sure **Show Overlays** is turned on there, as well.

The following are three other useful marker tricks I want to share before the end of this exercise:

18 **Ctrl+click** with the **Selection** tool in the timecode bar of the **Timeline**. At the bottom of the shortcut menu is a list of all your **Timeline** markers. Choose the marker you want to jump to, and the **playhead** moves there instantly.

I use this navigation technique constantly to move to specific points in the Timeline, such as the start of an act, or a clip that needs further attention.

19 Move to a marker and press **M** to open the **Edit Marker** dialog box. There are three large buttons in the lower half:

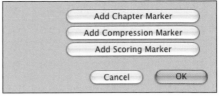

- **Add Chapter Marker** adds a special marker that indicates the start of a DVD chapter. When you export your project, which you'll learn about in Chapter 13, *"Output Your Project,"* this marker can be read by iDVD, DVD Studio Pro, or Compressor and turned into a DVD chapter marker. The advantage to setting chapter markers inside Final Cut is that they are frame-accurate, unlike setting chapter markers in the DVD programs themselves.

- **Add Compression Marker** is used as a flag to force Compressor to set an "I" frame at a particular spot to improve the compression of a particularly active transition or scene. In general, I don't use these—the default settings in Compressor are fine for my work.

- **Add Scoring Marker** adds a special marker that is displayed inside Soundtrack to help you flag particular sections of your video within Soundtrack.

---

20 You can move a marker by positioning the **playhead** to the right of a marker and placing it on the frame you want the marker to move to. Then choose **Mark > Markers > Reposition**, or press **Shift+`**, and the marker jumps to the **playhead**.

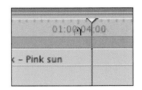

Although this is cool, sort of, it's not that useful. Markers move only to the right, never to the left. So, if you want to move a marker earlier in the **Timeline**, open the **Edit Marker** dialog box and type in the new timecode location for the marker.

---

21 Finally, Timeline markers do have one limitation. They don't move when you move clips on the **Timeline**. For instance, grab the clip **Track – Red Sun** and move it. Notice that the **Timeline** markers don't move.

Generally, this isn't a big deal. However, there is no way to link a marker on the Timeline to a clip so that if the clip moves, the Timeline marker moves with it.

---

22 That ends this exercise on markers. You don't need to save your work; you won't be coming back to this sequence again.

7 | Creating Subclips

In this exercise, you'll learn what a subclip is, how to create a subclip, how to use DV Start/Stop Detect to identify scenes on your tape, and a clever technique, using markers and subclips, that makes working with long sections of footage a lot easier.

---

1 To get started, open **Chapter 05 Lesson** and load **Seq – Markers** to the **Timeline**. The sequence may be empty, which is perfectly OK. Double-click **MS Brown coat** to load it from the **Browser** to the **Viewer**. If there are any **Ins** or **Outs**, delete them (press **Option+X**). Notice that the clip has a total duration of **13:01**.

Imagine that this clip, instead of being 13 seconds long, is actually 13 minutes long. Further, imagine that you want to work only with a small portion of the clip, and you want to pull multiple shots from that small section. One technique that works really well is to turn just the portion of the clip you want into a subclip. A subclip acts like it's a real, stand-alone clip. But, in point of fact, it's just "pointing" into a small section of the much larger media file on your hard disk.

Subclips make working with large files much easier, without requiring any changes to your master media files or even any additional disk space for new media.

---

2 Using the **MS Brown coat** in the **Viewer**, set an **In** at **01:01:30:24**. Then, set an **Out** at **01:01:39:15**. Notice that the clip has a new duration of **8:22**. So far, this is nothing new.

---

3 Choose **Modify > Make Subclip** and watch what happens. The shot in the **Viewer** remains unchanged. But, in the **Browser** a new icon appears with the name **MS Brown coat Subclip**.

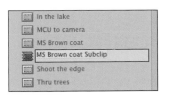

4 Double-click this new subclip and look at it in the **Viewer**. Notice that where the **Out** was in the first clip is now the end of the subclip, indicated by the sprocket holes on the right edge.

What you've done is create a new version of this clip, where the old In and Out have been replaced by the new clip's media start and media end. It's as though you had just captured this clip directly from tape. But you didn't; you just pointed to the original media file and created a new clip from it—not by duplicating the actual media files, but by creating a new pointer file that just points to a small section of the media file.

Subclips are a great way to make large, lengthy media files usable within Final Cut.

5 You edit with subclips exactly as you would a regular clip. Set an **In** and **Out**, and edit it to the **Timeline**. Trim it. Move it around. It acts just like a regular clip. With one added feature: Double-click the subclip to load it back into the **Viewer**. Then, choose **Modify > Remove Subclip Limits**.

The Viewer goes black, indicating the subclip is no longer a separate entity from the master clip it came from.

6 Double-click **MS Brown coat Subclip** in the **Browser** to load it back into the **Viewer**. With the sub-clip limits removed, this clip is an exact duplicate of **MS Brown coat**.

7 That ends this exercise, so you can close this project. You don't need to save your work; you won't be coming back to this sequence.

There's another really useful feature of Final Cut Pro that involves a combination of markers and subclips. But to use it, you first need to understand DV Start/Stop Detect.

Using DV Start/Stop Detect

When you are shooting DV video, every time you press the Record button, your camera records a special, invisible signal on the tape saying, "Hey! Somebody pushed the Record button!!" (Or, you know, something reasonably close to that, anyway.)

These record flags, as they are called, are transferred when you capture your DV footage into Final Cut as part of the metadata that's transferred along with the audio, video, and timecode. (**Metadata** is data that describes other data, similar to the way you would use words like height, weight, and hair color to describe a person.) These record flags, by the way, exist only in DV. If you are capturing SD or HD footage, this technique won't work.

When you run **Mark > DV Start/Stop Detect**, you are telling Final Cut to put a clip marker in the clip everywhere it finds one of those record flags. When this process is done, a marker indicates every time you pushed the Record button on your camera during production.

I don't have any long clips with record flags, so rather than create an exercise, I'll just show you how this works, so you can practice on your own tapes. For the sake of this explanation, pretend that **MS Brown coat** is a long DV clip with record flags indicating the start of multiple different shots.

To run DV Start/Stop Detect, load the clip into the **Viewer**. Then, choose **Mark > DV Start/Stop Detect**. In just a few seconds, your entire tape is scanned and every place the Record button was pressed has a marker.

continues on next page

NOTE:

Using DV Start/Stop Detect *continued*

Once these markers are added to the clip, over in the **Browser** there's a small, right-pointing triangle next to the clip name indicating that the **MS Brown coat** clip has markers. Twirl down the triangle to view the list of markers.

Here's the neat part: Create a new bin in the **Browser** and name it, say, **MS Brown subclips**. Then, select and *drag* just the markers from **MS Brown coat** in the **Browser** into the **MS Brown subclips** folder.

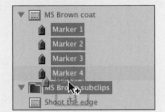

Twirl open the folder. Every marker has been converted into a subclip that starts at the marker and ends the frame before the next marker. In other words, you've just created subclips that start when the Record button was pushed and end the frame before the Record button was pushed, again. You've just divided your whole video in separate scenes, where each subclip is a scene.

These are very powerful ways to locate and organize your shots—all using markers, subclips, and DV Start/Stop Detect.

You can test this for yourself by capturing a long tape, containing multiple shots, into Final Cut, loading it into the **Viewer**, and running **Mark > DV Start/Stop Detect**.

Even better, you don't need to use DV Start/Stop Detect to create the markers. Simply create your own clip markers and use this technique to create subclips in exactly the same way.

Very cool. Very fast. Very slick.

Helpful Keyboard Shortcuts

Shortcut	Action
Up arrow	Moves playhead back to In of previous clip
Down arrow	Moves playhead forward to In of next clip
Shift+left arrow	Moves playhead back 1 second
Shift+right arrow	Moves playhead forward 1 second
Left arrow	Moves playhead back one frame
Right arrow	Moves playhead forward one frame
A	Selects the Selection tool
Z	Selects the Zoom In tool
ZZ	Selects the Zoom Out tool
Option+click with Zoom tool	Zooms in opposite direction
Cmd+A	Selects all (clips on Timeline, for example)
Shift+Cmd+A	Deselects all (clips on Timeline, for example)
Cmd+click	Selects whatever is clicked and adds it to a selection group
Shift+click a clip	Selects a range of clips in the sequence
G	Selects the Edit Selection tool
GG	Selects the Group Selection tool
GGG	Selects the Range Selection tool
Cmd+Z	Undos a change
Shift+Cmd+Z	Redos an Undo
Delete	Deletes a selected clip(s) and leaves a gap
Shift+Delete	Deletes a selected clip(s) and removes the gap
Shift+G	Moves playhead to next gap in Timeline
Option+G	Moves playhead to previous gap in Timeline

continues on next page

Helpful Keyboard Shortcuts *continued*

Shortcut	Action
Cmd+X	Cuts selected clip(s) to the clipboard
Cmd+C	Copies selected clip(s) to the clipboard
Cmd+V	Creates an Overwrite edit at the playhead from the clipboard
Shift+V	Creates an Insert edit at the playhead from the clipboard
F	Opens a match frame clip in the Viewer to match the Timeline (or vice versa)
Shift+F	Displays the source clip in the Browser for the clip in the Timeline that contains the playhead
X	Marks an In and an Out for the clip on the Timeline that contains the playhead
Option+X	Removes both the In and the Out
F11	Performs Replace edit
HH	Selects the scrolling Hand tool—used for viewing thumbnails
M	Creates a marker at the position of playhead
MM	Opens Edit Marker dialog (playhead must be sitting on top of marker)
Shift+M	Goes to next marker
Option+M	Goes to previous marker
Cmd+`	Deletes a marker
Shift+`	Repositions marker (moves downstream only)
Ctrl+`	Deletes all markers
Cmd+U	Creates subclip based on In and Out of a clip

Summary

In this chapter, you learned how to reorganize and replace clips on the Timeline, all with the goal of telling your story as concisely and powerfully as possible. The last step in the initial story-building process is to look at each edit point and trim it to make it as tight and perfect and invisible as possible. That's next.

Trim Your Story

Chapters 4, 5, and 6 are at the heart of editing with Final Cut Pro 5. In Chapter 4, *"Build Your Story,"* you learned how to select clips and edit them to the Timeline. Chapter 5, *"Organize Your Story,"* showed you how to move them around and get them organized. In this chapter, you will learn how to trim your edit points to perfection.

Although there is lots more still to cover, these three chapters will give you the skills and confidence to edit anything.

What Is Trimming?

Trimming is the process of removing or adding frames to the beginning and end of your clips so that the edits flow naturally, maintaining your story without calling attention to your editing. This is because the best editing is invisible. Your viewer should get absorbed into your story and not be thinking, "Wow! Killer cuts!"

An edit point has three "sides" that can be adjusted:

- The Out of the outgoing clip
- The In of the incoming clip
- The In and the Out simultaneously

To select an edit point, click it with the **Selection** tool, or press **V** to jump the **playhead** to the

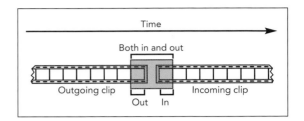

nearest edit point. You can toggle between the three sides of an edit point by pressing **U**.

In this chapter, you will learn, first, about general-purpose trimming tools, then tools that trim just one side of an edit, then tools that trim both sides of an edit. This chapter concludes with exercises in how to trim using timecode and using the Trim Edit window.

DVD MOVIE: **trimming.mov**

If you want to see examples of trimming in action, watch the movie **trimming.mov** in the **movies** folder on the **Final Cut Pro 5 HOT DVD.**

The Importance of Having Handles

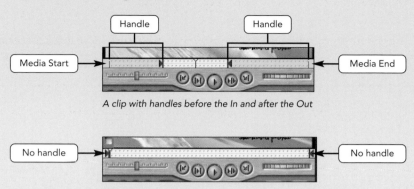

A clip with handles before the In and after the Out

A clip with no handles

Understanding and using handles is critical to successful editing. **Handles** are defined as extra media between the media start and the In and, again, between the Out and media end. The reason these are so important is because when you trim an In by moving it earlier, you are actually using frames located in the handle. If you started your clip at the exact beginning of the media, there would be no extra frames you could use to move the In earlier.

In Chapter 2, "*Understanding the Final Cut Pro Interface,*" you learned about media start and media end. These vertical line indicators at the beginning and end of your clip show the start and end of the media file stored on your hard disk. The goal in capturing media is to capture a few extra seconds before and after the portion of your clip you want to use so that you have some additional footage to work with in adjusting where your edits occur. This extra footage is called the "handle."

Without handles, you can't add transitions, extend shots, or start an In sooner or an Out later. Making sure you capture your media with handles is just really, really important.

1 | General Trimming Tools

There are two general-purpose trimming tools: the **Selection** tool (which looks like an arrow) and the **Razor Blade**. Both are more flexible than you might think, as you'll discover in this lesson.

---

1 Open **Chapter 06 Lesson**. This is a slightly modified version of what you were working on in the last chapter.

---

2 Duplicate **Seq – Snowboard start** by **Ctrl+clicking** the sequence title and choosing **Duplicate** from the shortcut menu.

The reason for duplicating a sequence is that it allows you to make changes to a sequence without running the risk of messing up the work you've already done.

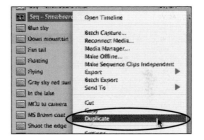

---

3 Name this newly duplicated sequence " **Seq – Trimmed 30**". Again, note the use of the leading space in the name to make sure it sorts to the top of the **Browser**.

The video in this sequence currently runs over 55 seconds. Your goal is to get it down to exactly 30 seconds, ready for broadcast. To do this, you need to trim all your edits.

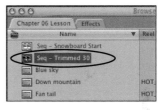

---

4 Click the **Selection** tool (or press **A**, because it looks like an arrow), grab the **In** of the first clip, **Gray sky red sun**, and drag it to the right to timecode **1:00:02:24** in the **Timeline**. Notice how the yellow tooltip shows you in real-time how much you are trimming? When you reach **2:24**, stop dragging and let go of the mouse.

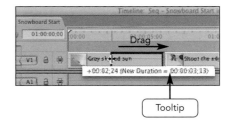

Tooltip

---

5 The advantage of using the **Selection** tool is that it is easy. Just grab the edge of a clip where the cursor turns to a double-pointing arrow and click and drag. The disadvantage to using the **Selection** tool is that it always leaves gaps. So, to get rid of this gap, click in the gap to select it and press **Delete**. The gap is removed, and all downstream clips are moved up (to the left).

Good. You are now 2:24 closer to reaching your goal of a 30-second commercial.

Selection Tool Summary

Key command	A (think *Arrow*).
Advantages	Easy to use.
	Tool readily available.
Disadvantages	Moving a clip's edge always leaves gaps.
	Can't move an In earlier when blocked by preceding clip.
	Can't move an Out later when blocked by following clip.
	Only moves one side of an edit, not both.
Tool options	Holding down Option key turns the tool into the Pen tool.
Impact on sequence	No change in the duration of the sequence.

Next, the end of the **Gray sky red sun** clip runs too long. This time, instead of using the Selection tool to trim it, you'll use the Razor Blade tool to cut the clip.

6 Drag the **playhead** until the snowboarder seems about to be swallowed by the plume of snow (timecode **01:00:03:04** in the **Timeline**).

There are actually two different timecodes associated with this shot: the timecode of the shot in the Timeline (01:00:03:04), and the timecode of the original shot (which you can't see at this point).

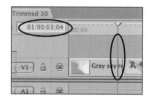

7 However, seeing the timecode of the source tape is often helpful in trimming. To turn the display of the source timecode on, go to the **Canvas** window, click the third pop-up menu, and choose **Show Timecode Overlays (Option+Z)**. To see timecode overlays, **Show Overlays** must also be turned on.

The numbers at the bottom of the screen show the time-code of the source video and audio clips at the position of the playhead in the Timeline. In this case, the playhead is at timecode 1:00:59:26 of the source clip located on track V1. (The clip timecode is called "Source Timecode.")

8 Click the **Razor Blade** tool (or press **B**) to select the single-bladed tool.

9 Click the **Razor Blade** where the **playhead** passes over the clip. The clip is cut, but the excess footage still remains on the **Timeline**.

10 Select the **Selection** tool (or press **A**), click the excess footage to the right of the **playhead** to select it, then delete it by pressing **Shift+Delete** to remove the clip and close the gap.

11 When you delete the excess footage, the **playhead** displays the first frame of the second clip. To make sure you cut the first clip at the correct spot, press the **left** arrow key to back up one frame. Your **Canvas** should look similar to this screen shot at timecode **1:00:59:25**.

The Razor Blade always cuts at the start of the frame. In other words, if you click the Razor Blade on frame 26, the cut occurs between frame 25 and frame 26.

Razor Blade Tool Summary

Key command	B (think Blade).
Advantages	Cuts clips anywhere in Timeline.
Disadvantages	Difficult to align with playhead unless snapping turned on. Removing cut footage is a multistep process. When cutting, removes the frame under the Razor Blade tool.
Tool options	Multitrack Razor Blade tool (RR) cuts all tracks simultaneously. Holding down Shift key toggles between the single and multitrack Razor Blade tool.
Impact on sequence	No change in the duration of the sequence by cutting a clip.
Secret keystroke	Ctrl+V cuts all clips at playhead without using the Razor Blade tool.

12 To see the results of your changes so far, click once in the **Timeline** and press **Shift+Z**. This fits the entire sequence into the **Timeline** window. I use this keyboard shortcut *constantly*.

---

13 That ends this exploration of trimming using the general-purpose tools of the **Selection** tool and the **Razor Blade**. Save your work, but leave this exercise open—you'll need it next.

NOTE:

The Red Bow Tie

When you first cut a clip, a small red bow tie appears. This icon indicates a **Through edit**—a cut in a clip where there is no change in the timecode, no change in the video, and no change in the audio. In other words, to the Viewer, this edit point is invisible.

In this chapter, you are using the Razor Blade tool to cut and remove unwanted portions of a clip. In later chapters, you'll use the Razor Blade tool to cut a clip so you can apply an effect to one part of a clip, without affecting other parts.

If seeing little red bow ties in your Timeline drives you nuts, you can turn off their display (but not their existence) by clicking the small, right-pointing arrow at the bottom of the **Timeline** and deselecting **Show Through Edits**.

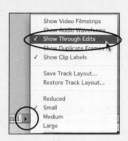

By the way, to delete a **Through** edit, thereby reconnecting the entire clip, just select the **Through** edit with your mouse and press **Delete**. Or, **Ctrl+click** on the edit point and choose **Join Through Edit**.

What Is Snapping?

Have you noticed when you move the playhead or a clip, it wants to "jump" to the end or beginning of a clip whenever it gets close? This is due to snapping.

Whenever the playhead, or a clip, gets within 15 frames of the edge of another clip, snapping jumps the two of them together.

Snapping is a truly wonderful feature when you are building and organizing clips on the Timeline, because it helps you align clips so that the end of one clip touches the next, with no flash of black. Snapping also quickly positions the playhead to the beginning or end of a clip.

For trimming, however, snapping is a pain in the neck. Why? Because almost all the trims you make are just a few frames here, a few frames there. And snapping keeps interfering.

Fortunately, there are three quick ways to toggle snapping on or off:

- Choose **Sequence > Snapping**.

- Click the **Snapping** button in the upper-right corner of the **Timeline**. Green is "on," and gray is "off."

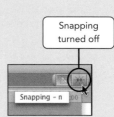

Snapping turned off

- Press **N**. This is my favorite, because using this keyboard shortcut allows you to turn snapping on, or off, in the middle of dragging a clip. The menu and button don't allow this flexibility.

Snapping, by the way, works for both audio and video clips on all tracks. With snapping turned on, whenever a clip or the playhead gets within 15 frames of any edit point of any clip on any track, snapping jumps them so they align.

You'll see examples of how to use snapping throughout the rest of this book, just not in the rest of this chapter.

2 | One-Sided Trimming

In this exercise, and for the rest of this chapter, you'll work with tools designed specifically for trimming. I don't use these tools all the time, but when I need them, they are very handy. In this exercise, you'll learn about a one-sided trimming tool called the **Ripple** tool and a way to change the duration of a clip on the Timeline.

One-sided trimming means to adjust *just* the In or *just* the Out of an edit point. The Selection tool is a good example of a one-sided trimmer. The problem with using the Selection tool for trimming is that, when a clip is surrounded by other clips, the Selection tool can't make an In start sooner, only later. Also, the Selection tool can't make an Out run later, only sooner.

The Ripple tool solves this problem.

---

1 Open **Chapter 06 Lesson**, if it isn't open already. Load the sequence, **Seq – Trimmed 30**, which you created in Exercise 1, into the **Timeline**.

---

2 Before you start trimming, press **N** to make sure snapping is turned off.

---

3 Select the **Ripple** tool from the **Tool** palette—it's the one with a single roller—or press **RR**.

The Ripple tool allows you to change an In or an Out in ways you can't with the Selection tool.

---

4 For example, click the **In** of **Shoot the edge** and drag it to the *left*.

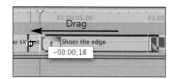

Notice the yellow tooltip that appears, showing you how much the shot is altered. Also, the dark brown box (wireframe) that represents the size of the clip grows larger as you move the In earlier.

When you're working with Timecode, negative numbers mean something is moving earlier, to the left, on the Timeline. Positive numbers mean something is moving later on the Timeline. In this case, the In has moved 18 frames earlier, making the clip 18 frames longer. It's longer because you didn't change the Out for the clip when you changed the In.

---

5 Using the **Ripple** tool, drag the **In** to the *right* until the tooltip says you've moved the **In 13** frames later (+13).

Notice how the brown wireframe gets shorter as you move the In later. This may look like you are adjusting both the In and the Out. You aren't. You are simply making the whole clip shorter or longer, by adjusting where the In starts.

Look up into the Canvas. As you move the Ripple tool, two small pictures appear.

The left picture shows the Out of the outgoing clip. The right picture shows the In of the incoming clip. As you move the mouse, the right picture changes, showing you the results of moving the In. This is a very helpful visual reminder of how you are changing the edit point, and it allows you to visualize the best place to cut between these two shots.

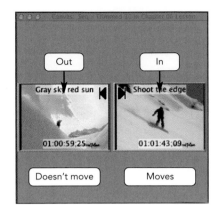

6 Watch what happens when you move the **Ripple** tool **+13** and let go of the mouse. See how the **Shoot the edge** clip is automatically shortened, the gap is removed, and all the clips later in the sequence are moved up to fill the gap?

This is the big benefit of using the Ripple tool to trim frames; either adding them or removing them. In both cases, it does not leave a gap in the Timeline.

The Canvas displays your new In as 1:01:43:09.

A **linked clip**, by the way, is a clip where the audio and video are linked together; this generally means a clip where audio and video are in sync, such as a talking head.

Ripple Tool Summary

Key command	RR
Advantages	Trims one side of an edit longer or shorter without leaving gaps.
	Can be used for video-only, audio-only, or video and audio clips.
Disadvantages	Trimming just the video or just the audio of a linked clip will cause the clip to go out of sync, which FCP won't allow.
Tool options	Holding down the Shift key toggles between the Ripple and Roll tool. (You'll learn about the Roll tool in the next exercise.)
Impact on sequence	Rippling always changes the duration of the sequence.

There's another "tool" that can be used for trimming. In writing this chapter, I realized that I use this technique a lot, but never considered it a trimming tool—mainly because it isn't a tool, it's the **Duration** dialog box.

7 Select the **Selection** tool, then **Ctrl+click** on the **Shoot the edge** clip. Notice that the fourth line down in the contextual menu displays the duration of the clip.

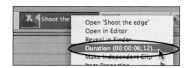

8 You need to change this duration to **4:29**. To do so, select **Shoot the edge** and choose **Modify > Duration** (or press **Ctrl+D**).

The Duration dialog box appears with the current duration (6:12) of the clip preset.

9 Change the **Duration** to **4:29** and click **OK**.

The duration of **Shoot the edge** is instantly reduced and all the downstream clips are automatically moved up to the left.

I use this technique to change the length of titles, graphics, still frames, and shots that don't have any significant movement in them, such as wide shots.

10 Now you need to trim up the rest of the clips in this sequence. Using all the tools you've learned so far, make the following changes to these clips:

Actions to Clips in the Sequence

Clip	Action
MCU to camera	Set duration to **3:05**.
Blue sky	Delete the clip—leave a gap in the **Timeline**.
Down mountain	Move this clip ahead of **Track the gap**, and start it at **01:00:15:01** on the **Timeline.** The starting source timecode of the clip is **1:00:15:03** and its duration is **5:27**.
Track the gap	Starts on the **Timeline** at **1:00:20:28** at source timecode **1:02:33:03** with a duration of **3:26**.
In the lake	Starts on the **Timeline** at **1:00:24:24** at source timecode **1:01:06:18** with a duration of **5:06**.
White coat jump MS	Leave as is.
White coat jump WS	Leave as is.

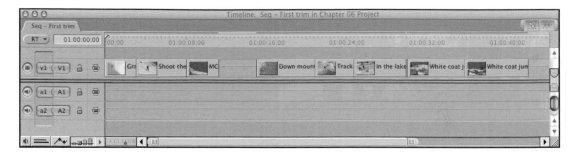

11 When you are done, your sequence should match **Seq – First Trim**. When you press the **End** key to jump to the end of the sequence, the timecode should be **1:00:42:07**.

12 This completes this exercise. Save your work, but leave everything open. You aren't done yet. Your commercial still runs over 12 seconds long.

NOTE:

Ripple Delete

There is one other one-sided trimming function that you learned about in the last chapter. Although you don't need to cover it, again, in detail, I want to mention it here for the sake of completeness: the **Ripple Delete**.

Selecting a clip and pressing **Delete**, or choosing **Sequence > Lift**, deletes the clip and leaves a gap. Deleting a clip does not change the duration of the sequence. This is called a **Lift edit**.

Selecting a clip and pressing **Shift+Delete**, or choosing **Sequence > Ripple Delete**, deletes the clip, removes the gap, and pulls up all the clips to the right (downstream) of the gap. Ripple deleting always changes the duration of the sequence.

Which brings me around to why the Ripple tool and the Ripple Delete are both called "Ripple;" both of them create results that "ripple" through the rest of the sequence.

When Rippling Doesn't Work

Rippling works great when you are trimming a video-only clip, an audio-only clip, or a clip with video and audio linked together.

Where it doesn't work is when you want to trim just the video, or just the audio, of a linked clip. In this case, one of two things will happen:

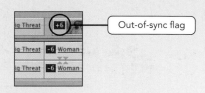

Out-of-sync flag

Your audio and video will go out of sync, indicated by the red flags.

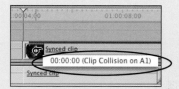

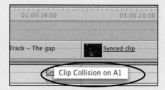

Or, you'll get an error message saying "Clip Collision."

You'll learn how to deal with sync issues in Chapter 8, *"Audio—The Secret to a Great Picture,"* including a *much* better way to trim a linked clip.

To solve the "Clip collision" message, however, you need to "lock" the tracks you *don't* want to change.

For instance, if you want to adjust a video edit point, and you know you won't force any of your audio tracks out of sync, you can lock your audio tracks. Locking a track tells Final Cut to ignore it when making changes to other tracks. In fact, locking a track is a good way to prevent yourself from making changes to a track, because as long as it is locked, *you* can't make any changes to that track either.

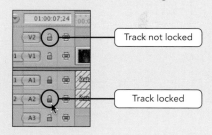

Track not locked

Track locked

To lock a track, click the small **padlock** at the left side of the **Timeline**.

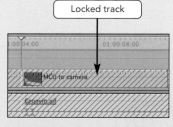

Locked track

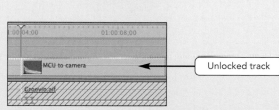

Unlocked track

A locked track has diagonal lines running through all the clips on the track. An unlocked track, which is the default, has no diagonal lines.

To unlock a track, click the **padlock** icon again.

3 | Two-Sided Trimming

In this exercise, you'll learn about tools that adjust both the In and the Out simultaneously: the Roll, Slip, and Slide tools.

The **Roll** tool allows you to move both sides of the edit point simultaneously.

The **Slip** tool allows you to change the content of a clip while keeping its duration and location in the Timeline unchanged.

The **Slide** tool allows you to change the location of a clip in the Timeline in relation to the clip before it and after it, while keeping its content and duration unchanged.

---

1 Start by opening **Chapter 06 Lesson**, if it isn't already open. Then, if you did all the work in the last exercise, open the **Seq – Trimmed 30** sequence. If not, open the **Seq – First trim** sequence.

---

2 Move the **playhead** so it is between the first and second clips. This step, which is optional, helps you remember which edit you are working on.

---

3 In the **Tool** palette, click the **Roll** tool (or press **R**).

The Roll tool icon has two rollers, implying that it is changing two sides of the edit at once.

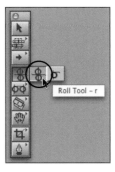

---

4 Click the **Roll** tool on the edit point containing the **playhead**.

What you are going to do is to tweak the placement of the edit point to improve the flow between two shots by simultaneously changing both the In and the Out.

---

5 Drag the **Roll** tool to the left. Notice the changing numbers in the tooltip.

---

6 Now, drag the **Roll** tool to the right. Watch the tooltip and the two images in the **Canvas**. The left picture shows the changes to the **Out** of the outgoing clip. The right picture shows the changes to the **In** of the incoming clip. Stop when your numbers match those in the screen shot.

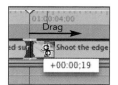

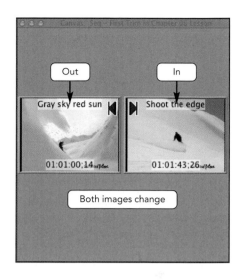

7 Let go of the mouse and press the \ (backslash) key.

The backslash is a fast way to preview the location of the playhead, which is why I had you position the playhead at the edit point in Step 2. The default setting is for playback to start 5 seconds before the playhead and end 2 seconds after.

NOTE:

Changing Playback Preview Settings

The settings for Playback Preview are set in **Final Cut Pro > User Preferences**.

General	Editing	Labels	Timeline Options	Render Co
Still/Freeze Duration:	00:00:10:00			
Preview Pre-roll:	00:00:04:00			
Preview Post-roll:	00:00:03:00			

The default settings are 5:00 pre-roll and 2:00 post-roll. I prefer **4:00** and **3:00**. You can set them however you like in the **Editing** tab.

Roll trims are excellent when the action in both shots matches, and you are just trying to find the best place to make the cut.

Roll Tool Summary

Key command	R
Advantages	Trims both sides of an edit simultaneously. Can be used for video-only, audio-only, or video and audio clips.
Disadvantages	Moves the edit point exactly the same amount for each clip, though in opposite directions.
Tool options	Holding down the Shift key toggles between the Ripple and Roll tools.
Impact on sequence	Rolling never changes the duration of the sequence.

The next trim tool you will learn is the Slip tool. This is often a tricky tool to get your mind around because it is not initially intuitive.

8 Put the **playhead** between the first and second shots and play the second clip. Notice how the snowboarder doesn't get completely out of frame before he skis into the third shot?

What you are going to do is keep the second clip the same length and at the same location in the Timeline, but change the content of the shot itself, by simultaneously changing the In and the Out of the second shot.

9 Select the **Slip** tool from the **Tool** palette (or press **S**).

10 Click in the middle of **Shoot the edge** and drag slowly left and right.

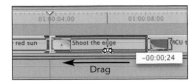

11 Watch the **Canvas** images to see your changes. The left image shows the changing **In**, and the right image shows the changing **Out**, both from **Shoot the edge**. See how you are changing the content of the shot, without changing the duration or its location on the **Timeline**?

Drag to the left until the tooltip says **–:24** and the snowboarder is just leaving the frame in the **Out** image.

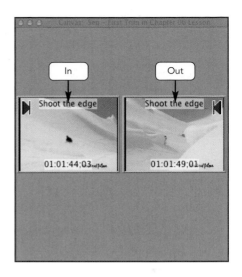

12 Press \ (backslash) and preview the edit.

Hmmm…something doesn't feel right. The cut feels "jumpy."

13 Grab the **Slip** tool and slip the clip back two frames (**–:02** in the tooltip).

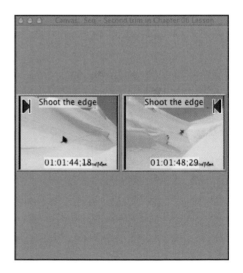

14 Preview the edit again.

Much better! For some reason, many edits flow better when you don't perfectly match the action, but take out a few frames between the end of the first shot and the start of the second to slightly speed the action.

Slip Tool Summary

Key command	S
Advantages	Changes the content of a shot (by simultaneously shifting the In and the Out of a clip in the same direction) without affecting its duration or location on the Timeline.
Disadvantages	Hard to understand conceptually. Slips only one clip at a time.
Tool options	Holding down the Shift key toggles between the Slip and Selection tool.
Impact on sequence	Slipping never changes the duration of the sequence.

The Slide tool is, essentially, the opposite of the Slip tool. The Slide tool maintains the current duration and content of a clip, but slides it along the Timeline by simultaneously adjusting the Out of the preceding clip and the In of the following clip. It's a concept that has been known to drive strong men to drink.

15 Select the **Slide** tool from the **Tool** palette (or press **SS**).

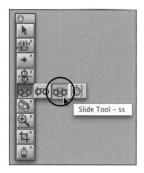

16 Click in the middle of **Track – The gap** and drag left and right. Watch as the location of the clip shifts on the **Timeline**. Drag the clip to the left, and you'll discover a point where you can't drag it anymore. This is because you have run out of handles on the **In the lake** clip. Without handles, you can't slide the clip any further.

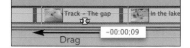

17 Slide the clip to the left nine frames (**–:09**) until the snowboarder in the right image, the **In**, disappears from the frame, but not his shadow. The images in the **Canvas** represent the changing **Out** of the outgoing clip on the left, and the changing **In** of the incoming clip on the right.

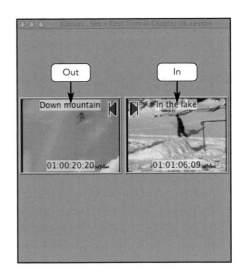

18 Let go and preview the edit. Giving a little more time to the last shot helps to pay off the joke of him skiing into the lake (showcasing, I guess, a new approach to water skiing).

Slide Tool Summary

Key command	SS
Advantages	Trims the Out of the preceding clip and the In of the following clip simultaneously so that the clip in the middle changes location on the Timeline. Can be used for video-only, audio-only, or video and audio clips.
Disadvantages	Can't completely cover up the preceding or following clip. Clip movement is limited by handles of bordering clips. Can't jump over a clip.
Tool options	Holding down the Shift key toggles between the Slide and Selection tools.
Impact on sequence	Sliding never changes the duration of the sequence.

19 This ends the exercise. Save your work. But keep everything open because even with all this trimming, your commercial is still heavy (um, TV-speak for "way the heck too long"). In the next exercise you'll finally bring it into time.

4 | An Alternate Way to Edit

In this exercise, you'll learn an alternate way to edit that is especially useful in documentaries and other "talking head" programs—editing using multiple tracks.

NOTE:

How Final Cut Handles Multiple Tracks

Final Cut allows up to 99 tracks of video and 99 tracks of audio in each sequence. There are so many that track count is, essentially, unlimited. The highest number of video tracks I've ever used was 32 and, in a different project, I used 21 audio tracks.

Final Cut reads video tracks from the top to the bottom. That is, it displays video on V99 on top of V98 on top of V97 down to V1. Further, if video on a higher-numbered track is full-screen and fully opaque, it totally blocks any video below it. Since you won't be learning about how to change opacity or image size until Chapters 10 and 11, any video that you put on a higher-numbered track now will totally block any underlying clips.

You can take advantage of this in your editing. If I am doing dramatic work, I try to keep all my clips on one track. It makes trimming and editing easier. If I am editing a documentary, corporate training, or news story, I often put my video on two tracks: V1 and V2.

This exercise shows you how.

---

1 Start by opening **Chapter 06 Lesson**, if it isn't already open. Then, if you did all the work in the last exercise, open the **Seq – Trimmed 30** sequence. If not, open the **Seq – Second trim** sequence.

---

2 Add a second video track by **Ctrl+clicking** in the gray area above the **V1** track and choosing **Add Track** from the shortcut menu.

---

3 By the way, you can delete a track, whether there are clips on it or not, by **Ctrl+clicking** between the track label (V1, V2, and so on) and the **padlock** icon and choosing **Delete Track** from the shortcut menu.

---

4 Drag **White coat jump WS** up to **V2**. Then, drag **White coat jump MS** up to **V2**. (A faster way to do this is to select the two clips and press **Option+up arrow**. This moves the selected clips up one track.)

---

5 Turn on snapping for this next move, then turn it back off when you are done. (Remember, the easiest way to do this is to press **N**, to toggle snapping.)

---

6 Grab both clips on **V2** and drag them until the first clip, **White coat jump WS**, lines up with the end of **MCU to camera**. Because snapping is on, you'll see two triangles at the edit point indicating that the ends of the clips line up.

---

7 Play the sequence.

The playhead starts out by playing the clips on V1. When it reaches the clips on V2, FCP jumps up and plays them. Then, for the period of time that the clip on V2 covers the clip on V1, Final Cut continues to play just V2 video. Only when V2 is empty is the video on V1 displayed.

---

8 Next, use the **Selection** tool to drag the **Out** of the second clip back until it ends at source timecode **01:02:49:12**. Notice, as you do so, that the image and timecode for the **Out** you are dragging show up in the **Canvas**.

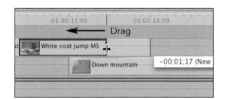

---

9 Play the sequence again, and you'll see that **White coat jump WS** and **White coat jump MS** are two different angles of the same jump. What you are going to do is use what you've learned about trimming to figure out the best place to cut between these two shots.

---

10 Select the **Ripple** tool and drag the **Out** of the first clip back.

Hmmm...what's wrong? Why a clip collision? Because there is video on track V1, and Final Cut doesn't know whether to pull it up with the ripple or leave it alone. When FCP is uncertain, it prevents you from doing a trim.

---

11 To fix this problem, recall what you learned earlier about locking tracks. Lock **V1**.

---

12 Using the **Ripple** tool, drag the **Out** of **White coat jump WS** back until you reach timecode **01:02:56:03**. Again, the **Out** and **In** are displayed in the **Canvas**.

Play the sequence. Cool—but he jumps twice. This is not ideal. In fact, it's considered an editing faux pas. You need to fix it.

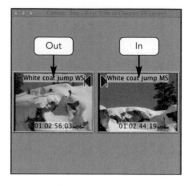

13 This time, unlock track **V1** and select the **Selection** tool. Why? Just to give you a different way to do a trim.

14 Drag the **In** of the second clip, **White coat jumps MS**, to the right to tighten the shot until you reach timecode **1:02:45:16**. Delete the gap by clicking in it and pressing **Delete**.

Oops! Deleting the gap moved video on *both* **V1** and **V2**. Undo.

Again, the objective is to delete the gap on **V2**. However, pressing **Shift+Delete** deleted the gap across *all* tracks. So, either remove the gap on **V2** by locking **V1**, then using **Shift+Delete** to delete the gap, or grab the second clip on **V2** with the **Selection** tool and drag it next to the clip on **V1**. Again, turning on snapping will help with the alignment.

15 Preview the edit by pressing \ (backslash). Then, unlock **V1**.

Sigh…. It looks simple when you trim edits this way, but I will confess that when I was writing this exercise, figuring out the best place to put that edit took me about 30 minutes. To give you an example of the difference in feeling that results from where an edit hits, select the edit point in the middle of his jump with the **Roll** tool. Roll the edit point around and watch what a difference a change in timing makes.

16 Ta-da! Your commercial is done for time. Press the **End** key and notice the timecode: **1:00:30:00**.

In Chapter 8, *"Audio—the Secret to a Great Picture,"* you'll add music. Chapter 9, *"Transitions—Making Change Beautiful,"* adds a couple of flashy transitions. Chapter 10, *"Text, Titles, and Graphics,"* shows you how to add opening and closing text. And, finally, Chapter 12, *"Filters and Keying,"* adds some interesting effects.

But, in terms of editing, you are done.

17 Save your work. You can keep Final Cut open for the next exercise, but you'll be using a different sequence.

You'll see more examples of using two video tracks for editing in Chapter 8, *"Audio—The Secret to a Great Picture."*

5 | Trimming with Timecode

In this exercise, you'll discover some power trimming techniques that can significantly improve the speed and precision of your trims.

You'll learn how to select edits using just the keyboard, how to harness timecode or the keyboard to make edit adjustments, and how to perform a high-speed editing technique to do a Roll edit, called the Extend edit.

On a personal note, although all the tools illustrated earlier in this chapter are important, the techniques in this exercise are the ones I use every day to get my work done.

---

1 Open **Chapter 06 Lesson** and load **Seq – 3 Clips** to the **Timeline**. This is a simple three-clip sequence that you will use to experiment with these techniques.

---

2 Drag your **playhead** to timecode **1:00:05:00**. Took you a while, didn't it?

---

3 Press **Home**, then click in the timecode box at the upper-left corner of the **Timeline** and type **1.0.05.0**, then press **Return**.

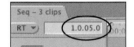

Notice that you don't need to enter double zeros, just one. And periods instead of colons. This is a much faster way to move the playhead, when you know where you are going.

---

4 You already know how to use the **up** and **down** arrow keys to jump between clips. Now, press **V**. The **playhead** jumps to the nearest edit and selects it.

---

5 Now, press the **up** and **down** arrow keys. See how the playhead not only moves between clips, but also selects the edit it lands on?

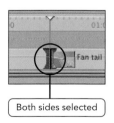

Both sides selected

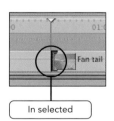

In selected

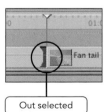

Out selected

6 Watch this: with an edit selected, press **U**. This selects one side of an edit, specifically the **In**. Press **U** again. Now the **Out** is selected. Press **U** a third time. Both sides of the edit are selected.

---

7 Here's the cool part. Press **U** until only one side of the edit is selected. Now, use the **up** and **down** arrow keys to move between clips and watch what happens. Right! The **playhead** jumps to the next edit and selects it in the exact same way it selected the edit point it just left.

This is a really fast way to trim a number of different clips.

---

8 Here's why. Go to the edit point between the first and second clip. Press **U**, until the **In** is selected. Be sure the **Selection** tool is selected.

---

9 Now, press the period key (**.**) and watch the **In** trim to the right one frame. You are doing a **Ripple** edit, using the keyboard.

---

10 Press the comma key (**,**) and watch the **In** trim to the left, also by a frame.

---

11 Press **U** until both sides of the edit are selected. Now, press the comma and period keys and watch the location of the edit shift. You are doing a **Roll** edit, totally under keyboard control!

---

12 But wait! There's more. Continue to keep both sides of this edit point selected. Press the **plus** key on the keypad or **Shift++** (plus key) on the keyboard. Next, type **15** and press **Return**. The edit point just moved 15 frames downstream, to the right.

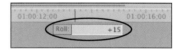

By the way, these are called "timecode offsets," and you can use either the keyboard or the keypad.

---

13 Press the **minus** (**–**) key. Type **20** and press **Return**. The edit point shifts to the left 20 frames.

OK, truth be told, although you *do* need to press the minus key, you don't really need to press the plus key. Final Cut assumes a positive number, unless you tell it otherwise. But I like pressing **Shift++** because it reminds me which direction I want the edit point to move. An edit point must be selected to be moved.

14 Press **U** until only the **Out** is selected. Press the **minus** key, then type **20**, then press **Return**. You instantly trimmed the **Out** by 20 frames.

For me, this is an amazing timesaver. Using only the keyboard and timecode, you can ripple or roll any edit point in your sequence—up to the limit of your handles. (You do remember about handles, right?)

---

15 Click the last clip, **Track - Jump**, to select it. Press **Option+up arrow** to move it to track **V2**. Make sure the clip remains selected.

---

16 Press the **minus** key, type **60** and press **Return**. The entire clip moves left 60 frames. Press the **plus** key on the keypad, type **20** and press **Return**. The entire clip moves right 20 frames.

---

17 One more thing to try. Grab the clip on **V2** and bring it back down to **V1** so that it edits tightly to the end of the **Fan tail** clip (meaning no gaps).

---

18 Next, make sure no clips or edit points are selected. Move the **playhead** out somewhere near the middle of the sequence; the exact location doesn't matter. Now, press the **plus** key, type **25** and press **Return**. Watch the **playhead** move a relative amount—in this case, 25 frames to the right.

Earlier in this exercise, you moved the playhead to an absolute timecode location: 01:00:05:00. Here you told it to move 25 frames downstream from wherever it was at that moment, and it moved.

These timecode keyboard shortcuts make editing fly. Using timecode offsets, you can move the play-head, clips, groups of clips, or edit points, as long as they are selected and they have room on the Timeline to move. Oh, yes—and as long as the edit points have handles.

There's one more technique to cover in this exercise: the Extend edit, which is my favorite edit. It's a Roll edit on steroids, which, um, have not yet been banned by the World Editing Federation.

---

19 Select the edit point between clips 2 and 3.

---

20 Put your **playhead** at **1:00:10:10** and press **E**. The edit point jumps to match the position of the **playhead**.

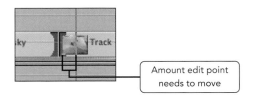

Amount edit point
needs to move

The Power of the Extend Edit

There are three situations where I find the Extend edit really useful:

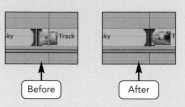

- A fast way to do a Roll edit between two clips on the same track

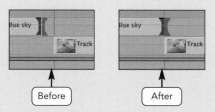

- A really fast way to extend the length of a B-roll clip

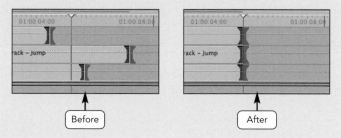

- A really, really fast way to get multiple clips on multiple tracks to start or end at the same time

You'll learn more about this third way of using an Extend edit in Chapter 10, "Motion Effects."

21 That wraps up this exercise on power trimming tools. Quit Final Cut if you are done, otherwise keep everything open for the last exercise in this chapter. If you are quitting, you don't need to save your work.

6 | Trim Edit Window

OK. Here's another confession. I am such a keyboard shortcuts junkie that I thought the Trim Edit window was more pain that it was worth. Then, two things happened: Apple added an incredible improvement in Final Cut 4, and I heard Walter Murch (a multiple-Oscar-winning editor) give a talk on how he edits using Final Cut Pro. Suddenly, the Trim Edit window made a whole lot more sense.

In this exercise, you'll learn how to use it and understand what makes it a unique editing tool within Final Cut.

---

1 If it isn't already open, start Final Cut, open **Chapter 06 Lesson**, and load **Seq – 3 clips** to the **Timeline**.

Since this is a tutorial for you to learn a technique, you won't need to use more than three clips.

The Trim Edit window has three big benefits not easily available by editing on the Timeline:

- It allows you to adjust your Ins and Outs in real time, while the video is playing.

- It allows you to see your edits in a larger window.

- It allows you quick access to a variety of precise controls to trim your edits.

---

2 **Double-click** the edit point between clips 1 and 2 to open the **Trim Edit** window (or select the edit point and press **Cmd+7**).

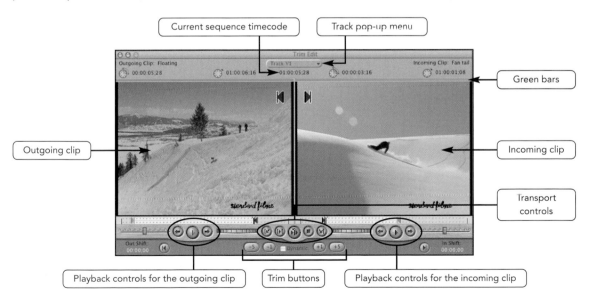

The Trim Edit window opens with each window the exact size of the Canvas. If you want the Trim Edit window to be bigger, make your Canvas window bigger before opening the Trim Edit window.

There are six main sections to the Trim Edit window:

- The outgoing clip window on the left
- The incoming clip window on the right
- Playback controls for the Out on the lower left
- Playback controls for the In on the lower right
- Edit point controls at the bottom middle
- Green bars that indicate what type of trim is being performed at the top

The Trim Edit window is designed, as its name indicates, to trim edits. There are three types of trims you can do in this window:

- Rolls (the default setting when the window opens)
- Ripples
- Slips

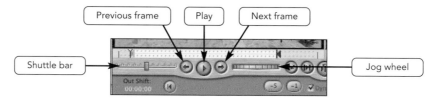

3 At the bottom of each image are the playback controls. Although the shuttle bar and jog wheel are similar to those in other windows, the arrow controls are different. Click the left-pointing arrow to go back one frame. Click the right-pointing arrow to go forward a frame. Click the center arrow to play the clip from the position of the **playhead** at normal speed.

In all cases, clicking these arrows does not change the placement of the In or the Out.

4 The green bars at the top indicate what type of trim is being performed. Click inside the right window (the incoming clip). Notice that your cursor turns into the **Ripple** tool pointing to the right, and the green bar over the right window lights up. This indicates that you are making a **Ripple** edit on the incoming clip.

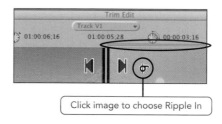

5 Click inside the left window (the outgoing clip). Your cursor turns into the **Ripple** tool pointing to the left, and the green bar over the left window lights up. This indicates you are making a **Ripple** edit on the outgoing clip.

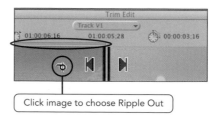

6 Click the vertical bar separating the two windows. Both bars light up, which means you are now doing a **Roll** edit to both clips.

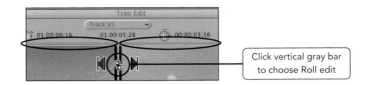

Click vertical gray bar to choose Roll edit

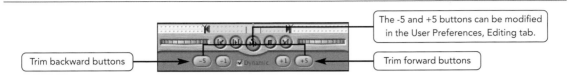

The -5 and +5 buttons can be modified in the User Preferences, Editing tab.

Trim backward buttons

Trim forward buttons

7 At the bottom center of the window are the trim buttons. Click the vertical bar to set the **Trim Edit** window to a **Roll** edit, then click the **–5** button.

You just rolled the edit point back five frames, as indicated by the Out Shift and In Shift indicators in each of the corners. These provide a running total of all your edit point changes.

8 Click the **+5** button to get back to where you started. You can trim in multiple frames or single frames, depending upon which button you click.

Roll

Ripple out

Ripple in

9 Another way to make changes is to put your cursor on top of the **Out** (or the **In**).

If both green bars are lit, dragging the **Out** (or **In**) left or right makes a **Roll** edit.

If the left green bar is lit, dragging the **Out** makes a **Ripple** edit on the **Out**.

If the right green bar is lit, dragging the **In** makes a **Ripple** edit on the **In**.

In all cases, the results of your changes show up in the indicators in the lower corners.

10 Just above the trim buttons are the playback controls.

Click the far-left button to go to the previous edit point.

Click the far-right button to go to the following edit point.

Click the second-left button to play from the **In** to the **Out** and stop (**Shift+**).

Click the middle button to preview the edit and repeat it (**spacebar**).

Click the second-right button to stop playback.

Out

In

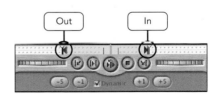

11 Here's where the magic of the **Trim Edit** window appears. Click the **Dynamic** check box to turn it on. (It is off by default.)

---

12 Now, follow these instructions exactly (in fact, read these before you do it):

a. With both windows in the **Trim Edit** window selected—that is, they have a green bar over them— press **J** to play backward for a few seconds.

b. Press the **spacebar** to stop.

c. Press **L** to play forward.

d. Watch the left window. When the snowboarder comes in for a landing, press **K** to stop playback. At the instant you pressed **K**, the **In** and the **Out** were rolled to match the position of the playhead.

Using the J, K, and L keys, you can watch and set your edit points in real time. Use J and L to play the edit. Every time you press K, the edit points are updated.

If you are doing a Roll, both the In and the Out update.

If you are doing a Ripple, only the side being rippled is updated

You've known how to use the J, K, and L keys for a while. The magic of the Trim Edit window is that, with the Dynamic check box checked, you are able to use the J, K, and L keys to adjust your edit points in real-time. It is this combination of precision, using trim buttons and dragging, using real-time trimming, and utilizing the J, K, and L keys that makes the Trim Edit window so useful.

---

13 Take a minute to experiment with different trims, both **Ripples** and **Rolls**, and watch how using the **J**, **K**, and **L** keys works.

Here are some tips to keep in mind:

- Using the spacebar to stop playback does not change the edit point.
- Using the spacebar to start playback and the K key to stop does not change the edit point.
- Using the J, K, and L keys in the Timeline does not change the edit point.
- Only using the J, K, and L keys in the Trim Edit window resets the edit point—provided the Dynamic check box is checked. Otherwise, no real-time update occurs.
- You can change edit points playing forward or backward.
- You can play forward in slow motion by holding down the K and L keys simultaneously.
- You can play backward in slow motion by holding down the K and J keys simultaneously.
- Edit points change when you press the K key, alone.

I don't use the Trim Edit window for every edit. But when I need to see how an edit looks in real time and make tweaks quickly, the Trim Edit window is my first choice.

---

14 This ends this exercise and chapter. You don't need to save your work from this exercise. Feel free to quit Final Cut and take a break, because we are moving on to something new for Final Cut 5—multi-camera editing. And, as you'll discover, multicam builds on everything you've learned so far.

NOTE:

Setting Trim Edit Preferences

There are two preference settings that affect how the Trim Edit window works. You can find them in the **Editing** tab of **User Preferences**.

The Dynamic Trimming check box, which is off by default, controls whether the Dynamic check box is turned on when the Trim Edit window opens. If the Dynamic Trimming check box is *off*, the Trim Edit window opens with the Dynamic check box unchecked. If it is *on*, the Trim Edit window opens with the Dynamic check box on.

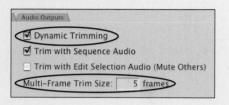

The Multi-Frame Trim Size setting allows you to change the default trim setting in the small ovals at the bottom center of the Trim Edit window from 5 frames (the default) to any number between 1 and 99. (I like setting mine at 6. Why? Because, for some reason, trimming in multiples of three frames works best for me.)

Summary

One-sided trimming tools *always* change the duration of a sequence. Two-sided tools do not. And, because trimming is such an integral part of editing, Final Cut provides lots of options for trimming your clips.

Helpful Keyboard Shortcuts

Shortcut	Action
V	Moves playhead to nearest edit point and selects it
U	Toggles between the three sides of an edit: In, Out, or both
Shift+Z	Depending on which window is selected, scales video in Viewer or Canvas to fit into the window, or scales sequence to fit entirely in Timeline window
A	Selects Selection tool
Option+click with Selection tool	Turns Selection tool into Pen tool
B	Selects the Razor Blade tool (single-track)
BB	Selects the Razor Blade tool (multitrack)
Shift+click with Razor Blade tool	Toggles between single- and multitrack mode
Z	Selects the Zoom In tool
ZZ	Selects the Zoom Out tool
Option+click with Zoom	Toggles between Zoom In and Zoom Out tool
R	Selects the Roll tool
RR	Selects the Ripple tool
S	Selects the Slip tool
SS	Selects the Slide tool
N	Toggles snapping on or off
Ctrl+D	Opens Duration dialog for clip or transition on Timeline
Shift+F4	Locks all video tracks
Shift+F5	Locks all audio tracks
\	Plays a clip or sequence from a few seconds before the current location of the playhead to a few seconds after
Shift+\	Plays a clip from the In to the Out
Option+up arrow	Moves selected clip, or clips, up a track
Option+down arrow	Moves selected clip, or clips, down a track
Comma	Moves selected clip or edit point back one frame
Period	Moves selected clip or edit point ahead one frame
Cmd+7	Opens the Trim Edit window

7

Multiclips—Many Views of the Same Thing

NEW▶ Multiclip is brand new with Final Cut Pro 5. Multiclip allows you to see and cut between multiple angles of the same scene in real time. It is very cool and, once you figure it out, a lot of fun to use. This chapter shows you how.

What's So Great about Multiclip?

In the past, the only way we could edit clips to the Timeline was one at a time. Open a clip in the Viewer, set an In, set an Out, edit the clip to the Timeline, and repeat. Over and over and over again.

Now, there's nothing wrong with this approach. Nothing, that is, until you shoot something like a concert or dance with multiple cameras. Then, editing one shot at a time is not what you want to do at all. Instead, what you *want* to do is see all your different angles at once in real time and select the best shot using the mouse or a key while the whole sequence is playing.

Well, now in FCP 5 that's exactly what multiclips allow you to do. Here's the process:

1. Import your clips and link into a multiclip.

2. Load the multiclip into the Viewer.

3. Set the In and Out of the multiclip.

4. Edit the clip to the Timeline.

5. Sync the Timeline to the Viewer.

6. Set your starting track for audio in the Viewer.

7. Set your starting angle for video in the Viewer.

8. Select the Timeline and play the clip.

9. Edit the clip by cutting between the different angles in the Viewer during playback.

10. Trim individual clips as necessary.

11. Sit back and bask in the applause.

Now that you have the overall picture in mind, let's get started.

1 | Creating a Multiclip

A multiclip builds on everything you've learned so far, then adds the ability to view multiple angles simultaneously in real-time. In this exercise, you will learn how to create a multiclip and synchronize the individual clips in it. You'll also learn the difference between a multiclip and a multiclip sequence.

(This footage is courtesy of Greene HD Productions (**www.greenehdtv.com**) from their program *Moscow on Ice*. This material was first shot on HD using four cameras with matching timecode, then downconverted to DVCAM and captured using Capture Clip. Cameras 2 and 4 recorded audio direct from the mixing board; Cameras 1 and 3 recorded crowd noise using their camera mikes.)

Also, multiclips need a fast hard disk. If you run into lots of dropped frames, move the media files for this lesson to your second hard disk.

---

1 Open **Chapter 07 Lesson**. (Just in case you've forgotten, this is in the **Lessons** folder inside **FCP 5 HOT Files**.

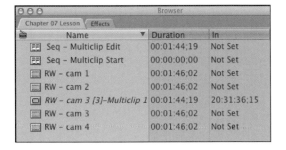

The four camera angles are in the Browser. Feel free to open each one and view it. In this example, they are named "RW – cam 1" through "RW – cam 4". (The letters "RW" stand for the red-and-white colors of their costumes.)

---

2 To create a multiclip, select all four camera angles. Be careful not to include any sequences or the existing multiclip by mistake. Although these clips are all the same duration, in real life your clip durations don't have to match. (Tip: Use the **Command** key to select clips that are not next to each other.)

---

3 Choose **Modify > Make Multiclip**, or **Ctrl+click** one of the selected clips and choose **Make Multiclip**.

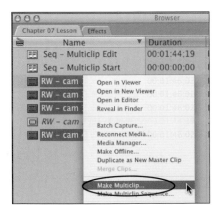

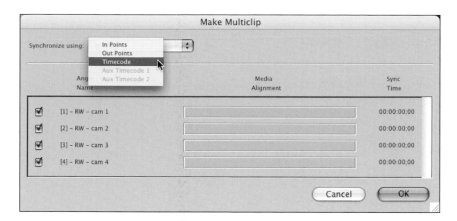

4 The **Make Multiclip** dialog appears, allowing you to determine how to sync your clips. Syncing tells Final Cut how to align the clips so they have a common starting point. You can align clips based upon the **In** or the **Out** (which you would need to set on each clip *prior* to creating the multiclip), or on matching timecode. In this case, choose **Timecode** from the **Synchronize using** pop-up menu.

---

5 The blue check boxes on the left indicate whether you want to include a clip in the multiclip. To exclude a clip, simply uncheck the check box. The blue bars indicate the alignment of the clips; in this case the length of all clips is identical, and the timecode all matches. The far right column indicates the time of the starting timecode.

In this case, **UN**check the check box for the **RW – cam 4** clip, and click **OK**.

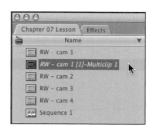

You've now created a multiclip containing three clips—cameras 1, 2, and 3. See how FCP automatically named the clip (though your name may vary slightly)? And did you notice the spiffy new **Multiclip** icon?

6 Double-click or drag the clip to load it into the **Viewer**. Choose the number of angles you want to view from the third pop-up menu (the **View** menu) at the top of the **Viewer**. Set this to **Multiclip 4-Up**. (You view multiclips using four different preset layouts: 1, 4, 9, or 16 angles.) However, watching more than four angles of DV will most likely require a RAID, because a single hard drive isn't fast enough.

7 From the same menu, choose **Show Multiclip Overlays** to see overlays showing the angle, file name, and timecode.

I find leaving these on to be useful when cutting a show. They are hidden during playback.

8 To rearrange angles within the **Viewer**, hold down the **Command** key, and drag the clip where you want it to appear.

This is useful when you want to change the order of clips in a multiclip.

9 To delete an angle, for instance **RW – cam 2** in the upper-right corner, hold down the **Command** key and drag the picture *out* of the **Viewer**. You won't be able to delete an angle that has a colored rectangle around it. (The next exercise explains what the rectangles mean and how to change them.)

10 Deselect any clips you have selected in the **Browser**. Add a new angle to this existing multiclip by holding down the **Command** key and dragging **RW – cam 4** from the **Browser** into a blank space in the **Viewer** not occupied by another clip. Choose **Insert New Angle** by dragging the clip on top of the overlay menu that appears. Be patient and wait for the pop-up menu; otherwise, you'll replace the multiclip with the clip you just dragged to the **Viewer**.

You actually have two choices when adding a new angle. If you want to *replace*, instead of *insert*, an angle that is already in the multiclip, **Cmd+drag** the new clip from the **Browser** on top of the angle in the **Viewer** you want to replace and choose **Overwrite Angle** by dragging the clip on top of the overlay menu.

11 That's it. Multiclips are easy to create, and in the next exercise you'll learn how to set one up for editing. Save your work and take a break if you need one.

DVD MOVIE:

multiclip.mov

If you want to see a demo of creating and editing a multiclip, be sure to watch **multiclip.mov** in the **movies** folder included on the **Final Cut Pro 5 HOT DVD** in the back of the book. It covers most of the material in this chapter.

Creating a Multiclip Sequence

As I was debating what footage to use for this chapter, I discovered the multiclip sequence. A multiclip sequence allows you to quickly create one, or multiple, multiclips based upon the starting or overlapping timecode of your clips.

Multiclip sequences are useful when you have a variety of camera angles with only some timecode in common that you need to build into a single multiclip, or when you have a series of angles that you want to build into separate multiclips.

An example of the first option is a parade, where you have two cameras at the beginning, two cameras in the middle, and three cameras at the end of the parade route. Here, you want to build all these different angles into a single multiclip that spans the length of the parade that you can edit into your finished program.

An example of the second option is a dance concert, where each dance is covered by four cameras that you want to integrate into a single program as a series of separate multiclips. In both these cases, you link these clips based on timecode.

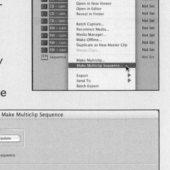

Here, for instance, are two different dances from *Moscow on Ice*. I selected all eight clips (two dances times four cameras), then **Ctrl+clicked** on any one of them to choose **Make Multiclip Sequence**.

The **Make Multiclip Sequence** dialog appears and allows you to sync clips based on Starting Timecode or Matching Timecode. Notice that here FCP has created two separate multiclips: one for dance number one (RW) and one for dance number two (CB). If this were a parade, it could create one multiclip with all the cameras placed by timecode into a single multiclip. Adjusting the **Starting timecode delta**, at the top of the dialog, controls if clips are placed into one, or multiple, multiclips. If you need to use an In or Out as a sync point, you need to use the **Make Multiclip** dialog instead. The rest of this dialog works the same as the Multiclip dialog. When you click **OK**, FCP creates as many different multiclip sequences as needed.

Also, see this small check box up in the upper-left corner—**Automatically edit new multiclip(s) into a new sequence?** Although it is on by default, I recommend you **UN**check it. Rarely will I want all my clips edited into a sequence automatically. I prefer the control of adding them myself. For this reason, I've developed the practice of creating all my multiclips at once but editing each one to the Timeline, as you are about to learn.

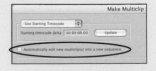

2 | Setting Up a Multiclip

Now that you have your multiclip assembled, it's time to set it up for editing. This exercise shows you how to determine your opening shot, separate your audio and video so you don't switch both, edit the clip to the Timeline, and get everything ready to edit.

---

1 If it isn't open already, open **Chapter 07 Lesson**. Please open the multiclip you created in the last exercise, or double-click **RW – cam 3 [3] – Multiclip 1** in the **Browser** to load it into the **Viewer**.

Now for two definitions:

- The **source angle** is the starting angle for a multiclip; there are two—one for audio and one for video.

- The **active angle** is the angle to which you are currently viewing or listening.

By default, the initial source angle is the first angle in your multiclip—the upper-left corner—and it is indicated by a blue-green rectangle surrounding the clip.

In this example, you will set the audio source angle to one camera and never change it. That way, your audio quality won't switch every time you change cameras. The video source angle, however, simply determines the opening shot. After that, you'll switch between a variety of active angles as you build the visual look of your show.

---

2 Go to the **Sync** pop-up menu (the one in the middle) in the **Viewer**. This menu totally changed from FCP HD. It determines source angles, whether you are switching audio, video, or both. The **Sync** menu also controls **ganging**, or connecting, the clip in the **Viewer** with the clip in the **Timeline**.

By default, the **Sync** pop-up menu is set to edit audio and video simultaneously, with the upper-left angle, called "Angle 1," as your default opening shot. From the **Sync** pop-up, choose **Audio > All**.

This allows you to change your audio source without affecting your video source angle. I've found it best to set the audio first, then set the video.

---

3 Click the upper-right picture (**RW – Cam 2**). See how the image is now bordered by a green rectangle? This indicates the audio source. In other words, until you change it, all your audio for this multiclip will come from camera 2—the direct feed from the audio board.

4 Now, go back to the **Sync** pop-up menu and choose **Video**. Next, click the lower-left window (**RW – cam 3**). See how it instantly displays a blue rectangle? This indicates your video source angle is set to camera 3. If you have things set up properly, your middle pop-up menu should look like the one shown above on the right.

5 Next, mark and edit your multiclip to the **Timeline**. This is *identical* to editing a normal clip. Here are the steps:

- In the **Viewer**, set an **In** at 20:31:37:15.

- In the **Viewer**, set an **Out** at 20:33:21:05. (Verify your duration is 1:43:19.)

- Click the red **Overwrite** button in the lower-left corner of the **Canvas** to edit the multiclip to the **Timeline**.

6 Make sure the Viewer and Timeline playheads are both at the start of the clip. If you miss this step, things get weird. Then, go to the Sync pop-up menu and choose Open. This links the Viewer and the Timeline so they play simultaneously. This means that when you select an angle in the Viewer, that shot change is reflected in the Timeline.

7 Finally, make sure your RT settings match this illustration. You change them from the RT pop-up menu in the upper-left corner of the Timeline.

- Set **Playback Video Quality** to **Dynamic**. (**Low** also works well on my PowerBook.)

- Set **Playback Frame Rate** to **Dynamic**.

- Turn on **Multiclip Playback**.

- Turn on **Scrub High Quality**.

8 That's it. You have everything prepped and ready to edit. In the next exercise, you slip into the Director's chair and cut your own show. That's next.

Multiclip Performance

I wrote this book on a G5, while running Final Cut Pro 5 on a PowerBook. This is exactly the *opposite* of what I should have done, but to be honest, I didn't want to lose my main system due to a software glitch. Plus, it allowed me to see how well the software worked on a slower computer. And the results are that it worked pretty well.

Multiclips require Dynamic RT. Also, multiclips work best when played from your fastest scratch disk. Never store multiclips on your boot disk (the one with your **Applications** folder). You will never get the performance you need.

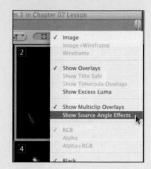

Remember, your goal in editing a multiclip is not playback quality, but to see all the clips at once. If you are still having problems, load the multiclip into the **Viewer**, go up to the **Sync** pop-up menu, and make sure **Show Source Angle Effects** is unchecked.

NEW▶ What Is Dynamic RT?

Dynamic RT is new with Final Cut 5. Building on the strength of Unlimited RT, Dynamic RT allows for real-time playback of effects by profiling your computer to see how fast it is. Then, when a particularly difficult effect is encountered, Dynamic RT will decrease video quality or playback frame rate, or both, so that you can see your effect in real-time.

This decrease in frame rate or video quality is only for playback. When you lay your final project down to tape, FCP will first render all effects, then output at the highest quality. The thing I like about Dynamic RT is that it works in the background and kicks in only when necessary. Also, running in Dynamic RT allows me to see composite modes in real time.

In order for Dynamic RT to work, you must first be in Unlimited RT. For most editing, set RT playback to **Unlimited RT**, with both **Dynamic Video Quality** and **Dynamic Frame Rate** turned on. This will dramatically decrease the time you spend rendering. If you want to see your effects exactly as they will appear on output, set RT to **Safe**. The trade-off is that you'll need to render (or use **Option+P**) to see your effects.

You can adjust both frame rate and quality levels between Dynamic, High, Medium, and Low from the RT pop-up menu in the upper-left corner of the Timeline. The High, Medium, and Low settings are left over from earlier versions of FCP. Dynamic is new with FCP 5. Remember, regardless of setting you still need to render your sequence prior to final output.

3 | Editing a Multiclip

In this exercise, you'll edit a multiclip. Finally.

But first, a definition. As Final Cut defines it, a "switch" is a change in the source angle. When you are editing, you are rarely changing the source angle. A "cut" is an edit in a multiclip, resulting in a change of shots in the Timeline.

Now, as an old...um, scratch that...as an *experienced* live video director, I view these terms as synonyms. However, Final Cut does not. What you want to do is set your source angles, then cut your clip. And that's what you are going to do now.

---

1   If, for some reason, you've closed the current sequence, please reopen **Chapter 07 Lesson**. Double-click **Seq – Multiclip Edit** to load it into the **Timeline**. If you closed this sequence or project, make sure you sync your clip between **Timeline** and **Viewer** by repeating Steps 6 through 8 in the last exercise. If you don't, things won't work.

---

2   With the **playhead** at the beginning of the clip, select the **Timeline**. Press the **spacebar** to play the multiclip. (If both the **Viewer** and **Timeline** aren't playing, be sure you have the **Timeline** selected.) Then, using the number keys **1**, **2**, **3**, and **4** on your keypad (not the keyboard) select between the four shots you see playing in the **Viewer**.

---

3   When you are done, press the **spacebar** to stop playback. Each time you pressed a key, it created a shot change. Now, all your shot changes are reflected in the Timeline.

When I first ran multiclip, I spent a half-hour just doing different cuts of the same sequence. Over and over and over again. Compared to editing multiple angles in previous versions of Final Cut, creating shot changes was amazingly easy. And, when I remembered what it was like directing live cameras in a remote truck, well, it took me fifteen minutes to stop giggling. This is *very* cool!

When you press the **spacebar** to stop, all your edits show up in the Timeline as though you edited each clip individually. You can stop at any time to view your sequence, you don't need to wait until the end.

You play a multiclip sequence the same way you play a regular clip—put your **playhead** where you want playback to start and press the **spacebar**. Notice that because they are synced, both the Viewer and Timeline still play simultaneously.

---

4 There are two ways to change a shot or range of shots in an edited multiclip in the **Timeline**

1. Put your **playhead** in the middle of the clip you want to change and click the shot you want to replace it with in the **Viewer**. This is the best choice when both the **Viewer** and **Timeline** are still synced together.

2. Select the clip(s) you want to adjust, then **Ctrl+click** one of the selected clips. When the **Adjust Angle** sub-menu appears, choose the replacement shot. This is the best choice when the **Viewer** and **Timeline** are no longer synced together.

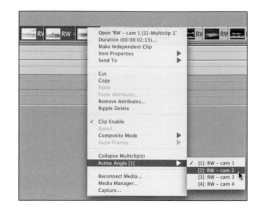

5 A "red bow-tie" between two clips means that it is the same shot on both sides of an edit. This is called a **Through** edit. To delete the **Through** edit, click the edit point to select it and press **Delete**. There is not a fast way to delete multiple **Through** edits at the same time.

If you want to trim your edit points, you won't be able to ripple, because that would throw the video out of sync with the audio. Instead, use the **Roll** tool to move an edit point. If you've forgotten how, refer back to Chapter 6, *"Trim Your Story."*

Because the benefit of multiclip is the ability to cut a sequence in real time, there is an infinite number of ways to cut a sequence. Play **Seq – Multiclip Edit** to see one way that I've cut this.

6 If you need to change your edits, in other words, to recut a portion of the sequence, select the clips you want to reedit on the **Timeline**, **Ctrl+click** the selected clips, and reset them from **Adjust Angle** submenu back to a single shot. Put your **playhead** at the start of the portion you wish to recut, press the **spacebar**, and edit as you did earlier.

7 And that's it. You can edit a multiclip as many times as you want. Just reset the active angle back to the same shot, and have at it again.

Also, a multiclip retains all its different clips until you collapse it (**Modify > Collapse Multiclip**). The benefit to collapsing is that each clip acts as a stand-alone clip, which means you are no longer playing all these clips in real time from your hard disk. In general, it's a good habit to collapse your multiclips when you are done editing and trimming. Your hard disk and **Timeline** performance significantly improve.

Summary

In this chapter, you learned how to create an edited sequence from a series of synced clips using multiclip. Best of all, once a multiclip is on the Timeline, you trim it just like a regular clip. This finishes the editing portion of this book. From here, you move into audio and, after that, effects.

Multiclip Buttons and Keyboard Shortcuts

You can cut between shots in a multiclip using the

- Mouse—In the **Viewer**, click the shot you want to use. This is my preferred way to edit a multiclip.

- Keypad—Use the number keys to select that angle.

- Buttons—Choose **Tools > Button Bars > Multiclip**, then click buttons in the **Timeline** to change shots.

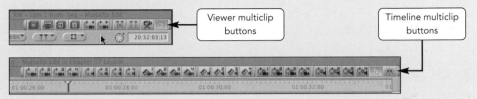

But, there isn't an easy way to use the keyboard of a laptop. And, because my laptop didn't have a keypad, it looked like I was out of luck. Then, I remembered I could remap the keyboard (**Tools > Keyboard Layout > Customize**) so that I could use the number keys on my laptop (1, 2, 3, and 4) to cut between shots.

In case you've forgotten how to do this, refer back to Chapter 2, *"Understanding the Final Cut Pro Interface."*

Helpful Keyboard Shortcuts

Shortcut	Action
Keypad	Cuts between angles in a multiclip; keypad numbers correspond to angle numbers. Maximum clips that can be switched is nine.
Shift+keypad	Switches between different source angles. Maximum number of angles is nine.
R	Selects Roll tool.
S	Selects Slip tool.
SS	Selects Slide tool.
Cmd+1	Selects Viewer.
Cmd+3	Selects Timeline.
Q	Toggles between Viewer and Canvas.

8

Audio—The Secret to a Great Picture

Editing audio for video could fill an entire book just on its own. In many productions, the audio (what people say) is far more important than the visuals (how they look). Yet, far too often, audio is virtually ignored during the production process.

In this chapter, you will learn a basic audio editing workflow, how to edit and trim audio clips, set basic audio levels, add music and effects, then mix everything together so it sounds great.

NEW▶ Soundtrack Pro is new with this version of Final Cut and is destined to play a significant role in your audio post-production. Although I don't have room in this book to cover Soundtrack Pro, at the end of this chapter I've added an exercise that shows you some fast ways to move your sequences between Final Cut and Soundtrack Pro.

Still, for all the audio tools, flexibility, and power that Final Cut provides, keep in mind that in the end, it all comes down to your ears. Be an active listener. Concentrate on building a "sound picture" in your mind using your audio track. Because the better your audio sounds, the better your picture looks.

The Workflow of Editing Audio

Editing audio goes hand-in-hand with editing video. In fact, as you'll see in these exercises, when you have clips with synced audio and video, you edit both the audio and video at the same time.

However, there are many, many times when you want to adjust the timing of the audio differently from the video. Or use one transition for video and another for audio. Or add music and effects to your sequence.

For all these reasons, I've found it helpful to follow a workflow for editing supplementary audio, similar to what you learned in Chapter 1,

"*Get Organized,*" for Final Cut itself. This audio workflow consists of five steps:

1. Edit the audio to the Timeline.
2. Trim the audio.
3. Add transitions.
4. Add effects.
5. Mix.

The exercises in this chapter directly follow this editing workflow, with the exception of audio transitions, which are covered in the next chapter, to help you learn a *process* for editing, as well as specific techniques.

The Math of Audio

But, first, you need to understand some of the math behind the audio. Why? Because, when it comes to audio, what you don't know can make your life really unpleasant.

You've probably tossed around terms like "96K," "48K," "44.1K," "32K," or "8-bit," "16-bit," even "24-bit." But, what do those terms mean? When I ask my students, I either get "quality," or some seriously blank looks.

But understanding what these terms mean has a direct impact on your audio—especially when, as a marketing ploy, many inexpensive DV cameras ship from the factory with the wrong audio settings for digital editing.

So, sharpen your pencil and grab an extra cup of coffee. This stuff is important and won't take long to read.

Frequency 101

In order to understand digital audio, you first need to understand "normal" audio.

All audio is analog—variations in air pressure that cause your eardrum, or a microphone diaphragm,

to vibrate. Those vibrations are translated by our brain, or the mic, into electrical signals, which can then be heard or recorded.

The "normal" range of human hearing is 20 to 20,000 cycles per second. This is called the *frequency response* of human hearing. However, human hearing changes with age. As people get older, they tend to lose the ability to hear higher frequencies. A middle-aged man, for instance, can only hear frequencies up to 12,000 to 14,000 cycles. Women tend to lose high-frequency hearing more slowly than men.

A deep pipe on an organ, or bass guitar, is in the 60 to 100 cycle range. Much below that, and you'll feel the vibration, but not hear the tone.

Human speech is in the range of 300 to 4,000 cycles per second, with some sounds, like "S" and "F," going a bit higher.

Orchestral triangles are in the 8,000 to 12,000 range.

Why is this important? Because if you want to emphasize the loudness of a ship's horn (which

I did in a recent video for a cruise line), you can either increase the volume for the entire clip (which raises the overall noise) or just increase the frequencies for the horn (which makes it louder, without affecting anything else). You'll learn how to do this later in Chapter 12, *"Filters and Keying."*

Sample Rate

The first set of terms, "96K, 48K, 44.1K, and 32K," all have to do with the frequency response of a digital audio clip.

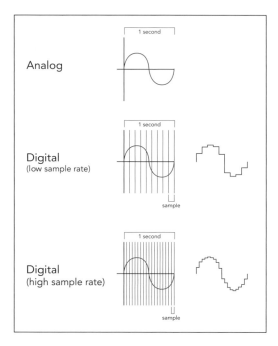

By their very nature, analog signals are infinitely variable, like the smooth curve of the sine wave in this illustration. And, although our ears can deal with analog signals perfectly well, a computer can't. It needs to convert these infinite changes into discrete numbers that it can store and process.

This conversion is called *quantizing*, and it works like this: The computer "listens" to an incoming audio signal and, every so often, records the average level of the sound it "hears." If those digital samples are far apart, as in the second illustration, only a very rough digital image of that sound is recorded. However, if those samples are very close together, as in the third example above,

then a much more accurate picture of the sound is recorded.

The sample rate is the measure of how many digital samples are recorded by the computer. The higher the number of samples per second, the more accurate the picture of the sound is captured by the computer.

According to the Nyquist Theorem (which I'm sure you remember from high school physics), the frequency response (or range of frequencies a clip contains) of a digital audio signal is equal to half its sample rate. Thus, a 32K sample rate contains a range of frequencies from 20 to 16,000 cycles. A 48K sample rate ranges from 20 to 24,000.

The default setting for Final Cut does not like editing 32K audio files. It works much better on 44.1K and 48K sample rates. However, many inexpensive digital cameras are set to 32K sample rates for weird marketing reasons. So, make sure the production crew sets the audio sample rate on the camera to 48K (the digital standard). This is often listed in camera menus as 16-bit. This simple change will make your editing life much easier.

Dynamic Range

The second set of numbers, "8-bit, 16-bit, and 24-bit," all have to do with dynamic range, the amount of difference between the softest and loudest sound in a clip.

But where did the word "bit" come from? Not surprisingly, it came from the computer. Since all computer numbers are recorded in binary ones and zeros, an 8-bit audio file means that all its different volumes are represented by a series of numbers that range from 0 to 255—or 256 different values. Why 256 values? Because 256 is equal to 2 to the 8th power, where 8 represents the bit-depth of the audio file. The standard for CDs, 16-bit audio, has 65,536 discrete volume settings (2 to the 16th power). And 24-bit audio, used in DVD-Audio and theatrical films, has 16,777,216 discreet settings (2 to the 24th power).

This means that an 8-bit sound with a level of 1 is very, very, *very* soft. A sound with a level of 255 is as loud as it can get; because in an 8-bit environment loudness can't be greater than 255. In audio, loudness, or gain, is expressed in decibels, where 0 db is "as loud as possible." Softer volumes are shown as negative numbers smaller than 0. If your audio track gets too loud, so that the combined signal is greater than 0 db on the audio meter, your audio gets clipped and parts of the signal are thrown away.

As a warning, Final Cut lights these two small clips lights to tell you your audio is too "hot," or loud.

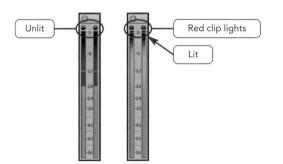

Why are these lights important? Because audio mixing is additive. As you add more tracks, the additional signals increase the overall volume, which makes it very easy for those levels to get too high. Then, because the computer does not have any more numbers to use to represent this extra loudness, it throws that excess audio away, leaving flat-top waveforms where audio should be.

This missing signal creates digital distortion. Little computer bits, flying out of your computer, landing higgledy-piggledy on the floor. Homeless. (Well, OK, maybe they don't really fly out of your computer. But digital distortion sounds *awful*, and if you output it to tape, there is no technology on the planet that can fix your audio to make it sound good.)

So, watch your audio meters! Be very, very careful those clip lights don't light. Not once. Not even flicker.

Dynamic Range Table

Bit Depth	# of Levels	Dynamic Range	Common Use
8-bit	256	0 to –96 db	Internet, broadcast TV
16-bit	65,536	0 to –124 db	CD-ROM, digital video
24-bit	16,777,216	0 to –143 db	Theatrical films
Human hearing	N/A	0 to –120 db	Life

NEW ▶ New in FCP 5 is support for 96K sample rates and 24-bit audio. Final Cut can edit WAV or AIFF files, 8-, 16- or 24-bit depth, with sample rates from 8 to 96 kHz.

DVD MOVIE: | **audio.mov**

For audio tutorials illustrating this chapter, check out **audio.mov** in the **movies** folder on the **Final Cut Pro 5 HOT DVD**. This audio tutorial shows you how to set audio levels and use the Audio Mixer within Final Cut.

1 | Building the Audio Story

In this exercise, you will learn how to read audio waveforms, how to add audio to the Timeline, and how to trim clips based on the audio.

In this chapter, you will work with news footage from CNN ImageSource showing the 1999 preparations for Hurricane Irene in Florida to create a promo for an upcoming documentary on hurricanes. The editing techniques presented here are especially useful in documentaries, education, training, or whenever you have to illustrate what someone is talking about.

---

1 Open **Chapter 08 Lesson 1**. It's in **FCP Projects > FCP 5 HOT Files** folder you created at the beginning of this book. Double-click **Seq – Talking Head start** to load it into the **Timeline**.

Save this project under a new name (**File > Save As**). Call it **Hurricane**, and save it in your **FCP Projects** folder.

NOTE: | **Talking Head**

Talking head is an old newsroom term that refers to video showing a close-up of the person talking. *B-roll* is an even older film term that refers to pictures that are used to illustrate what the talking head is talking about. You work with both in this exercise.

---

2 Open the bin named **Heads**, and double-click the clip **Easley – Get safe** to load it into the **Viewer**. Notice that a new tab appears at the top: **Stereo (a1a2)**. Click it to display the audio associated with this clip.

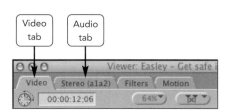

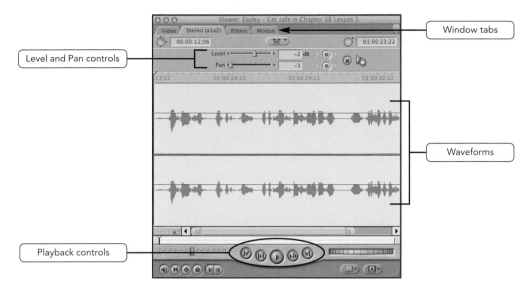

Window tabs

Level and Pan controls

Waveforms

Playback controls

Final Cut displays audio as a **waveform**. A waveform shows the volume of the audio. Where the waveform is thin, the audio is quiet. Where the waveform is thick, the audio is loud. Although a waveform doesn't indicate either the quality or the frequency of the sound, being able to read a waveform is really, really helpful in editing audio.

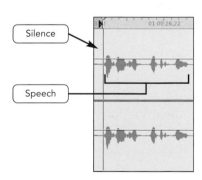

Here, for example, right at the beginning, are the words, "Now's the time to ask people to please…." Human speech is "bursty," meaning that there is always a slight pause between syllables and words. This makes it possible to edit audio by looking to see where phrases begin and end.

---

3 Now, move the **playhead** to just before he starts to speak, and set an **In**. Press the **spacebar** and notice that he starts speaking immediately.

Silence

Speech

Hmmm, a bit *too* immediately, actually. Move your **playhead** back to the **In** and move it to the left about two frames and reset the **In**. Play this again.

See how much better this sounds? This brief pause gives the start of your sequence a little room for your audience to see the visual before the audio starts. Also, later, it will give you room to add a brief audio fade-in to make the start sound more natural. (Your new **In** should be at **Viewer** timecode **01:00:24:07**.)

---

4 Edit this clip to the **Timeline** by grabbing the hand and dragging the clip from the **Viewer** to the **Overwrite** overlay in the **Canvas**, or use another automated tool you learned about in Chapter 4, *"Build Your Story."*

This is one of the great strengths of Final Cut. Whether you are editing video, audio, or audio and video, all the tools work exactly the same. So, everything you learned about editing clips to the Timeline— organizing them once they are on the Timeline and trimming your clips to remove the parts you don't need—still applies when you add audio into your sequence.

---

5 Play the end of the clip on the **Timeline**. Notice the extra words at the end? Trim this. You can do this several ways, but, remember, for trimming, *always* turn off snapping (press **N**). Otherwise, snapping keeps jumping you to the nearest edit point.

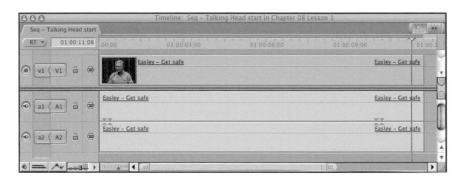

6 First you need to find the revised **Out**, so grab the **playhead**, back it up before the end of the clip, and play it. Stop when he says, "ride the storm out" (**Timeline** timecode: **01:00:11:08**).

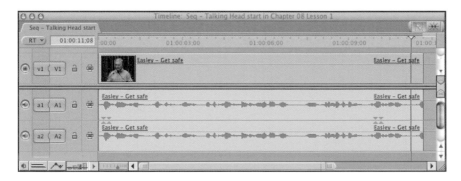

7 Often, when editing audio, turning on audio waveforms in the **Timeline** is helpful. You can do this by pressing **Option+Cmd+W** or…

…by clicking the small right-pointing arrow in the lower-left corner of the **Timeline** and turning on **Show Audio Waveforms**.

Keep in mind, however, that there is a performance hit in Final Cut when you have audio waveforms on. Turn them off when you are editing video so your system will perform faster.

8 Now you have several choices for trimming the end of the clip:

- Turn on snapping, grab the end of the clip, and drag it to the **playhead**.

- Turn on snapping, select the **Razor Blade**, cut the clip at the **playhead**, and delete the unused portion on the right.

- Turn on snapping, select the **Ripple** tool, and ripple the end of the clip to the **playhead**.

- Press **Ctrl+V** to cut the clip at the **playhead** and delete the unused portion.

- Select the edit point and press **E** to jump the edit point to the **playhead**.

Pick one of these methods and delete the excess audio and video.

---

9 Double-click **Devanas – Big story** to load it into the **Viewer**. This time, you'll set both the **In** and the **Out** in the **Viewer**, so you won't need to trim it on the **Timeline**.

Set the **In** so that it is right after the "Uh," and the **Out** to the end of his sound bite. (This term comes from radio news where a "sound bite" is a short clip of someone talking, in this case, Mr. Devanas. It is a "small bite of sound.") Your **Viewer** timecode points should be close to an **In** of **01:00:05:09** and an **Out** of **01:00:13:20**.

Cutting out the "uh" at the beginning of the sound bite makes it sound better.

Hmmm… these two quotes sound jumpy. I think it would flow better if I put a clip between these two. You'll do this with an Insert edit.

---

10 Double-click **Bush – Major threat** to load it into the **Viewer**. Click the **Stereo (a1a2)** audio tab, and then find the beginning of the audio, where he says, "The major threat…". Set your **In** three frames before he starts speaking (**01:00:00:08**).

Again, you are giving a little breathing room to the clip to make the audio sound more natural and less "clipped."

---

11 Go to the end of the clip, where he says, "…to be rainfall." Using the arrow tools can help find the exact end of the audio. Again, add three more frames and set the **Out** (**01:00:04:00**).

---

12 Using the **Up Arrow** key, move the **playhead** between these first two clips (**Timeline: 01:00:11:08**). Then, using one of the automated tools, *Insert* edit this clip to the **Timeline**. It should appear at the position of the **playhead**. If you have problems editing using one of the automated tools, be sure you don't have an **In** or **Out** set on the **Timeline** (press **Option+X**). Play the two clips and watch the video.

---

13 Now, position your **playhead** to the end of the sequence and add the remaining four sound bites to the sequence. Use the order in the following table. You should be able to listen to each clip and decide where to set the **In** and the **Out**, but, if you want to check yourself, the table lists the **In** and **Out** for each clip.

Building the Sound Bites		
Clip Name	Source Timecode In	Source Timecode Out
Easley – Get safe*	01:00:24:07	01:00:35:14
Bush – Major threat	01:00:00:08	01:00:04:00
Devanas – Big story	01:00:05:09	01:00:13:20
Myers – Flooding	01:00:35:28	01:00:45:21
Bush – Emergency	01:00:14:03	01:00:19:10
Jerrill – Big threat	01:00:43:03	01:00:52:16
Woman – We're safe	01:00:54:21	01:00:57:05

* The politically astute reader undoubtedly noticed that Gov. Mike Easley has nothing whatever to do with Hurricane Irene in Florida, since he is the governor of North Carolina, and is talking about a different hurricane. Two liberties were taken in selecting video for this chapter. The first is pretending Gov. Easley had something to do with Hurricane Irene, when he didn't. The second is using B-roll from a variety of hurricanes. My reasoning is that the purpose of this chapter is to teach you how to edit with audio, not to teach you the ethics of editing.

14 When you are done, your sequence should look like **Seq – Talking Heads finished**, and end at **01:00:50:14**.

15 In looking at this sequence one more time, I realized that the second Bush clip is too long. Using the **Ripple** tool, trim it back so that it ends when he says, "…of emergency in Florida" (**01:00:34:14** on the **Timeline**).

Now, your whole sequence should end at **01:00:46:14** in the **Timeline**.

16 Another idea to experiment with is using the **Move** (or **Swap**) edit you learned about in Chapter 6, *"Trim Your Story."* Shuffle the clips around to see if it improves the clarity of the story.

The key point to this exercise is that the editing tools you've already learned work exactly the same way when you are editing audio. It's just that now, when you are building an audio-driven story, you need to make your edits based on what's being said in the audio, not the visuals in the video.

---

17 In the next exercise, you'll learn how to add B-roll to illustrate what the speakers are talking about. For now, though, save your work. You'll be using this exact same sequence in the next exercise.

NOTE: **Audio Scrubbing**

Audio scrubbing is a quick way to review audio while you are editing.

You turn audio scrubbing on (or off) in the **View** menu, or by pressing **Shift+S**. When it's on, dragging the playhead across clips in the **Timeline**, **Viewer**, or **Canvas** allows you to hear snippets of the audio. When scrubbing is off, dragging the **playhead** is silent.

NOTE: **The Benefits of Two-Track Editing**

When I'm editing dramatic material, I tend to keep the video to one track because it helps me to see the pacing of a scene.

However, when I'm editing anything that's a talking head with B-roll, two-track video editing is far easier. First, because moving B-roll clips is as easy as dragging them from one spot to another on the V2 track, this means I don't have to mess with the trimming tools. Second, I can easily see my jump cuts in V1. (A "jump cut" is a sudden, unjustified change in position. Put the two Bush clips together, and you'll see what I mean.) Third, using two tracks of video makes it easier for me to checkerboard my audio clips, which you'll learn about in Exercise 5. Finally, keeping my talking heads on V1 makes it easier to see where I need to put my lower-third supers and IDs, because I can see where the shots change. (You'll learn about text and titles in Chapter 10, *"Text, Titles, and Graphics."*)

You can, of course, edit your pieces any way you like. However, this two-track system works well for me.

2 | Adding B-Roll for Illustration

In this exercise, you'll learn how to use a second video track to provide B-roll coverage for a talking head, how to use the Timeline patch panel, and some basic approaches to laying out your audio tracks in a sequence.

1 Open the **Hurricane** project, if it isn't open already. Then, **Ctrl+click Seq – Talking Head finished** in **Browser** and choose **Duplicate** from the shortcut menu. This makes a copy of the sequence so you can make changes without damaging the original sequence. Name the new sequence " **Seq – B-roll added**".

First, in this style of editing, you are going to keep your talking head video on v1 and add additional video to v2. I call this multitrack editing.

2 So, you need to add one more video track and two more audio tracks. There are several ways to do this, but when you are adding multiple tracks, the fastest is to choose **Sequence > Insert Tracks** and fill in the two **Insert** fields.

Next, in order to use the automated tools for editing a clip from the Viewer to the Timeline, you need to change the settings in the patch panel, on the left side of the Timeline.

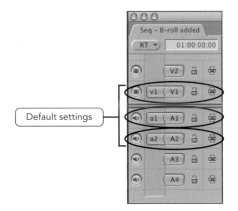

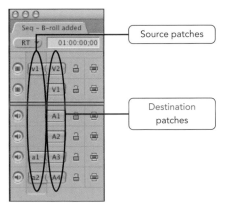

Default settings

Source patches

Destination patches

3 The default settings work fine, when all your video is on **V1** and your audio is on **A1** and **A2**. However, in this case, you want to put your B-roll video on **V2** and the natural sounds from it on **A3** and **A4**.

To do this, move the **v1** on the *left* side up to match **V2** on the *right* side. This means that the video from the **Viewer** (which comes into the patch panel from the left on **v1**) goes out to the **Timeline** using the **V2** patch. (If you wanted to put the video on **V3** on the **Timeline**, you'd move the left **v1** patch up to **V3**, thus connecting the **Viewer** on the left to the **Timeline** on the right.)

Similarly, you need to move the audio patches so that the audio from the **Viewer** (which, again, comes in from the left on **a1** and **a2**) goes out to the **Timeline** on **A3** and **A4**.

In brief, the patch panel controls how signals are routed from the Viewer to the Timeline.

NOTE:

The Patch Panel

The patch panel tells Final Cut how to route the audio and video from the Viewer to the Timeline when you use the automated editing tools (such as dragging to the Canvas overlay, pressing F10, or clicking the red button). The patch panel is "smart," meaning that it knows what type of clip is in the Viewer and adjusts itself accordingly.

Normally, the default settings are fine—but not when you want to put video or audio on other tracks. The patch panel is also highly useful when you want to do an audio-only or video-only edit with a clip that contains both audio and video.

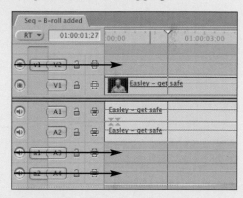

Video only

Here, a video-only clip is loaded into the Viewer, and only the v1 patch is available on the Viewer side of the patch panel.

Audio only

Here, a two channel audio-only clip is loaded into the Viewer, and only the a1 and a2 patches are available.

continues on next page

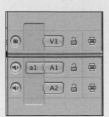

A1 only

Here, a mono audio file is loaded into the Viewer, and only the a1 patch is available.

Audio and video

This is an audio and video clip, loaded into the Timeline. All three signals (v1, a1, and a2) are patched through to the Timeline. The next two examples, though, are more interesting.

Video, no audio

Here's the same clip, but only the video is connected. See that small gap between the two audio patches on the left and right? You create that gap by clicking the a1 or a2 patches on the left. When you click them, Final Cut disconnects the signal. In this case, only the video is passed from the Viewer to the Timeline.

Audio, no video

Here's the opposite situation. There's a clip with audio and video in the Viewer, but the patch panel is allowing only the audio to go through. See that small gap between v1 on the left (the Viewer) and V1 on the right (the Timeline)? This tells Final Cut to block the video but let the audio go through.

Whenever you use an automated editing tool to move a clip from the Viewer to the Timeline, it always passes through the patch panel.

4 Move the **playhead** to just before Gov Easley says, "…ask the people…" (**01:00:01:24**) and set an **In**. You are going to establish who is speaking, then almost immediately cover them with hurricane footage.

---

5 Open the **B-roll** bin and double-click the clip **B – sandbags CU** to load it into the **Viewer**.

Notice how all the B-roll shots start with "B"? I did this intentionally because it helps me sort B-roll video from interviews. Feel free to steal my idea and use it yourself.

---

6 Set an **In** at the beginning of the clip. Set a duration of **2:07**. Once you have the clip marked, press **F10** to edit it to the **Timeline**.

Notice how Final Cut automatically puts the video on V2 and the audio on A3 and A4? This is why you use the patch panel in combination with the playhead—they give you precise control over where clips get placed. And, as you've come to expect when editing video, the playhead automatically moves to the end of the clip, positioning itself for the next edit (**01:00:04:01**).

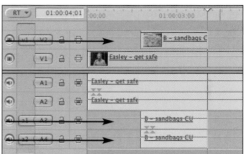

<table>
<tr><td>

NOTE:

</td><td>

How Final Cut "Reads" Video Tracks

Clips laid out horizontally on the Timeline play one after the other. Clips stacked vertically play at the same time.

Final Cut has a rule for reading stacked video tracks: The video on the higher numbered track covers the video on the lower numbered track. Thus, V2 totally blocks video on V1.

However, there's an addition to this rule: Video on higher tracks blocks video on lower tracks, *provided the video on the higher track is 100 percent opaque and 100 percent full-screen*. Changing those settings is the whole idea behind compositing and motion effects. You will learn about these rules in Chapter 11, *"Motion Effects."*

</td></tr>
</table>

7 OK. Now that you have the first B-roll shot in the sequence, the following table shows the rest of the clips and the timecode at which they start. Given what you know, you should be able to easily edit these to the **Timeline**.

To make it easier to edit, all the rest of the B-roll clips are trimmed, so you don't need to set **Ins** or **Outs**.

B-Roll Clip Order

Clip Name	Timeline Start	Duration
B – sandbags WS	01:00:04:01	4:11
B – board carry	01:00:08:12	3:04
B – board saw	01:00:11:16	3:06
B – board drill	01:00:14:22	2:07
B – storm trees L	01:00:16:19	3:00
B – storm trees R	01:00:19:29	2:22
B – storm road	01:00:22:21	2:29
B – storm light	01:00:25:20	4:06
B – storm waves	01:00:29:26	3:01
B – storm trees	01:00:32:27	2:19
B – storm boats	01:00:35:16	3:14
B – storm police	01:00:39:00	3:01
B – storm flood	01:00:42:01	4:14

Perfect. Except, um, the B-roll ends one frame later than the video on v1. Here's a quick trick to fix it. Remember the Extend edit you learned about in Chapter 6, "*Trim Your Story*"? It is ideally suited to getting clips on multiple tracks to end at the same time.

8 Select the **Zoom** tool (press **Z**) and zoom into the end of the sequence until you can see a difference between the ending of the shots on **V1** and **V2**.

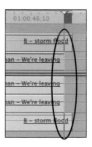

9 Move the **playhead** so that it is sitting on the **Out** of **V1**. Then, select the **Selection** tool, and click to select the **Out** of **V2**, which also selects the audio on **A3** and **A4** because the clips are linked.

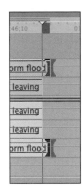

10 Press the letter **E**, and watch as the selected tracks instantly line up at the position of the **playhead**. No muss. No fuss.

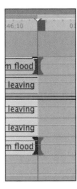

11 That's a lot to cover in one exercise. In the next exercise, you'll learn how to trim the audio without touching the video. But, for now, save your work and take a break.

3 | Trimming Audio While Staying in Sync

In this exercise, you'll learn how to trim audio separately from video, while still keeping everything in sync.

1 If it isn't already, open the project **Hurricane**, and double-click **Seq – B-roll finished** to load it into the **Timeline**.

2 Position the **playhead** so it is at the start of the B-roll. Then, zoom in so that the first clip (also called the *A-roll clip*) and the two B-roll clips fill the **Timeline**. (A quick way to have a selection fill the **Timeline** window is to select what you want to zoom in on, then press **Shift+Option+Z**.) Be sure you can see all six tracks.

3 Play the beginning of the sequence. Hear how the audio energy drops after the first B-roll clip?

What you are going to do in this exercise is remove the audio from the second B-roll clip, and extend the audio from the first clip to cover both B-roll clips.

4 Go to the upper-right corner of the **Timeline** and click the **Link** button to deselect it (gray).

5 Now, grab the video from the first B-roll clip and drag it to the left a few frames. (You may want to turn off snapping before trying to move the clip.)

See those red flags? It means you've just moved the video of this clip out of sync!

A Rant on the Link Button

This Linked Selection button drives me absolutely nuts! *Why* would anyone put a button on the Timeline that, when you use it, almost assuredly allows you to get your clips out of sync?!?

I grant that, in certain instances, being able to control linking is necessary. But it is *not* necessary on the Timeline as a button. This thing is bad and needs to be destroyed!

First, click the button to turn it back on (green).

Then, grab the button from the **Timeline** button bar, drag it out and let go. *Poof!* It's gone and good riddance. If you really need to mess with linking, you can select it in the **Modify** menu.

But this button is just stupid!

Oh, what is linking, you ask? A **linked clip** is one where the audio and video are locked in sync, or *linked*.

You can tell if clips are linked because the name of the video clip and the names of the audio clips are under-lined. Generally, but not always, linked video and audio clips have the same name, as well.

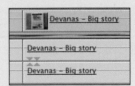

If just the audio clip names are underlined, it means that the two audio clips are linked as a stereo pair but are not linked to the video. A music clip is a good example of a stereo pair.

(By the way, it's easy to convert a clip from dual mono to a stereo pair and vice versa. Just choose **Modify > Stereo Pair**, or press **Option+L**.)

Clicking any part of a linked clip selects the entire clip. This is great, if you want to move the entire clip. However, it's a pain in the neck if you want to adjust the video or audio separately. There's a better way—and that's the whole point of this exercise.

(Sigh…OK, if you are feeling badly about the poor trashed Linked Selection button, you can always put it back in the button bar by rereading Chapter 2, "*Understanding the Final Cut Pro Interface.*" But I really wish you wouldn't.)

6 There's an extra-secret way of moving one side (meaning the video side or the audio side) of a linked clip without getting everything out of sync. But, first, you need to get your video clip back in sync. However, because linking is on, whenever you click one side of a clip, the whole clip gets selected.

So, deselect everything. Then, hold down the **Option** key and click the out-of-sync video clip to select it. Then, with just the video clip selected, **Ctrl+click** the red sync flag and choose **Move into Sync** from the shortcut menu. (Be sure to click only the red flag, not the edit point or elsewhere in the clip.)

The Option key is the secret. You can use it to get rid of one side of a linked clip, or trim just a video In, or change an audio Out. Whenever you need to work with just one side of a clip, the Option key makes it possible. The Option key temporarily overrides linking. The benefit to using the Option key is that, once you let go, linking is back in force. This reduces the opportunity for unintentional mistakes.

---

7 Hold down the **Option** key and click once to select *just* the audio for the second B-roll clip.

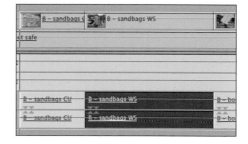

---

8 Delete the selected audio and leave a gap.

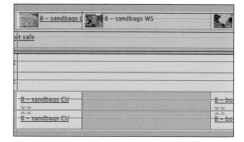

---

9 Next, hold down the **Option** key and select the audio **Out** of the first B-roll clip.

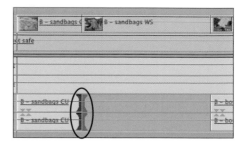

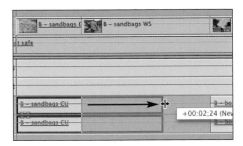
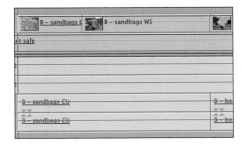

10 Now, while still holding down the **Option** key, drag the **Out** all the way to the right to fill the gap.

11 Play the first part of the sequence.

Hear how the B-roll audio carries the energy and excitement of the first B-roll clip through the second B-roll clip?

12 This is such an incredibly important technique that I want you to discover one more way you can use this. As additional practice, **Option+click** the video **In** of the first B-roll clip. Drag it to the right.

See how you can move the edit point of a clip, yet the audio and video elements of the clip stay in sync? Using the Option key to move an edit point or select just the audio or video of a clip is far, FAR better than using the Linked Selection button.

NOTE:

Split Edits

Split edits are where the video and the audio edit occur at different times. There are two types of split edits: an *L-edit* and a *J-edit*.

An L-edit is one where the audio edit occurs later than the video edit. It's called an L-edit because the shape of the end of the outgoing clip looks like the letter L.

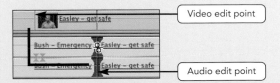

The easiest way to create an L-edit is to **Option+click** the video (or audio) edit point with the **Roll** tool, then **Option+drag** the edit point with the **Roll** tool so the video **In** occurs *before* the audio **In**.

continues on next page

Split Edits *continued*

A J-edit is one where the audio edit occurs earlier than the video edit. It's called a J-edit because the shape of the edit points form the letter J.

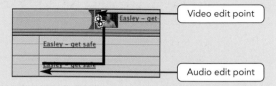

The easiest way to create an J-edit is to **Option+click** the video (or audio) edit point with the **Roll** tool, then **Option+drag** the edit point with the **Roll** tool so the video **In** occurs *after* the audio **In**. In fact, the process of creating a J-edit is identical to creating an L-edit. The only difference is the direction you drag the edit point.

Split edits are used constantly, whenever you want to see one thing and hear another.

---

13 That ends this exercise. Save your work, but keep everything handy. You're going to use this same exercise again.

When Should You Use the Link Command?

I don't like the Linked Selection button, because it gets too many people into trouble. But the **Link** command (**Cmd+L**) is very useful—in certain situations.

As you've probably surmised, I don't recommend unlinking a clip when you can use the **Option** key instead.

However, a good use of the Link command is when you have two different clips, and you want to connect them (for instance, a video-only clip and an audio-only sound effect).

Linking them together tells Final Cut that it should treat these two clips as being "in sync." That way, whenever you move one side of the clip—the video, for example—the sound effect follows.

To link a clip, align the two clips so that the sound and video play together with the right timing. Then, select both clips and choose **Modify > Link**. Both clip names become underlined, and for the rest of that **Timeline**, they move together.

There's also a reason to *unlink* a clip. Say you want to use the audio from a clip several times in a sequence. (For example, it could be traffic noise you want to use as background.) Unlinking the audio from the video makes it easy to move the audio around as its own separate clip; because you never want to use the video, maintaining sync is irrelevant.

4 | Setting Audio Levels

In this exercise, you will learn the difference between a stereo and dual-mono audio file, how to read the audio meters, and how to set proper audio levels. You'll also get an introduction to keyframes.

NOTE:

Stereo vs. Dual-Mono Audio files

In Chapter 3, *"Gather Your Media,"* you learned about capturing audio and video. Audio can be captured in two ways: stereo and dual-mono.

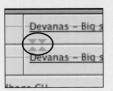

A stereo file has both channels linked for sync (their clip name is underlined) and displays a little green bow-tie between the clips. Channel 1 is panned all the way to the left and Channel 2 is panned all the way to the right. Additionally, the audio levels are linked. Changing the level on one track automatically changes the level on the other track by the same amount. Stereo is the correct file choice when you care about the spatial relationship of the sound, that is, whether it is on the left, right, or center. Music is a good example.

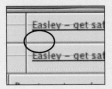

A dual-mono file has both channels linked for sync, but without the green bow-tie. Both channels are panned to the center, and there is no link between their audio levels. Changing one does not affect the other. Dual-mono is the default setting for audio capture and is used when the spatial relationship of the sound is not important, for example, in an interview.

You can easily convert between a stereo file and dual-mono by selecting the audio clip and choosing **Modify > Stereo Pair**, or pressing **Option+L**. There is no loss in quality by turning stereo linking on or off.

---

1 Open **Hurricane**, if it isn't already open. Then, double-click **Seq – B-roll finished** to load it into the **Timeline**.

---

2 Play the sequence and watch the **audio meter**. (Don't worry about the overall mix at this point.) Notice that the audio levels bounce between **–6** and **–12 db**, with a little yellow bar floating over the top of the green meters. The yellow bar is called the **peak indicator**. This shows you the level of your loudest sound during the last 3 seconds. The green bars indicate the sound level of your left and right audio channels.

The peak indicator is handy because it is often hard to see the levels of the green bars since they are bouncing so much.

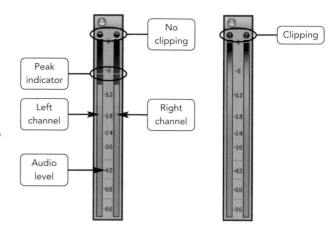

By default, all odd-numbered channels are assigned to the left channel, and all even-numbered channels are assigned to the right channel.

As the audio gets louder, the green bars get taller. When the audio is too loud, even for an instant, the red clip lights light. *It is critical that you adjust your audio levels so that the clip lights never light.*

Generally, for dialogue, you want your meters to bounce between –6 and –12. They can go higher than this occasionally, but this is a good range for average levels. Running your audio at this level allows you plenty of headroom for loud sounds and sudden changes in volume. Set your volume (called "audio gain") much lower than this and it is hard to hear what is being said.

There are at least four ways to set audio levels for a clip, plus two more when you learn about the Audio Mixer. Which one is best? Whichever one helps you get your work done.

3 Double-click the **Easley** clip in the **Timeline** to load it into the **Viewer**. Play the clip. Notice the audio levels are low, down between **–12** and **-18 db**? These levels need to be increased so the speaker's audio is between **–6 db** and **–12 db**.

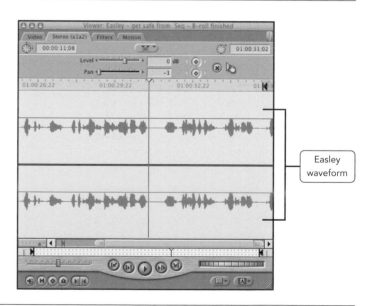

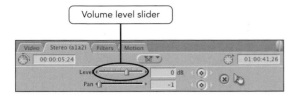

Volume level slider

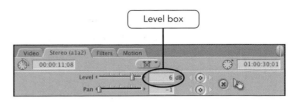

Level box

4 One way to change the level of a clip in the **Viewer** is to slide the volume **Level** slider left (to decrease volume) or right (to increase it) until the audio level is where you want it. In this case, drag the **Level** slider to the right until the audio level is bouncing between **–6** and **–12**.

5 Another way to change the level in the **Viewer** is to click in the **Level** box to the right of the **Level** **slider** and type a number. In this case, increasing the level to **6** brings the volume up appropriately. Every clip is different; the key is to make decisions by watching the meters.

6 A third way to change the level of a clip in the **Viewer** is to grab the red horizontal lines running through the middle of each waveform and drag them up (to increase the audio level) or down (to decrease the level). (These horizontal lines are also affectionately called *red rubber bands*.)

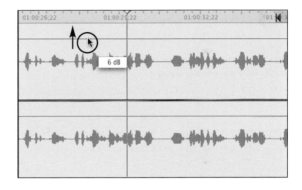

Try this and see how, as you move these rubber bands, the Level slider moves, and the number inside the level box changes

These are all great tips to know. However, I don't use any of them, because there is an easier way.

7 Click the button at the bottom left of the **Timeline** that looks like a mountain range. This toggles on (or off) clip overlays. See the red rubber bands in the audio clips on the **Timeline**? You can easily set audio levels directly in the **Timeline** by adjusting these bands. (These lines get their

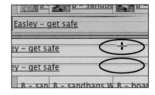

name, "rubber bands," for their flexibility, which you'll understand better as you start to set keyframes a little later in this chapter.)

These volume rubber bands exist in both the Timeline and the Viewer. They work the same way. You can use whichever is the easiest for your method of working.

8 Play each of the clips in the **Timeline** and set the levels so that the meters are bouncing between **–6** and **–12**. When you play the sequence now, all the voices should sound about the same, in terms of volume.

What do you mean, you can't hear the voices because the B-roll audio is too loud? Oh, yeah. You should probably fix that.

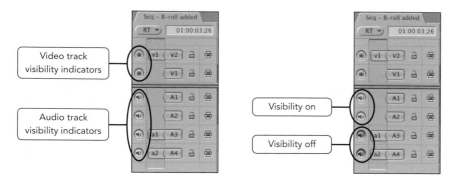

Video track
visibility indicators

Audio track
visibility indicators

Visibility on

Visibility off

9 On the extreme left side of the **Timeline** are green visibility indicators. When these lights are lit, you can see the contents of a video track, or hear the contents of an audio track. Turn the visibility indicator off for audio tracks **A3** and **A4**, and you'll be able to hear the voices a *lot* better. (Try clicking an indicator holding the **Option** key and watch what happens.)

NOTE:

Clip Enable vs. Visibility Indicators

Turning off visibility indicators deletes any render files for the entire track. For audio, this isn't a big deal. Audio render files don't take long to rebuild. However, as you'll learn in Chapter 10, *"Text, Titles, and Graphics,"* video render files are a different story. Many times, you won't want to delete all your video render files because they take so long to calculate.

Instead of using the visibility indicators, another way to turn off a clip is to **Ctrl+click** it and deselect **Clip Enable** (or press **Option+B** or choose **Modify > Clip Enable**). This makes a clip invisible for video, or inaudible for audio, without deleting render files for the entire track. However, it *does* delete the render files associated with that clip. Still, this is often far better than having to redo all your render files for the entire sequence.

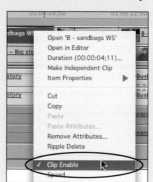

10 Turn on the visibility indicators for **A3** and **A4** and off for **A1** and **A2**, because you now need to adjust the audio levels of the B-roll. Better yet, turn on all visibility indicators and turn on the **Solo** buttons for **A3** and **A4**.

The Solo button automatically mutes a1 and a2 and allows a3 and a4 to play.

NOTE:

An Alternative to Visibility Indicators

There is an audio alternative to the track visibility indicators—audio solo and mute controls.

Click the small speaker icon in the lower-left corner of the **Timeline**.

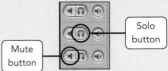

This turns on the audio **Mute** and **Solo** buttons. To silence an audio track, click the **Mute** button, on the left. To silence all tracks, except one, click the **Solo** button, on the right. You can mute or solo multiple tracks, so you can listen to exactly the tracks in your sequence you want to hear. (Try clicking a button holding the **Option** key and watch what happens.)

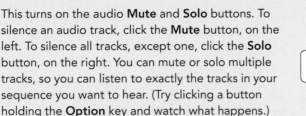

The benefit of using the Mute and Solo buttons is that neither destroys render files, unlike the visibility indicators. Solo and mute controls are also available in the Audio Mixer, which you'll learn about in Exercise 7.

11 Go to the last B-roll clip, **B – storm flood**, and play it. First, bring the audio level up a bit so you can hear it better.

Hmmm…the truck is going from the left to the right, but the audio stays centered. Panning the audio from left to right as the truck moves would improve this effect.

12 Double-click the clip to load it into the **Viewer**. Click the audio tab (**Mono a1**) to display the waveform. This audio is really quiet, so bring the audio level up to, say, **8**. (Note, this is a positive 8, not a negative 8.)

Now, this truck clip, unlike the other clips, has only one audio track: a mono track that is panned to the center. And the audio waveform is so small as to be almost invisible. Sigh. Not all audio is great quality.

13 Drag the **Pan** slider left and right and watch the dark-purple line in the center of the waveform window move. This purple line indicates the pan of this clip from left to right.

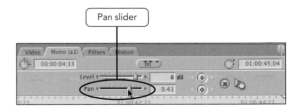

Simply dragging the pan to a new position doesn't give you the effect you want, because dragging the line moves the sound to the left, or right, and parks it there. You want it to change over time. Change requires keyframes.

Definition: Keyframe

Understanding keyframes is one of the critical concepts necessary to getting the most out of Final Cut Pro 5. They rank right up there with timecode and handles.

A **keyframe** is a specific setting of a specific parameter at a specific point in time. And, you'll always use keyframes in pairs. Keyframes are required if you want something to change over time, such as the pan or volume of a clip, or any kind of animation. For example, to change the pan of this truck, you need to indicate where the sound starts, on the left, and where it ends, on the right. You do this with keyframes.

In this example, you will set two keyframes: one on the left when the truck drives in and one on the right when the truck drives out. Final Cut will calculate all the settings in-between to make your effect happen.

14 Drag the **Pan** slider until you can see the purple line clearly, somewhere in the middle of the window. Select the **Selection** tool and hold down the **Option** key so that it turns into the **Pen** tool (or just select the **Pen** tool). Click near the end of the line to set a keyframe. Drag this keyframe up near the top of the waveform window.

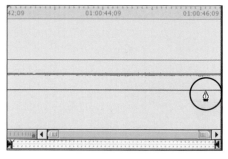

To repeat, you create keyframes by **Option+clicking** with the **Selection** tool or clicking with the **Pen** tool.

Final Cut, unlike virtually every audio program I've ever used, puts the left pan on the bottom and the right pan on the top.

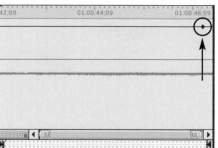

15 Make sure the **playhead** is at the start of the clip, then drag the **Pan** slider down to **–1** and watch the angle of the line change. (You could set a second keyframe at the start of the clip, however, FCP automatically creates a second keyframe, located at the playhead, whenever you change a setting that already has one keyframe created.)

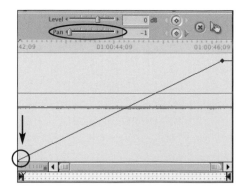

What you've done is set two keyframes—one at the beginning of the clip, using the Pan slider, that puts the sound on the extreme left, and one at the end of the clip, using the Pen tool, that puts the sound on the extreme right.

Because the two locations are different, the sound moves from side to side during the playing of the clip.

16 Increase the volume level of the clip to **12** (all the way up) and play the clip. (The technical term for volume level is "gain.")

Hear how the truck now sounds like it's moving from left to right? Final Cut automatically calculated all the intermediate steps so that the sound moves smoothly from one side of the screen to the other. This technique is used all the time to have sound effects reinforce movement on the screen.

Every audio clip, both mono and stereo, has pan controls. Feel free to experiment with other clips.

Pan Settings

Setting	What It Means in Mono	What It Means in Stereo
–1	Clip panned left	Normal stereo effect
0	Clip panned center	Clip panned mono
1	Clip panned right	Reversed stereo (left goes right and right goes left)

17 You'll be working a *lot* with keyframes for the rest of this book. However, for now, take a break. Save your work. Next you'll be working with music and effects.

NOTE:

A Faster Way to Check Audio Levels

Here's a very fast way to check the audio levels of a clip to see if they are too hot:

1. Double-click a clip to load it into the **Viewer**.

2. Choose **Mark > Audio Peaks > Mark**.

Final Cut will quickly check the entire file and put a clip marker everywhere it finds an audio level that is too hot (that is, greater than 0).

This is the fastest way to check a clip for audio hot spots, much better than playing the entire clip.

To get rid of these markers, choose **Mark > Audio Peaks > Clear**.

5 | Adding Music or Effects

Music often provides the emotion of a scene. In other cases, music is what drives a scene. In still other cases, effects are what make a particular scene sound believable, or comically unbelievable. In all cases, adding music and effects can significantly enhance a project.

In this exercise, you will learn about track layout and checkerboarding audio clips, how to add music and sound effects, and how to convert audio files for use with Final Cut.

---

1 Open **Hurricane**, if it isn't already open. Then, double-click **Seq – B-roll added** to load it into the **Timeline**.

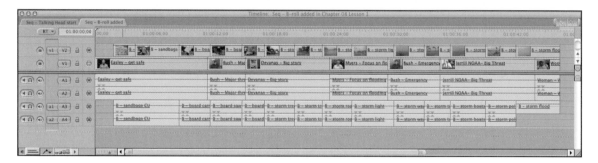

2 Look at the **Timeline**. See how the audio tracks are organized? This is called the **track layout**.

Now, audio, unlike video, doesn't care which track is on top, because there is no concept of one track "blocking" another. Rather, sounds are principally perceived based on volume; louder sounds are closer, softer sounds are further away. Still, I've found that the way you organize your tracks makes a difference in mixing and in understanding what you did when you return to a project after a long absence.

Laying Out Your Audio Tracks

You can lay out your audio tracks in any order. But I strongly suggest you follow a plan. If you don't have your own a plan, the following table outlines one you can use.

Sample Track Layout	
Audio Tracks	**Content**
1 and 2	Sync sound from V1 (talking heads or key actors)
3 and 4	Sync sound from V2 B-roll
5	Narration
6, 7, and 8	Sound effects and other wild (not synced to video) sounds
9 and 10	Music track
11 and 12	Music track

The two music tracks allow you to fade out one piece of music at a different rate than the second music clip fades in.

Leaving multiple tracks free for effects allows you to group and organize your effects in a way that makes sense to you and your project.

This process of putting different types of audio, sync sound, effects, and music on different tracks is called *checkerboarding*, because it resembles a checkerboard. A major motion picture takes this concept to extremes, where audio is scattered across dozens of tracks—often over 100. In this case, though, I just want you to think about how putting related audio on related tracks can help in organizing your project.

Obviously, not all Final Cut projects need as many as 12 tracks, though some may use more. For instance, this project uses only six. The goal is to approach your audio layout logically so that when you go to reedit an old project, you don't need to spend time figuring out where you put stuff.

Plus, there is no penalty for leaving black space on tracks—audio track gaps don't take any memory or storage.

Because all our B-roll has audio, we don't need to add any special audio effects. However, if you wanted to emphasize the strength of the storm you could add more wind howling effects, or distant sirens, or…well, anything your imagination suggests, actually.

In this case, we want to add some music to emphasize the emotional response we want viewers to have with the story.

3 To do this, drag **Hurricane.aif** from the **Music** bin in the **Browser** to below track **A4** in the **Timeline**.

Notice that Final Cut automatically creates two tracks to hold it. Why two tracks? Because the audio clip is stereo, which means it has two audio tracks in it—one for the left channel and one for the right. Almost all tracks you capture will also have two tracks, as will most music and sound effects. However, as you have already seen, not all sounds require two tracks.

Later in this chapter, you'll worry about setting levels for all this audio. For right now, the job is to get everything in the right place—both on the right track and at the right time.

Notice, also, that I had you drag the clip from the Browser to the Timeline. Although I strongly recommend you use the Viewer to preview all your Timeline elements, there's nothing that prevents you from dragging a clip from the Browser to the Timeline.

---

4 And that's it. A nice, simple exercise. Final Cut makes adding music and effects to a sequence very easy. Simply preview it, set any necessary **Ins** and **Outs**, then put it on the **Timeline**—either by dragging or, preferably, using the automated tools.

Save your work. But read the next Note before you take a break. It will help you prevent future audio problems. Then, you can close this project, because the next exercise uses a different project file.

N O T E :

Converting Audio Files

Final Cut can handle a wide range of audio sample rates and bit-depth. You can even combine different files on the same Timeline without needing to render. Audio from CDs is fine as long as you copy the audio files to your hard disk before using them in FCP.

Audio Formats

Where things get tricky is if you are using iTunes to store your audio files. Final Cut likes AIFF and WAV files. From my experience, I've had the best results using AIFF files. Noticeably absent from this list are MP3 and AAC—the two audio formats most common over the Web and in iTunes. This omission is not an accident—Final Cut *hates* MP3 and AAC files.

They pop. They crackle. They sound flat-out terrible. In short, they need to be converted.

continues on next page

Converting Audio Files *continued*

You can buy expensive audio software to handle this conversion, but, truth be told, you already have everything you need bundled with your Mac—it's called iTunes. Here's how to use iTunes to convert MP3 or AAC files into AIFFs for Final Cut.

1. Open iTunes.

2. Choose **iTunes > Preferences**.

3. Click the **Importing** icon.

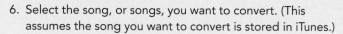

4. Choose **AIFF Encoder** from the **Import Using** pop-up menu.

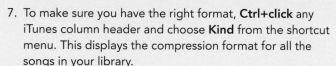

5. Close the **Preferences** window.

6. Select the song, or songs, you want to convert. (This assumes the song you want to convert is stored in iTunes.)

7. To make sure you have the right format, **Ctrl+click** any iTunes column header and choose **Kind** from the shortcut menu. This displays the compression format for all the songs in your library.

8. Choose **Advanced > Convert to AIFF**. iTunes converts the selected clips to AIFF and puts them in your iTunes folder.

9. When the conversion is complete, drag the file name from the iTunes playlist to where you want to store it, import it into Final Cut (**Cmd+I**), and you're all set.

CD Audio

In OS 9, and earlier versions of Final Cut, converting CD audio into something FCP can read was, well, tricky. In OS X, that is no longer the case.

To convert any audio file on CD into something Final Cut can read, simply drag it from the CD into your computer. The operating system converts it so that Final Cut can play it smoothly.

Important note: Never import an audio file directly from CD into Final Cut, for two reasons. First, that means the CD needs to be in your drive whenever you edit that project, and, second, CD players are not as fast as hard drives and, many times, that lack of speed can cause dropped-frame issues. Always copy all media files to your hard disk for editing.

By the way, it goes without saying that you should have permission from the copyright holder to use any copyrighted materials. All the clips in this book have been licensed—which is often a time-consuming process. But licensing is far, far better than dealing with lawyers and facing potential civil and criminal penalties because you borrowed a clip you didn't have permission to use. If you didn't create it, then someone else owns it, and you'll need to request permission to use it in any project you create.

6 | Using the Voice Over Tool for Narration

In this exercise, you will learn how to record narration using the Voice Over tool. However, in order to record narration, you also need to have a microphone connected to your Mac. Since many readers won't have mics connected, this section has been written so you can work through the exercise, or simply look at the pictures. Either way, when you are done, you will understand how this tool works.

1 Open **Chapter 08 Lesson 2**, which is in the **FCP 5 HOT Files** lessons folder. This is the same project you completed at the end of Chapter 6, *"Trim Your Story."* Double-click **Seq – Snowboard Final** to load it into the **Timeline**.

2 Put the **playhead** at the beginning of the sequence, if it isn't already there. What you are going to do is to record an introductory narration for the beginning of the snowboard commercial.

You don't need to be James Earl Jones to be successful as a narrator. Nor do you even have to like listening to your recorded voice. Of all the actors I've worked with, none have ever liked the sound of their voices. That isn't the point. The point is do *other* people like listening to the sound of your voice?

A narrator needs to be easy to understand at first hearing and seem interested in the material he or she is presenting. Most importantly, his or her voice should complement the emotional tenor of your project.

3 Because this is the intro, move the **playhead** between the second and third shots and set an **Out**. This tells the **Voice Over** tool to stop recording when it hits the **Out**.

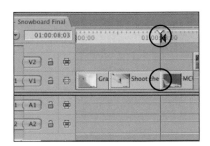

4 Choose **Tools > Voice Over** to open the **Voice Over** tool. The tool opens on top of the **Viewer**, though in its own window. (Secret tip: Changing the size of the **Viewer** changes the size of the **Voice Over** tool when it opens.) You can drag this **Voice Over** window wherever you want and resize it.

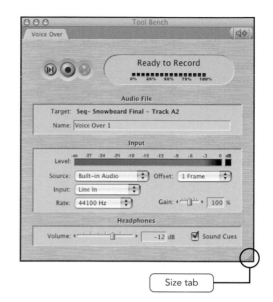

Size tab

The lower half of the window allows you to set the following:

- The **Input** and **Source** (which vary depending upon how your microphone is connected to your computer).

- The sample **Rate** (default is 44,100 Hz); I set mine to 48,000 to match the audio sample rate of my Final Cut Timeline.

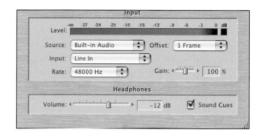

- **Gain**, which controls how loud or soft your mic volume is. Again, try to get your narration to record around the –6 level.

- **Offset**, which allows you to adjust for the delay between the time you talk and the time it gets recorded. This, too, varies by computer and operating system version, though the default of 1 Frame is a good place to start.

At the bottom of the window is the **Volume**, which adjusts headphone volume, and a check box to turn on, or off, audible countdown beeps. Turn these on if you are wearing headphones; turn these off if you are listening through speakers.

These audio beeps count you down to zero during recording, so that you can time the narration to end on time.

---

5 The top half of the window shows you where the recorded narration will appear in Final Cut. (Voice-over narration is always placed on the **Timeline** in the track immediately *below* the last used track—in this case, **A2**.)

Plus, this is where you enter the name of the soon-to-be-recorded clip. In this case, type **Snowboard Intro**.

6 When everything is ready, click the **Record** button.

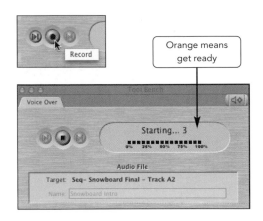

Orange means get ready

The Voice Over tool flashes orange in its status screen, counting down to when the recording starts.

7 During the recording, the **Voice Over** status window turns red, the **Timeline** plays, the **Audio Meter** bounces, and…

…as you get near the end, the status screen counts down the final 10 seconds.

Red means recording

If you are wearing headphones, you will also hear beeps in your headset that count you down. When I do voice-over recording, I find myself concentrating on the script and the reading; I don't have time to watch the screen for a countdown. These audible beeps are really helpful to me in bringing the reading in on time.

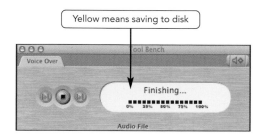

Yellow means saving to disk

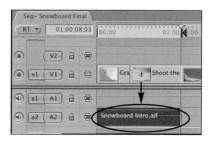

When the recording is complete, Final Cut records it to disk and drops it on the Timeline into the track *below* the last used track.

Voice-over recordings are stored in memory during recording. When recording is complete, they are permanently saved into the **Capture Scratch** folder. If I am working on a machine with limited memory, I make it a point to keep my recordings short.

Also, Voice Over tool recordings don't show up in the Browser unless you drag them from the Timeline to the Browser.

---

8 That's it for this exercise. If you recorded anything you want to keep, save your project. Otherwise, close this project because we are going back to the **Hurricane** project for the next exercise in this chapter.

---

7 | Mixing Your Project

Now that you have assembled all your elements, sync sound, effects, music, and narration, it's time to mix them all together and make it sound right.

Cleve Landsberg, an Oscar-nominated sound editor, once wrote: "Sound is perceived emotionally, as well as intellectually. Each genre, such as comedy, action, or drama, demands its own approach and sound sensibilities."

There's no such thing as a perfect way to mix. But here are some techniques you can use to improve your own mixing skills. There are three ways you can mix your project: using Final Cut, using Soundtrack Pro, and using an application such as DigiDesign's ProTools.

In this lesson, you'll learn how to mix inside Final Cut, using keyframes to control audio levels and the Audio Mixer for real-time mixing. In the next exercise, you'll learn how to export your project into Soundtrack Pro. And in Chapter 13, *"Output Your Project,"* you'll learn how to export your audio into a program like ProTools.

---

1 Open **Chapter 08 Lesson 1**, or **Hurricane**, if it isn't already open. Then, double-click **Seq – Ready to mix** to load it into the **Timeline**. This is a version of the documentary you've been working on earlier in this chapter. I've added room at the beginning for a title and additional shots at the end to bring it to 1 minute in length.

---

2 Take a minute and play this sequence. Listen to all the elements carefully.

You started the process of mixing this project in Exercise 4 when you listened to the talking head clips and set audio levels so the audio meters were bouncing between –6 and –12 db.

---

3 One way to automate your mix is to use keyframes.

Click

Keyframes provide a quick way to control audio levels. Zoom in to the front of the project and click the small gray-and-blue bar chart in the lower-left corner of the **Timeline** to expand the height of the tracks. What you need to do is start the music up full (that is, at full volume), then bring it down and under when the first speaker starts speaking.

This is a perfect opportunity to use keyframes.

---

4 Select the **Selection** tool and **Option+click** near the start of **Hurricane.aif** on the red rubber band to set a keyframe for the start of the music. You change the level of a keyframe by dragging it. Raise the level to **3 db**.

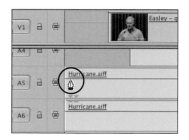 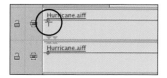

The benefit to using the Option key with the Selection tool is that it is a fast way to set keyframes. However, you can't get exactly to the edit point of a clip, because the Selection tool turns into a trimming tool. If you need to move closer to the edit point, either zoom in closer or select the **Pen** tool (press **P**). In this case, we don't need the keyframe right at the beginning of the edit.

NOTE:

When Is Zero Not Equal to Zero?

When you are comparing a zero reading on the audio meter with a zero level on the red rubber band for an audio clip, the two are not the same.

The audio meter shows an *absolute* reference to sound level (which is what "db"—an abbreviation for decibels, a measure of sound loudness—measures).

When you drag an audio level rubber band up or down, the tooltip shows a *relative* reference to changes in sound level. 0 db means that you are not changing the level of the audio from the level at which it was recorded. Positive numbers (which range from 0.1 to 12 in Final Cut) mean you are amplifying, or increasing, the loudness of the sound compared to the level at which it was recorded. Negative numbers (which range from –0.1 to –infinity db) mean you are attenuating, or decreasing, the loudness of the sound compared to the level at which it was recorded.

The audio meter shows the *absolute* audio level and cannot go above zero. The tooltip shows the *relative* change in level and can wander all over the map.

---

5 Set a second keyframe just before the first sound bite. (Keyframes are set in both track **A5** and **A6** because these two tracks are a linked stereo pair.) Set a third keyframe just after the first sound bite starts. Leave the second keyframe unchanged and drag the third keyframe down to around **–6 db**. (Hold the **Command** key to "gear down" while dragging, which moves the red rubber band in smaller increments.)

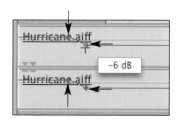

6 Play the sequence. Hear how the music starts nice and loud, to get your attention, then ducks down so you can hear the speakers? Perfect.

Except…audio in Final Cut is clip-based. So, you need to go through every clip and set the level. This is only a 60-second project, but it has 25 sound files that need adjusting. There has to be an easier way!

---

7 There is an easier way—it's called the **Audio Mixer**. There are two ways to find it:

- Choose **Tools > Audio Mixer**.

- Choose **Window > Arrange > Audio Mixing**.

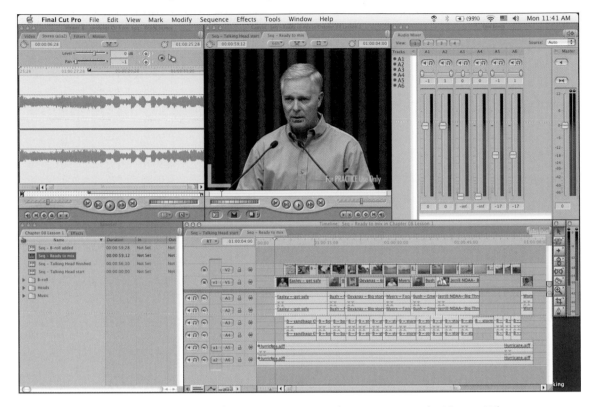

When you use the first choice, the Audio Mixer pops up at the same size as the Viewer. When you use the second choice (my personal favorite), all the windows get rearranged so the mixer has room to work. I like that.

Pick a method that works with your size monitor and select the Audio Mixer. (At the end of this exercise, on page 253 is a more detailed look at the Audio Mixer. Please refer to it if you need an orientation before continuing this exercise.)

OK. Now it's time to get this sequence mixed.

---

8 First, though, get rid of the keyframes you've already set in the music by double-clicking the music track to load it into the **Viewer**. Then, click the small red **X** in the circle. This removes all keyframes from a clip. (This is a very handy way to reset a clip back to its default setting and clear keyframes, not just for audio, but for any effect or filter that uses keyframes.)

---

9 Next, go to the top-right corner of the **Audio Mixer** and click this small, insignificant little button. It's *this* button that turns on the real power of the **Audio Mixer**. (I'll explain what this button does after step 16.)

10 Position your **playhead** in the **Timeline** at the beginning of the sequence and play the first few seconds to get a sense of when the first sound bite starts, relative to the music.

11 Now, again, reset the **playhead** to the beginning, but this time, put your mouse on the slider for **A5** and play the sequence. Just before you get to the start of the sound bite, drag the fader down to around **–18**.

Because A5 and A6 are linked as a stereo clip, both A5 and A6 faders move together. If there was no link, only the A5 fader would move.

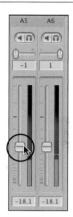

12 After the speaker starts talking, stop playing and look at the music clip. The **Audio Mixer** added keyframes to the audio clip every time you moved the fader. Best of all, if there are too many keyframes, as there are here, you can remove them by **Option+clicking** them with the **Selection** tool.

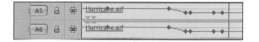

13 Remove all the extra keyframes until the start of your audio looks like this. (The audio level of the second keyframe is **–18 db**.)

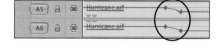

14 Jump forward to the end section where there is a break between speakers. Here the music needs to come up full, then duck down in time for the last speaker, the woman, to be heard.

15 Again, using the **Audio Mixer**, play the sequence, set the level of the music, and trim your keyframes until it looks like this.

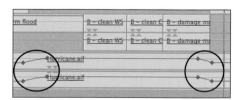

16 You can use the **Audio Mixer** to set the levels of not just one clip, but all the clips on a track. This technique is a whole lot faster than adjusting each clip manually.

If the **Record Keyframes** button is lit, every time you move a fader you'll set a keyframe. If the **Record Keyframes** button is not lit, every time you move a fader, you'll set the volume for the entire clip. In mixing, you'll toggle between these two options, depending upon whether you want to hear the audio level to vary, or remain the same.

For now, experiment with the **Audio Mixer** and mix down this entire sequence. The best way to do this is to mix one track, or linked pair of tracks, at a time. Remember to keep an eye on your levels. At *no* time should the clip lights blink; if they do, change the level to fix it. The clip lights will reset the next time you play the sequence.

---

17 Mixing is an art that takes practice. Whether you adjust individual clip levels or use the **Audio Mixer**, the ultimate judge of which method works best is how the sequence sounds. As always, practice makes perfect.

You can hear my mix of this sequence by opening **Seq – Finished mix**.

This ends this exercise. Save your work if you wish. In the next exercise, you'll learn how to get your audio out of Final Cut and into Soundtrack Pro.

A Quick Tour of the Audio Mixer

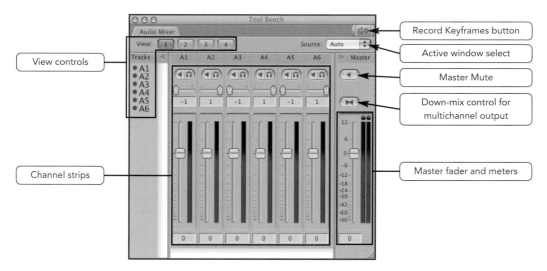

View controls — View controls

Channel strips — Channel strips

Record Keyframes button

Active window select

Master Mute

Down-mix control for multichannel output

Master fader and meters

The Audio Mixer looks more complex than it really is. It actually isn't frightening once you understand it. On the far left is a list of all the audio tracks in your sequence. In the middle are the channel strips—one for each audio track. Each channel strip is identical to all the others, so once you know how one works, you know how they all work. On the far right is the master fader and a duplicate set of audio meters.

There are four areas of the mixer that can be explained quickly:

- Master fader
- Master audio meters
- View controls
- Pop-up menu

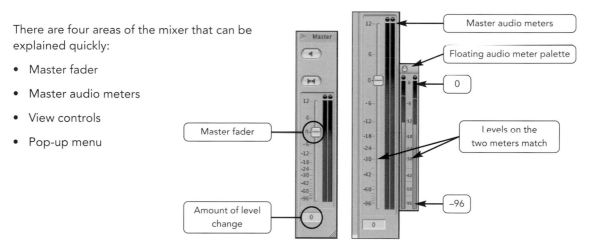

Master fader

Amount of level change

Master audio meters

Floating audio meter palette

0

Levels on the two meters match

–96

First is the master fader, which controls the master audio levels for all of Final Cut! Here's the rule for the master fader: *Don't touch it!* Leave it at 0 and pretend it doesn't exist. If you have problems with your mix, fix them by adjusting individual tracks, not the master. Adjusting the master is a bad habit that will get you in trouble, because you aren't adjusting just this one sequence, you are adjusting *all* audio for *all* projects.

The master audio meters, next to the master fader, correspond directly with the meters on the floating audio meter palette. Both zeros are equal. The master audio meters, though, show how far over zero a particular sound has gone. If left unchanged, your audio will still distort. It will still sound bad on tape. But, at least now you know how far you need to lower the volume to correct the clipping.

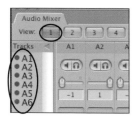  

The View controls (across the top) allow you to display a subset of your audio tracks in the sequence. This is especially helpful when you have more audio tracks than you have room to display in the mixer.

Here's how this works:

1. Click the **2** button.

2. Unclick audio tracks **A3**, **A4**, **A5**, and **A6**. See how the number of tracks displayed in the mixer decreases? The tracks aren't gone, they simply aren't displayed in the Mixer.

3. Click the **3** button.

4. Unclick the **A1** and **A2** tracks. See how **A1** and **A2** disappeared?

5. Click the **1** button. All your audio tracks are displayed in the Audio Mixer.

6. Click the **2** button. Only tracks A1 and A2 are displayed in the Audio Mixer.

7. Click the **3** button. Only tracks A3 through A6 are displayed in the Audio Mixer.

The pop up menu in the top corner is best left set to **Auto**. This means that when you click the Viewer, the mixer shows you the audio tracks in the Viewer. When you select the Canvas or Timeline, the mixer shows you the tracks in the Timeline. However, you can force it to always show the Canvas or Viewer by selecting it in this pop-up menu.

The heart and soul of the Audio Mixer is the channel strip. Every channel strip is identical in layout and operation. You change the level by sliding the large fader up and down. You change the pan by sliding the small fader from side to side. The numbers below each show the amount of change. Setting the level to the thick, black line, labeled "Unity," means you are making no change to the audio level of a clip.

The Mute and Solo buttons are identical in look and operation to those you learned earlier in this chapter in the Timeline.

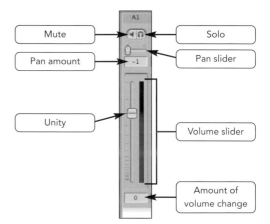

Moving Audio from Final Cut into Soundtrack Pro

NEW ▶ In this exercise, you'll learn how to move your audio between Final Cut and Soundtrack. The audio mixing and editing capabilities in Soundtrack are far superior to those in Final Cut, so it's worth your time to learn how they work. But, that's a story for a different book (sigh…). In this exercise, you'll learn how to move and update files between the two applications. (This lesson assumes you own Soundtrack Pro. If you don't, feel free to skip ahead to the next chapter.)

There are two types of Soundtrack files:

- Audio files

- Multitrack files

You use an audio file when you want to edit or repair the audio in a single clip, or a group of clips you want to treat as a single clip. You use a multitrack project when you want to mix a collection of clips into a single soundtrack.

Additionally, there are three ways to move audio out of Final Cut into Soundtrack:

- Export

- Open in Editor

- Send to Soundtrack Pro

Which option you choose depends upon whether you are editing a clip or mixing a project and whether you want to edit destructively or nondestructively. **Destructive** audio editing means that the changes you make to a file are permanent and cannot be removed. **Nondestructive** editing means that even after you've saved a file, you can still go back and undo all your changes, even to the point of returning a file to its original state. Nondestructive editing is significantly better and more flexible, but prior to Soundtrack, almost impossible to do.

Let's look at all three options, starting with exporting.

---

1 Open **Chapter 08 Lesson 1**. Double-click **Seq – Ready to mix** to load it into the **Timeline**.

---

2 To export this sequence into Soundtrack, or any other audio application, choose **File > Export > For Soundtrack**. Give the file a name and save it somewhere you can find it again.

---

3 **Open** Soundtrack. Choose **File > Open** (or press **Cmd+O**) and select the file you just saved.

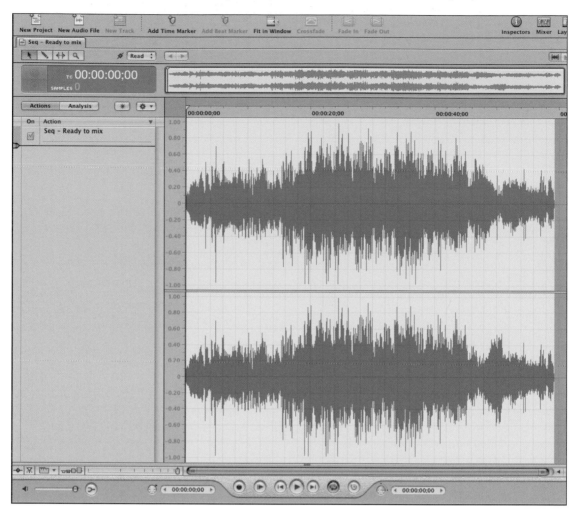

It opens into Soundtrack as an audio project. That's the good news. The bad news, though, is significant:

- There is no way to edit individual clips, because they are all merged into one giant AIFF file.

- All tracks are merged into a single stereo file.

- There is no way to update Final Cut automatically with your revised Soundtrack file. You need to import it manually.

- All editing is destructive. Once you save the Soundtrack file, all your changes are permanent.

For all these reasons, exporting is not a good choice. You have better options.

This time, you'll explore a feature first introduced in Final Cut Pro HD: **Open in Editor**.

4 The Appendix covers this feature in more detail, but for now, choose **Final Cut Pro > System Settings** and click the **External Editors** tab. Set **Audio Files** to **Soundtrack Pro**. You do this by clicking **Set**, then selecting **Soundtrack Pro** in your **Applications** folder. This tells Final Cut what audio application to use when you choose **Open in Editor**.

5 **Option+click** the audio for **Easley – get safe** to select just the audio portion of the clip. Then, **Ctrl+click** the audio and choose **Open in Editor**.

Soundtrack starts automatically and loads the selected clip.

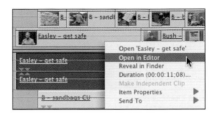

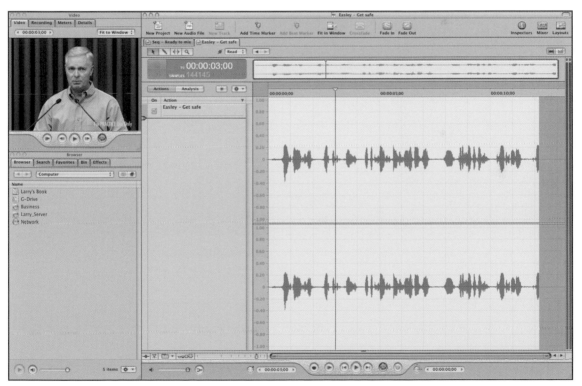

At this point, you can make whatever changes you want to the clip. However, in order to get it back into Final Cut you must save the file, which will make all your changes permanent. In other words, using Open in Editor forces Soundtrack into destructive editing mode.

6 To return this clip to Final Cut from Soundtrack, choose **File > Save**. This replaces the old version of the clip with the new version.

---

7 Finally, switch back to **Final Cut**, choose **File > Import > File**, and select your file from the **Import** dialog.

This is a good procedure to use when you need to make only limited changes to a file. But there's a better option, called **Send**, which you'll learn next.

---

8 Go back to Final Cut and **Option+click** the audio for **Easley – get safe** to select just the audio portion of the clip. Then, **Ctrl+click** the audio and choose **Send To > Soundtrack Pro Audio File Project**.

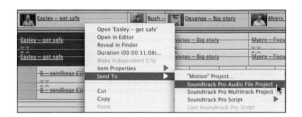

---

9 A dialog appears, asking you to save the audio into a separate file. I just accept the default name and click **Save**.

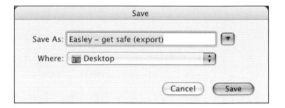

---

10 Soundtrack opens and loads the clip as before. And, as before, you make changes to your clip. When you are done, click **File > Save**.

Soundtrack saves your file and, behind the scenes, creates an audio render file, which is loaded into your Final Cut project automatically.

See? Easley's audio has been replaced by the new Soundtrack audio file—**Easley – get safe (export)**. The benefit to using **Send** is that you can make multiple modifications to a file.

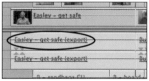

However, and this is a **VERY** important point, the next time you want to send this file to Soundtrack, choose **Open in Editor**. That opens the already-existing audio export file and allows you to make changes. Don't use **Send**, otherwise you'll create multiple export files for the same clip, and everything will get very confused very quickly.

There's one more way to get clips out of Final Cut and into Soundtrack, and that's as a Soundtrack Pro multitrack project, which you use to mix your clips.

---

11 Either select your sequence in the **Browser**, or select all the clips in your **Timeline (Cmd+A)**, **Ctrl+click** any clip, and choose **Send To > Soundtrack Pro Multitrack Project**.

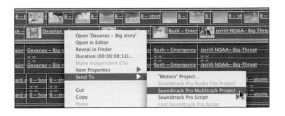

12 In the dialog that pops up, give this export a name (I usually use the default), and be sure both options are checked. **Open in Soundtrack Pro Multitrack Editor** makes sure your clips end up in the multitrack part of Soundtrack. **Include Background Video** creates a small movie of your sequence that you can watch while mixing.

Click **Save**, then be prepared to wait for a bit as your files are saved, the movie is created, and everything gets imported into Soundtrack.

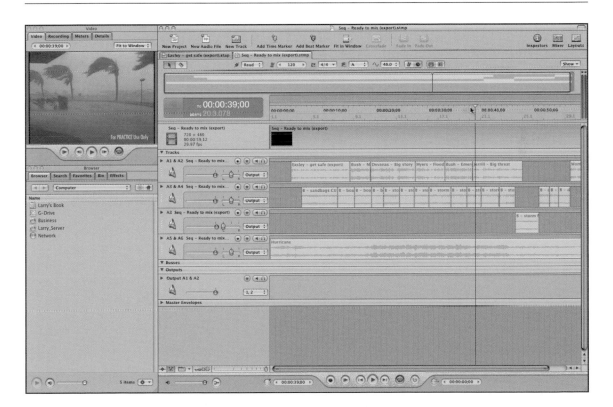

13 Soundtrack opens your file in the multitrack editor with all clips (and their handles) intact. From here, you can mix your file.

14 When your mix is complete, choose **File > Save** to save your work as a Soundtrack project. Then, choose **File > Export Mix** to export the final mix ready to import into Final Cut.

15 Name your mix and select a location to store it. Using a 16-bit depth and 48 kHz sample rates are the best choice for most video projects.

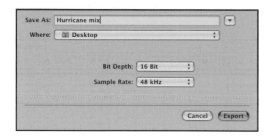

16 Switch back to Final Cut and choose **File > Import > File** and import your mix. Drag it to the Timeline, and place it on A7 and A8, below all existing audio tracks. Be sure it starts at the beginning of your sequence.

17 Then, turn off all the green visibility lights for all audio tracks, except your mix. The fastest way to do this is to **Option+click A7**, which turns off all other visibility lights, then click **A8**. This permanently mutes all tracks except for A7 and A8.

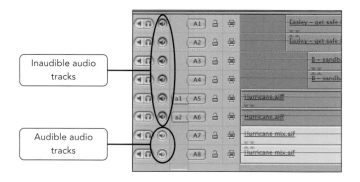

18 If you need to adjust your mix, **Ctrl+click Hurricane mix.aif** and choose **Open in Editor**. (Remember, the first time you export a file, use **Send**. Every time thereafter, use **Open in Editor**.) Make your changes in Soundtrack, then go back to Step 14 to export your mix back into Final Cut.

19 That's it. You're done. Save your work and take a well-deserved break. Whew! That was a lot to cover.

Helpful Keyboard Shortcuts

Shortcut	Action
N	Toggles snapping on and off.
Shift+S	Toggles audio scrubbing on and off.
Shift+Option+Z	Zooms selected clips to fill Timeline window.
Shift+L	Toggles linked selection (generally, a bad thing).
Cmd+L	Turns linking on and off (another dangerous thing).
Option+drag	(On edit point.) Selects and moves either the audio or video side of a linked clip without allowing the clip to go out of sync (a much, much better thing).
Ctrl+click	(On red sync flag.) Moves clip back into sync (menu choice).
Option+L	Toggles between making an audio clip stereo or dual-mono.
Option+click Selection tool	Toggles between Selection and Pen tool.
Option+click Fader	(In Mixer.) Resets the level and/or pan control to 0.
Shift+Cmd+K	Toggles between recording and not recording keyframes in the Audio Mixer.
Option+6	Displays Audio Mixer.
Option+0 (zero)	Displays the Voice Over tool.
Option+Cmd+W	Toggles audio waveform display on and off in the Timeline.
Option+W	Toggles clip overlays on and off.
P	Selects the Pen tool to create and move keyframes.
PP	Selects the Negative Pen tool to remove keyframes.
Option+B	Makes a clip visible (enabled) or invisible (disabled).

Summary

This chapter has covered a huge amount of material in a very short time. In this chapter, you started with audio editing and ended with mixing—with a whole lot of terminology and technique in the middle. Next you learn about audio and video transitions in Chapter 9, *"Transitions—Making Change Beautiful."*

9

Transitions—Making Change Beautiful

A transition means a change—a change in scene, a change in level, a change in perspective, or content, or text, or…well, just about anything. A cut is a transition. But in this chapter you will see that "transition" means more than that. This chapter is all about how to make the transition from shot 1 to shot 2.

In this chapter, you will learn how to create audio and video transitions, how to edit a transition, and how to harness power tools to create favorite and default transitions.

"Everything Is a Transition"

A few years ago, an effects wizard told me that the secret to his success was in understanding that everything is a transition. And, the more I thought about it, the more I realized how true this is. Everything is always moving—going from one place to another.

In this chapter, you will learn how to add transitions to your edit points. Also with this chapter, you make a transition as well. You are moving out of editing, which is covered in the first half of the book, into polishing, which is the second half of the book.

And the best way to start is to segue into your first exercise.

Creating an Audio Transition

All transitions are created in the Timeline. In this exercise, you will learn how to create an audio transition, then build on that knowledge by working on video transitions for the rest of the chapter.

1 Open **Chapter 09 Lesson 1** and double-click **Seq – Ready to mix** to load it into the **Timeline**. It's in the **FCP Projects > FCP 5 HOT Files** folder you created at the beginning of this book. This is the same hurricane project you were working on in Chapter 8, *"Audio—The Secret to a Great Picture,"* but I removed the keyframes because using keyframes to create transitions is what the first part of this exercise is all about.

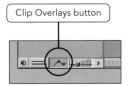

Clip Overlays button

2 There are three ways to create a transition using the mouse, plus several more using keyboard shortcuts. Here's the first, which is a review from Chapter 8. Select the **Zoom** tool (press **Z**) and zoom in on tracks **A5** and **A6**. Then, choose the **Pen** tool (press **P**) and set two keyframes at the beginning of the music. Remember, you always use keyframes in pairs.

(If you don't see the red "rubber bands," display them by clicking the **Clip Overlays** button in the lower-left corner of the **Timeline**. It's the icon that looks like a mountain.)

3 Using the **Pen** tool, drag the first keyframe down and to the edge of the clip. This brings the volume "rubber band" down so that the audio will fade in starting at the first keyframe and ending the fade at the second keyframe.

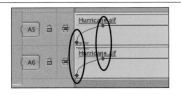

You've just created your first transition: a fade up from silence to full audio. Using keyframes is a common way to create level changes. I use them all the time because they're reasonably fast and quite accurate.

4 However, there's still a bit more to learn, so double-click the music track to load it into the **Viewer**, then click the red **X** in a circle (the **Reset** button) to remove the keyframes and reset the clip to its opening state.

5 Here's the second way to create a transition. Again, remember that transitions are created in the **Timeline**, so select the **Selection** tool (press **A**), and select the edit point in the **Timeline** where you want the transition to appear.

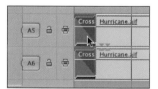

6 Now, choose **Effects > Audio Transitions > Cross Fade (+3dB)**. Immediately, a transition appears at the selected edit point.

This is the big benefit of using the Effects menu. You select an edit point, choose a transition from the Effects menu, and the transition appears on the selected edit point.

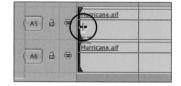

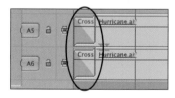

7 Click near the center of the gray transition to select it, and press **Delete**. (If you, by accident, double-click the center of the transition, you'll open the **Trim Edit** window.)

This is how you get rid of any transition—select it and press **Delete**. (Remember the first interface rule from Chapter 2: you **select** something, then you **do** something to it. That rule still applies, all these chapters later.)

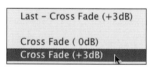

8 Here's the third way to create a transition. Using the **Selection** tool, make sure nothing is selected on the **Timeline**. Then, go up to the **Browser** and click the **Effects** tab. This is a duplicate of all the effects available in the **Effects** menu, with one new benefit: you don't need to select the edit point before you apply your transition.

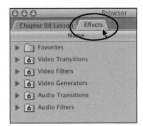

9 Twirl down the **Audio Transitions** folder, select **Cross Fade (+3dB)** and drag it down on top of the first music edit point.

Poof! The transition is immediately applied to the edit point.

This is the really big benefit to pulling transitions from the Effects tab—you don't need to select the edit point first, you just drag the transition to any edit point you

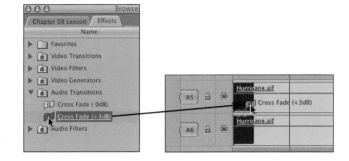

want. Which of these three ways of creating a transition is better? That's entirely your opinion. I use all three, switching between them depending upon where I am and what I want to do.

One of the cool things about using a transition, as opposed to setting keyframes, is that it is easy to change the duration of the transition.

10 First, because you need to make a small adjustment, be sure to turn off snapping by clicking the **Snapping** button in the upper-right corner of the **Timeline**, or by pressing **N**. Using the **Selection** tool, grab an edge of the transition and pull it to the right. See how the duration changes?

Drag this out until the new duration is **2:00** (2 seconds).

It is not possible to use keyframes to create a dissolve between two audio clips—well, not with both clips on the same track, that is. But this is not a problem because it is far easier to create dissolves using the Effects menu and the Effects tab, as you are about to learn.

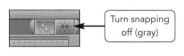

Turn snapping off (gray)

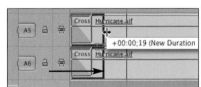

What's the Difference Between a Cross Fade (0 dB) and Cross-Fade (+3 dB)?

Unlike video, there are only two audio transitions to choose from: 0 dB and +3 dB. What's the difference?

The **Cross Fade (0 dB)** option is called an *equal gain* cross fade. This transition fades the first clip down in a smooth straight line, while fading the second clip up, also linearly. Due to the physics of audio, this smooth fade makes the volume dip (get softer) in the middle of the dissolve.

The **Cross Fade (+3 dB)** option is called an *equal power* cross fade. Instead of fading the volume using a straight line, Final Cut fades the volume using a slight curve to bump the volume up a little bit in the middle of the transition. To the ear, this makes the cross fade sound smooth.

My recommendation is to use the +3 dB cross fade. If it doesn't sound quite right to you, though, use the other transition. I use the +3 dB cross fade exclusively and am quite happy with it. This is also the default audio transition for FCP, as well.

---

11 Scroll until you can see the edit point between the second and third clips on **A1** and **A2**. Because you are working only on these two tracks, turn on the **Solo** buttons for these two tracks on the far-left edge of the **Timeline**. Then, highlight the edit point.

(If the **Mute** and **Solo** buttons are not visible, display them by clicking the **Audio Controls** button in the lower-left corner of the **Timeline**.)

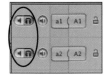

---

12 Choose **Effects > Audio Transitions > Cross Fade (+3 dB)**. It appears on the selected edit point.

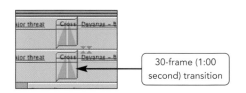

30-frame (1:00 second) transition

4-frame transition

13 Double-click the gray transition icon, and the **Duration** dialog opens. This is another way to change the duration of a transition. Many times, I've found it very useful to add a very short audio dissolve between two sound bites to smooth out the transition in background noise (called **room tone**) between the two cuts.

For this reason, my favorite audio transition is four frames. Enter the number **4** and click **OK**. See how the transition got smaller? (By the way, you can open the **Duration** dialog at any time, for either a clip or transition, by **Ctrl+clicking** the clip and choosing **Duration** from the shortcut menu, or by selecting the clip, or transition, and pressing **Ctrl+D**.

---

14 Play the first section of this piece with the first two tracks soloed. Can you hear how the transition makes the cut between the two voices sound less jarring? That's the point behind using this dissolve—it makes your audio sound smoother.

---

15 That's it for this introduction to transitions. For the rest of this chapter, you'll be working with video. Save your work, if you want, and close this project.

NOTE:

About Handles

Handles are critical to trimming and transitions—because if you don't have a little extra footage at the beginning and end of each shot, you can't trim, and you can't add a transition.

Why?

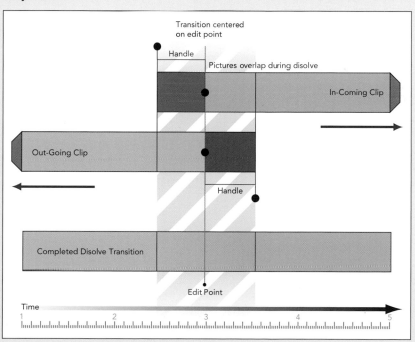

For the duration of any transition, whether a dissolve, wipe, or awe-inspiring 3-D effect, there are two images on the screen at once. This means you need to have enough footage on the end of each clip for them to overlap for the duration of the transition.

continues on next page

NOTE:

About Handles *continued*

For instance, a 30-frame dissolve, centered on the edit point, requires an extra 15 frames of video after the Out on the outgoing clip and 15 frames before the In of the incoming clip.

Although you can't tell whether a clip has handles just by looking at it on the Timeline, it's easy to tell once you load a clip into the Viewer, Here are two examples:

| Handle | Handle | Handle | No handle |

The clip on the left (**Thru trees**) has plenty of video before the In and some video after the Out. This is enough handle for virtually any transition. The clip on the right (**MS Brown coat**), although having plenty of handle before the In, has no handle after the Out. Without a handle, you can't do a transition; unless you change the transition alignment. You'll read about this next.

Handles are just really, really important.

2 | Creating a Video Transition

In this exercise, you will build on what you just learned about audio transitions to explore the power of video transitions.

Consistency in how you do things (the Final Cut interface) is one of the great features of Final Cut Pro 5. Everything you've already learned about creating an audio transition also applies to a video transition. Also, although this chapter is about transitions, you'll learn later in this book that everything you've just learned about keyframes also applies to using keyframes for motion and filter effects.

---

1 Open **Chapter 09 Lesson 2**, and load **Seq – Snowboard final** to the **Timeline**. It's in the **FCP Projects > FCP 5 HOT Files** folder you created at the beginning of this book. This is the same snowboard project you were working on in Chapter 8, *"Audio—The Secret to a Great Picture."*

---

2 You've been editing for a long time. Are you in a hurry to add a dissolve? OK, here it is, in two steps:

Select the edit point between the first two clips (timecode: **01:00:03:04**).

Press **Cmd+T**.

Poof. Instant dissolve. You've just applied the default transition, a 1-second cross-dissolve, to the selected edit point. (If you've changed your default transition, your default will appear instead of the cross dissolve.) You will learn in Exercise 3 how to change the default transition.

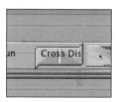

That is, without a doubt, the fastest way to apply a dissolve to an edit point. But there's a lot more power available to you, if you can afford a few extra seconds.

---

3 Delete any transition by clicking slightly *off* center on the icon to select it, then press the **Delete** key.

---

4 Select the edit point, and choose **Effects > Video Transitions > Slide > Multi-Spin Slide**. The **Multi-Spin Slide** edit appears at your edit point.

---

5 A fast way to change the duration of a transition is to grab the edge of the transition icon and drag it to the length you want. In this case, drag it shorter so that it is **20** frames long. (If you can't drag the edge of the transition, zoom into the **Timeline** a bit more.)

---

6 This next technique, though probably obvious to you, took me years to learn. Click the center of the edit point to select it. (You may need to zoom in on the transition for this to work.) Notice that the cursor turned into the **Roll** tool? Even though you have applied a transition to the edit point, you can still trim the edit using the trim tools you learned about in Chapter 6, "*Trim Your Story.*"

7 Turn off snapping (press **N**) and drag the edit point from side to side. Press **U** to select the three different sides of an edit. You can roll or ripple the edit point as though the transition wasn't even there!

Gosh, I wish I knew this several years ago! Back then, when I needed to change an edit point, I'd remove the transition, correct the edit point, then reapply and adjust the transition. Trimming under the transition is just *so* much faster!

As you might expect, Final Cut provides a number of ways to apply transitions. The benefit to using the **Effects** menu is that it automatically applies the transition to whatever edit point you have selected. This is especially handy if you want to apply the same transition to more than one clip at the same time.

8 Here's an example. Scroll down until you see the two clips stacked on top of each other (timecode **01:00:11:09**). Click the lower edit point, then hold the **Command** key and click the upper edit point so that both are selected.

9 Choose **Effects > Video Transitions > Dissolves > Cross Dissolve**. Again, poof! Multiple transitions.

Final Cut will not allow you to select more than one edit point on a track. But if you had, say, five video tracks, you could select one edit point on each track and apply the same transition to all tracks all at once.

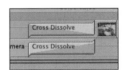

10 OK, undo that last double transition (press **Cmd+Z**) and go back to the first edit point again. It's between the first and second clips (timecode: **01:00:03:04**).

11 Select the **Multi-Spin Slide** transition by clicking it, slightly off center. Remember when, earlier, you changed its duration to 20 frames? Put the playhead in the middle of the transition; this allows you to watch as you change a transition.

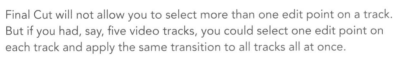

12 Go up to the **Browser** and click the **Effects** tab. Twirl down the **Video Transitions** folder. Twirl down the **Wipe** folder.

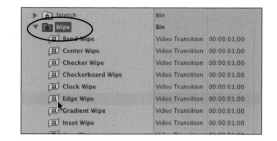

13 Select the **Edge Wipe** transition. Notice that it has a default length of **1:00** (1 second). Now, drag it from the **Effects** tab and place it on top of the existing **Multi-Spin Slide** transition. Notice that the new transition inherits all the timing and alignment characteristics of the old, selected, transition.

Another advantage of using the Effects tab to place transitions is that you can put a transition anywhere on the Timeline, regardless of whether the edit point is selected or not.

Transitions are remarkably flexible, if you know where to look. Here's where:

14 Double-click *near* the center of the icon for the **Edge Wipe** transition (but *not* at the center) to open it in the **Transition Editor**. Although the settings in the **Transition Editor** vary by transition, the window contains the following sections:

- Transition duration and alignment

- Transition bar

- Transition settings

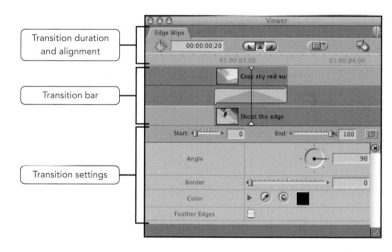

The transition bar shows the location of the transition, which allows you to make changes to the transition or the edit point beneath it. The dark blue/gray bar indicates video displayed in the clip. The light blue/gray bar indicates clip handles, and a white bar (not shown in this example) indicates where there is no video.

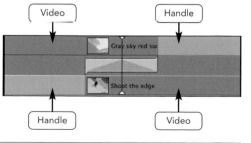

15 Grab the edge of the transition and drag to change its duration.

16 You can also trim the edit point by using the trim tools. Click the **playhead** in the **Transition Editor** and drag to do a **Roll** edit.

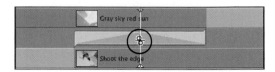

Or, click the end of one of the dark-gray video clip bars to do a **Ripple** edit.

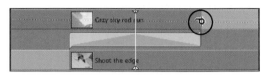

At the top of the window, you can set the transition's duration and alignment, display a list of recent items, or grab the drag handle (the hand) and move the transition (more on this in Exercise 4).

The transition alignment buttons are very useful—especially when one of your clips doesn't have handles. Click the left-hand alignment button and watch the transition in the Timeline. This button aligns the transition so that it *starts* at the edit point.

 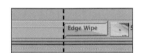

17 Click the middle button. This aligns the transition so that the *middle* of the transition is at the edit point.

18 Click the right-hand button. This aligns the transition so that it *ends* at the edit point.

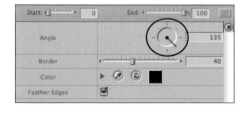 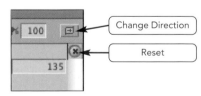

19 In the middle of the **Transition Editor** are all the transition settings, which you can use to alter the look of the transition. These settings vary depending upon which transition you are editing.

In the case of this **Edge Wipe**, change your settings to match mine. (You can grab the hands of the clock and twist to change the **Angle** setting.) **Feather Edges** blurs the edges of the wipe, **Border** adjusts the width of the blurred edge, or the width of the border that wipes between the two clips. **Color** adjusts the color of the border. Personally, you have to work very, VERY hard to convince me that a bordered wipe should be seen in polite society.

There are two very, very small buttons on this screen that you should also notice: the **Reset** button (the tiny red **X** in a circle) and the **Change Direction** arrow just above it. Click the **Reset** button to reset all the transition settings to their default. Click the **Change Direction** arrow to change the direction of a wipe.

Press the **backslash** key to play the results of your work.

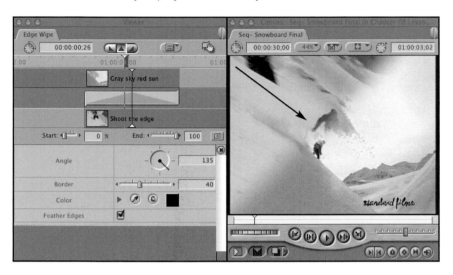

As you play the transition, the wipe travels in the same direction as the snowboarders (downhill to the right) and at about the same speed, making for an interesting transition between the two shots.

---

20 Feel free to add other transitions to the shots in this sequence. Use wipes sparingly, though. A wipe, by definition, is designed to call attention to itself. If you do your editing correctly, you don't want people watching your wipes, you want them watching your program.

Once you are done playing, sorry, intensively practicing this exercise, you can save your work (or not, depending). The remaining exercises in this chapter are a series of brief techniques you can use to make working with transitions more efficient.

DVD MOVIE:

transitions.mov

For examples on using the Transition Editor, watch **transitions.mov** in the **movies** folder on the **Final Cut Pro 5 HOT DVD** included at the end of this book.

Understanding Rendering

Depending upon the speed of your computer, when you create a transition, you will see one of three colored bars at the top of the Timeline. These bars are called **render bars**. They indicate whether a transition or effect will play in real-time or require rendering.

"Rendering" is simply a fancy word that means that the computer needs to calculate the effect you are creating before it can play it in real-time. Many effects, such as dissolves, most motion effects, or some filters, can play perfectly in real-time without needing to be rendered first. On the other hand, drop shadows and motion blurs always require rendering.

Although it seems like there's a whole rainbow of render bar colors, there are only three you really need to pay attention to: green, orange, and red.

Green render bars indicate that an effect or transition can be played in real-time, without requiring rendering, until you are ready to output to tape.

Orange render bars are only displayed when you are using Unlimited RT. They indicates an effect that can be played in real-time, but not perfectly. For instance, drop shadows, soft wipe edges, or video quality may be dropped to view this effect in real-time. This is helpful for previewing, but not for judging final quality.

Red render bars indicate that your computer is not fast enough to play the effect in real-time. In order to see an effect that requires rendering, you need to do one of three things:

- Render the effect (**Sequence > Render All**, or **Sequence > Render Selection**).
- Press **Option+P** to play the clip, however, this plays slower than real time.
- Choose **Tools > QuickView**.

The QuickView window opens to the same size as the Viewer with a little timer at the bottom. Starting at the position of the playhead, it plays your effect forward for half the time indicated on the timer. Then, it backs up the full distance of the timer and plays the effect in real time in the small QuickView window. What QuickView does is build a RAM preview of your effect; in other words, the first time through an effect it calculates and stores it temporarily into memory. The second time through plays at real time.

The benefit to QuickView is that, after the first time through calculating your effect, you'll see the effect in real-time. The thing I don't like about it is that it requires me to put my playhead in the middle of the effect, then calculate how much time I want to view the effect. Plus, it won't play anything longer than 10 seconds.

For these reasons, I almost never use QuickView, but use **Option+P** all the time.

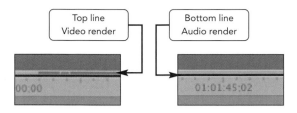

Top line
Video render

Bottom line
Audio render

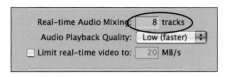

If you look really closely at the render bar line, you'll notice it's divided into two sections. Video renders are indicated in the top half and audio renders in the bottom half. An audio render is required if the number of audio tracks (or effects) exceeds the computer's capability to play them simultaneously in real time.

You can set the number of real-time audio tracks your computer can play in **Final Cut Pro > User Settings > General**. (The **Audio Playback Quality** setting determines the quality of audio playback on the **Timeline**. The **Low** setting is a good choice; allowing more CPU time for processing video. Audio quality is always **High** for final output. Chapter 13, *"Output Your Project"* covers this in more detail.)

NOTE:

How Do You Render Something?

Final Cut provides three ways of rendering:

Render Selection (Cmd+R) is my favorite. By selecting the clips I want to render, then selecting this option, I render only what I need at this moment. If an option is checked, it will be rendered. To check an option, click it with the mouse. The dialog will disappear, which is a pain, so you'll need to select it a second time to render your selection. Or, you can do what I do, which is select all the options, then invoke the menu by pressing **Cmd+R**.

Render All (Ctrl+R) renders everything in your sequence. I'll use this when everything is done, or I'm leaving the office for a bit, and want things to render while I'm gone. I prefer manually rendering before outputting, because that way the render files are saved with the project, in case I need to output again.

Render Only allows you to select a specific render format to render. I should use this, I guess. But, for some reason, I don't. **Ctrl+R** renders all Preview (green) bar clips.

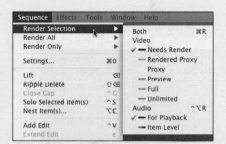

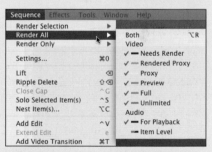

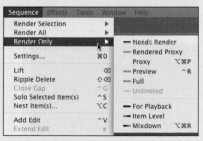

NEW► Real-Time Playback

There's one more thing you need to understand and that's **Safe RT** versus **Unlimited RT** versus the brand-new **Dynamic RT**. You change the setting in the upper-left corner of the **Timeline** using the **RT** pop-up menu.

Apple has worked really hard to bring more real-time effects to Final Cut. Obviously, the more real-time effects, the less time you waste waiting for the computer to render. The thing is, see, there's real-time and "real-time."

New with FCP 5 is **Dynamic RT**. Dynamic RT checks to see how fast your computer is during FCP's startup. Then, based on these results, it automatically plays back your effects in real time at the highest possible quality. However, in order to achieve real-time playback, it may lower the video quality, or alter the frame rate.

Dynamic RT is the default Timeline playback setting, with **Video Quality** set to **Dynamic**, and **Frame Rate** set to **Full**. The benefit to you is that by using Dynamic RT, virtually every effect you create will play in real time, though video quality and/or frame rate may decrease if your effect is really complex.

For me and my system, I like the defaults.

Safe RT plays all green render bars in real-time, exactly as it will output. Anything that doesn't have a green render bar needs rendering before it will play back. If you want to see all your effects perfectly, this is the best choice. Prior to FCP 5, I used Safe RT exclusively.

Unlimited RT gives you more real-time effects by dropping calculation-intensive portions of the effect. For instance, drop shadows, motion blurs, and feathered edges are all calculation-intensive effects. The problem with Unlimited RT is that it drops stuff I'd like to see, like frames and parts of your effect.

The only benefit to using Unlimited RT is that it will, most likely, play Motion and LiveType projects imported into FCP without rendering. This is cool, but not cool enough for me to want to use it.

Important Last Point: Although all these RT settings affect video playback on the Timeline during editing, the default setting for FCP 5 is to ALWAYS output or export your sequences at the highest possible quality. In other words, these three RT settings have no effect on final output.

3 | One More Way to Create a Transition

In this exercise, you'll learn one more way to create a transition—using keyframes. In this case, you will change the opacity of a clip to fade it from black to full screen.

Opacity is the measure of transparency of a clip. A clip with an opacity of 0% is completely transparent (invisible). A clip with an opacity of 100% is fully opaque. (You'll work more with opacity in Chapter 11, "*Motion Effects*.")

---

1 Open **Chapter 09 Lesson 2** and load **Seq – Keyframe** into the **Timeline**.

---

2 In the bottom left of the **Timeline**, click the third bar in the bar chart (it turns blue) to expand the vertical height of all tracks. Then, click the **Clip Overlays** button, next to it on the left, to turn on clip overlays.

You used this button in Exercise 1 to set audio volumes using the red rubber bands inside each clip. This time, you'll use it to set the video opacity for a clip.

In these illustrations, I adjusted the Timeline so that the small pictures at the beginning of a video clip are not displayed (**Sequence > Settings > Timeline**). This makes it easier to illustrate how to use keyframes to set a fade in/fade out.

---

3 Select the **Pen** tool (press **P**) and set a keyframe near the leading edit point of this clip.

---

4 Set a second keyframe about 1 second later. The exact time is not important.

---

5 Drag the first keyframe down until it reaches the bottom of the clip. The tooltip will show **0**. This sets the opacity of the first keyframe to **0** (fully transparent), while the second keyframe remains at **100**, which is fully opaque. Remember, you always use keyframes in pairs.

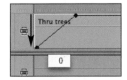

---

6 Play the clip and see how the clip fades in from black to full screen. Final Cut calculates all the transparency levels between the first keyframe and the second so that the clip fades in from black.

Where did this black at the beginning come from? The double gray bar below the video clip that separates the video from the audio acts as video and audio black (unlike other editors, which often force you to put a black clip next to a video clip whenever you want to fade to or from black). The rule is that this double gray bar acts as black as long as there is a clip after it in the Timeline. When the end of all clips is reached (that is, there's no clip later in the Timeline), Final Cut no longer uses the double gray bar as black, but instead stops playing the Timeline.

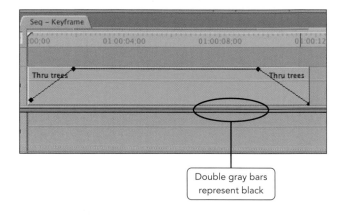

Double gray bars represent black

7 Set two more keyframes at the end of the clip and watch as the clip fades to black at the end.

Whew! Finally, an exercise that takes less than 10 steps! I use opacity settings a lot in animation and compositing. And, although I almost always use regular transitions for fade in/fade out, as you'll learn in Chapter 13, *"Output Your Project,"* using a keyframe fade in/out has significant benefits when you are working with multiple levels of video. And this is the reason I mention it now—just to put all transition descriptions together in one place.

8 That's the end of this exercise. You can save your work if you want, but it isn't necessary. You won't be coming back to this sequence.

4 | Changing the Default Transition

In this exercise, you'll learn how to change the default transition. You can only have one default video transition and one default audio transition. This exercise shows you how to change both of them. On my system, my default video transition is a 20-frame cross-dissolve, and my default audio transition is a 4-frame +3dB cross fade.

---

1 Open **Chapter 09 Lesson 2** and load **Seq – Snowboard final** into the **Timeline**. You'll be working principally in the **Browser** for this exercise.

---

2 Go to the **Browser** and click the **Effects** tab. Click the triangle to twirl down **Video Transitions**, then twirl down **Dissolves**. Assuming you haven't changed your default transition, **Cross Dissolve** should be underlined. (And, if you have changed your default transition, then skip ahead to the next exercise.)

See how the name **Cross Dissolve** is underlined? This marks it as the default transition. In this case, you need to change the duration of the default transition from **1:00** (indicated in the **Length** column on the right) to **20** frames.

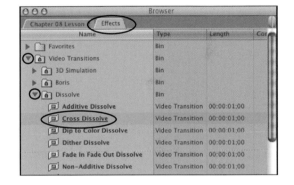

---

3 Double-click the duration in the **Length** column to select it. Then, enter **20** for the new **Duration**. Press **Return** to make the change permanent.

---

4 The last step is to save this as the new default. Select **Cross Dissolve** in the **Effects** tab, then click the **Effects** menu and choose **Video Transitions > Set Default**, and Final Cut will make this transition your new default transition. (Or, **Ctrl+click** the name of the transition and choose **Set Default** from the shortcut menu.)

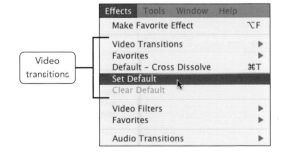

The nice thing about default transitions is that you can apply them with a keystroke: **Cmd+T** applies the default video transition to any selected edit point or points. If you wanted to make a different transition your default, simply select it, make any duration changes you need, go to the **Effects** menu, and choose **Set Default**.

---

5 Changing the default audio transition is similar. In this case, twirl down **Audio Transitions** and select **Cross Fade (+3dB)**.

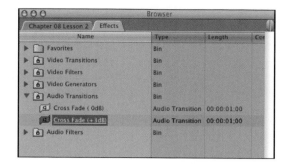

6 Change the **Duration** to **4** (for four frames) and press **Return**.

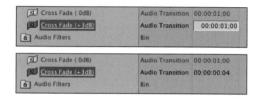

7 Select **Cross Fade (+3dB)** and click the **Effects** menu, and choose **Audio Transitions > Set Default**. (Be sure you are in the **Audio Transitions** section.)

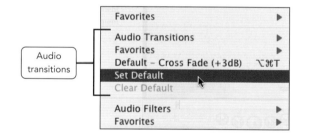

Audio transitions

Ta-da! That's it. Another "less-than-10-stepper." To apply the default audio transition, select an audio edit point and either use the **Effects** menu or press **Option+Cmd+T**.

You don't need to save your work, default audio and video transitions are saved automatically in your **Preferences** files.

NOTE:

A Caution About Preference Files

Here's a quick heads-up on all this Preferences stuff. One of the maintenance procedures you'll do fairly frequently with Final Cut is to trash your Preferences files. (See Appendix A for instructions on how to do this.)

This means that anything that is stored *only* in Preferences files will be lost or reset when those files are trashed. For this reason, I tend not to spend a lot of time obsessing over setting my default transition, creating Favorite effects (there are three: Transitions, Motions, and Filters).

So, use favorites if you want, just keep in mind that you'll need to redo your defaults and favorites every time you trash your Preferences.

5 | Create a Favorite Transition

In this exercise, you'll learn how to take a transition you particularly like and turn it into a favorite transition—and why you may not want to.

---

1 Open **Chapter 09 Lesson 2** and load **Seq – Snowboard final** into the **Timeline**. You'll be working principally in the **Browser** for this exercise.

---

2 You already know how to do most of this:

- Select an edit point.

- Apply a transition. For instance, I've used a **Stretch > Cross Stretch** transition.

- Double-click the transition to load it into the **Viewer**.

---

3 Change your settings to match mine. (Not that mine are all that great, but, hey, it shows that you can create a customized favorite transition.)

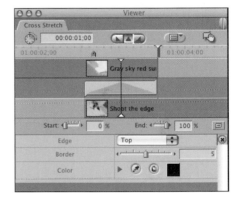

---

4 See the small hand in the upper-right corner? It's called the **drag handle**. Grab it.

---

5 Drag the drag handle to the **Effects** tab in the **Browser** and drop it on the **Favorites** folder. (OK, maybe I should have told you to locate this folder before you dragged the transition. Let go of the transition, click the **Effects** tab, locate the **Favorites** folder, and drag the transition into the folder again. Sorry.)

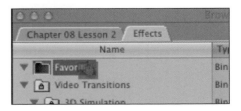

Chapter 9 : **Transitions—Making Change Beautiful** |

6 Twirl down the **Favorites** folder to see your new favorite transition inside.

---

7 Go to the **Effects** menu. Choose **Favorites**, and see? There's your latest favorite transition with a keyboard shortcut already assigned.

This, too, is stored in your **Preferences** folder.

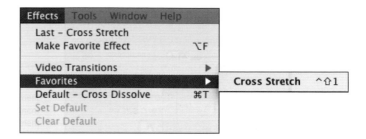

---

8 To apply a favorite transition, either select your edit point, then choose **Effects > Video Transitions Favorites > [pick your transition]**, or drag it from the **Favorites** folder in the **Browser Effects** tab.

Wow! Eight steps. Very cool. You don't need to save your work; Favorites are saved automatically in the Preferences files.

---

6 | Bonus Transition: A Gradient Wipe

In this exercise, you'll learn an interesting effect that makes one image "melt" into another. Consider it a bonus for all the hard work you've been doing.

1 Open **Chapter 09 Lesson 2** and load **Seq – Snowboard final** into the **Timeline**. You'll be working principally in the **Browser** for this exercise.

2 If there's a transition between the first two clips, delete it.

3 Select the **Browser**, choose **File > Import > File** and import **Gradient.tif** from the **FCP 5 HOT Projects > Media > Graphics** folder.

4 Double-click **Gradient.tif** to load it into the **Viewer**. Final Cut has a special wipe that uses the shading (gradient) of white to black for a wipe. It's called the **Gradient Wipe**, and it's easier to understand when you see it than for me to explain it.

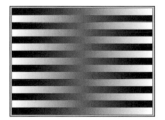 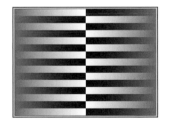

I started with a simple series of gradient bars in Photoshop and then twirled them, using a Photoshop filter. I then exported this as a TIF image. This is what you imported into Final Cut.

You can easily create your own gradient images; just remember to use only shades of black and white.

5 Apply the **Video Transitions > Wipes > Gradient Wipe** transition to the first edit point. The default length of **1:00** is OK. You can use either the **Effects** menu or the **Effects** tab. The wipe is the same; the only thing that changes is how you apply it.

---

6 Double-click the transition to open it into the **Transition Editor**. If you feel adventurous, change the **Softness** setting to **10**.

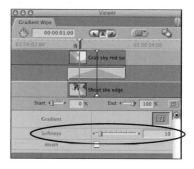

---

7 Drag the **Gradient.tif** image from the **Browser** into the **graphics well** in the **Transition Editor**. This image will be what creates the wipe. Like I said, it's easier to see than to explain.

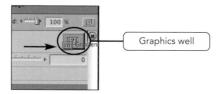

Graphics well

---

8 Your transition will require rendering. I used **Option+P** to view this transition without rendering, but you can use any of the three render options: **Sequence > Render Selection**, **Option+P**, or **Tools > QuickView**.

Voilá! A really cool, if somewhat "Batman-and-Robinish," gradient wipe. All in only eight steps. You are getting *really* good!

Helpful Keyboard Shortcuts

Shortcut	Action
Cmd+Z	Undos the last event (default setting tracks the last 10 events)
P	Selects Pen tool to add keyframes
PP	Selects Negative Pen tool to remove keyframes
Option+click	Use with the Pen tool to toggle between Positive and Negative Pen tool
Option+8	Opens the QuickView window
Z	Selects Zoom tool
N	Toggles snapping on and off
G	Selects Edit Selection tool, used for selecting edit points on multiple tracks
Ctrl+D	Opens the Duration dialog for selected clip or transition
Cmd+T	Applies default video transition to selected video edit point
Option+Cmd+T	Applies default audio transition to selected audio edit point
Cmd+R	Renders selection
Option+R	Renders everything
Option+P	Plays an effect that needs rendering as fast as it can be calculated, without first rendering the effect (my *favorite* keyboard shortcut)
Cmd+click	Select multiple edit points (one edit point per track)
Option+click	Use with Selection tool to set keyframes if they don't exist, or delete keyframes if they do exist; click audio volume overlays (red rubber bands) or video overlays (black opacity lines)

Summary

In this chapter, you've switched gears from editing into making your projects look beautiful. And, in so doing, you've learned many of the basic elements you'll be working with throughout the second half of the book: keyframes, renders, opacity, and transitions. In the next chapter, you'll work with text and graphics so you can really drive your message home.

10

Text, Titles, and Graphics

Text and graphics are often as important an element in telling your story as music, effects, or even B-roll. Identifying a speaker establishes his or her credibility. Showing a map of a historic battle is far better than wide shots for establishing relationships.

In this chapter, you will learn how text and graphics for video are different from graphics for print or the computer screen (and they differ significantly!). You will learn how to create titles for your programs. You will also learn how to integrate Photoshop, LiveType, and Motion files into your sequences.

1 | Creating a Main Title

In this exercise, you will learn how to create a full-screen title using Final Cut Pro 5's built-in text generator. FCP's built-in text capability, although very limited, is still useful in a wide range of titling applications. This lesson shows you how it works.

---

1 Open **Chapter 10 Lesson 1**. It's in the **FCP Projects > FCP 5 HOT Files** folder you created at the beginning of this book. Double-click **Seq – Ready to Title** to load it into the **Timeline**.

Notice at the beginning of the sequence there's a 4-second gap. This gap is where you will put the opening title for this scene.

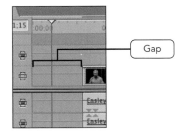

---

2 Start by placing the **playhead** anywhere in this gap. This tells Final Cut where to locate the text clip you are about to create.

---

3 Click the small pop-up menu in the lower-right corner of the **Viewer** that has the letter "A" inside it. This is the **Generator** menu. Scroll down and choose **Text > Text** (or press **Ctrl+X**).

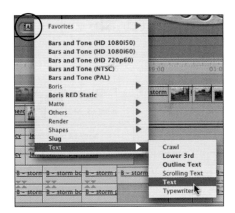

Text Clips

Creating and editing a text clip to the Timeline is where most people have problems working with text in Final Cut. Because of this, let me first give you this three-step process so you understand it clearly. Then, you'll do it as part of this exercise:

Step 1: Put the **Timeline playhead** in the clip over which you want to superimpose your text. Click the **Generator** pop-up menu and choose the text you want to create.

Step 2: Before entering any text, drag the newly created text clip from the **Viewer** to the **Superimpose** overlay in the **Canvas** (or press **F12**).

Step 3: Immediately double-click the new text clip in the **Timeline** to load it back into the **Viewer**.

The advantage to using this three-step process is that you not only automate the process of creating a text clip, placing it on the **Timeline**, and trimming it to the correct length, but you also are able to see in the **Canvas** all the changes you make to the text clip because the **playhead** is already located in the middle of the new text clip.

I use this technique, or a modification you'll learn in the next exercise, virtually every time I work with text.

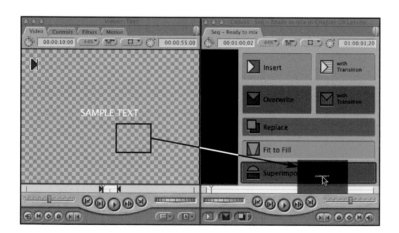

4 *Before* you enter any text, drag the new text clip from the **Viewer** to the **Canvas** and drop it on the **Superimpose** overlay.

The text clip is immediately placed **above** the gap in the **Timeline** where the **playhead** is located and trimmed so that both are the exact same length. Notice, unlike with most other edits, you did not need to set an **In** or **Out**, or even move the **playhead** to the start of the clip. Final Cut calculates all that for you automatically.

For those who demand exact technical precision, Final Cut places the text clip in the next track above the Viewer patch panel setting (in this case **v1**), trimmed to match the lower clip for time and location (in this case, it wasn't a clip, it was a gap). In most cases, this means your text super (TV jargon for a title "superimposed" over video) will appear on **V2**, timed to match the clip, or gap, on **V1**.

5 Next, double-click the text clip to load it back into the **Viewer**.

6 With the clip loaded into the **Viewer**, notice that a new tab (**Controls**) has appeared at the top. Click this tab to make adjustments to the contents and formatting of the text in this clip.

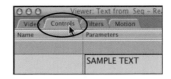

The top half of the **Controls** window is where you enter text. The bottom half is where you control how it looks and where it is placed on the screen.

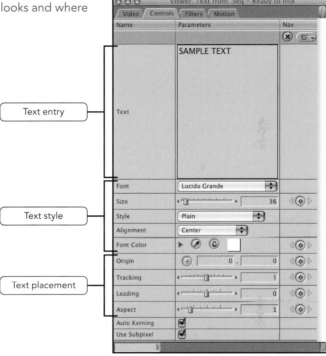

Text entry

Text style

Text placement

7 Start by entering the title of this sequence: **Hurricane Irene 1999**. At the end of each word, press **Return** to insert a line break. This forces each word to appear on its own line of the screen.

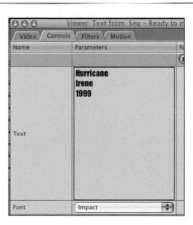

8 From the **Font** pop-up, choose the typeface **Impact**. (If **Impact** doesn't exist on your system, use **Arial Black**. However, by using **Arial Black**, you may need to adjust some of the formatting from that shown in these illustrations.)

9 Next, change the font **Size** to **70**, and adjust the **Tracking** to **1.5** and the **Leading** to **–5**.

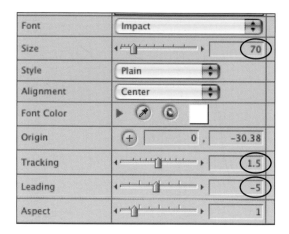

Tracking is the spacing between characters. (Smaller numbers mean closer text.) Leading is the spacing between lines of text. (Smaller numbers mean closer lines.)

Finally, you need to move the text so it centers properly on the screen. The best way to do this is to use the **Origin** control.

10 Click once in the circle containing the crosshair to select it. Then, go to the **Canvas** and click where you want the center of the graphic to be located. **Continue holding the mouse** and drag to move the text around the **Canvas**. When you are happy with the location, let go of the mouse to position the text.

This technique of using the crosshair to set the position of text, graphics, or an effect is used a lot throughout the rest of this book.

NOTE:

Don't Use the Motion Tab to Set Font Size or Position

Some inexperienced FCP editors use the **Motion** tab, which you'll learn about in Chapter 11, "Motion Effects," to set font size and location. This is *really* not a good idea. The **Controls** tab works with text as vectors, whereas the **Motion** tab converts it to bitmaps, which means using the **Scale** command puts jagged edges on your text. Also, moving text using the **Motion** tab makes it easy to unintentionally crop the edges of letters. Use the **Controls** tab for all text sizing and placement. It *always* looks better.

---

11 To precisely set the position of text or graphics, you can also enter the coordinates directly into the **Origin**. The first number sets the horizontal position; the second sets the vertical.

In this case, enter **0** in the first box to center the text horizontally and **–31** in the second box to move the text up a little bit.

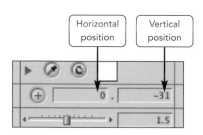

A Quick Word on Coordinates

Final Cut uses the coordinates **0, 0** to represent the exact center of a frame of video in pixels. (Photoshop, on the other hand, uses **0, 0** to represent the top-left corner of an image.) So, when you enter numbers into the Center parameter, you are telling Final Cut to move the center of the *selected* clip to those coordinates.

The top-left corner for DV video is at coordinates **–360, –240**. The bottom-right corner for DV video is at coordinates **360, 240**.

To move an image to the left, type a negative number in the first box.

To move an image to the right, type a positive number in the first box.

To move an image up, type a negative number in the second box.

To move an image down, type a positive number in the second box.

In other words, up and left are negative, down and right are positive, and the numbers represent pixels.

---

12 Because this is the beginning of the sequence, you need to put a quick fade up on the beginning of the title and dissolve from the title to the first video. To do this, select the **In** of the title and apply a 20-frame **Cross Dissolve**.

---

13 One way to set the duration of a transition is to select it, and press **Ctrl+D**. Then enter the new duration into the **Duration** dialog. (Your dissolve duration may default to 20 due to your work in the last chapter.)

---

14 The **Out** of the text clip isn't long enough to support a dissolve. You need to extend it. A quick way to do this is to select the **Out** of the text clip and press the **+** key on either the keypad or keyboard. Then type **20** and press the **Return** key. This extends the **Out** 20 frames. (Why 20 frames? Because we needed to add a handle to the text equal to the length of the transition so the dissolve doesn't start over black.)

---

15 Finally, apply a 20-frame **Cross Dissolve** to the **Out**, and you are done.

You could have moved the clip down to **V1** and put a dissolve between the two clips. However, most text is keyed over a clip, which you'll do in the next exercise, which means text is almost always on a different track from your video. (Yes, I know the text keyed over his face looks ugly. Don't panic, this changes in Exercise 6.)

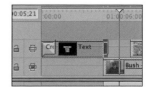

---

16 Save your work and quit Final Cut if you want to take a break. However, there is still more you can do with text, as you'll learn in the next exercise.

NOTE:

Action Safe, Title Safe, and Full Screen

As you will soon discover, this chapter is filled with "Wouldn't it be nice if...?"

In this case, wouldn't it be nice if all the elements in your program could go to the edge of the screen? Well, they can't, mainly because of the way television sets are manufactured and the way they age.

TVs, as you can imagine, are produced in huge quantities under a variety of conditions and quality control. Experience has taught that, essentially, every set loses some of the picture at the edge of the frame. This is because consumers want to see as big a picture as possible, and don't like seeing black around the edges. So manufacturers zoom the picture slightly so it fills the screen. However, because this zooming is not absolutely precise, some edges of the picture are often lost.

To compensate for this, Final Cut, and other professional video tools, draws a rectangle around the picture 5% in from each edge. This rectangle is called **Action Safe**. It is the area, 5% in from all edges, within which you need to keep all essential action; otherwise, some percentage of TV sets out there will not be able to see it.

To compound matters, as TV sets age, their picture tubes zoom in, losing even more of the picture around the edge. To compensate for this additional picture loss, Final Cut has a second rectangle, drawn 10 percent in from each edge, called **Title Safe**. When you are creating titles, company logos, sponsor phone numbers, or any other essential text information, be sure it entirely fits inside the **Title Safe** rectangle.

You toggle the display of these rectangles by choosing **View > Show Title Safe** or the **View** pop-up menu in the **Canvas** (or **Viewer**).

Tips on Designing Video Graphics

There isn't room, in a single book, to cover designing television graphics in the detail it deserves. So, rather than explain each of these in detail, here are some key guidelines you can use to improve the look of your graphics:

- All video, in all formats, worldwide, everywhere, all the time, period, is fixed resolution. In other words, you see the same amount of information on a 60-inch monitor as on a 9-inch monitor—the pixels just get bigger or smaller. Video is low-resolution. Printing is high-resolution. You cannot get the same look in video that you can create on your computer screen or a printer. Just accept this as a fact and move on.

- Avoid text with very thin lines in the font, like the bar in this "e." The bar disappears on video and makes the character impossible to read. This font does not work well at small point sizes. If you must use a font like this, make sure to set the text large on the screen; generally 24 points or more.

- Avoid text that's so ornately scripted you have to look at the letter several times to figure out what it is. Your viewers don't have that much time. Even if you make the font really large, you won't see the smooth curves you expect, but lots of tiny little stair steps along the edges of each curved line.

- Avoid fonts with little "feet" or "bars"—called *serifs*—at the end of the characters. These serifs often flicker and make the text hard to read.

- Use sans serif fonts, like Arial, Futura, Gill Sans, Lucida Grande, Impact, Machine, and others for maximum readability. They aren't particularly fancy, but they work really well.

- Avoid using text in point sizes smaller than 24 point.

- Avoid using highly compressed or condensed fonts; they are too hard to read.

- Avoid using lines thinner than 4 pixels; they will flicker.

- Avoid using highly saturated colors. In Exercise 4, you'll learn how to use scopes to make sure your colors are safe.

- Avoid using pure white (more on this later). Again, in Exercise 4, you'll learn how to use the Waveform Monitor to maintain good video levels.

- Always add drop shadows (and remember to change FCP's default settings to match my suggestions, which you'll learn in about four pages).

- Basically, if someone who hasn't seen your design can't read it in less than 4 seconds, your design is too fancy. Figure out a way to make it simpler. Remember, video is *low*-resolution.

2 | Creating Lower-Third and Upper-Corner Titles

In this exercise, you'll learn how to create two more workhorse titles: the lower third and the upper corner.

---

1 Open **Chapter 10 Lesson 1**. You'll find it inside the **Lessons** folder on the **Final Cut Pro 5 HOT DVD** included with this book. Double-click **Seq – Ready to Title** to load it into the **Timeline**. It should have the opening title you created in the last exercise. If not, open, **Seq – Ready for lower third**.

---

2 Set an **In** on the **Timeline** at the start of Gov. Easley's statement. Set an **Out** just before the B-roll starts. (Remember, if you use the down arrow to find the start of the B-roll, you need to move **back** one frame to set the **Out**.)

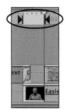

---

3 Click the **Generator** menu and choose **Text > Lower 3rd**. (If you can't see the **Generator** menu, click the **Video** tab at the top of the **Viewer**. If the **Transition Editor** is showing in the **Viewer**, double-click any clip from the **Timeline** or **Browser** to display the **Video** tab.)

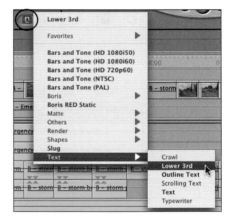

---

4 **Ctrl+click** in the gray area above **V2** and select **Add Track**. Then, move **v1** on the left side of the patch panel to match track **V2** (on the right). Remember, your clip will be placed on the track immediately *above* where the **v1** patch is located.

---

5 Change the third button at the bottom of the **Canvas** from **Replace** to **Superimpose** by clicking the small arrow to the right of the button and dragging to select the purple **Superimpose** button from the pop-up menu. Then, click the **Superimpose** button to edit the text clip to the **Timeline**. Select the **Timeline** and press **Option+X** to remove the **In** and **Out**.

6 Because you want the lower-third super to dissolve *in* at the same rate that the title graphic is dissolving *out*, copy the transition at the end of the main title by **Option+dragging** it from the end of the main title to the beginning of the lower-third. Dragging the transition would simply move it.

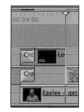

Option+dragging a transition makes a copy of the transition and moves it to the edit point you drop it on. (I find **Option+dragging** to be the fastest way to copy a transition.) You don't need to add a transition at the end of the clip because the title ends at a shot change.

(If you can't **Option+drag** a transition, you can always select the edit point and apply the transition using the **Effects** menu. Or, you may have bad **Preferences** files, which was a problem I ran into while writing this chapter. See the Appendix, *"Additional Resources,"* for instructions on how to delete and restore your **Preferences** files.)

7 Place the **playhead** in the middle of the lower-third text clip and double-click it to load into the **Viewer**.

8 Click the **Controls** tab.

The Controls window for a lower third is different than the Controls window for full-screen text. This is a good example of how windows change to reflect different attributes of a clip, effect, or transition. This window has sets of controls for the first line of text, the second line of text, and a background effect.

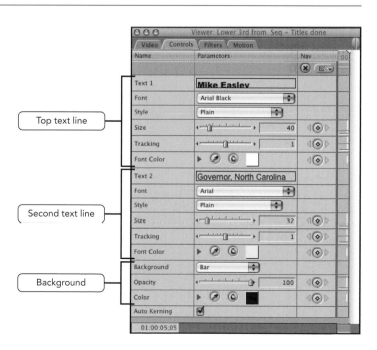

9 Enter **Mike Easley** into **Text 1**. Set the **Font** to **Arial Black** and the **Size** to **40** point.

10 Enter **Governor, North Carolina** into **Text 2**. Set the **Font** to **Arial** and the **Size** to **32** point.

11 Change the color of the second line by clicking the white color chip for the second line of text and selecting a rich yellow color. Pick something a little back from the edge of the color circle.

12 You can save a color to reuse later by dragging the color from the color bar at the top and dropping it into one of the color chips at the bottom. Since this color picker is a system-level utility, *any* application that opens this color selector is able to select the same color by clicking the small chip at the bottom.

The lower-third text clip has a background you can use to add additional separation between the text and the clip. You can select either a solid color block or a very thin line. Both are not, um, ideal.

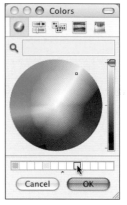

13 Choose **Bar** from the **Background** pop-up menu. This adds a red line between the two lines of the title. (Adjusting the opacity makes it translucent.)

There's one more setting you need to adjust, which I use for all my text: a drop shadow. Drop shadows make text *much* more readable.

14 To create a drop shadow, click the **Motion** tab and check the **Drop Shadow** check box near the bottom of the window.

15 Adjust your shadow settings to match mine. I've found these settings make for the most readable text: **Offset = 1.5, Angle = 135, Softness = 30,** and **Opacity = 90.** Write these down, I recommend them highly!

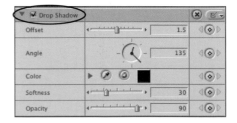

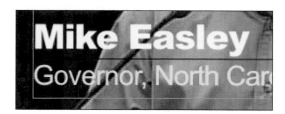 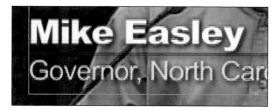

Drop shadows are *essential* in video. The image on the left has no shadow; the image on the right does. While it may be hard to see in print, in video, drop shadows are highly effective and essential for making text readable.

You have one more task in this exercise, which is to add an upper-corner super to the first B-roll shot to identify it as historical footage (often called **file footage**).

---

16 Create a full-screen text clip, set its duration to **2:17** seconds, and edit it to the **Timeline** on **V3** immediately after the lower-third super you just completed. (Notice that it ends at the same time as the first B-roll clip. Coincidental? I think not.) Double-click it in the **Timeline** to load it into the **Viewer**.

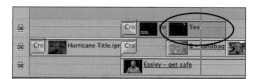

---

17 Enter **Florida**, press **Return** for a line break, then enter **1999**. Set the rest of the settings to match this screen. Use the same color yellow as the earlier super by clicking on the small yellow color chip at the bottom of the color picker. Then, drag the text into position using the **Origin** crosshairs or enter **285** for the horizontal position and **–170** for the vertical.

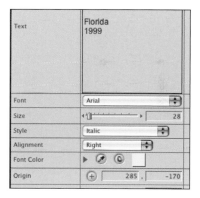

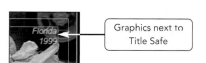

Graphics next to Title Safe

See how it lands nicely against the Title Safe gridline? Click the **Motion** tab, add a drop shadow, and you're done.

---

18 Save your work. You'll be using this project again later. Quit Final Cut if you need to take a break. Otherwise, keep everything open for the next exercise.

Video Graphics Anxiety, Part I—Square Pixels

Wouldn't it be nice if…video and computers displayed the same things the same way?

Well, they don't.

In fact, there are six principal ways computer video differs from television video. Some of these I have already discussed; the rest will be presented here:

- Computer monitors display more data as they get bigger. Standard television sets display the same image, regardless of picture size. We say that video has a "fixed" resolution.

- Computer video is progressive—it displays every horizontal line of pixels in order from top to bottom. Television video is interlaced—it displays all even-numbered lines, then all odd-numbered lines.

- Computers display a full-range of grayscale from pure black to pure white. Television video displays a more limited range of grayscale from "almost black" to "almost white."

- Computers display all colors as RGB values. Television video displays grayscale and color values using YUV, where Y is the grayscale value and U/V are the color values. YUV colors do not have the same range as RGB colors.

- Computers display all colors uncompressed, that is, each pixel is uniquely described using discrete red, green, and blue values. Television video, in order to squeeze more information onto a tape, displays colors using a variety of color sampling schemes: 4:2:2, 4:2:0, and 4:1:1. This color sampling further restricts the amount of color information contained in a video clip.

- And, finally, the key difference that drives editors the most nuts: computers display images using square pixels, whereas video displays images using rectangular pixels. This last point is the one I'll discuss here.

Computers display images as a series of square pixels. Video displays images as a series of rectangular pixels. This means that if you are creating graphics for video, you need to allow for this difference.

To make matters worse, Final Cut expects graphics in one size if they are a single layer, such as a scan of a photograph, and a different size if they are a multilayer Photoshop file (more on this later in this chapter). Rather than spend pages explaining this, here is a table you can use to make sure your graphics are the right size.

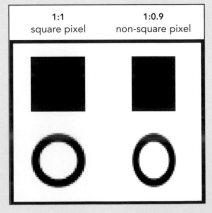

continues on next page

Video Graphics Anxiety, Part I—Square Pixels *continued*

By the way, there used to be a big brouhaha about whether to create your images in Photoshop, and then alter the image size in Photoshop before importing into Final Cut. My experience indicates you get the same result either way. So, keep it simple: create your graphic in Photoshop at the size indicated in the following table, save it, import it into Final Cut, and let Final Cut do any necessary resizing. The quality is fine.

By the way #2, I use TIFFs as my preferred file format for single-layer images, and I use PSD (Photoshop documents) for multilayer images.

By the way #3, Final Cut Pro changed how it calculates pixel aspect ratios with the HD version. The following table is correct for both FCP 5 and FCP HD.

Graphic Image Sizes
(create all graphics at 72 pixels per inch)

Video Format	Single-Layer (TIFF or PNG)	Multilayer Photoshop (PSD)
DV – NTSC	720 × 540	720 × 480
DV – NTSC (16 × 9)	853 × 480	720 × 480
DV & SD – PAL	768 × 576	720 × 576
DV & SD – PAL (16 × 9)	1024 × 576	720 × 576
601 – NTSC	720 × 547	720 × 486
601 – NTSC (16 × 9)	853 × 486	720 × 486
720i/p high definition	1280 × 720	1280 × 720
1080i/p high definition	1920 × 1080	1920 × 1080

3 | Creating a Credit Roll

In this exercise, you will create a simple credit roll for the end of the Hurricane sequence.

---

1 Open **Chapter 10 Lesson 1**. You'll find it inside the **Lessons** folder on the **Final Cut Pro 5 HOT DVD** included with this book. Double-click **Seq – Ready to Title** to load it into the **Timeline**. It should have all the graphics you've created so far during this chapter. If not, open **Seq – Ready for credits**.

---

2 Create a scrolling text clip by choosing **Text > Scrolling Text** from the **Generator** pop-up menu in the lower-right corner of the **Viewer**.

---

3 Go to the **Timeline** and put your **playhead** at the **In** of the fourth clip from the end, **B – clean WS**. Then, repatch the video so that **v1** source connects to **V2** destination.

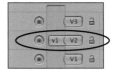

---

4 Superimpose the text clip to the **V3** track of the **Timeline**, then drag the **Out** with the **Selection** tool so that the credits text covers the three clips prior to the final sound bite. Double-click it to load it into the **Viewer**.

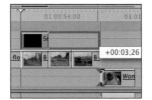

---

5 Enter your credit list in the top half of the **Controls** panel. Put asterisks between the titles and names as a separator. Final Cut turns this into the correct spacing automatically using the **Gap Width** setting in the next step.

You can change the font, size, and color as you like. In this case, use **Lucida Grande**, **32** point.

The speed of the scroll is determined by the length of the clip.

---

6 At the bottom of the **Controls** panel are some new settings:

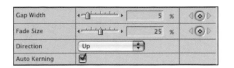

Gap Width controls the size of the horizontal gap, indicated by the asterisk, between the title and the name.

Fade Size fades the text at the top and bottom of the screen. This is a percentage of the entire screen. Adding a slight fade makes the credit roll look nicer, to my way of thinking.

Direction controls which way the text scrolls.

Auto Kerning improves the spacing between letters. I always leave this on.

---

7 Add a drop shadow to your text and move your **playhead** near the middle of the clip to see what the credits look like. (Pretty darn nice, if you ask me!)

Note fade

---

8 Save your work, and you're done. There's more to come next, so keep everything open.

NOTE:

Video Graphics Anxiety, Part II—What Color Is White?

Wouldn't it be nice if…computers and video used the same white and black levels?

Well, they don't.

When you hear terms like "8-bit video" and "10-bit video," the bits refer to the number of levels between maximum black and maximum white (or the maximum/minimum values of a color). Eight-bit video has 256 discrete levels, and 10-bit video has 1,024 levels.

Digital black

Digital white

This means pure black on the computer has an RGB value of 0,0,0, and pure white on the computer has an RGB value of 255, 255, and 255.

continues on next page

Video Graphics Anxiety, Part II—What Color Is White? *continued*

The problem is that video doesn't have a range that wide. In 8-bit video, video black in the U.S. is only 16 (as measured on the RGB scale) and video white is 235. To complicate matters, video is measured in IRE (as audio is measured in db, or frequency in Hz), where 7.5 IRE equals black, and 100 IRE equals white.

The reason you need to know this is that you can create graphics on your computer that are too white. When they are broadcast, they visually distort and make the audio buzz. Not good. If you are creating professional-level video, this results in your tapes getting rejected for poor technical quality.

There is some good news, however. First, create all your graphics with black set to 0. Your capture card or DV deck handles the conversion to the proper level of black automatically.

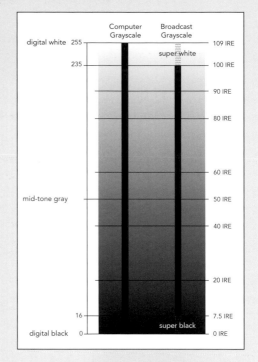

With white settings, it isn't so easy, though Final Cut adds a preference to help. Choose **Sequence > Settings** (or press **Cmd+0**) and click the **Video Processing** tab.

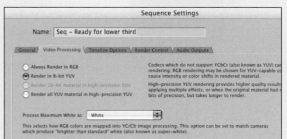

Here's the rule: if you are outputting to DV, set this pop-up to **Super-White**. If you are outputting to any other format, such as Betacam, set this pop-up to **White**.

What this menu tells Final Cut to do is "clamp," or automatically reduce, all imported graphics so that their white levels match the tape format to which you are recording. This setting affects only imported graphics, and not video, but, still, it's a great help. (You'll learn a way to clamp video white levels at the end of the next exercise.)

Understanding Video Scopes

In this exercise, you'll learn how to read the video scopes supplied with Final Cut, as well as when to use a Waveform Monitor and when to use a Vectorscope. Why study scopes now? Because the computer can create colors that cannot be safely recorded to tape. As we transition out of editing and into effects, you need to make sure that what you are creating can be safely output. The Video Scopes can help.

1 Open **Chapter 10 Lesson 1**. You'll find it inside the **Lessons** folder on the **Final Cut Pro 5 HOT DVD** included with this book. Double-click **Seq – Ready to Title** to load it into the **Timeline**. It should have all the graphics you've created so far during this chapter. If not, open **Seq – Ready for credits**.

2 Position your **playhead** at **01:00:16:01**—the shot of the lady in the blue top holding a sheet of plywood.

3 Select the **Video Scopes** by choosing **Tools > Video Scopes** (or press **Option+9**).

Final Cut has four Video Scopes: Waveform Monitor, Vectorscope, RGB Parade, and Histogram. These last two scopes, although helpful, are nowhere near as important as the first two. So, you will concentrate on the Waveform Monitor and Vectorscope in this exercise.

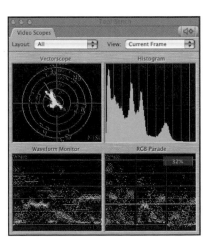

4 Choose **Waveform** from the pop-up menu in the upper-left corner of the **Video Scopes** window.

The Waveform Monitor shows all the pixels in the picture in the Canvas, ranging from black, at the bottom, to white, at the top. Various shades of gray are in the middle. Pixels on the left edge of the image are on the left edge of the Waveform and pixels on the right side of the image are on the right side of the scope.

A properly exposed picture has pixel values that range from top to bottom. Images that look washed out are missing black levels. Images that are gray and dull are missing white levels.

Although you can't recognize specific images in the Waveform, you can recognize the various gray levels of shapes. For instance, it's easy to spot the highlights on her hat, the midtones of the plywood, and the darker shadows under the hedge.

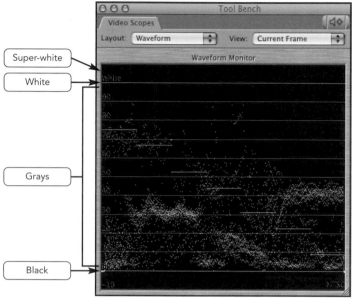

5 Move the cursor inside the **Waveform** and watch as the yellow guidelines make it easy to measure the level of grayscale.

The Waveform Monitor is how you measure your video levels, which is why this scope is so important: video levels are "TV-safe" when their white levels do not exceed 100% (100 IRE). The only time they can exceed 100% is if you are outputting to DV.

However, the Waveform Monitor tells you nothing about color. For that, you need to open the Vectorscope.

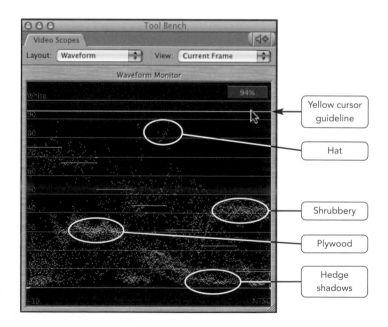

6 Choose **Vectorscope** from the pop-up menu.

The Vectorscope tells you everything about color and nothing about grayscale. In fact, all blacks, whites, and shades of gray are a single dot in the center of the scope. The Vectorscope displays color in two dimensions: hue is represented by the angle of the color, red is at the top left, magenta at the top right, green near the bottom left, and cyan near the bottom right. Saturation is represented by how far out from the middle the color is.

For instance, it is easy to see the colors in the picture by looking at where the pixels clump: the small jet of blue from her top, the red/yellow of the plywood, the green from the shrubbery, and a small jet of yellow from the tops of her gloves.

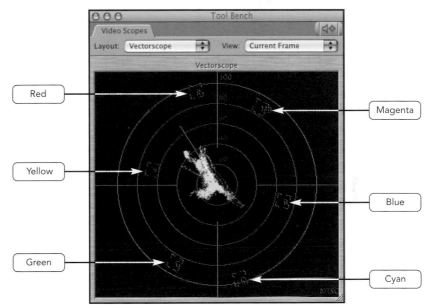

7 Move the cursor around the **Vector-scope** and watch as the yellow guidelines allow you to easily measure the distance and angle of a color.

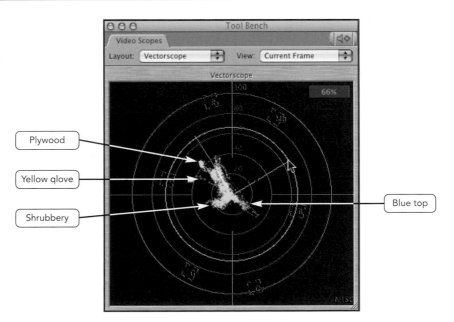

The Vectorscope measures your color levels, which is why this scope is so important: color levels are "TV-safe" provided that they do not exceed a rectangle drawn connecting the tops of each of the six color boxes.

However, not all the boxes are the same distance from the center. Red and cyan are the farthest out and allow the greatest color saturation. Yellow and blue are the closest in and allow the least color saturation. It is *very* easy to create a graphic on the computer whose colors are well outside video color safe. The best way to tell is to use the Vectorscope.

If a color exceeds this "box," it will not play back safely on videotape or DVD. (The video distorts, or "tears," and often creates an audio buzz caused by how the video and audio signals are processed inside most TV sets.) You must correct any illegal colors before outputting.

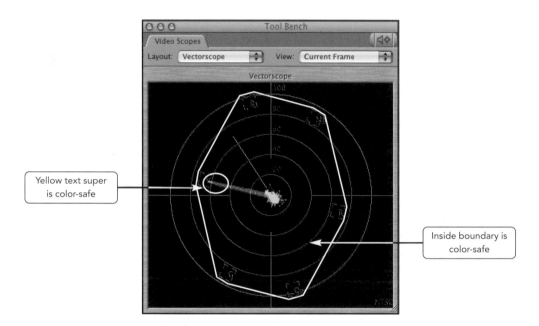

8 Remember in Exercise 2 when you created the yellow upper-corner graphic, and I told you to select a color near the edge of the color wheel? Put your **playhead** over the text clip and look at it on the **Vectorscope**.

If you got too close to the edge, your color would exceed the yellow color range. If this is the case, open the text clip in the **Viewer** and change the color of the super until the **Vectorscope** indicates it's OK. The yellow color in this screen shot has about the maximum saturation you can have without exceeding color limits.

9 That's it for this exercise. If you changed the color on your graphic, save your work. Otherwise, quit Final Cut if you need to take a break.

NOTE:

Clamping Video Levels

Earlier in this chapter, you learned how to set the video rendering for a sequence to clamp (or reduce) white levels that were too high in imported graphics. There's also a filter you can use that does the same thing for video. (Remember, if you are outputting to DV, you don't need to worry about this.)

You will learn how to apply filters in Chapter 12, *"Filters and Keying,"* which talks about filters in detail, but the Broadcast Safe filter is important enough to discuss here.

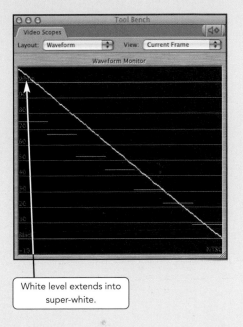

Here's a video test signal that ramps from white, on the left, to black, on the right. The white is too white. Whites that are too white are called *super-white*. You can clamp this video level so that it doesn't exceed 100% by applying the **Broadcast Safe** filter (**Effects > Video Filters > Color Correction > Broadcast Safe**).

White level extends into super-white.

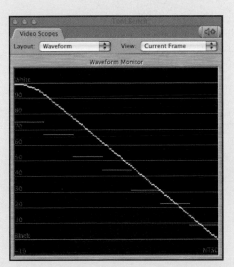

White is clamped at 100%.

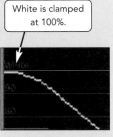

When this filter is applied, all the super-white levels are pushed down to 100%, although the remaining levels in the picture are not changed. You can use this filter whenever you need to control video levels for lots of different clips and don't want to color-correct each one.

NOTE:

Video Graphics Anxiety #3: Color Sampling Drives Me Nuts

Wouldn't it be nice if computers and video displayed the same colors?

Well, as you have probably guessed, they don't.

Computers display all pixels individually at full value. Video compresses color information to reduce file size and make transmission easier. This process is called *color sampling*.

Imagine a blonde actor in front of a green screen. The image is made up of pixels. Each pixel is defined by three numbers: Y defines the luminance or grayscale value; U and V define the color.

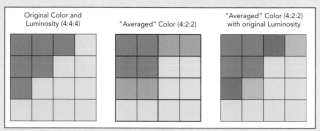

In 4:2:2 color sampling, the colors of 2 adjacent pixels are "averaged" into 1 color for both pixels.

Uncompressed video uses unique Y, U, and V values for each pixel, as shown in the image on the left, which is called *4:4:4 color sampling*—four pixels using independent Y, U, and V values. This is normal for your computer, but it is never used in SD video; the file sizes and transmission requirements are too big. (4:4:4 DV video, if it existed, would require a data rate of slightly more than 31.1 MB per second for playback. Some high-end HD video does use uncompressed 4:4:4 color sampling; the file sizes, though, are ENORMOUS!)

To save space, video engineers decided to average the color values of adjacent pixels. Rather than display them using discrete values, they would average the color between two horizontal pixels—called *4:2:2 color sampling*. Four pixels still had four discrete Y values, but only two discrete U and V values, because colors were averaged over two pixels. This reduced the data rate about 25%. DigiBetacam and DVCPRO-50 both use 4:2:2 color sampling. The middle picture illustrates this averaged color.

Since the human eye is very sensitive to changes in luminance, that is, to changes in brightness, these engineers realized they could improve image quality by averaging color, but leaving all luminance levels alone.

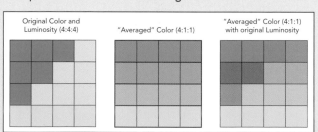

In 4:1:1 color sampling, the colors of 4 adjacent pixels are "averaged" into 1 color for all 4 pixels.

This is how SD video is broadcast today with unique luminance values for each pixel, with color averaged between two pixels.

continues on next page

NOTE:

Video Graphics Anxiety #3: Color Sampling Drives Me Nuts *continued*

When it came time to create DV, keeping image quality high was important, however, using small file sizes was even more critical. To do this, engineers again compressed the color space by averaging the color values of *four* horizontal pixels. So, now, each pixel in a group of four pixels each had a unique luminance (Y) value, but shared one common color value. This is called *4:1:1 color sampling*. This reduced the data rate to less than 4 MB per second. And, although DV video uses additional compression techniques to minimize the data rate, this color sampling is the one with the most direct impact on effects.

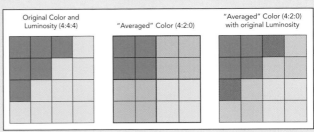

In 4:2:0 color sampling, color is shared between two lines of video, in groups of two pixels.

One more illustration: HDV and DVD-video use *4:2:0 color sampling*, which is even more compressed than DV, because it averages color between two horizontal pixels *and* two video lines.

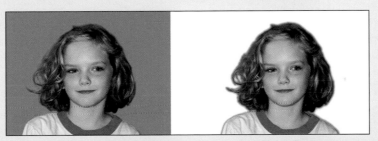

Color sampling can produce undesired results such as a "halo" when keying an image.

Normally, color sampling is not a big deal. However, when you start doing color correction, chroma key, gradients, or composites, you very quickly learn that DV or HDV video just doesn't have enough color information in it to create good-looking effects. The image above illustrates this. The girl on the left is the source image, the girl on the right sports a green halo after chroma-keying. This halo is an exaggerated example of the effects of color sampling when creating a chroma-key using either DV or HDV source video.

So, if creating high-quality color effects is your goal, you might want to change to a video format that uses less compressed color sampling.

5 | Working with Adobe Photoshop Graphics

In this exercise, you will learn how to work with a layered Photoshop (PSD) graphics file and, more importantly, what makes a layered graphic especially useful in Final Cut. Plus, you'll learn how to change the default duration of all imported graphic files. In the next chapter, you'll learn how to do a "pan-and-scan" move on a still image.

1 Open **Chapter 10 Lesson 2**. You'll find it inside the **Lessons** folder on the **Final Cut Pro 5 HOT DVD** included with this book. Double-click **Seq – Snowboard Final** to load it into the **Timeline**.

2 Blaine Albios, a very talented graphic artist, created an opening Photoshop graphic specifically to use at the beginning of this sequence. I've already imported it, so go to the **Browser** and twirl down **Graphics**, then double-click **Snowboard Title** to load it into the **Viewer**.

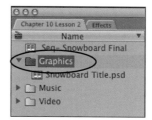

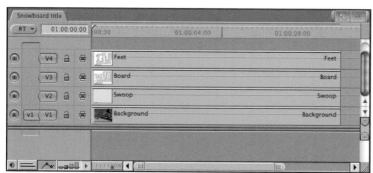

Whoops! What happened? It didn't load into the **Viewer**, it loaded directly into the **Timeline**! That's because imported Photoshop graphics that contain layers are treated as sequences, with each layer acting as a separate video track. Best of all, the alpha (transparency) channel information is retained by Final Cut.

3 This time, *drag* the graphic from the **Browser** to the **Viewer** to load it into the **Viewer**.

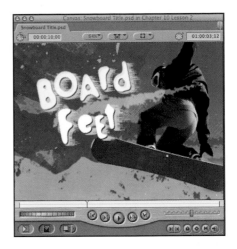

4 You are going to replace the first shot in the Snowboard sequence with this graphic, so **Ctrl+click** the first clip, **Gray sky red sun**, to read the duration: **3:04**. Then, delete the **Gray sky red sun** clip.

5 Now, go to the **Viewer** and change the duration of the graphic to **3:04**.

6 Edit the graphic from the **Viewer** into the space at the beginning of the **Timeline** where the first shot used to be.

Now, you *could* stop there. But, since this graphic came in layers, take advantage of an opportunity to create some simple animation to finish off this exercise.

7 Double-click the graphic to open it into the **Timeline** as a sequence. Notice the graphic opened as a sequence, with its own tab in the **Timeline**.

8 Select the top three layers (**Board**, **Feet**, and **Swoop**), then type **+20** and press **Return**.

9 See how all three layers moved downstream **20** frames? Now select the top two layers and move them downstream another **20** frames. Then, move the top layer an additional **20** frames.

You should now have a staircase effect at the beginning of the graphic sequence.

10 Add a 20-frame dissolve to the beginning of each track.

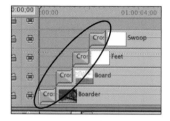

11 On the **Timeline**, click **Seq – Snowboard Final** to make it active. Add a 10-frame dissolve between the graphic and the first video shot. Render everything and play the sequence.

This technique is a very simple, but effective, way to create a feeling of animation for images like maps and complex drawings.

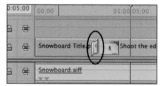

12 One other thing before you finish. All imported graphics default to a duration of **10:00** seconds. You can change this default setting by choosing **Final Cut Pro > User Preferences**, clicking the **Editing** tab, and changing the **Still/Freeze Duration** to whatever you like. I usually leave it at 10 seconds, unless I am importing an image sequence for animation, in which case I'll change this setting to one or two frames.

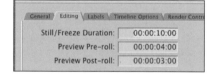

13 That's it for the still image exercises. In the next two exercises, you'll work with images that *move!* Save your project, if you wish. However, you won't be coming back to this example again.

NOTE:

Viewing Correct Video Aspect Pixels in Photoshop CS

Photoshop CS and CS2 add the ability to view images on your computer in the correct aspect ratio for video. To see this on screen, create a graphic in Photoshop and choose **View > Pixel Aspect Ratio Correction**. To export an image from Photoshop with the pixels correct, choose **File > Export > Video Preview**.

6 | Working with LiveType Projects

Final Cut Pro 5 integrates LiveType smoothly into your FCP project. Although it's beyond the scope of this book to give you a proper introduction to LiveType, in this exercise you'll learn how to export video from Final Cut for use in LiveType, change preference settings in LiveType for DV, import a LiveType project, and easily make changes in a LiveType project by using "round-tripping."

1 First, let's export some video we can use in LiveType to create our opening titles. Open Chapter 10 Lesson 3. (You'll find it inside the **Lessons** folder on the **Final Cut Pro 5 HOT DVD** included with this book.) Double-click **Seq – Export** to load it into the **Timeline**.

2 Place your **playhead** in the middle of the first clip (**B - storm waves**) and press the letter **X**. This marks the clip with an **In** and an **Out**.

3 Choose **File > Export > For LiveType**. Give the file a name, **Hurricane video**, and select where you want it saved. In this example, I'm using the **Desktop**. You can save it anywhere convenient.

Notice that we are exporting this file as a QuickTime reference movie, because **Make Movie Self-Contained** is not checked. Reference movies are very small and export very fast. You'll learn more about this in Chapter 13, "Output Your Project." Your exporting is now complete. Next, let's open LiveType and change its preferences so it works better with DV footage, then input the movie to create an opening animation.

4 Start LiveType. It automatically opens with a new, empty, project. Choose **Edit > Project Properties**. These default settings are for SD images, not DV. Creating a DV image using these settings will degrade the quality of your animation.

5 Change the top pop-up menu to **NTSC DV 3:2** (it's near the bottom). Notice how the image size changed from 720 × 486 to 720 × 480. Those six pixels make a big difference!

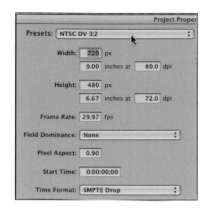

6 There's one other preference you need to watch: near the bottom of the screen is a check box labeled **Render Background**. If this is **Off**, which it is by default, when you import your LiveType project to Final Cut, all background images in LiveType are not included. If this is **On**, all LiveType backgrounds are included in the project file sent to Final Cut. For now, set it to **Off** (unchecked).

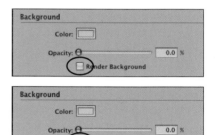

That takes care of adjusting LiveType's preferences. Next, you'll place a video clip on the background of a LiveType file, add a simple animated title, and send it over to Final Cut.

7 In LiveType, choose **File > Place Background Movie** and find the movie (Hurricane video) you exported out of Final Cut. Highlight the name of the clip and click **Choose**. See how the clip shows up in the Canvas and at the bottom of the LiveType Timeline?

8 Grab the Out indicator, which defaults to the 6-second mark, and drag it so that it is just inside the right end of your clip. This sets the duration of the clip that will ultimately end up in Final Cut, in this case 3:01. This is actually a big deal—if you don't move the Out indicator, LiveType exports black between the end of your animation and the Out.

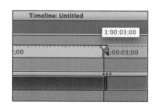

9 Click in the middle of the **01 text track** to select it. Type **Hurricane** in the text entry box immediately to the right of the video image in the **Canvas**. There are two of them, you can use either one.

10 Grab the right edge of the text clip, on the top track, and drag it so that it is the same length (duration) as your video clip on the lower track. The duration for both clips should be **3:01**.

11 Select either the text track or the text you just typed, then select **Itchy** from the **LiveFonts > Collector's Edition** menu. Click **Apply**, in the lower-right corner of the Media Browser, to apply that animation to the text. You'll need to readjust the length of the text track after you apply the animation.

12 Here's the best part—you don't need to render your movie. Instead, choose **File > Save As** and save your project; in this case, use **Hurricane Title**. Although you could save this LiveType project anywhere, if I were doing this for real, I'd save it in the relevant project folder inside FCP Projects. That way all the elements for this Final Cut project are stored in the same place.

13 Now, switch to Final Cut. Choose **File > Import > File** and import the LiveType project you just saved. Notice that it is loaded into the Browser. **Double-click** the clip to load it into the Viewer, then edit it to the **Timeline** at the beginning of the sequence.

Voilá! One opening animated title! And, Final Cut handles all the rendering. (If you only get text on a black background, I'll explain how to fix that problem in a minute.)

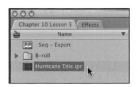

14 But, what is most exciting is what happens when you want to make changes. You can use a new feature of Final Cut called **round-tripping**. This allows you to quickly and easily change a LiveType, Motion, or Photoshop file directly from the FCP Timeline.

For instance, I want to replace the footage of the hurricane with some animation (or I want to replace the black background with animation). To do this, **Ctrl+click** on the LiveType clip in your FCP Timeline and choose **Open in Editor**. FCP automatically starts LiveType and loads the project into it.

15 Click once on the **Hurricane Video** file in the bottom track to select it, then delete it. Go over to the **Media Browser**, click the **Textures** tab, click the **Category** pop-up menu and change it to **Smoke**, then select **Contrail**. Click the **Apply to New Track** button at the bottom of the Inspector to move it into the LiveType Timeline. Grab the right end of the animation and drag it so that it is as long as the text clip above it; again, that's **3:01**.

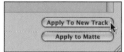

16 Save your project and switch back to Final Cut. Sha-zaam…? Um, maybe not. What happened to the background texture? Well, remember the Render Background preference that we left UNchecked a few steps back? Well, when that preference is not checked, everything below the thick gray line in LiveType is not imported into FCP. Go back to **Edit > Project Properties** and check **Render Background**.

Now, save your project—saving your project is critical—and switch back to Final Cut.

Ta-DA! The animation is immediately updated with the new background. This is very, very cool!

17 One last thing to try. **Ctrl+click** the LiveType clip in your FCP Timeline and choose **Open in Editor**. (This turns on the round-tripping feature.) Switch to **LiveType**, choose **Edit > Project Preferences** and uncheck **Render Background**. Save the LiveType project and switch back to Final Cut. Your background is no longer included in the animation.

Now you know how to export a movie from Final Cut, import it into LiveType, create a simple animated title, save the project and re-import it back into Final Cut. Plus, depending upon how the Render Background preference setting is set, your LiveType background either will, or won't, be included as part of the animation.

This is very cool and, while it doesn't begin to scratch the surface of what LiveType can do, this tells you everything you need to know to use LiveType and Final Cut together on a project.

---

18 That ends this exercise and chapter. Save your work, if you feel so inclined. We won't be coming back to this exercise again.

NOTE:

Round-Tripping Files Between FCP and Motion or Photoshop

I don't have enough room in this book to show you how to round-trip files to Motion and Photoshop, but the process is exactly the same:

1. Create the file (for example, in Motion).

2. Save the Motion project or Photoshop file.

3. Import the file into Final Cut and edit it to the **Timeline**.

4. **Ctrl+click** the clip and choose **Open in Editor** to load it back into its source application.

5. Make your adjustments.

6. Save the file.

7. Switch back to FCP, and your changed file is automatically updated.

Very cool—and a HUGE timesaver!

Helpful Keyboard Shortcuts

Shortcut	Action
Ctrl+X	Creates a new full-screen text clip in the Viewer
F12	Superimposes a clip in the Timeline based on patch panel settings and trims it to match the length of the clip playhead is located in
W	Toggles the selected window (Canvas or Viewer) between displaying the Image, Image+Wireframe, or just Wireframe
Q	Toggles between selecting the Viewer and the Canvas
Option+9	Displays Video Scopes
Option+drag	(On a transition) Makes a copy of the transition onto another edit point
Cmd+R	Renders whatever clips are selected
Ctrl+R	Renders entire sequence
Cmd+0 (zero)	Opens Sequence Settings dialog

Summary

In this chapter, you learned how to create text from within Final Cut, create a simple animation using Photoshop layered graphics, and integrate a LiveType project. In the next chapter, you'll build on this foundation as you move further into effects by creating motion effects.

11

Motion Effects

This chapter is about how to create motion effects inside Final Cut Pro to animate your projects. This chapter is part one of a two-part look at Final Cut effects.

In this chapter, you will learn how to use the Motion tab and keyframes to bring movement to your images. Making things move is often essential to creating a visually interesting program. Chapter 12, *"Filters and Keying,"* rounds out this exploration of effects by showing you how to change the actual look of your video, or the sound of your audio, through the use of filters.

What Is a Motion Effect?

A motion effect is a special visual effect where an image, or text, changes its size, shape, opacity, or position during the course of the effect. Sometimes, just one image changes. Other times, many images are moving all over the place. It all depends upon the needs of your project.

Which brings to mind a quote from my favorite professor when I was studying television production in graduate school at the University of Wisconsin. Dr. Richard Lawson kept stressing: "Never make an aesthetic decision for technical reasons." Or, as I like to say, "Just because you can, doesn't mean you should."

Just because these effects exist doesn't mean you should use them. Many programs are produced without any special effects. But, for those times when you are editing a deadly dull show, and you are praying for something, anything, to move, it's nice to know that Final Cut can deliver the goods.

There are two types of motion effects: the first is where images don't change during an effect, and the second is where they do. The classic example of the first type is a newscaster with graphics over his or her shoulder. The size and placement of the graphic is preset and nothing changes position. This is the effect you'll create in the first exercise.

The second effect is where an image changes size, shape, position, or opacity during its time onscreen. Examples of this include virtually every commercial and music video on the air today. You'll create these type of effects starting with the second exercise.

Our eyes and brain are programmed to respond to movement. If something moves, our eyes move to it instinctively. As editors, we can use this to lead the viewer's eyes to the specific part of the screen we want them to watch.

NOTE:

Programs Are Horizontal, Effects Are Vertical

So far, you have created programs that start on the left of the Timeline and finish on the right, one clip immediately following the other. In other words, everything is horizontal.

When you are working with effects, though, you start working vertically in the Timeline. In other words, to put multiple images on the screen at the same time, you stack them.

For instance, to put two images onscreen at the same time, you would stack two clips. To put five images on the screen at the same time, stack five clips.

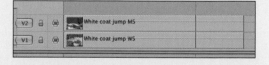

By default, a video clip is 100% full-screen and 100% opaque. Final Cut reads video tracks from the top down. This means that the clip on the highest numbered track will totally block anything below it. You discovered this for yourself when

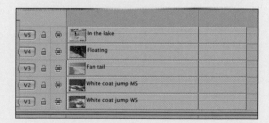

continues on next page

NOTE:

Programs Are Horizontal, Effects Are Vertical *continued*

you edited the B-roll of the hurricane footage in Chapter 8, *"Audio—The Secret to a Great Picture."* Clips on higher numbered tracks are in front of clips on lower numbered tracks. Final Cut allows up to 99 video and 99 audio tracks.

So, in order for multiple images to be onscreen at once, in addition to stacking clips on multiple tracks, you also need to change the size, shape, position, or opacity of the clips on higher numbered tracks so the clips beneath them can be seen.

NOTE:

Tips to Creating Effects

As you can probably imagine, entire books are devoted to creating effects. Still, here's a quick set of guidelines you can use to help make your effects work easier:

- Start by planning your effect—even if only for a minute in your head. Thinking about what you want to do helps to clarify how you want to go about doing it; especially in deciding what clip goes on what track.

- The best effects are short in length. The goal in creating an effect is to have your audience believe your effect is real. An effect is a failure if your audience turns to you and says, "Yep, by golly, *that* was really an effect!"

- I've found it faster to start with the finished effect and construct backwards. In other words, start where you want to end up.

- Finally, create your effect in small steps. This allows you to check things in process and fix them before they get out of control.

DVD MOVIE:

motion_efx.mov

For tutorials illustrating this chapter, check out **motion_efx.mov**, located in the **movies** folder on the **Final Cut Pro 5 HOT DVD**. These tutorials show you how to create picture-in-picture effects, move images along a motion path, and create curved motion paths.

1 | Creating a Picture-in-Picture Effect

In this exercise, you will learn how to create a picture-in-picture effect showing two different angles of the same snowboard jump. To do this, you'll learn how to stack clips, use markers to indicate sync points, change the speed of a clip, and explore the Motion tab.

---

1 If Final Cut is not running, start it and open **Chapter 11 Lesson**. It's in the **FCP Projects > FCP HOT Files** folder you created at the beginning of this book. Double-click **Seq - Pix in Pix** to open it. Don't panic, this sequence is supposed to be empty. You'll soon add the content yourself.

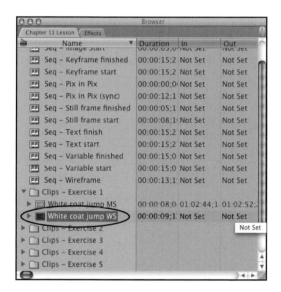 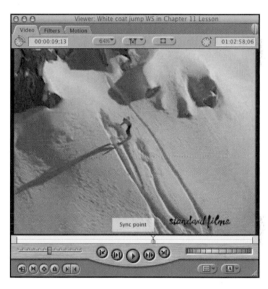

2 Twirl down the bin **Clips - Exercise 1** and double-click **White coat jump WS** to load it into the **Viewer**. (To save typing, I'll call this the **WS** clip.) Notice that I've added a marker, labeled **Sync point**, to the clip. Edit this clip, in its entirety, to **V1** on the **Timeline**. This shot is the wide shot. (And, just to clarify, when I say, "edit a clip," I mean for you to move a clip from the **Viewer** to the **Timeline**. In other words, edit it into its position on the **Timeline**.)

3 Before adding the next shot, you need to set another marker. Move the **playhead** down through the clip on the Timeline and watch for the point where the snowboarder crosses the track of another boarder.

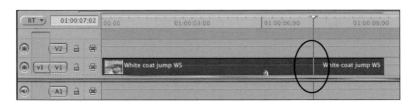

4 Be sure the **WS** clip on **V1** is selected and press **M** to set a clip marker at the **playhead**. (The timecode of this marker is **01:00:07:02**.)

5 Double-click **White coat jump MS** to load it into the **Viewer**. (I'll refer to this shot as **MS** because it is the medium-wide shot that will be shown inside the wide shot.) Notice that I've added a marker to this clip as well, labeled **Sync point**.

6 Go to the patch panel on the left side of the **Timeline** and drag **v1** (the source) up so it connects to (touches) **V2** (the destination). This patches the video from the **Viewer** (the left **v1**) to the **V2** track of the **Timeline**.

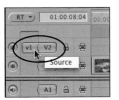

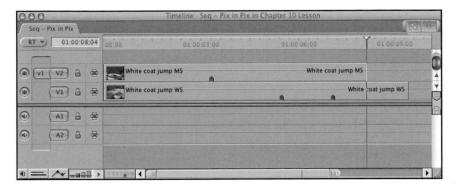

7 Move the **playhead** to the beginning of the **Timeline** and edit this clip to the **Timeline** by clicking the red **Overwrite** button in the lower-left corner of the **Canvas**. Notice that the clip markers traveled with each clip.

These two shots are two angles of the same jump; one wide (**V1**) and the other medium-wide (**V2**). The point where he lands in each shot is indicated by the marker labeled **Sync point**. You will make the **MS** clip on the top track smaller and tucked into a corner of the wide shot so viewers can see both angles at once.

8 Be sure snapping is turned on (press **N**), then select the bottom clip and position the **playhead** exactly on top of the first marker. (A fast way to do this is to press **Shift+M**, to move *right* to the next marker or **Option+M**, to move *left* to the next marker, depending upon the position of the **playhead**.)

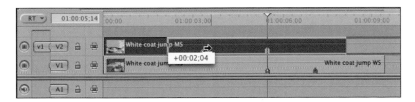

9 Drag the top clip so that its first marker aligns with the **playhead** and the first marker of the **WS** clip. (The clip should move **2:04** down the **Timeline**, according to the tooltip.)

10 Select the top clip and slide the **Timeline playhead** down until the boarder crosses the same track you marked in the **WS** clip. (The timecode of this spot is **01:00:07:17**.) Be sure the top clip is selected and set a marker at the **playhead**.

Hmm…the two sets of markers don't line up. This is not good. In this case, I happen to know that the folks at Standard Films (who shot this sequence) filmed the top clip in slow motion. So, you need to slow down the bottom clip to match it.

11 Select the bottom clip (**WS**). Choose **Modify > Speed** and set the **Speed** to **75** percent. This slows down the bottom clip to 75 percent of its normal speed.

(By the way, if you want to reverse a clip, you use this same menu to do so. Simply click the **Reverse** check box, and your clip plays backwards, from **Out** to **In**.)

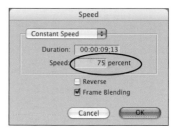

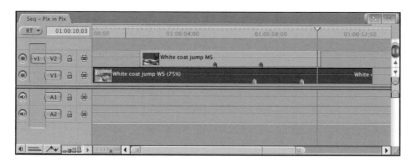

Oh, my goodness. Things just got worse! Now the bottom clip is much longer, and none of the markers match.

This is normal. When you apply a constant speed change to a clip, it will always change duration based on the speed change. Clips that are slowed down get longer. Clips that are sped up get shorter. As well, the audio changes with the video. Slower video means deeper-pitched audio. Faster video means higher-pitched audio. (As you will see in Exercise 6, these rules are different when you make a variable speed change to a clip.)

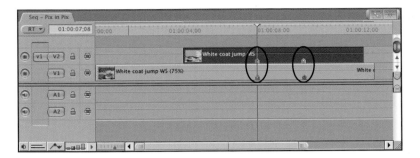

12 Turn on snapping to help align the clips. Select the bottom clip and press **Option+M** to move the **playhead** to the first marker. Next, drag the top clip so the first two markers align, and you will see that the second markers now align as well. (If you are having problems getting your clips to align, double-click **Seq – Pix in Pix (sync)** and use it instead.)

You have now matched the speed of both clips and aligned them so they are running in sync; that is, they are both showing the same portion of the jump at the same time. You are ready to create the picture-in-picture effect.

---

13 Double-click the **V2** clip to load it into the **Viewer**. Click the **Motion** tab to display the **Motion** menu. You'll be working a lot with this menu during this chapter, but for now, concentrate on the top portion, labeled **Basic Motion**.

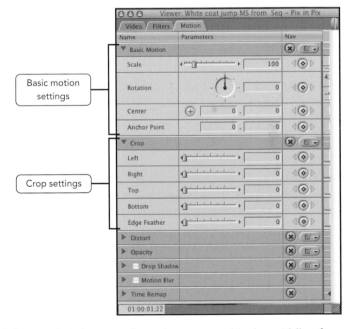

There are four Basic Motions:

- **Scale**, which controls the size of the image

- **Rotation**, which controls the rotation of the image

- **Center**, which controls the position of the image

- **Anchor Point**, which controls the point around which the image rotates

The default settings are 100 percent size (full-screen), 0 degrees of rotation, centered in the middle of the screen, and rotating around the center of the image. Final Cut defines the Center coordinates of the center of the image as 0,0.

You need to change two View settings in the Canvas in order to finish this effect. In the past, you've used the Canvas principally to review the results of changes you've made in the Viewer or Timeline. Now, you are going to use the Canvas to actually create some of your motion effects.

14 From the **View** menu at the top of the **Canvas**, choose **Show Title Safe**. (You learned about Action Safe and Title Safe in Chapter 10, *"Text, Titles, and Graphics."*)

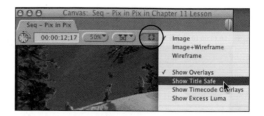

15 Go back to the same menu, and choose **Image+Wireframe**.

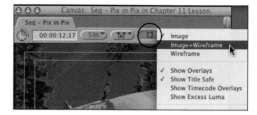

NOTE:

Image, Image+Wireframe, and Wireframe Modes

The View pop-up menu in the Canvas and Viewer is a shortcut for the View menu in the main menu bar, duplicating many of the menu bar choices in a more convenient location.

You learned about Title Safe and Action Safe in Chapter 10, *"Text, Titles, and Graphics,"* but I want to explain the Image, Image+Wireframe, and Wireframe settings now.

When the Canvas is in **Image** mode, it simply displays whatever frame is under the playhead in the Timeline. When you are editing, this is the normal mode for the Canvas.

When you want to create motion effects, switching to **Image+Wireframe** allows you to manipulate the image in the Canvas as an object. As you will learn in Exercise 2, you can resize, move, rotate, crop, and distort images, all in the Canvas, without having to use the Motion tab in the Viewer at all. When I am doing compositing, which means combining two or more images to form a single, new image, I almost always use Image+Wireframe mode.

When I have a particularly complex effect that takes a long time to render, switching to **Wireframe** shows just the outline of an image, without filling in the image itself. This is a very fast way to watch how the shapes of images move during an effect, without needing to render first. In this exercise, switching to Wireframe mode won't help a lot, because, while the snowboarders are moving, the images that show the snowboarders are stationary. In Exercise 4, as you animate the movement of your clips, you'll get a better understanding of how helpful the Wireframe mode can be.

You can easily toggle between these three settings by selecting either the **Canvas** or the **Viewer**, then pressing **W**.

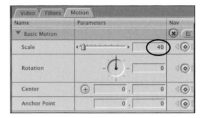

16 Click the **Motion** tab and change the size by typing **40** into the **Scale** field, then pressing **Return**.

The size of the **MS** clip is immediately reduced in size and centered in the screen.

17 Using the **Selection** tool, grab near, but *not* at, the center of the smaller image and drag it up and to the right until the edges of the image align with the upper-right **Action Safe** corner.

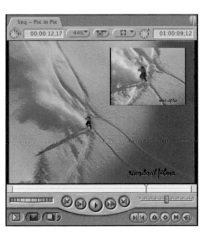

18 Deselect all clips on the **Timeline** and play the sequence. Most motion effects are real time, so you shouldn't need to render this effect to see it.

Congratulations! Your very first motion effect.

19 Except…those black borders on the side of the small image are driving me nuts. So, double-click the top clip to load it into the **Viewer** and twirl down **Crop**.

Crop allows you to trim your image from the top, bottom, left, and right edges so that you can hide elements of your image. In this case, you want to eliminate the black borders.

20 In the **Crop** menu, drag the **Left** slider in a little until the left black border disappears. (A value of **3** should do it.) Then, drag the **Right** slider until the right black border disappears. (Again, a value of **3** should be fine, as well.)

Much better.

Except, well, now without that black border, the two images seem to blend into each other too much. You need to separate them.

21 Look further down in the **Motion** menu and check **Drop Shadow**.

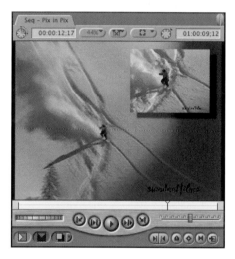

22 Ta-DA! Much better. Drop shadows always require rendering, so either render the sequence, or use my favorite keyboard shortcut—**Option+P**—to play the sequence without rendering.

Option+P plays an unrendered effect—slightly slower than real time, but without waiting for it to render first. I use **Option+P** constantly when I am building effects. I still need to render for output, or to see things in real-time, but using **Option+P** for testing my effects is a HUGE time-saver.

23 That's it for this exercise. Watch your sequence a couple more times to admire your handiwork, then save your project (**Cmd+S**). Quit Final Cut if you wish, but in the next exercise, you'll be using this project again.

Working with Wireframe Mode in the Canvas

In this exercise, you'll learn how to alter the shape of an image using the Wireframe mode in the Canvas, plus discover a few little-known tips to make shape-shifting easier.

---

1 Open **Chapter 11 Lesson**, if it isn't already open. Double-click **Seq – Wireframe** to load it into the **Timeline**.

(You can use these techniques anywhere in the clip. However, if you want your screens to match mine, put your **playhead** on the marker contained in this sequence.)

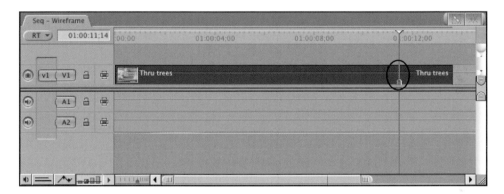

2 Select the **Thru trees** clip. In order for these techniques to work, you must have the clip selected, and you must be working in the **Canvas**.

The normal setting for the **Canvas** is to display all images as **Fit to Window**. This is the best way to display images while editing. However, when you are working on motion effects, you need to create some space around the edges of the image.

---

3 In this case, choose **25%** from the **Scaling** pop-up menu (upper-left menu in both the **Canvas** and **Viewer** windows).

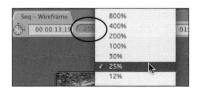

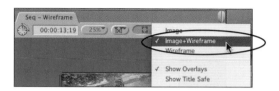

The gray area around the picture is *outside* the image area, but it provides room for you to manipulate the image size and position. It's like a visual pasteboard—an area where you can position clips that you want to have enter or exit a frame. You'll work with this more in Exercise 3.

4 To allow you to directly manipulate the size and position of the image, choose **Image+Wireframe** from the **View** pop-up menu.

With the clip selected on the **Timeline**, there is now a cyan border, with two diagonal white lines, around the image. And, if you look carefully at where the two diagonal lines cross, the number indicates the video track in which the clip is located.

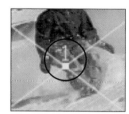

5 Press **A** to select the **Selection** tool, then click one of the corners. (In this case, I used the top-right, but any corner will do.) While holding down the mouse, drag the corner and scale (resize) the image larger and smaller.

Scaling Shortcuts

Shortcut	What It Does
Shift+drag corner with Selection tool	Scales asymmetrically
Cmd+drag corner with Selection tool	Scales and rotates at same time

6 Press **Cmd+Z** to undo that size change. With both the **Selection** tool and the clip still selected, click *near* a corner and drag to rotate the image. (See how the shape of the cursor changes to a rotating, um, thingy?)

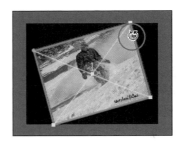

Rotation Shortcuts

Shortcut	What It Does
Shift+drag *near* corner with Selection tool	Constrains movement to 45-degree angles
Cmd+drag corner with Selection tool	Scales and rotates at same time

7 Press **Cmd+Z** to undo that rotation change. With both the **Selection** tool and the clip still selected, click *near*, but not *at*, the center of the image and drag to reposition the image on the screen.

In the case of this screen shot, I first made the image smaller, then dragged it up to the upper-right corner. This is another way to achieve the same effect you created using the Motion tab in Exercise 1.

Positioning Shortcut

Shortcut	What It Does
Shift+drag position	Constrains movement to horizontal or vertical only

8 You don't need to keep undoing each of these moves, but I've found starting each move fresh helps make them easier to understand. So, press **Cmd+Z** and undo your positional changes. Remember, with Final Cut, you have multiple levels of undo, depending on how you set your **User Preferences** in Chapter 1, *"Get Organized."*

There are two tools in the Tool palette that can help modify the shape of an image: **Crop** and **Distort**.

9 Press **C** to select the **Crop** tool, then click a corner and drag to crop two sides of an image.

Crop Tool Shortcuts

Shortcut	What It Does
Click+drag corner	Crops adjoining sides simultaneously
Click+drag edge	Crops one side
Shift+click+drag corner	Crops image and retains 4:3 aspect ratio
Cmd+drag edge	Crops opposite sides symmetrically
Cmd+drag corner	Crops all sides symmetrically

10 Undo, as usual, then press **D** to select the **Distort** tool. (I don't use this tool very often, but it creates a way cool effect when I do.)

The Distort tool allows you to put a forced perspective into your video, as though it was projecting on the side of a building, viewed from the side.

Using this tool, you can precisely control where each corner of your video is located, in a process called *corner pinning*. Or just alter the overall shape of your clip. It is easier to see than to explain.

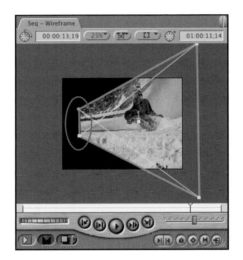

11 Be sure the video clip is selected, then, in the **Canvas**, grab the lower-left corner with the **Distort** tool and drag. See how the corner moves, distorting the rest of your clip? Undo that, then hold the **Shift** key and drag a corner again. See how the whole clip develops a forced perspective?

Distort Tool Shortcut

Shortcut	What It Does
Shift+drag corner	Distorts all four corners symmetrically to create perspective

One last thing. Sometimes, an effect just isn't working and you want to reset everything back to the beginning. Here's a fast way to do it:

12 Double-click the clip to load it into the **Viewer**. Choose the **Motion** tab. Then, click the small, red, circled **X** for the parameter you want to reset. To reset all effects, click each of the seven circled **Xs** in the **Motion** tab.

The red **X** is the **Reset** button. You will find it in all filters, motion effects, transitions, and audio waveforms in the Viewer, and wherever other fine visual effects are sold.

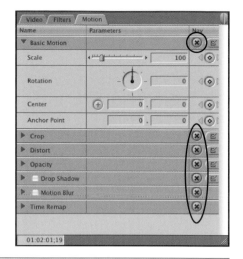

13 That's it for this exercise. In most exercises, I use numbers in the **Motion** tab so it's easier for your work to match mine. However, many times in real life, clicking and dragging a wireframe is faster and works just as well. And now you know how to do it.

You're done with this exercise. Don't save your work. Quit Final Cut if you need to take a break. Otherwise, in the next exercise, you are going to make images fly.

NOTE:

Fit to Window Menu

As you noticed, the Fit to Window menu allows you to zoom in or out on an image. You can also zoom using the Zoom tool (press **Z**). Keep in mind, however, that if you zoom in on an image, Final Cut will no longer display it in your external NTSC monitor.

So, if your external (meaning not your computer) monitor suddenly goes black, it's probably because you are zoomed in too far on an image in either the Canvas or Viewer.

To fix this, and get your image back, use one of these three steps:

- Choose **Fit to Window** from the pop-up menu.

- Click once in the zoomed-in window to select it and press **Shift+Z**.

- **Option+click** in the zoomed-in window with the **Zoom** tool to zoom back out.

A quick indicator that you are zoomed too far into a window is when you see scroll bars. If you see scroll bars, video to your external monitor will be turned off.

3 | Moving Images with Keyframes

In this exercise, you will learn how to move images around the frame using keyframes, and you'll learn how to create favorite motions. These techniques are used a lot in commercial work.

In this example, you are creating part of an opening title sequence where, during a long downhill run, a variety of images slide into and out of the frame. You can see the finished effect by playing **Seq – Keyframe finished**. (You may need to render this before it plays.)

---

1 Open **Chapter 11 Lesson**, if it isn't open already. Double-click **Seq – Keyframe start** to load it into the **Timeline**.

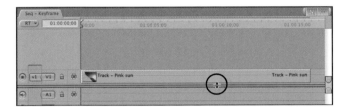

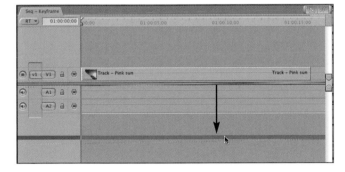

2 Because there will be a number of images onscreen at once, give yourself some room to work by dragging down the horizontal double bar in the middle of the **Timeline**.

---

3 Choose **Sequence > Insert Tracks** and add **4** new video tracks. Then, in the **Canvas**, turn on **Image+Wireframe** and **Show Title Safe** to help you align the images. (If you've forgotten how to turn these on, refer back to the previous exercise.)

4 Start by opening the **Clips – Exercise 3** bin and loading **MCU to camera** into the **Viewer**. (Notice that I've already added the **In** and **Out**, as well as two markers, and set the duration to **5:00**.)

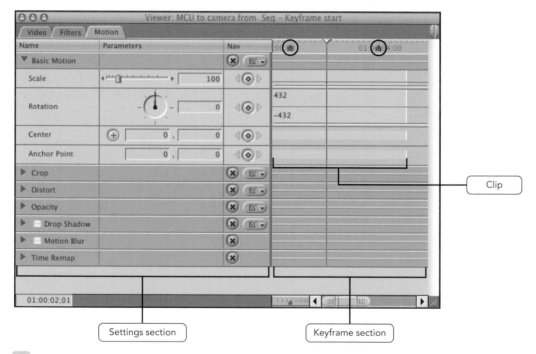

Settings section

Keyframe section

Clip

5 Position your **playhead** at the beginning of the **Timeline** and edit the **MCU to camera** clip to **V2** in the **Timeline** (remember to use the patch panel). Then double-click the clip on **V2** to load it back into the **Viewer**. Click the **Motion** tab to select it and drag the **Viewer** wider so you can see the keyframe section on the right.

The light-gray area in the keyframe section indicates the duration of the clip you are editing. Markers are pink and displayed at the top of the Motion tab.

A Keyframe Review

Keyframes are essential to creating motion effects. Although they were introduced earlier in the book, here's a quick summary of what you need to know about keyframes, all in one place:

Definition: A keyframe is a specific setting of a specific parameter at a specific point in time, and you always use keyframes in pairs.

Description: A keyframe is required whenever you want to make something move or change over time. They are very granular. In other words, a keyframe for one parameter (such as position) has no effect on a keyframe for a different parameter (such as color desaturation). In order for multiple things to happen at once, you need to add multiple keyframes. The minimum number of keyframes you need is two: one for the starting position and one for the ending position.

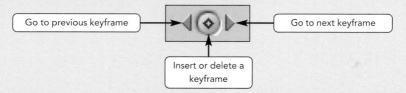

To create a keyframe: Option+click with the Selection tool where a keyframe does not exist, click the Insert/Delete Keyframe button, click with the Pen tool, or press Ctrl+K.

To go to a keyframe: Click the little left and right arrows on each side of the **Keyframe** button, press **Shift+K** (next keyframe), or press **Option+K** (previous keyframe).

To move a keyframe: Grab it with the mouse and drag it.

To delete a keyframe: Drag it straight down with the mouse, **option+click** the keyframe with the **Selection** tool, click with the **Pen (minus)** tool, **Option+click** with the **Pen (plus)** tool, or place the **playhead** on the keyframe and click the **Keyframe** button.

To delete all keyframes: Click the red **X** reset button.

---

6 First, change the **Scale** to **10**, and press **Return**. The image on **V2** shrinks in size.

---

7 To change the position of the **V2** image, press the **Home** key to go to the beginning of the clip in the **Viewer**. Set a keyframe at the beginning of the clip by clicking the **Keyframe** button for **Center**.

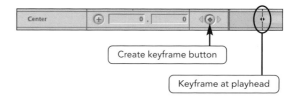

8 Move the clip so that the lower-right corner of the clip is positioned on top of the lower-right corner of **Action Safe**. (If you can't move the clip, be sure **Image+Wireframe** is selected in the **Canvas** pop-up menu.)

9 As you move the clip, watch the coordinates change in the two **Center** boxes. You have positioned the clip correctly when the left box (showing the horizontal position) reads **180** and the right box (showing the vertical position) reads **120**.

Because you want everyone at home to see your animation, you must make sure to keep everything contained inside **Action Safe**. If this were a sponsor's logo or phone number, you should keep it inside **Title Safe**.

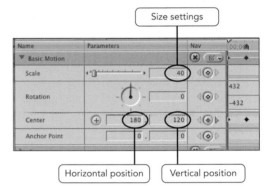

10 Because you were parked on a position keyframe when you moved the clip, the keyframe is automatically updated with the revised position of the clip. Next, move **20** frames ahead, either by dragging the **playhead** or typing **+20**, and press **Return**. (You should be lined up with the marker.) Set a second keyframe for **Center**.

11 Move to the end of the clip (press **Shift+O**), or drag the **playhead**. Personally, I like using **Shift+O** because that way I know I am on the last frame of the clip. Many times, the **Viewer** is so small, it's hard to tell precisely where the **playhead** is positioned. (Notice that the **playhead** is just inside the lighter-gray area, which indicates the duration of the clip.)

Set another center keyframe. (This is the third.)

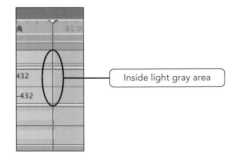

12 Move back from the end of the clip **30** frames. (Yup, you guessed it, type **−30** and press **Return**.) Set another center keyframe.

Your two interior keyframes should line up with the markers.

OK, you've sized and moved the clip into its final position onscreen and set four keyframes that will move it into and out of position. Now, you need to set the first and last keyframe so the clip will slide *into* frame at the beginning, and slide *out* of frame at the end.

NOTE:

Is All This Precision Really Necessary?

The difference between a good effect and one that makes you cringe is in the details. If all I wanted to do was move one clip around the screen, I wouldn't be this precise.

However, in this case, you are creating a master movement that will be copied to multiple clips that will chase each other across the screen. The only way this effect will be believable is to concentrate on getting the details right as you build the effect. In other words, yes, precisely aligning clips and setting keyframes exactly is pretty much standard.

Oh, and a little planning wouldn't hurt, either.

13 Zoom the **Canvas** back so the image size is **25%**. Use the **Scaling** pop-up menu. (A large computer monitor may allow you to work at **50%**. The results are the same.)

14 Position the **playhead** at the beginning of the clip. Hold down the **Shift** key and, with the **Selection** tool selected, drag the clip to the right until the left edge of the clip touches the right side of the main image. In other words, you dragged it offscreen right (**Center** coordinates: **510, 120**). You can type these directly in the **Center** fields, if you need to correct your coordinates.

Holding down the **Shift** key makes sure the clip doesn't move vertically when you are dragging it.

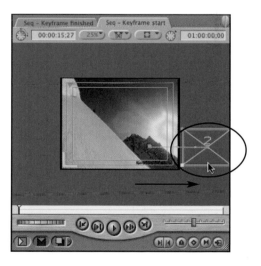

15 Move the **playhead** so it is parked on the last keyframe. Hold down the **Shift** key and drag the clip to the left until it is offscreen left (**Center** coordinates: **–510, 120**).

16 Since motion effects are real time, select the **Timeline** and position the **playhead** to the start of the sequence and play it.

Cool! The snowboard skids onto the screen in 20 frames, glides for about 3 seconds, then dashes off in 30 frames—all while the background boarder is kicking up some huge fantails.

Now what you need to do is duplicate all that effort into four more clips. The good news is that Final Cut makes that process easy.

17 Select the **V2** clip on the **Timeline** and position the **playhead** over the last marker (press **Option+M**).

18 Double-click **Track – Jump** to load it into the **Viewer**. Adjust the patch panel so **v1** (source) connects to **V3** (destination). Do an **Overwrite** edit (**F10**) to edit the **Track – Jump** clip to the **Timeline**.

You stacked the two clips because, for a brief period, you have three images on the screen at the same time (including the clip on **V1**). You

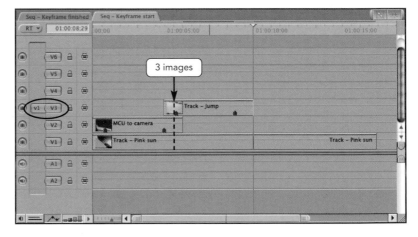

shifted the **V3** clip downstream because, although it uses the same movement as the **V2** clip, that movement does not occur at the same time, but slightly later, than the clip on **V2**.

These two concepts, stacking and staggering, are used all the time in creating motion effects. The markers help to position the clips, and they help me remember what it is that I am doing.

19 On the **Timeline**, select **MCU to camera**, and choose **Edit > Copy** (or press **Cmd+C**). Select **Track – Jump** and choose **Edit > Paste Attributes** (or press **Option+V**).

Uncheck **Scale Attribute Times**, check **Basic Motion**, and click **OK**.

20 Play the sequence. Watch how all the position attributes of the first clip were copied into the second. This is looking better; the second clip almost pushes the first clip offscreen.

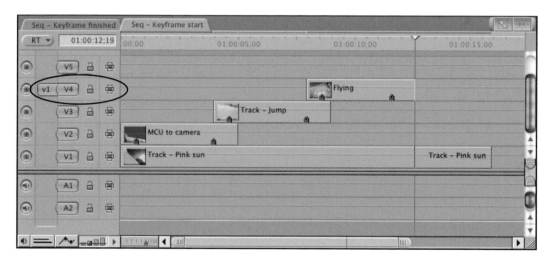

21 Double-click **Flying** to load it into the **Viewer**. Adjust the patch panel so **v1** (source) connects to **V4** (destination). Position the **playhead** to the last marker of the **V3** clip and do an **Overwrite** edit (**F10**) to put the **Flying** clip on the **Timeline**.

22 This time, double-click **MCU to camera** and click the **Motion** tab to make it active. Choose **Effects > Make Favorite Motion**.

The motion path you created for **MCU to camera** is saved to the **Effects > Favorites** folder of the **Browser**, available to you whenever you need it. Like, um, now.

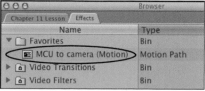

23 Select the **V4** clip (**Flying**) and choose **Effects > Motion Favorites > MCU to camera (Motion)**.

24 Play your sequence and watch how one clip chases the other off the screen.

NOTE:

Paste Attributes vs. Favorite Motion

You've used two different ways to copy a motion from one clip to another: Paste Attributes and applying a Favorite Motion. Is there a difference? Yes, and they are significant.

Paste Attributes allows you to select which attributes you want to paste from the dialog. **Favorite Motion** pastes all motion attributes regardless.

More significant is the **Scale Attribute Times** option within Paste Attributes. Double-click **Flying** to load it into the **Viewer** and choose the **Motion** tab. Using the **Zoom** tool, zoom in on the second marker. See how the second set of keyframes doesn't line up precisely with the marker? They are early by two frames.

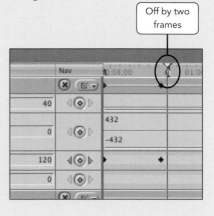

Off by two frames

This is because the **Flying** clip runs **4:21**, and all the other clips run **5:00**. Favorite Motion scales keyframe timing to match the length of the clip. In this case, it shortened the second set of keyframes by two frames and lengthened the third set of keyframes by a frame. Unless all your clips are the same length, using Favorite Motion isn't precise.

Favorite Motion *always* scales keyframe timing. Paste Attributes gives you the *option* of scaling keyframe timing.

Finally, Favorite Motions are stored as part of your preferences. When you trash your Final Cut preferences (and I said "when," not "if"), all your Favorite Motions will be lost.

For all these reasons, I use Paste Attributes almost exclusively.

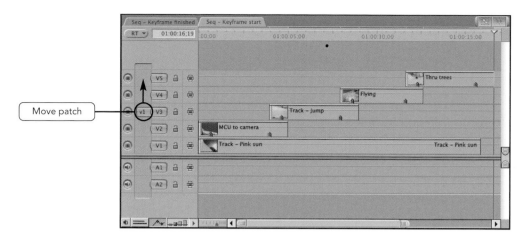

25 You have one last clip to add. Double-click **Thru trees** to load it into the **Viewer**. Adjust the patch panel so **V1** (source) connects to **V5** (destination). Position the **playhead** to the last marker of the **V4** clip and do an **Overwrite** edit (**F10**) to put the **Thru trees** clip on the **Timeline**.

---

26 Again, select **MCU to camera**, copy it to the clipboard, select the **V5** clip, and choose **Edit > Paste Attributes** (or press **Option+V**). Uncheck **Scale Attribute Times**.

---

27 Play your sequence. You just need to trim up the end of the last shot, and the sequence is done.

28 Put the **playhead** at the end of the **V1** clip (press the **up** arrow). Select the ending edit point of **V5**, and press **E**. The edit point jumps to the position of the **playhead**.

(See? I told you in Chapter 6, *"Trim Your Story,"* there was a reason for learning this shortcut. I use it constantly when working with effects.)

---

29 Double-click the **V5** clip to load it into the **Viewer** and remove the last two keyframes so the image doesn't start to move at the end of the sequence, and you are done.

30 Play your sequence and compare it to **Seq – Keyframe finished**.

What do you mean, they don't match? Oh. Well, yeah, they don't. I adjusted the timing of the keyframes in **Flying** to match the other clips, cropped the left and right edges of each of the moving images, then added a drop shadow. But you learned how to do that in Exercise 1. Add them again here, and the two sequences match.

31 Whew! Finished. That was a lot to cover. Save your work because you are going to use this project in the next lesson. Quit Final Cut if you need to take a break.

Cool Way to Fade to Black

The sequence you just finished is designed to cut to another shot, which is why everything ends so abruptly.

However, let's say you wanted to fade everything to black at the end. How would you do it?

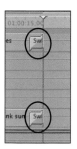

Well, you could simply select the ending edit points for the clips on **V1** and **V5** and add a cross fade to black for each of them. But, what if you had lots more tracks? Is there an easier way? Well, depending upon how you define easier, the answer is *Yes*.

This process works best if you have lots of tracks, say more than four, that all need to fade at the same time.

---

1 In the **Viewer**, choose **Slug** from the **Generator** pop-up menu in the lower-right corner of the **Viewer**. ("Slug" is an old-fashioned word from the molten-lead printing days of the early 1900s that means "blank space." In Final Cut Pro 5, it means "audio and video black.")

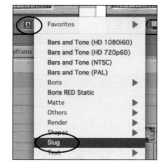

---

2 Change the duration of the slug to **20** frames, or whatever length you want for your fade to black.

---

3 Click the **a1** and **a2** sources on the patch panel to disconnect them.

Note gap

---

4 Edit the slug to the **Timeline** so that it ends at the *end* of your sequence.

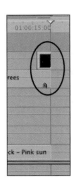

5 Turn on **clip overlays**.

6 **Option+click** with the **Selection** tool to set keyframes at the beginning and end of the slug.

7 Drag the first keyframe all the way down, to make the slug transparent. The thin black line controls *clip opacity*. When the line is at the top, the clip is opaque. When the line is at the bottom, the clip is fully transparent. When the line is in the middle, the clip is varying amounts of translucent. You can use opacity keyframes to vary the translucency of any video clip.

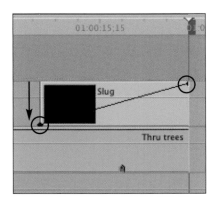

8 Play the sequence. Instant fade to black. (Well, mostly instant.)

Again, if you have only one or two clips to fade, this second way is slower. If you have lots of clips to fade, this second way is much faster and much more flexible, because all you need to do to change the duration, or location, of a fade is change the length, or position, of the slug.

NEW▶ New Render Options

New with this version of Final Cut is significantly improved rendering, which means higher-quality image scaling, rotation, and movement when using the Motion tab.

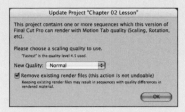

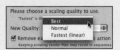

The first indication of this new feature occurs when you open a project created in an earlier version of Final Cut and this dialog appears.

If you do nothing and just accept **Normal**, you are *already* working at a higher render quality than all earlier versions of FCP. These settings *only* affect motion rendering. They have no effect on the quality of any clips that are not rendered. However, they really make a difference. Here's what these quality levels mean:

- **Fastest:** This renders the fastest, but the image quality is relatively low. This was the only render option for FCP HD.

- **Normal:** This is the default setting for FCP 5. It provides a nice balance between rendering speed and image quality. It's a good place to start.

- **Best:** This is the highest-quality setting. Apple says, "this performs very high-quality motion transformations on your clips." It's their suggested quality for final output.

Can I tell a difference? Oh, my goodness, yes!! However, you pay a price—higher-quality rendering takes longer. In my purely unscientific test, if a **Fastest** render takes 10 seconds, **Normal** takes 35 seconds, and **Best** takes 46. Keep in mind that file sizes remain the same, regardless of quality.

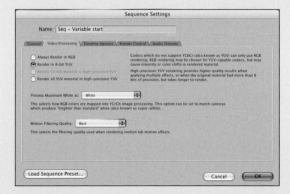

To change the render settings in an existing sequence, load it to the **Timeline**, choose **Sequence > Settings (Cmd+0)** and click the **Video Processing** tab. Make your selections in the bottom pop-up menu, then re-render (**Option+R**) your sequence.

4 | Moving Text with Keyframes

In this exercise, you will build on the movement skills you just learned and animate a simple text title to fly in as the images are moving along the bottom. Additionally, you will learn how to create a curved motion path for the text movement.

---

1 Open **Chapter 11 Lesson**, if it isn't open already. Double-click **Seq – Text start** to load it into the **Timeline**.

This sequence is identical to the one you just finished, except I deleted the last shot on **V5**, created a text clip on **V6**, and added some keyframes to the text clip—all using techniques you learned earlier in this chapter.

---

2 Double-click the text clip to load it into the **Viewer**. Click the **Motion** tab and widen it so you can see the keyframe section. Slide the **Zoom** control to the left to zoom in a little on the keyframe section so that you can easily see the keyframes that are already set.

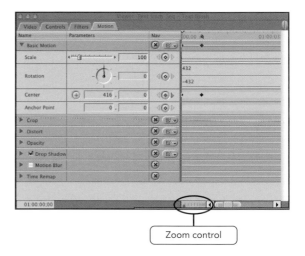

Zoom control

---

3 Switch the Canvas to **25%** view (use the **Scaling** pop-up menu) and widen it to give you room to move the text clip around.

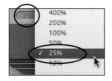

---

4 With the text clip selected and the **playhead** at the start of the clip, hold down the **Shift** key (to constrain movement to only horizontal or vertical) and drag the clip to the right until the text disappears off the screen.

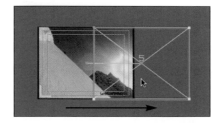

5 Put the **playhead** on the first marker of the text clip. Since the sequence needs rendering, rather than wait for rendering when you are only previewing the initial part of the effect, choose **Tools > QuickView**. This opens a window (the same size as the **Viewer**) that allows you to preview effects without rendering.

Use the default **Range** setting of **2** seconds and play your effect in the **QuickView** window.

NOTE:

The QuickView Window

The QuickView window first temporarily builds your effect into memory (RAM). This means that the first time you play an effect in QuickView it will be slow, because Final Cut needs to calculate the effect and store it. QuickView always plays your effect as a loop, so starting with the second time through, since the effect is stored in memory, QuickView plays the effect in real time.

The QuickView window works a bit differently from other windows in that it always starts in the middle.

See the Range slider at the bottom of the QuickView window? This slider allows you to select how long a clip you want to preview. The default is 2 seconds. The maximum is 10 seconds.

Say you have a 4-second duration selected on the Range slider. The QuickView window starts at the location of the playhead and plays for 2 seconds (half the time indicated on the Range slider). Then, it backs up to 2 seconds *before* the location of the playhead and plays for the full 4 seconds.

The great thing about the QuickView window is that you can see your effects in real time. But, because it always centers on the playhead location, I find it awkward to use, which is why I like **Option+P** more, because it *starts* at the playhead, rather than *centers* on the playhead.

For me, it's a matter of convenience. They both work great. Pick your favorite.

6 Now you need to set keyframe positions for the text to exit. Position the **playhead** on the last keyframe and drag the text clip down and left until it exits screen left (**Center** coordinates: **–628, 215**). Play the ending of the sequence.

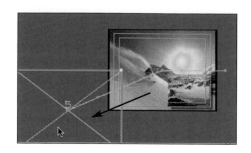

Hmmm…it's OK, but not great. The text makes too straight a line, and it travels right over the body of the snowboarder in the video clip. What you need to do is get the text to curve, so that it misses the snowboarder.

Notice how Final Cut displays keyframes in the **Canvas** as green dots? Knowing this is helpful in finding keyframes.

Position keyframe

7 **Ctrl+click** the last (far left) keyframe and choose **Linear** from the shortcut menu. (It makes no difference if the **playhead** is on the frame or not. The important point is to click the correct green keyframe.)

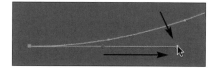

Two new blue dots now appear along the motion path (they are often hard to see). The one nearest the green keyframe controls acceleration; the other one controls the shape of the motion path using Bezier controls. I call it the **Bezier controller**.

The Bezier controller is always the outside dot, and the acceleration controller is always the inside dot.

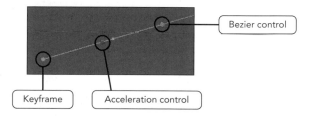

Bezier control

Keyframe

Acceleration control

8 Grab the furthest keyframe, the **Bezier** controller, and drag it down and to the right. See how the motion path converts from a straight line to a curve?

9 Next, move the **playhead** to the third keyframe. Your text image moves back to the center of the frame. (Positioning the **playhead** makes sure you are changing the correct keyframe, since there are two keyframes at this position.) **Ctrl+click** the keyframe and choose **Linear** from the shortcut menu.

10 Drag the **Bezier** controller down and to the right so you form a smooth curve for the motion path. Hmmm…that's really hard to see.

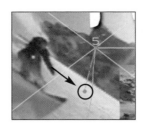

11 Sometimes, its easier to adjust an image when you can't see it. Click the **View** pop-up menu and choose **Wireframe**.

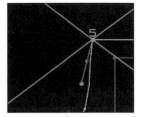

This hides the image, but displays the wireframe.
A wireframe shows the shape and position of an image without showing the image itself. Wireframes never require rendering, so previews are always in real time.

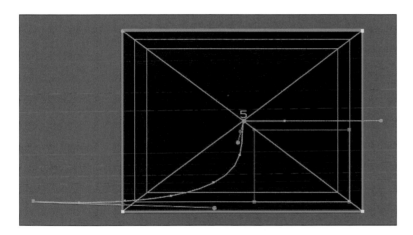

Setting Bezier curves is an art, because you can't type in specific keyframe numbers. When the motion looks right to you, you are done. Here's the motion path I created for this sequence. You can view it in **Seq – Text finished**.

12 There's a lot you can do with Bezier curves and motion paths, so feel free to experiment. At least now, you know where to click and what to do. Save your work. Quit Final Cut if you need a break.

In the next three exercises, you will learn several quick techniques that also relate to motion.

5 | Creating a Still Frame from a Clip

In this short exercise, you will learn how to create a still frame and add it to the end of a clip to freeze movement. You will also learn the best way to export a still frame.

---

1 Open **Chapter 11 Lesson**, if it isn't open already. Double-click **Seq – Still frame start** to load it into the **Timeline**.

---

2 Position the **playhead** on the marker and choose **Modify > Make Freeze Frame** (which I never use) or press **Shift+N** (which I always use).

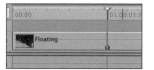

Final Cut creates a still frame (or freeze-frame, if you prefer) at the position of the **playhead** and loads it into the **Viewer**.

---

3 The still frame appears in the **Viewer** with a default duration of **10:00**, which you can change by choosing **Final Cut Pro 5 > User Preferences** and clicking the **Editing** tab.

---

4 Change the duration of the still frame in the **Viewer** to **3:00** for this example.

---

5 Without changing the position of the **playhead**, edit the still frame back to the **Timeline**—press **F10**, or click the red **Overwrite** button.

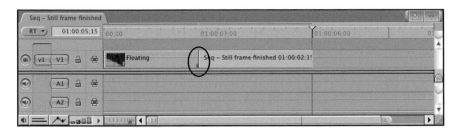

6 The still frame is edited back to the sequence at the position of the **playhead** using an **Overwrite** edit, so that the video flows smoothly up to the point of the freeze-frame, then freezes. The middle of the **Floating** clip was covered (deleted) by the **Overwrite** edit. If there is any of the **Floating** clip left over at the end, delete it.

Done.

---

7 If you want to export this still frame from Final Cut to edit in another program, here's how to do so: Load the still frame into the **Viewer** and make sure the **Viewer** is selected.

---

8 Choose **File > Export > QuickTime Conversion**.

---

9 In the **Export** dialog, give your still frame a file name, then change the **Format** pop-up to **Still Image**.

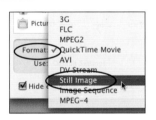

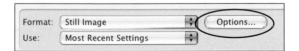

10 Although PNG is a good image format, and the default, I am old-school enough to prefer TIFF images. So, click the **Options** button and change the format from **PNG** to **TIFF**.

---

11 That's it. You can compare your still frame with mine in **Seq – Still frame finished**. Save your work, if you feel so inclined. Quit if you want to; otherwise, there are two more techniques to go.

In this exercise, you will learn how to create variable speed changes in a clip.

In Final Cut, there are several ways to create variable speed clips, including the **Time Remap** tool. I find all of them very confusing, complex, and difficult to teach. I learned this procedure from Ken Stone a while ago and found it clean, simple, and easy to understand—which is the reason I'm teaching it to you now.

---

1 Open **Chapter 11 Lesson**, if it isn't open already. Double-click **Seq – Variable start** to load it into the **Timeline**.

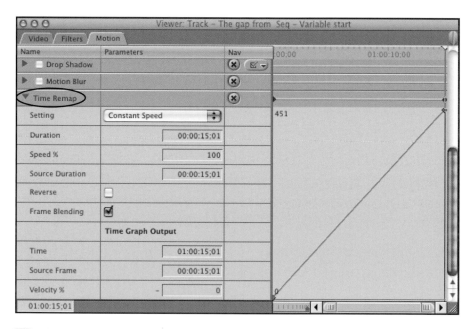

2 Double-click **Track – The gap** to load it into the **Viewer**. Click the **Motion** tab to make it active. Expand the width of the **Viewer** so you can see the keyframe section. Twirl down **Time Remap** so you can see the green diagonal line from beginning to end.

This green line represents the speed of your clip, with the two keyframes at the beginning and end representing the **In** and the **Out** of the clip.

The Angle of the Time Remap Line

When it comes to changing the speed of a clip, the precise angle of the green line is not important. What is important is that the green line *has* an angle.

You change the speed of your clip by setting keyframes and changing the angle of this green line.

Angle Table

Angle	What It Does
Equal to original line	Clip runs at normal speed.
Less than original line	Clip runs slower than normal speed.
Greater than original line	Clip runs faster than normal speed.
Flat line	Clip freezes.
Diagonal down-right	Clip runs in reverse, faster as the angle steepens.

A few other notes:

- A constant speed change *always* changes the duration of a clip; a variable speed change does not.

- A constant speed change *always* changes the audio; a variable speed change does not.

- And, finally, when you make a constant speed change to a clip, only those frames between the In and the Out are affected. When you make a variable speed change to a clip, all frames before or after the In can be affected.

3 Using the **Selection** tool, **Option+click** where you want your speed changes to occur. In this example, place four keyframes, equally spaced along the line.

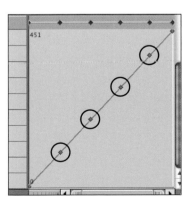

Again, this is art, not science, even Apple says this feature is a bit "quirky," so a little trial and error is necessary to find the best place to put keyframes. In this exercise, where you put your keyframes is not important, just try different places and watch what happens.

4 Now, to position your keyframes:

Drag the third keyframe down, slightly, so the angle of the line decreases.

Drag the fourth keyframe down, so that the line is flat compared to the third keyframe.

Drag the fifth keyframe down, so the line moves diagonally down and to the right.

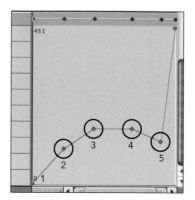

5 Variable speed changes are played back in real time, on most systems, so play your sequence and watch what happens as the angle of the line changes.

The first segment plays normally, the second slows down, the third stops, the fourth plays in reverse, and the final segment runs many times faster than full speed.

6 Adjust the angles and move the keyframes and watch the results. Then, set an **In** and **Out** and see what effect that has on where your clip starts and ends.

Right. The **In** had no effect. A variable speed change to a clip starts at the **In** and ignores the **Out** in order to give you the speed changes you request.

For instance, if you froze the first frame of a clip, the entire clip would consist of just the **In**.

If you ran the clip in reverse, the clip would start at the **In** and play backwards.

If you ran the clip forward at high speed, the clip would start at the **In** and play all the frames it needed, including those *after* the **Out**, in order to fulfill the duration of the clip.

7 That ends this exercise. Save your work, if you wish. Quit Final Cut, if you need to take a break. There's one more exercise still to come: making moves on still images.

7 | Moving a Still Image

Ken Burns, in his PBS series "The Civil War," popularized a technique of moving still images around in the frame to heighten visual interest. In fact, iMovie created the "Ken Burns Effect" so beginning editors could do the same thing. Although Final Cut doesn't have a prebuilt filter for this kind of movement, you can create the same effect with much more precision using keyframes and Bezier curves. This exercise shows you how.

In this example, you are going to do a simple move, starting in a lower corner, then tilt up and zoom in to a close-up. You'll also use an Ease-In, Ease-Out keyframe so that your image slows gently to a stop.

---

1 Open **Chapter 11 Lesson**, if it isn't open already. Double-click **Seq – Image start** to load it into the **Timeline**.

This sequence contains a scanned still image that is larger than full-screen, which allows you to move around inside it, while still maintaining a high degree of image quality.

NOTE:

On Image Size

Final Cut is designed to edit video, not large graphics or images. Although FCP has a fairly large image buffer, I've found it gets grumpy if you have a lot of images which are much larger than 2000 × 2000.

So, when you are scanning images for use in a video, pay close attention to the total pixel count. Video dots per inch (dpi) is always 72, so it isn't the dpi that matters; it's the total number of pixels.

Remember, also, in your scanning calculations, that filling a full-screen 4:3 NTSC DV frame requires a still image size of 720 × 540.

Image scanning tables can run dozens of pages, but the following table gives you a few numbers to start your thinking in the right direction. (This is for 4:3 NTSC DV video.)

Sample Scanned Graphics Sizes and Moves

DV NTSC Image Size	What You Can Do
720 × 540	Full screen, no movement
720 × 1080	Start full screen in bottom half, tilt up to top half
1440 × 540	Start full screen on one side, pan over to other side
1440 × 1080	Start in lower corner, pan and tilt up to opposite upper corner

All images are created at 72 pixels per inch. For the record, my favorite still image scan size is 1440 × 1080 at 72 pixels per inch, unless I have a specific move in mind.

2 Double-click the **Fred Kalbermatten.tiff** image clip from the **Timeline** to load it into the **Viewer**. Notice the duration of this clip is **5:00**. Click the **Motion** tab to make it active.

The scale is set to **50%** when the picture was edited to the Timeline. This is because Final Cut always imports a

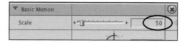

still image so that the entire image is visible in the Viewer or Canvas. This particular image was scanned at 1440 × 1080, so that it fits perfectly in a 4:3 aspect ratio.

Note: If you double-click the Browser image to load it into the Viewer without first editing it to the Timeline, FCP thinks the image is an HD still-frame and none of these settings work. To prevent this confusion, move the picture to the **Timeline** first, which tells FCP to scale the image for DV NTSC video, then double-click it to load it into the **Viewer**.

---

3 Set the **Canvas** to **Image+Wireframe** (or select the **Canvas** and press **W** to toggle to the **Wireframe** mode).

---

4 Position the **playhead** at the beginning of the sequence. In the **Motion** tab of the **Viewer**, set a **Center** keyframe and a **Scale** keyframe.

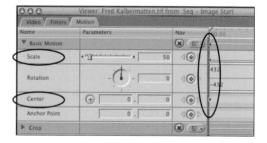

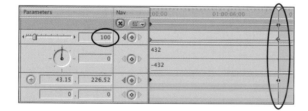

5 Position the **playhead** at the end of the sequence and change the **Scale** to **100%**. *Don't* create any keyframes. Using the **Selection** tool, drag the image in the **Canvas** until the snowboarder's body fills the frame. Notice that whenever you change a setting, Final Cut automatically sets new keyframes for the appropriate motion control.

6 Play the sequence. It looks nice, but it would be even nicer if the final move gently slowed down and "landed" on the close-up. To do this, **Ctrl+click** the green keyframe in the **Canvas** that represents the final **Center** keyframe and choose **Ease In/Ease Out**.

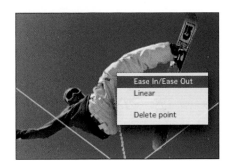

Play your sequence again. See how the motion gently slows down and stops? You can adjust this by dragging the inside control point closer to the keyframe (to speed up this landing) or further from the keyframe (to slow down the landing).

You may also notice that the image seems to "pop" when playback stops. This is because, during playback, Final Cut does not show the full resolution of the image in order to allow the CPU to create more real-time effects. Once playback stops, Final Cut displays the image at high-quality resolution, which makes the image seem to suddenly "pop" into focus.

Everything you've already learned about keyframes, Bezier control points, and curves also applies to moving graphics. The nice thing is that because they are larger than full-screen, you can move around inside them with no loss in quality—which is something you can't do with a video image.

You can compare your version to mine by playing **Seq – Image finish**.

---

7 That wraps up this chapter. Save your work, quit Final Cut, and take a break. You've earned it.

Helpful Keyboard Shortcuts

Shortcut	Action
Cmd+J	Displays the Constant Speed change dialog
Q	Toggles between selecting the Viewer and the Canvas
W	Toggles the Canvas, or Viewer, between Image, Image+Wireframe, and Wireframe modes
M	Sets a marker
MM	Edits a marker
Option+P	(My favorite keyboard shortcut) Plays a sequence requiring rendering without first rendering it
A	Selects the Selection tool
C	Selects the Crop tool
D	Selects the Distort tool
Shift+drag corner with Selection tool	(In Canvas) Scales a clip asymmetrically
Cmd+drag corner with Selection tool	(In Canvas) Scales and rotates a clip simultaneously
Shift+drag corner with Crop tool	(In Canvas) Crops a clip while maintaining 4:3 aspect ratio
Cmd+drag corner with Crop tool	(In Canvas) Crops all sides of a clip simultaneously
Shift+drag corner with Distort tool	(In Canvas) Distorts all four corners to create perspective simultaneously
Shift+drag position with Selection tool	(In Canvas) Constrains clip movement to horizontal or vertical
Shift+drag rotation with Selection tool	(In Canvas) Constrains clip rotation to 45-degree increments
Ctrl+K	Adds a Motion keyframe
Shift+K	Goes to next keyframe

continues on next page

Helpful Keyboard Shortcuts *continued*

Shortcut	Action
Option+K	Goes to previous keyframe
Shift+I	Goes to the In of a clip or Timeline
Shift+O	Goes to the Out of a clip or Timeline
Option+V	Pastes the attributes of one clip into a selected clip, or range of clips
Shift+N	Creates a still frame at the position of the playhead in either the Viewer or the Canvas
Cmd+R	Renders the current selection in the Timeline
Ctrl+R	Renders the sequence currently active in the Timeline
Cmd+0 (zero)	Opens Sequence Settings dialog

Summary

In this chapter, you've learned about motion effects—from changing the size of an image to creating keyframes and getting images and text to move around the screen. In the next chapter, you'll continue your exploration of effects by looking at filters and keying. And you'll start with a change of pace: creating an *audio* special effect.

12

Filters and Keying

Compositing is the process of combining two, or more, images to form a new image. One way to composite is using motion effects. Another is through filters and keying.

The difference between the motion effects you learned about in Chapter 11, *"Motion Effects,"* and the filters covered in this chapter is that, in general, motion effects change the size, shape, opacity, and/or position of a video clip; filters change the actual look of the video, or sound of the audio.

In this chapter, you will learn how to use audio and video filters, discover a simple way to color-correct a scene with color problems, and practice combining multiple images using a variety of keying techniques.

DVD MOVIE: | **filters_efx.mov**

For tutorials illustrating this chapter, check out **filters_efx.mov**, located in the **movies** folder on the **Final Cut Pro 5 HOT DVD**. These tutorials show you how to create a telephone audio effect, apply and keyframe a filter, perform a simple color correction, and create a chroma key.

NOTE: | **Audio Frequency 201**

You learned about audio frequencies in Chapter 8, *"Audio—The Secret to a Great Picture."* Here is some additional information you need to make this next exercise appear less like magic.

Large rooms sound different than small rooms. It isn't that they are noisier, necessarily, but the echoes they create are different. A large room has wider, louder, more noticeable echoes than a small room.

In the first exercise, you will adjust the echoes created by a voice to make it sound like he is moving from a large room in the first half of the clip, into a small room in the second half. This effect could be enhanced further with the sound effect of a door closing and the speaker saying something like, "Come in here, we need to talk."

Human hearing ranges from 20 cycles per second (very, *very* low-pitched sounds) to 20,000 cycles per second (extremely high-pitched sounds), provided you are about 18. As you get older, you lose some of your high-frequency hearing. (Sigh....) However, human speech falls into a much more limited range, generally, from 300 cycles to 4000 cycles per second, although some letters like "S" and "F," have frequencies that range up to 6500 cycles per second.

The telephone company knows this. So, in order to squeeze more phone calls onto a single wire, they limit the frequencies transmitted during a phone call to a range between 350 and 3500 cycles per second. This is why phone conversations, while still completely understandable, don't sound as nice as listening to someone in person.

In the second part of this exercise, you'll take advantage of this fact to create the illusion of a phone conversation, even though the audio was recorded in-person with a good mic.

Remember, your goal with all filters is subtlety. You want to make an effect believable, not suddenly jolt your audience awake with the feeling someone just turned on the echoes and set them to "stun."

1 | Using Audio Filters

Why, if you are learning compositing, am I starting with audio? Two reasons: first, because this helps make the concept of filters easier to understand and, second, because this is a neat technique to keep in your back pocket for when you need it.

In this exercise, you will first learn how to create the illusion of a speaker moving from a large room into a small room. Then you'll learn how to apply a filter to create the sound of a telephone conversation.

---

1 If Final Cut is not running, start it and open **Chapter 12 Lesson**. It's in the **FCP Projects > FCP 5 HOT Files** folder you created at the beginning of this book.

This Devanas clip shows a weather map, with a meteorologist discussing the upcoming hurricane at a press conference. In point of fact, the commentator is speaking at a press conference from a podium in the same room as the weather map. However, since he is not on camera at this moment, in this effect, you will make him sound like he is moving from a large room to a smaller room.

2 Double-click **Seq – Audio Echo start** to open it.

---

3 Select the **Razor Blade** tool (press **B**) and cut the clip at the marker. Turn on snapping (**N**) to help align the **Razor Blade** properly with the marker.

A linked clip is one where the audio and video are synced together. Final Cut indicates this by underlining the clip name in the **Timeline**. When you use the **Razor Blade** to cut a linked clip, both the audio and video will be cut, regardless of which side you click with the **Razor Blade**.

Cutting the clip, to create a Through edit, makes it easy to apply an effect to one portion of a clip, without affecting other parts of the clip.

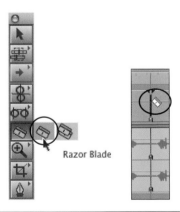

Razor Blade

4 Select the first portion of the clip and choose **Effects > Audio Filters > Final Cut Pro > Reverberation**. Double-click the clip to load it into the **Viewer** and click the **Filters** tab to make it active.

---

5 From the pop-up menu, choose **Room (Large)**.

---

6 The settings in the text boxes are a tad, um, *aggressive*. So, decrease the **Effect Mix** (the percent of the effect compared to the original source) to **12**. An **Effect Mix** of **0** is no effect, all original source; an **Effect Mix** of **100** is all effect with no original source. In this case, we want to sense a light flavoring of the room, not drown in it.

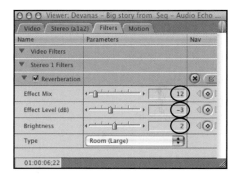

If you have good speakers, decrease the **Effect Level** to –3. If you have small multimedia speakers, leave this at **0**, which will make the effect easier to hear. If I were mixing this for real, I'd set it to –3.

Then, increase **Brightness** to +2. This increases the high frequencies, which are a significant component of echoes, to make them easier to hear.

---

7 Play the sequence and hear the transition from large room to small. Again, in this case, there's no justification for the movement, but this does illustrate how to prepare a clip for a filter and how to adjust the filter once it's applied.

You can compare your effect to mine by playing **Seq – Audio Echoes finished**.

---

8 Here's another example of using audio filters. Double-click **Seq – Audio Phone start** to open it.

(As usual, it is not a problem to have multiple sequences open at the same time in the Timeline.) In this part of the exercise, you'll create an audio effect to make it sound like the meteorologist is phoning in his report.

---

9 Select the **Razor Blade** tool (press **B**) and cut the clip at the marker.

In order for this to sound like a phone call, you need to eliminate all frequencies below 350 cycles and above 3500 cycles per second. In fact, to make this effect even more believable, it helps if you cut the low end at 500 and the high end at 2500.

There are several possible filters you could use to limit these frequencies. EQs come first to mind. However, an EQ filter principally enhances or de-emphasizes a range of frequencies. You want to totally eliminate them.

There is no single filter that does this. However, if you use *two* filters, this becomes very simple.

---

10 Double-click the *second* half of the clip to load it into the **Viewer**. With the clip still selected, choose **Effects > Audio Filters > Final Cut Pro > High Pass Filter**. Then choose **Effects > Audio Filters > Final Cut Pro > Low Pass Filter**. Finally, click the **Filters** tab.

---

11 See how both filters have been applied to the same clip? You'll work with multiple filters again in Exercise 3.

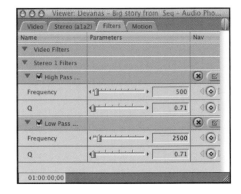

However, the frequency settings are wrong. You want the **High Pass** filter to allow (pass) all frequencies *above* 500 cycles. So, change this setting to **500**.

Next, you want the **Low Pass** filter to pass all frequencies *below* 2,500 cycles. So, change this setting to **2500**.

By the way, the **Q** represents the amount of feathering in an audio effect. A high **Q**, greater than 1.0, has very little feathering; the transition is very sharply defined. A low **Q**, less than 1.0, has more feathering, which softens the transition into the effect. In this case, you want a sharp edge to the frequency cutoff, so keep the **Q** levels high, say around 2.

---

12 Play the sequence. Hear how natural the voice is in the beginning, then, after the cut, how it sounds as if he's on the telephone.

Compare your sequence with mine by playing **Seq – Audio Phone finished**.

---

13 As a reminder, to close a sequence in the **Timeline**, **Ctrl+click** the tab containing the sequence name and choose **Close Tab**.

---

14 See? Even simple effects can be fun! Save your work, if you want. You are done with audio filters; it's time to move to video.

Thoughts on Audio Filters

Audio is one of the things I love, and an area that many video editors have limited experience with. With the release of Soundtrack Pro, we now have a whole arsenal of audio tools at our disposal. Still, there are times when using a filter in Final Cut is faster to use. So, here is a quick summary of the types of audio filters in Final Cut, along with suggestions on how to use some of them.

There are two collections of filters supplied with Final Cut Pro 5: Apple and Final Cut Pro. I tend to use the FCP filters because I like them better. The Final Cut audio filters fall into four broad categories:

- Equalizers

- Repair

- Dynamic control

- Echo and reverb

Equalizers are designed to alter selected frequencies, either to enhance or eliminate them. The more bands an equalizer has, the more adjustments it can make at one time. Equalizers include 3 Band equalizer, Band Pass filter, High Pass filter (this is the same as the Low Shelf filter), Low Pass filter (the same as the High Shelf filter), and Parametric equalizer. You've already learned how to use the High and Low Pass filters. Try using the Parametric EQ to warm a narration, that is, to enhance the low frequencies. Set it to a **Frequency** of **300**, **Q** of **1**, and **Gain** of **2.5**.

Repair filters are designed to fix problems like hum, or a speaker who is too close to the mic. Repair filters include DC Notch, Hum Remover, Notch, Vocal DeEsser, and Vocal DePopper. The audio repair facilities in Soundtrack are far superior to Final Cut, so I suggest you use FCP's Repair filters only as a "last resort."

Dynamic control filters are designed to control gain without creating distortion. These filters include Compressor/Limiter and Expander/Noise Gate. I don't like any of these filters—the controls in Soundtrack Pro, or ProTools, are far superior.

Echo and Reverberation filters are designed to make a singer's voice sound fuller, or give a better sense of the size of a room. Generally, you don't add echo or reverb to a narrator, cool though it may sound.

2 | Using Video Filters

In this exercise, you will learn how to apply, adjust, and delete video filters to achieve a certain creative look for your sequence. You will also learn how to create a favorite filter, as well as apply filters to multiple clips simultaneously.

---

1 If Final Cut is not running, start it and open **Chapter 12 Lesson**. Double-click **Seq – Video Open start** to load it into the **Timeline**. You may need to render it to play it.

This is the same exercise you worked with in Chapter 11, *"Motion Effects,"* a potential open for the Snowboarding sequence. The problem is, the background needs more excitement. You need to create a more unusual look.

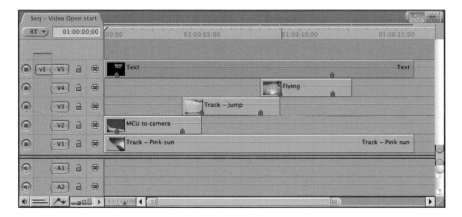

2 Play the sequence to get a sense of what it looks like.

Hmmm…to me, the foreground images are so interesting that my eye goes to the text title and the foreground; I'm not seeing the background at all. It feels flat. Since this is the open to my show, this needs to be fixed.

3 Select the clip **Track – Pink Sun** and choose **Effects > Video Filters > QuickTime > Color Tint**.

4 Not ideal. A black-and-white shot of a snow scene just doesn't make it. However, all Final Cut filters can be adjusted, so double-click **Track – Pink Sun** to load it into the **Viewer**. Click the **Filters** tab to make it active.

5 To toggle between applying and removing a filter from a clip, uncheck and check the blue check box near the name of the filter.

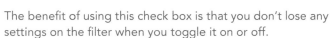

The benefit of using this check box is that you don't lose any settings on the filter when you toggle it on or off.

Sigh…the **Black and White** filter just isn't working.

6 Change the pop-up menu from **Black and White** to **Sepia**.

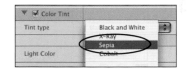

Oh, my goodness! Far worse!! Quick, delete it before somebody sees what you are doing.

7 Click the name of the filter in the **Filters** tab to select it, then the press the **Delete** key. (As usual, you "select something, then do something to it.")

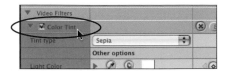

Whew! Although sepia tone images are wonderful for giving an image a romantic, nostalgic feeling, extreme snowboarding is not generally considered part of that category. Try again.

---

8 With **Track – Pink sun** selected in the **Timeline**, choose **Effects > Video Filters > Stylize > Posterize**.

---

9 Whoa! Much better. Press **Option+P** to play the sequence without waiting for it to render.

Now, my eye is jumping all over the screen. The background clip is much more predominant, due to this effect. This really makes the beginning of my program seem exciting.

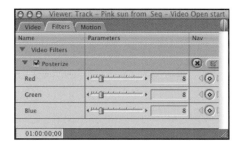

---

10 Double-click **Track – Pink sun** to load it into the **Viewer**, if it isn't already. Click the **Filters** tab to make it active, and change the **Red**, **Green**, and **Blue** settings to **5**, **5**, and **5**.

The lower the slider values, the greater the poster effect. The higher the slider values, the more the image looks "real." You can also experiment with different, and unequal, Red, Green and Blue settings to get an even more pronounced effect.

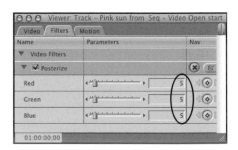

11 Much better. Select the entire **Timeline** using **Edit > Select All** (or press **Cmd+A**) and render it using **Sequence > Render Selection** (or press **Cmd+R**).

You *could* just choose **Sequence > Render Sequence** (or press **Option+R**). That, too, will render your sequence. But I prefer to select what I want to render, rather than always rendering everything. So, for me, my habit has always been to select what I want to render, then just render that selection, whether it's a transition, clip, or group of clips. You can use whichever system you prefer.

OK. So far, you've learned how to apply a filter, delete a filter, and modify a filter. And, just as you can create a favorite motion, you can also create a favorite filter. Here's how.

12 Select **Track – Pink Sun** on the **Timeline**. Choose **Effects > Make Favorite Effect**.

13 Look in the **Effects** tab of the **Browser**. Your effect is created and stored in the **Favorites** folder. The **Favorites** folder is empty, until you create your first favorite motion or favorite effect.

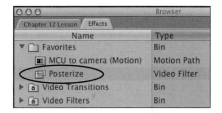

14 To apply this filter to another clip, select the clip and choose **Effects > Favorites > Posterize**, from the **Video Filters** section of the menu. The name of a favorite filter changes, depending upon which effects you are using. You can apply a favorite effect to a single clip or a range of selected clips.

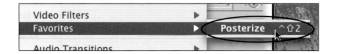

15 That's it for this exercise. Save your work, if you wish. Quit Final Cut, if you need to take a break. Otherwise, keep it open; you'll use it again in the next exercise.

Favorite Effects vs. Paste Attributes

In Chapter 11, *"Motion Effects,"* you learned how to paste attributes for motion effects. The same process applies here: you can paste attributes for filter effects as well.

Favorite effects, like favorite motions, are convenient, but I rarely use them for all the reasons discussed in Chapter 11. For me, the biggest negative is that favorites are lost when I trash Final Cut's preferences files. Also, favorites always scale keyframe timing, whereas Paste Attributes gives me the option to scale or not to scale. However, if the effect doesn't use keyframes, scaling is not an issue.

Just to be clear, when you trash preferences, you are *not* deleting any filters applied to any clip; you are only deleting the *reference* to the filter stored in the **Browser**, under the **Effects** tab, in the **Favorites** folder.

I think favorites are a great idea and, in the future, when Final Cut preferences are more stable, I look forward to using them more, but for now, I'll stick to Paste Attributes.

A Quick Way to Copy a Filter

OK, notwithstanding what I just said about Paste Attributes, here's a fast way to copy a filter to another clip:

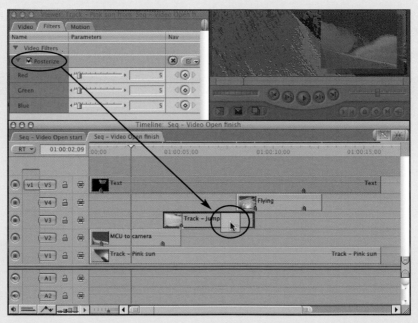

Double-click a clip with an effect you like, into the **Viewer**. Grab the name of the filter and drag it on top of the clip you want to copy the filter to. As long as you aren't using keyframes, this technique works great!

3 | Fancy Filter Tricks, Part I

I was going to call this exercise "Combining Multiple Filters," but how boring is that? In this exercise, you will learn how to combine multiple filters to create an effect, reorganize filters to change an effect, create a filter stack you can apply to other clips, and remove attributes from a clip.

This is an exercise in learning a technique, so you'll need to use only one clip.

---

1 If Final Cut is not running, start it and open **Chapter 12 Lesson**. Double-click **Seq – Video Fancy Filter 1** to load it into the **Timeline**.

2 Although you can create these effects anywhere you wish in the clip, if you want your screens to match mine, position the **playhead** on the *second* marker.

---

3 Select **MS Brown coat** in the **Timeline**, then choose **Effects > Video Filters > Border > Bevel**. Double-click the clip to load it into the **Viewer**, then click the **Filters** tab.

4 Click the color chip in the **Bevel** filter and select a light golden color. (Oh, no reason, I just like the color gold.) Notice that the bevel matches the color you selected. Twirl the **Bevel** filter up by clicking the small down-pointing triangle. This provides more room to work in the **Filters** tab.

---

5 Apply a second filter to this same clip. Choose **Effects > Video Filters > Blur > Gaussian Blur**. This blurs the image. (By the way, this is the *only* filter to use when you want to blur a clip. The other blur filters look pretty tacky.) For the purposes of this exercise, crank the **Radius** up to **20**.

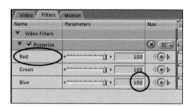

---

6 Finally, apply a third filter to this same clip. Choose **Effects > Video Filters > Image Control > Desaturate**. This removes all the color from the image.

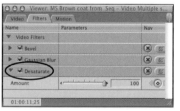

What you have created is a colored bevel around an image, then you blurred the whole image, including the bevel, and removed all the color from the image.

Here's the point of this exercise: you can combine multiple filters to create effects not possible with one filter alone. However, and even more important, the *order* of your filters directly affects your effect. Watch this...

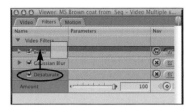
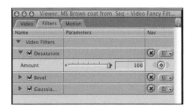

7 Click and drag the title of the bottom filter (**Desaturate**) to the top of the filter stack.

See the change? The image is desaturated *first*, then the color bevel is added, then the whole image is blurred.

NOTE: **Filter Processing**

Final Cut processes filters from the top down. In other words, the topmost filter is processed first, then the results of that filter are processed by the next filter down, then those results are processed by the next filter, and so on from top to bottom.

This means you can change an effect simply by changing the stacking order of your filters. And you move filters by dragging their names up or down the list.

There is no limit to the number of filters you can apply to one clip, though after you combine more than one or two filters, Final Cut will probably need to render your effect, rather than play it in real time.

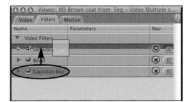
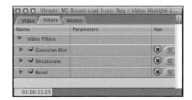

8 One more time to make the point. Drag the bottom filter, **Gaussian Blur**, to the top and watch how the new order changes the image.

---

9 Just as you can create a favorite filter, you can also create a favorite filter stack. (A stack is a group of filters, such as you've been working on here). To create a filter stack, select the clip containing the effects you like (**MS Brown coat**). Choose **Effects > Make Favorite Effect**.

---

10 In the **Browser**, click the **Effects tab**. Twirl down the **Favorites** folder and inside you will see a folder labeled with the name of your clip and the text, "**(Filters)**". This is now a favorite effect that can be applied to other clips. However, filter stacks can only be applied by dragging them from the **Favorites** folder, inside the **Effects** tab of the **Browser**. *Individual* favorite effects can also be selected from **Effects > Video Filters > Favorites** menu.

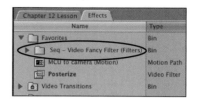

WARNING:

Don't Open a Filter Stack

A filter stack is represented by a folder in the **Effects** tab of the **Browser**. But be careful not to double-click this folder to open the stack. Why? Because the **Browser** sorts files in alphabetical order. Watch...

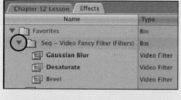

If you want to see what's in a filter stack, twirl down the folder. That maintains the order of the filters.

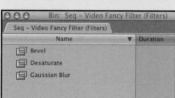

If you open the folder by double-clicking it, the Browser sorts all files in alphabetical order, thus totally rearranging your effect.

There's more to learn about filters, but, first, let me show you another way to remove attributes from a clip. It's called **Remove Attributes**.

11 Select **MS Brown coat** and choose **Edit > Remove Attributes**.

Remove Attributes is smart—it looks at the clip to determine what effects have been applied. In this case, you have only added filters, so only the Filters option is selected. If you had applied other effects, other options would be selected. The benefit to using this window is that you are able to remove some effects without removing all of them.

12 In this case, leave **Filters** checked and click **OK**.

All filters have now been removed from the clip. And this is a good thing, because you are about to work with this same clip in a new way.

13 That's it for this exercise. Don't save your work, unless you feel the need. Quit Final Cut if you want to take a break.

4 | Fancy Filter Tricks, Part II

In this exercise, you will learn how to keyframe a filter.

---

1 If Final Cut is not running, start it and open **Chapter 12 Lesson**. Double-click **Seq – Video Fancy Filter 2** to load it into the **Timeline**.

---

2 Select the clip and choose **Effects > Video Filters > Stylize > Posterize**. Double-click the clip to load it into the **Viewer**. Click the **Filters** tab.

---

3 Position the **playhead** at the beginning of the clip and set a keyframe for all three colors (**Red**, **Green**, and **Blue**).

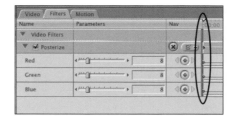

---

4 Move **30** frames forward (type **+30** and press **Return**) and set a second set of keyframes for all three colors.

---

5 With the **playhead** parked on the second set of keyframes, change the **Red** value to **6**, the **Green** value to **5**, and the **Blue** value to **7**. (If you have an image that is varying shades of black, white, or gray, you will get a more interesting posterization effect if the three color values are different.)

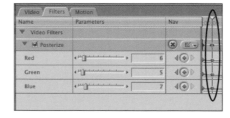

---

6 Press the **Home** key to move the **playhead** to the first set of keyframes. Set all three color values to **100**.

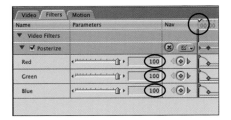

---

7 Play the clip, although you may need to render it first.

Just as you can keyframe motion, you can also keyframe filters—exactly the same way, with exactly the same navigation and control. This provides an enormous amount of control over your effects.

One other note: applying filters is mostly an art, not a science. There is no *magic setting* that you should use. If it looks good, in the context of your sequence, it probably is. Just remember to use your scopes (press **Option+9**) to make sure your video levels are within safe boundaries for white level and chroma.

---

8 That's it for this exercise. Save your work. Quit Final Cut if you want, but there's lots more good stuff still to come.

---

5 | Nesting Sequences

Sometimes you need to apply the same filter to multiple clips, for example, to create a widescreen look, or display timecode over a series of clips. In this exercise, you'll learn how to nest your clips into a sequence, apply a filter to all of them, then convert them back into individual clips.

---

1 If Final Cut is not running, start it and open **Chapter 12 Lesson**. Double-click **Seq – Video Nest** to load it into the **Timeline**. This is the open you created in Exercise 2.

What you need to do is apply a widescreen filter to all these clips to make this look as though it were shot 16:9, instead of 4:3. To do this, you need to create a nest. A nest is exactly the same as a sequence, except instead of editing the clips to it, as you would do normally, you create the sequence after all the clips have been edited.

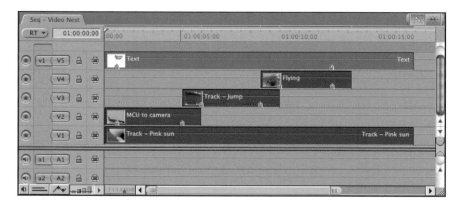

2 Select all the clips in the sequence by choosing **Edit > Select All** (or press **Cmd+A**).

---

3 Choose **Sequence > Nest Items** (or press **Option+C**).

---

4 Change the name of the suggested nest to " **Seq – Source Clips**". (Remember to use a leading space so all your sequences sort to the top of the **Browser**.) Click **OK** to create the new nest.

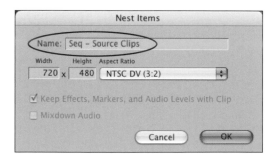

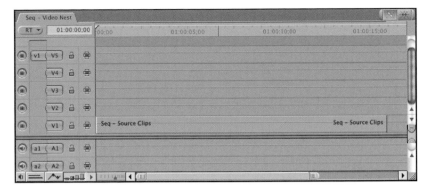

Notice that all your clips have coalesced into a single, new "master clip," called a **nest**, while in the **Browser**, a new sequence has appeared, called **Seq – Source Clips**. The master clip is the nest, and **Seq – Source Clips** contains all your original clips—intact and available for editing.

5 Select the nest and choose **Effects > Video Filters > Matte > Widescreen**.

This cuts off the top and bottom of the frame to make your images have a widescreen look. However, this isn't a true 16:9 aspect ratio. You need to change the filter settings to get the proportions right.

6 Double-click the nest to load it into the **Viewer**.

Oops, that didn't work. Normally, you double-click a clip to load it into the Viewer, But nests are different. Double-clicking a nest opens up the nest so you can see, and edit, the individual clips it contains.

Notice at the top of the Timeline there are now two tabs: one containing the original clips (**Seq – Source Clips**) and one that contains the nest itself (**Seq – Video Nest**). Click the **Seq – Video Nest** tab to get back to the nest.

7 This time, either **Option+double-click** the nest or highlight it and press **Return** to load it into the **Viewer**. Click the **Filters** tab, and choose **1.78:1** (which is the correct aspect ratio for 16:9 video) from the **Widescreen** pop-up menu.

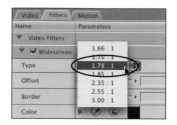

8 Play your nest. Given all the effects you are using, you will probably need to render this first.

The 16:9 filter has been applied to all the clips in the nest. Granted, now that you've changed the aspect ratio, you'll need to change the position of the clips, but that's easy to do.

9 To edit any clip in a sequence, double-click the sequence to open the nest. All your original clips are here, ready for you to edit. Best of all, any changes you make to the clips inside a nest are automatically reflected back to the nest itself.

In this case, you won't make any changes. However, it's nice to know you can. (Oh, OK, make some changes and see what happens.)

Nests are very useful when you want to apply a filter, or motion effect, to a group of clips.

10 As an additional exercise, you can use a nest to display timecode for an entire sequence. This is very useful when providing a client with a copy of your sequence to review. There are two timecode display filters in Final Cut: **Effects > Video Filters > Video > Timecode Generator** and **Video > Timecode Reader**.

Timecode Generator displays the timecode of the Timeline. Timecode Reader displays the timecode of the source clips in the Timeline. You apply a timecode filter to a nest in exactly the same way as illustrated in this exercise.

11 That's it for this exercise. Save your work, if you feel so inclined. After a brief discussion of color space, you are going to take a detailed look at a series of specialized filters that all relate to color and keying. Quit Final Cut now, if you need to take a break.

NOTE:

Deconstructing a Nest

Although nests are very useful, sometimes you may need to tear them apart and work with the original clips.

You can do this using copy-and-paste, but here's a much cooler, though little-known, method:

1. Create an empty sequence, or find an empty spot on an existing sequence.

2. Drag your nested sequence (such as **Seq – Source Clips**) from the **Browser** to the **Timeline**.

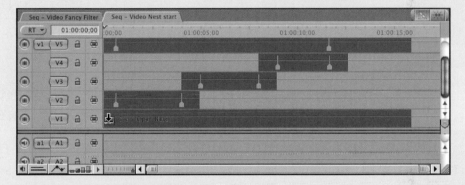

3. Once you *start* dragging, but *before* you get to the **Timeline**, press the **Command** key. This converts your sequence from a nest to a collection of its component clips.

4. Drop them on the **Timeline**.

Remember, don't press the **Command** key until *after* you start dragging.

The *Advanced Effects for Final Cut Pro* course textbook discusses color for 202 pages. However, in this exercise, we won't go into that much depth. Here, you'll learn a basic approach to solving color problems in seven steps.

Although this exercise is designed to teach you how to fix problems, there is a *lot* more that Final Cut can do with color. If you want to learn more, the Appendix lists other resources available to you.

WARNING:

NEW ▶ Matching Computer Color to Video Color

For this exercise, color correcting on your computer monitor will be just fine because you are learning the process of color correction. However, computer monitors don't display video images using the same colors as your TV set or, even better, a video monitor.

Video displayed to your computer looks dark and muddy. Shown on a TV set, it looks great. Computer images that look vibrant and colorful on your computer screen look washed out and lifeless on a TV set. Computer monitors further complicate this problem because they don't show video interlacing either.

In Final Cut Pro HD, Apple introduced Digital Cinema Desktop Preview (**View > External Video > Digital Cinema Desktop Preview**). This is a great way to preview your images on your computer monitor, but the colors are still not accurate and interlacing is still not shown. You need a video monitor.

In Final Cut 5, Apple introduced the ability to set the gamma of your computer to compensate for these differences. With some high-end graphics cards, FCP will make this change automatically. For graphics cards that don't support gamma correction, choose **Final Cut Pro > System Settings** and click the **Playback Control** tab. This gives you two options:

1. **Accurate** resets the gamma on your computer to more accurately match a video monitor. This is the default setting, however, it requires more CPU power to display.

2. **Approximate** is a better choice if you have a slower system. The colors are not as accurate, but this option requires fewer computing resources for playback.

For best results, use a calibrated video monitor. Otherwise, if your computer allows it, be sure the playback gamma is set to **Accurate**. Your worst choice is using a TV set. These are neither calibrated nor accurate.

You've been warned.

1 If Final Cut is not running, start it and open **Chapter 12 Lesson**. Double-click **Seq – Color Correct** to load it into the **Timeline**.

If you need help in reading the scopes inside Final Cut, please refer to Chapter 10, *"Text, Titles, and Graphics."*

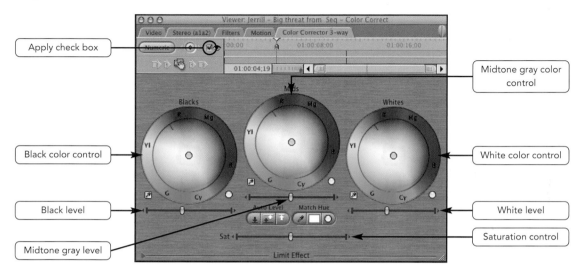

Here are the steps to fixing color problems with a clip:

1. Put the playhead in the middle of the clip you want to correct and select it.

2. Apply the **Color Corrector 3-way filter**.

3. Double-click the clip to load it into the **Viewer** and click the **Color Corrector 3-way** tab.

4. Choose **Window > Arrange > Color Correction**.

5. Set the black levels.

6. Set the white levels.

7. Color-balance the whites.

If necessary, you can copy these correction settings to other clips that have the same problem using the same techniques you use to copy other filters or effects.

---

2 Start by selecting the first clip, **Jerill – Big Threat**, and choosing **Effects > Video Filters > Color Correction > Color Corrector 3-way**.

The **3-way** filter is used for video and other YUV clips. The **Color Corrector** filter, also in that same collection, is used for correcting RGB and other computer graphics clips.

---

3 Put the **playhead** on the marker in the first clip, then double-click the **Jerill** clip to load it into the **Viewer**.

4 Choose **Window > Arrange > Color Correction**. (You can also open the scopes by choosing **Tools > Scopes**, (or by pressing **Option+9**), but using the **Window > Arrange** menu reorganizes all your windows to make color correction easier.)

Again, you can color-correct a clip using video anywhere within the clip; however, if you put your **playhead** on the marker, your screens will match mine.

The color in this clip is fine, but the black levels are too high, making it look washed out, and the color saturation is a bit low.

On the Waveform Monitor, the small white dots represent the grayscale values of all the different pixels in the image. Higher dots represent video levels that are whiter than lower dots. The highest dots are called the **white level**, and the lowest dots are called the **black level**.

5 Switch the scope to **Waveform** using the **Layout** pop-up menu in the upper-left corner.

See how the black levels, the white dots in the lower third of the scope, are seriously elevated? They are pushing 20%, which is way too gray. Black levels should be down near the line labeled **Black**.

Note: In Final Cut, black levels are always set to zero. For you TV engineers, 7.5 IRE setup for NTSC is added automatically when dubbing to analog tape. If you are not a TV engineer, just nod your head wisely and move on. In a digital environment, black equals zero.

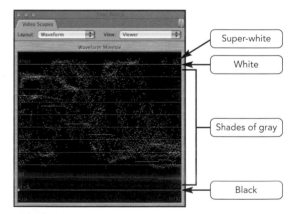

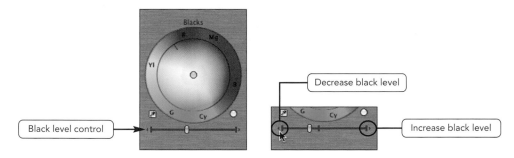

Black level control

Decrease black level

Increase black level

6 You fix this using small increments of change—not huge swipes with the mouse. In the **Viewer**, click the small left-pointing arrow at the left end of the line below the **Black** color circle on the **3-way Color Corrector**. This line adjusts black levels. Clicking the left arrow brings them down; clicking the right arrow brings them up. Most often, you are bringing down black levels.

In video, color correction is interactive. Making a change to any color affects all other colors. For this reason, I've found that I get the most consistent results by adjusting levels and colors in a specific order: first, black levels, then white levels, then, finally, color hue and saturation.

7 Click the left arrow until the black levels start touching the **Black** line. For me, this was about 37 clicks.

Again, I rarely use the slider because it doesn't have the precision I need. Small increments, slow and steady, work best for color correction.

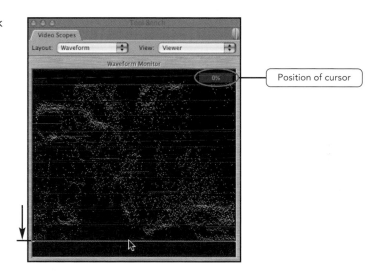

Position of cursor

8 Next, look at the white levels. Again, a little hot (meaning, too high)—around **103%**. Here's a tip to help you quickly set white levels: use **View > Range Check > Excess Luma** (or press **Ctrl+Z**).

Using Range Check

Range Check is a very helpful FCP utility that can tell you at a glance if your white levels or color saturation is out of spec.

Here's the basic guideline: if you are outputting to DV, or going directly to DVD, you don't need to worry about white levels. If you are outputting to a higher-quality video format for broadcast, you *do* need to worry.

Video levels for higher quality formats cannot exceed 100%. The Range Check tells you when they do. It has three different settings:

Excess Luma: Checks only for white levels that are too high.

Excess Chroma: Checks only for chroma levels that are too high (that is, too saturated).

Both: Checks for both excess white and chroma levels.

Range check uses three different icons and two zebra patterns to warn you of problems:

 Warning: Video or chroma levels are too hot (depending upon which setting you are using). Use your scopes to determine what needs to be controlled. The red zebra (vibrating lines) pattern shows where the video or chroma levels are excessive.

 OK: Video levels are OK with a maximum range between 90% and 100%. The green zebra patterns show where video levels exceed 90%.

 OK: Chroma levels are OK, or, if checking for Excess Luma, white levels are below 90%. (Did you notice that the small little arrow in the top left of the green circle is missing in this icon? That's the difference between these two green checkmarks.)

When I am adjusting my white levels, I use both the scope and Range Check. When the Range Check switches from the Warning to the OK icon, I click the white level control down three clicks more for safety and I'm done.

9 To adjust the white levels, click the white level bar underneath the **White** color circle. Click the left arrow to decrease white levels; click the right arrow to increase white levels. In this case, bring the white levels down until the vast majority are below the **100%** line at the top of the **Waveform Monitor**. When the **Range Check** switches from the **Warning** to the **OK** icon, click three times more to put your white levels into safe territory. For me, this was three clicks for the warning to disappear, plus three more for safety.

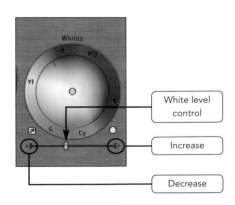

White level control

Increase

Decrease

10 Using the pop-up menu, switch to the **Vectorscope** to check your chroma (which means "color") levels.

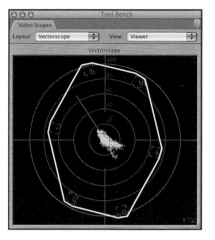

The chroma levels are well within safe guidelines, so you can safely increase saturation to warm up his skin tones.

---

11 Adjust saturation by clicking the small arrows at the end of the **Sat** line. The right arrow increases saturation, and the left arrow decreases it. For me, 10 clicks with the right arrow made him look good.

With saturation, in general, skin tones will fall between the first and second rings. So, make the person look good, while still maintaining safe color saturation levels on the Vectorscope.

Before

Toggle

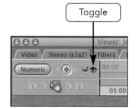

After

---

12 Play the clip. Compare what he looked like before and after correction by toggling on and off the blue checkmark in the upper-left corner of the **Color Corrector 3-way** window. Checked means the filter is on; unchecked means the filter is off.

In the second clip of this sequence, **Meyers – Bad color**, you need to correct one of the speakers at the press conference who has a decidedly purple skin tone.

13 Select the second clip, **Meyers – Bad color**, and position your **playhead** on the marker. Choose **Effects > Video Filters > Color Correction > Color Corrector 3-way**, and double-click the clip to load it into the **Viewer**. If you haven't done so already, choose **Windows > Arrange > Color Correction**.

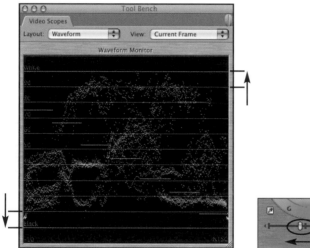

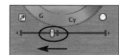

14 First, set the black level. Look at the **Waveform Monitor**. The black levels are up near **10%**. Too high.

Click the black level left arrow to pull the blacks back down to **0%**. (For me, this was about 23 clicks.)

15 Then, set the white level. Both the **Range Check** and the scope agree the white levels are OK. You might pull the white levels up a few clicks, just to brighten the image a bit. However, if the **Range Check** warning appears, you've gone too far.

Now that both black and white levels are set, it is time to correct the color. Remember, the most reliable way to color correct is to follow a strict order: set black levels, set white levels, then adjust color.

Switch to the **Vectorscope**. The pink line pointing diagonally up to the left is called the **flesh tone line**. All skin tones, regardless of race, will appear very close to this line, because the primary color of human skin is provided by red blood. Since everyone's blood is the same color, all flesh tones are, in the eyes of the **Vectorscope**, simply different amounts of red.

Flesh tone line

By looking at how far someone's skin tone diverges from the **Vectorscope flesh tone line**, it is easy to see what kind of color correction is necessary to bring them back to normal.

You also use the Vectorscope to determine proper color saturation. In general, most skin tones will fall along the Flesh Tone line between the first and second ring.

In the case of Mr. Meyers, his skin tone is rolled decidedly toward magenta, with very little saturation. This is the last of the three steps to color correction.

16 To color-balance a shot, click the small **eyedropper** in the lower-left corner of the **White** color wheel. Then, click something you believe to be white in the image. Try to pick a part of the image that is not overexposed. In this case, the shoulder of his shirt will work fine.

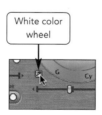

White color wheel

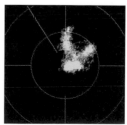

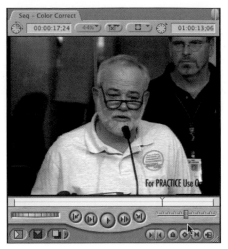

| *Before* | *After* |

As soon as you click the eyedropper, the color is immediately corrected. The skin tones are right on the flesh tone line. And you are done.

There is a school of thought that says color-correcting on a midtone gray is more accurate. Although I don't argue, my point is that finding a clean white in an image is easier than finding a clean mid-tone gray. This is why I teach this system—it's easy to use and provides dramatically improved results.

However, in this case, you can further improve the image by selecting the mid-gray eyedropper and clicking the gray window immediately to the left of his right ear. This improves both his skin tone and saturation.

---

17 Save your work, or not. As you wish. In either case, you are done with this exercise. Keep things open, though; there's still more to learn.

---

7 | Creating a Luma Key

A key is a special effect that removes portions of an image based upon certain values. In the case of a luma key, those values are based on luminance, or grayscale. In the case of a chroma key, those values are based on color. In this exercise, you will learn how to do a luma key.

In Chapter 10, *"Text, Titles, and Graphics,"* you learned how to key Photoshop graphics, which have built-in alpha channels. Luma keys are used when you have a graphic against a black or white background without an alpha, or transparency, channel. They are most often found when you download JPEG graphics off the Web.

---

1 If Final Cut is not running, start it and open **Chapter 12 Lesson**. Double-click **Seq – Key Luma** to load it into the **Timeline**.

---

2 This is a color graphic of a snowboarder, **Snowboard Luma.tif**, which you need to key into the background shot on **V1**. To do so, select the clip on **V2**. (Remember, effects are *always* applied to the top clip.) Choose **Effects > Video Filters > Key > Luma Key**.

Double-click the **Snowboard Luma** clip to load it into the **Viewer**, then click the **Filters** tab.

---

3 Because you want to remove the black background, choose **Key Out Darker** from the **Key Mode** pop-up menu.

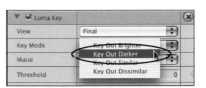

---

4 Since this black background was computer-generated, you can reduce the **Tolerance** to **0**. If you shot this graphic with a camera, you would decrease the **Tolerance** from **100** until the black background completely disappears.

To minimize the black lines that appear around the image, decrease the **Threshold** to **–65**.

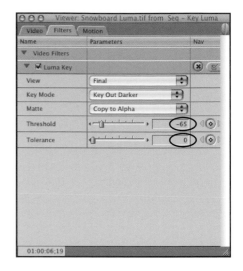

5 Play the sequence. Because video is bitmapped, some stair-stepping on smooth curves is unavoidable—that's the nature of video. You can minimize these jagged edges by avoiding lines or edges of objects that are almost, but not quite, vertical or horizontal (a rule that I violated in this instance with the edges of the snowboard).

6 That's it. A quick exercise. You don't need to save your work. Quit Final Cut if you want to take a break; otherwise, it's on to chroma keying.

8 | Creating a Chroma Key

In this exercise, you will learn how to remove a specific color and replace it with the background of your choice in a process called **chroma keying**.

---

1 If Final Cut is not running, start it and open **Chapter 12 Lesson**. Double-click **Seq – Key Chroma** to load it into the **Timeline**. Double-click **Track – Jump** to load it into the **Viewer**. Click the **Filters** tab to make it active. Position your **playhead** on the marker.

You are going to create a surreal sky as a background for a snowboarder. To do this, you will replace the blue sky with a computer-generated background.

A couple of notes before you start. First, the snowboarder was not shot with chroma key in mind. Because of this, you won't get a perfect key. Don't worry about perfection; concentrate on learning the process.

Second, I knew at the outset that I was not going to get a perfect key, so I selected a background that would hide any blue edges caused by a poor key. Inserting a background with a similar color to your chroma key color is a useful technique when you know that "pulling a clean key" (creating the effect) is going to be difficult.

Third, this effect can also be improved by color-correcting the snowboard shot. You already know how to color-correct a clip, so you can experiment with it for extra credit at the end of this exercise. For best results, I suggest you chroma key first, then add color correction.

---

2 The process of chroma keying involves three different filters, and they need to be applied in a specific order. So, select **Track – Jump**, then choose **Effects > Video Filters > Key > Color Smoothing - 4:1:1**. This filter tries to compensate for the loss of color created when compressing video to DV. This filter is either on or off. This is often subtle. Pick the setting that looks best—it varies with each key. In this example, leave it on.

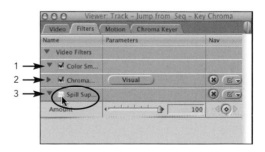

Next, choose **Effects > Video Filters > Key > Chroma Keyer**. This is the filter that does the heavy lifting.

Finally, choose **Effects > Video Filters > Key > Spill Suppressor (Blue)**. This filter compensates for blue (or green) spill around your subjects, spoiling the key. I've found this filter to be quite useful, but only at the end of the keying process. Because its default settings make the picture look worse, for now, turn it off.

3 Click the **Visual** button on the **Chroma Keyer** filter, or click the **Chroma Keyer** tab in the **Viewer**. This switches the filter from a numeric display to a visual interface.

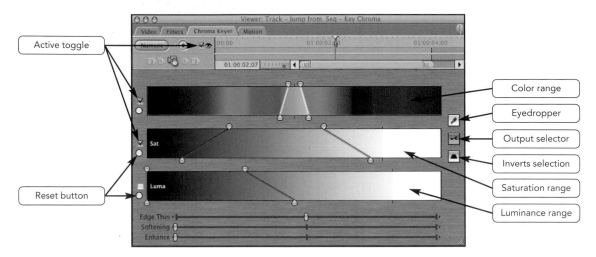

The chroma key filter is divided into three sections: color selection, edge enhancement, and controls. You'll work with all three in this exercise.

Each of the three bars has two small gray buttons at the top and bottom. The top two gray buttons determine the selection range. The bottom two buttons determine feathering, that is, what amount of adjacent values will be included.

Color Range: Used to select the hue of the color to be removed.

Saturation Range (Sat): Used to select the saturation range of colors to be removed.

Luminance Range (Luma): Used to select the luminance range of the colors to be removed.

Edge Thin: Use to restrict or expand the edges of the selected color.

Softening: Blurs the edges of a key. Use in *very* small increments (one to three mouse clicks).

Enhance: Tries to remove color fringes at the edges of a key by using a complementary color. Use this in very small increments, if at all (one to three mouse clicks).

---

4 The best way to work with this filter is from the top down. Set your color range to key out the greatest amount of color first, then improve your key using saturation, then, finally, adjust the luma settings. Don't jump around. Click the **eyedropper** to select the key color. (The "key color" is the color you want to remove.) Then, click in the dark-blue sky near the upper-right corner.

Instantly, part of your sky disappears and is replaced by the background.

5 Next, extend the range of your selected color by clicking the **eyedropper** again. Hold down the **Shift** key and click near the middle of the frame. I generally try to get two color samples when I start a key.

(Notice how the **eyedropper** has a very small plus sign next to it? This indicates it is *adding* to the selection.)

6 The light-gray edge between the trees and the sky is very difficult to remove. Still, there's more you can do to improve this key. Gently tweak the two white dots at the top of the color bar until the key looks as clean as possible. You won't need to move them much. The top two dots control color selection. The bottom two dots control the feathering between colors.

Now, it's time to move to the next two lines: **Sat** and **Luma**.

7 In order to see how well your key is progressing, click the **Key** icon. The **Canvas** changes from showing the final key, to a mass of white against the background. The white is the "matte," or the visual information you want to retain for your key. Your goal is to get this white matte as solid and firmly edged as possible. (This is far easier to write than it is to do.)

When you are viewing the *matte*, the **Key** icon is a black key on a light-gray button. When you are viewing the *source video*, the **Key** is red on a blue button. When you are viewing the *final composite*, the **Key** is red on a gray button. Click the **Key** icon to switch between these three variations.

8 I've also learned that not all three bars are necessary to pull a good key. For example, turn off **Sat** and see if the matte improves. Nope. Better leave **Sat** on.

9 Turn off **Luma** and see if the matte improves. In many keys, leaving **Luma** off *improves* it. In this case, due to the noise in the lower-right corner, the key is better with **Luma** on.

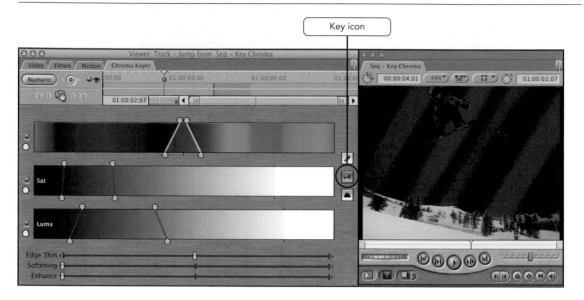

Key icon

10 Slowly tweak the buttons at the top of the **Sat** and **Luma** bars until your matte looks as solid as possible. I work first with **Saturation** until it looks as good as it can, then move on to **Luma**. Only when the key looks as good as you can make it should you start adjusting the sliders at the bottom. This screen shot shows the values I came up with when creating this key.

11 Switch back to the **Final** output of your key (click the **Key** icon) and start adjusting the **Edge Thin** slider. Generally, I move this wildly in both directions until I see which best improves the image. Then, I gradually narrow down the range of movement until the key looks as good as it can.

Finally, when everything else is set, click once or twice on the right arrow of **Softening**. This will blur the edges of your key. Any more than three mouse clicks and things deteriorate quickly. I generally use just one mouse click.

I rarely use **Enhance**—Spill Suppressor is much better. If I do use it, it's only one or two mouse clicks.

Before color correction

After color correction

12 You're done. Render and play your key. The image on the left is my key.

The image on the right is what I came up with after adding color correction. In correcting the image, I pulled down black and midtone levels, significantly boosted the whites, and increased saturation. The image is darker here due to the midtone correction. But this also got rid of the noise in the lower-right corner. You can view my version (without color correction) by playing **Seq – Chroma key finished**.

---

13 That's it for chroma key. Save your work and quit if you need a break. Otherwise, keep this project open. There's one more exercise to go in this chapter—one of my favorites: creating a travel matte.

---

9 | Creating a Traveling Matte

In this exercise, you will learn how to create an effect you've seen most of your life: video inside other video. Often, the video is inside text. In this case, you'll put the video inside a graphic image of a snowboarder. (As an interesting bit of trivia, traveling mattes are the only effect in Final Cut that require a minimum of three layers; all the rest can be done with two.)

1 If Final Cut is not running, start it and open **Chapter 12 Lesson**. Double-click **Seq – Travel start** to load it into the **Timeline**. Position your **playhead** at the start of the sequence.

2 Turn off the visibility indicator for **V3**, so you can see the image on **V2**. Double-click **Snowboard Travel.tif** to load it into the **Viewer**. (This is a TIFF image with an embedded alpha channel to separate the image of the snowboarder from the background. The problem is, the image is too big.)

Also, make sure all four **Auto Select** buttons are turned **on** (dark).

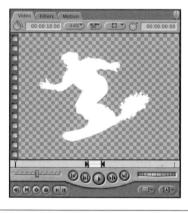

3 In the **Canvas**, turn on **Show Overlays**, **Show Title Safe**, and **Image+Wireframe**.

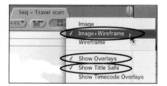

4 Go to the **Viewer**, click the **Motion** tab, and change the **Scale** to **50**. Then, in the **Canvas**, drag the image of the snowboarder to the lower-right corner and align it with the **Title Safe** border. Your **Center** settings should be about **110, 73**.

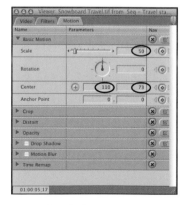

5 Turn on the visibility indicator for **V3** and double-click it to load it into the **Viewer**.

You are creating a three-layer effect: **V1** is the background, **V2** cuts a hole into the background, and **V3** fills the hole. To do this, you need to create a traveling matte, where the image on **V3** is inserted into the image on **V2**. Normally, this is done using text. In this case, you'll use a picture.

---

6 With the **V3** clip selected, choose **Modify > Composite Mode > Travel Matte – Alpha**.

The white image of the snowboarder has been filled with video from the **V3** clip. But you need to position the **V3** clip more precisely.

---

7 Click the **Motion** tab and change the **Scale** of **Thru trees** to **40**. Then, using the **Selection** tool, drag the **V3** image so it completely fills the still graphic on **V2**. The **Center** coordinates are about **100, 71**.

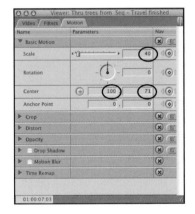

Render and play the clip. Very cool, but somehow a bit flat. This can be perked up with a drop shadow, but to do that, you need to add one more layer—just to create the shadow.

---

8 Select both the **V2** and **V3** clips. Press **Option+up arrow** to raise both clips a track and create a new **V4** track, all at the same time.

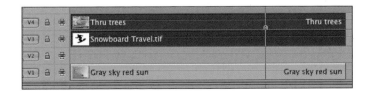

---

9 Select *just* the **V3** clip, **Snowboard Travel.tif**, and choose **Edit > Copy** (or press **Cmd+C**).

10 Turn *off* the **Auto Select** button for **V1**, which forces Final Cut to paste the clip to the lowest numbered track with a dark **Auto Select** button; in other words, **V2**.

Then move the **playhead** to the beginning of the sequence.

---

11 Choose **Edit > Paste** (or press **Cmd+V**). A copy of the **V3** clip is pasted into **V2**. Double-click the **V2** clip, also called **Snowboard Travel.tif**, to load it into the **Viewer**. Click the **Motion** tab, and click **Drop Shadow**.

---

12 The shadow helps a lot, but the **Offset** is too great. Twirl down the **Drop Shadow** triangle to adjust the drop shadow settings, and change the **Offset** to **3**.

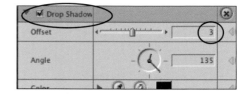

---

13 That's it. A four-layer effect! Congratulations. You are done. Save your work, if you wish. Quit Final Cut and take a break. That wraps up this chapter.

Um, what? Why is it called a "traveling matte" if it doesn't move? Well, it can. Take a look at **Seq – Travel traveling** and you'll see what I mean. There are a *lot* of ways you can use this effect.

NOTE:

Other Uses for Traveling Mattes

Traveling mattes are used a lot to put one image inside another image. Here are some other ideas to spark your creativity:

- Put video inside text for an opening title.
- Put video inside a generated shape (click the **Generator** pop-up menu, choose **Shapes**, and then choose a shape (**Circle**, **Oval**, **Rectangle**, or **Square**).
- Put a LiveType texture inside a graphic.
- Put a Photoshop image inside text to provide texture.

In other words, using a traveling matte, you can put any image or video clip inside text, a generated shape, an imported graphic, or anything else with an alpha channel.

Helpful Keyboard Shortcuts

Shortcut	Action
Option+Cmd+W	Toggles audio waveforms on and off in the Timeline
B	Selects the single-clip Razor Blade tool
BB	Selects the multiple-clip Razor Blade tool
Option+P	Plays a clip that needs rendering, without first rendering it
Option+R	Renders a sequence
Cmd+R	Renders the selected clip, clips, or sequence
Ctrl+R	Renders only Preview (green bar) clips
Double-click	(Nested sequence) Displays nest as series of individual clips
Option+double-click	(Nested sequence) Loads nested sequence into the Browser
Drag (nest), then Cmd	(Nested sequence in Browser) Converts nest into it's component clips when Cmd-dragged into Timeline. (Remember to press Cmd *after* you start dragging.)
Cmd+A	(Timeline or Browser) Selects all clips in Timeline, or all elements in Browser
Shift+Cmd+A	Deselects all selected clips
Option+C	Creates a nest from selected clips or sequence
Option+9	Opens the Video Scopes window
Ctrl+Z	Toggles on and off Range Checking for excess white levels

Summary

In this chapter, you learned a variety of special effects, all revolving around filters. This only scratches the surface of what Final Cut can do, but you now know everything you need to start creating some really incredible effects. That wraps up our look at effects. In Chapter 13, you'll learn how to output your projects—to the Web, CD, DVD, and videotape.

13

Output Your Project

Your project is done and ready to output. This chapter teaches you how to output your project to videotape or to a wide variety of digital formats.

Similar to Chapter 3, *"Gather Your Media,"* this chapter is partly an exercise in using your imagination, since your hardware configuration is probably different than mine. So, I'll show you the steps, and you can make any necessary adjustments specific to your system.

Definitions

There is a difference, to my way of thinking, between outputting and exporting. So, let me give you my definitions:

Outputting: Sending a project out of Final Cut Pro 5 and recording it onto videotape. Outputting involves converting between the digital files stored in the computer and videotape. The opposite of output is capture.

Exporting: Sending a project out of Final Cut, but keeping it in a digital form that can be read by the computer. The opposite of export is import.

Since I use these terms throughout this chapter, I wanted to explain to you at the beginning what they mean to me.

Getting Ready for Output

As I was writing this chapter, I realized that I use a lot of techniques to get ready for output that are not easily categorized. So, I gathered them here so you can easily find them all in one place.

A Simple Technique to Improve Output Reliability

Here's a quick tip that improves reliability: before you start the final output, do a **File > Save As** and save your project with a new name; for instance, **My Project v2**. As you will learn in the troubleshooting section of the Appendix at the end of the book, **Save As** fixes any internal problems with your files that can mess up output.

Doing a **Save As** every few days during editing is a good idea in general, just to keep project files clean. However, this is an especially good technique to make sure your outputs go smoothly.

Organizing Long Projects for Output

Many of the shows I edit are 30 minutes or longer. Although editing a 30- or 60-minute

show in a single sequence in Final Cut is possible, I rarely do it.

Instead, I break my show up into acts (or segments) and edit each act in its own sequence. This allows me to see my individual clips more easily, without having to zoom in and out along a huge Timeline.

Then, I create a new sequence as my "master sequence" and edit all my acts into it in order, all neatly arranged with room for commercial breaks.

Or, if I'm doing something without commercials, I simply butt two segments together with no break.

This practice of creating a master sequence of all the different acts makes final output to tape simple.

Rendering for Output

During editing, a variety of transitions and effects cause render bars to appear over your video or audio elements. Generally, green bars mean the effect can play in real-time.

Generally, that is, but not at output.

When you get ready to output your project, Final Cut renders *everything*. Chapter 9, *"Transitions—Making Change Beautiful,"* discussed rendering in detail. However, in order to guarantee quality, Final Cut makes one more rendering pass just before output.

This final rendering occurs after you complete the **Print to Video** or **Edit to Tape** dialog. And, sometimes, this rendering can take a while. I decrease my waiting for output by rendering my whole sequence first. Then, after everything is rendered, I save my project. This way if I need to cancel an output, I don't have to wait for FCP to re-render again.

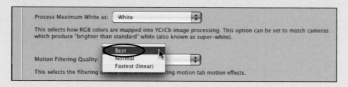

NEW ▶ Also, remember that new with FCP 5 is the ability to change render quality. If your project uses motion effects such as rotation or scaling, I suggest you change your render settings to **Best** quality (choose **Sequence > Settings** and click the **Video Processing** tab) before outputting. If you are just using filters or transitions, changing render quality won't make any difference; so leave it set to **Normal**. **Best** takes about 25% longer to render than **Normal**. FCP does not automatically change these settings for output, so the ultimate choice is up to you.

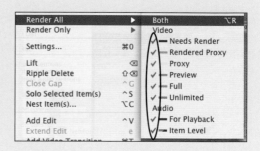

To render, choose **Sequence > Render All > Both** (press **Option+R**) and make sure all options are checked.

Choosing Between "Print to Video" and "Edit to Tape"

How do you decide whether to use **Print to Video** or **Edit to Tape** for final output? Well, it all comes down to timecode.

The rule is simple: *always* use **Print to Video** *unless* you need to record to a specific timecode

on the tape. If you need your project to start at a *specific* timecode on the record tape, use **Edit to Tape**.

For most DV editors, most of the time, **Print to Video** will be fine. For editors of broadcast projects, **Edit to Tape** will most often be a better choice. In either case, the quality is identical.

Don't Play the Timeline for Final Output

In versions of Final Cut prior to version 4, many users, including me, got used to the idea of playing the Timeline when we wanted to record to tape. This was because the **Print to Video** and **Edit to Tape** functions were not as robust as we would have liked. Many times, playing the Timeline was our only option; nothing else worked reliably.

In Final Cut Pro 5 that stratagem no longer works. This is because, in order to reserve more CPU power for real-time effects and audio mixing, the default output options for playing the Timeline are set to a lower quality for both audio and video.

Although these defaults can be changed, my personal feeling is that I like having the extra horsepower for editing. So, for me, it is time to change habits and use the Print to Video and Edit to Tape functions for my final output. In addition, Apple has worked hard to eliminate the bugs that made Print to Video and Edit to Tape unreliable.

Don't spend hours making your projects perfect, only to fall short at the last minute by playing the Timeline to tape. Learn how to do it the right way—read Exercise 1.

1 | Print to Video

In this exercise, you will learn how to output your project to tape using **Print to Video**.

---

1 Start Final Cut and open **Chapter 13 Lesson**. It's in the **FCP Projects > FCP 5 HOT Files** folder you created at the beginning of this book. Double-click **Seq – Snowboard Final** to load it to the **Timeline**.

This is my version of the commercial you've been working on during this book, plus a few extra goodies: a modified nested sequence for the open from Chapter 12, *"Filters and Keying,"* new transitions from Chapter 9, *"Transitions—Making Change Beautiful,"* and audio fades from Chapter 8, *"Audio—The Secret to a Great Picture."*

It's time to output this sequence to tape.

---

2 Either go to the **Browser** and select the sequence you want to output—in this case, select **Seq – Snowboard final**—or open the sequence you want to output into the **Timeline** and make sure the Timeline is selected.

---

3 Choose **File > Print to Video**, or press **Ctrl+M**.

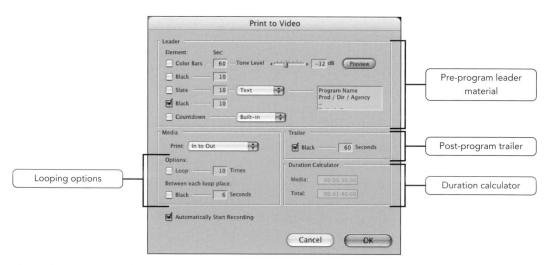

This is the **Print to Video** dialog. If you are outputting a tape for the client to review, or for your Aunt Joyce to show to the family, these settings are fine. Note, however, that I've made three changes from the defaults:

I checked **Black** in the **Leader** box. This adds 10 seconds of black at the beginning of my tape, which allows room for the tape to thread and guards against any tape crinkling damaging my program.

I changed the duration of the **Trailer** from **5** seconds to **60**. The Trailer setting determines how much black will be output by Final Cut after your sequence is complete. Five seconds is too short a time for someone to get up and turn off the tape. Sixty is more reasonable.

(If you are outputting to VHS tape, the industry standard is to fill the remainder of the tape with black, so that the viewer never sees "snow" at the end of the tape. That assumes, of course, you are using a tape length close to the length of your program. There's no advantage to outputting two hours of black just to fill the tape.)

The third change I made was checking **Automatically Start Recording**. By checking this box, if Final Cut has machine control over your deck (as is true with virtually all FireWire-connected decks), then it will switch your deck into Record

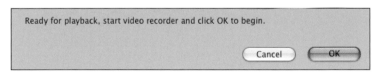

mode 3 seconds after rendering is complete. This means you don't need to wait; it can all be automatic.

Very cool. Except...um, I *like* watching this last playback to tape. Just to be sure nothing goes wrong. Not, of course, that it ever does. Much. So, I check this box, but I don't leave the room.

---

4 Click **OK**. Behind the scenes, Final Cut does a final mixdown of your audio to a stereo file and makes sure all video has been rendered.

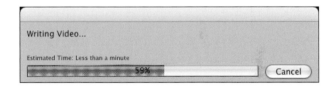

---

5 This dialog appears when FCP is ready to output. If **Automatic Record** is on, FCP will start recording three seconds after this dialog appears. (Or, if you're impatient, press **Record** on your deck and click **OK** in this dialog.) Then, sit back and watch your movie.

When the recording is done, Final Cut will switch your deck out of Record.

Ta-DA! Finished. Whew!

---

6 That's it for **Print to Video**. In the next exercise, you'll learn about a more sophisticated way to lay video back to tape, but for now, take a break. Quit Final Cut, if you wish. Otherwise, keep this project open—you'll use it again. Because you made no changes, there's nothing you need to save to disk.

Understanding Pre-Program Material

The last exercise introduced the concept of pre-program material. However, if you are planning to take your tape to duplication, broadcast, a trade show, or archiving, there are a few more steps you should complete before pressing the **Record** button on your tape deck or camera.

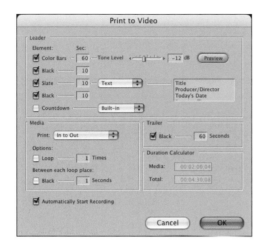

When I use **Print to Video**, these are the settings I use. Let's take a look at what they do and why you should use them.

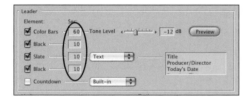

In the top half of the screen are the controls for pre-program, or leader, material. For a long, long time, standard industry practice has organized the beginning of a tape as follows:

- 60 seconds of color bars
- 10 seconds of black
- 10 seconds of slate (keep reading, I'll explain it shortly)
- 10 seconds of black
- Program start

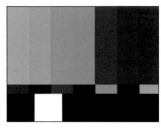

Color bars display an engineering test signal that allows a tape to be configured on playback so that the colors it plays back match the colors you recorded when you output your sequence. Recording 60 seconds of color bars allows an engineer sufficient time to properly set up your tape. Color bars have been used in broadcasting for decades. There's a good reason. Without them, there's no guarantee that the colors that play back from your tape will match the colors you recorded.

Along with color bars (called "bars" by those "in the know") goes **tone**. Tone is a 1000-cycle tone set at a fixed reference volume level. These reference levels are standardized by tape format, so that an engineer can set the tone at the proper level for playback. The default output level for tone in Final Cut is –12 dB.

Slate identifies your program. At a minimum, it should include a title and a running time (abbreviated **TRT**, for **T**otal **R**unning **T**ime). Most professional slates also including the name of the client/producer/director, the date the show was finished, and anything else relevant from an engineering point of view. Here, for example, I indicated this sequence uses drop-frame timecode (DFTC) with a stereo audio mix.

Reference Audio Tone Levels

Recording Tape Format	Tone Level
VHS	Output from Final Cut at –12, record at 0 dB.
DV (MiniDV, DVCAM, DVCPRO-25)	–12 dB
DigiBetacam, DVCPRO-50, DVCPRO-HD	–20 dB
Betacam SP	Output from Final Cut at –12, record at 0 dB.

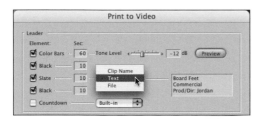

To create a slate, change the **Slate** pop-up menu to **Text** and type your information in the small text window on the right. Use hyphens (-) when you want to put a space between lines. You can also use this pop-up menu to select a file or clip to use as a slate.

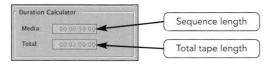

Running time, often abbreviated as **TRT**, is the length your show runs from fade-up to fade-down, excluding any commercial breaks. The **Duration Calculator** in the lower-right corner of this dialog gives you the answer. The top line (**Media**) shows actual program running time (30 seconds in the case of this commercial); the second line (**Total**) shows total running time including all the pre- and post-program material, 3:00:00, in this example.

One other neat goodie is the **Media** section. Many times, when I create materials for trade shows, the client wants it to repeat over and over…and over. Using these check boxes means I only need to create the sequence once, and Final Cut will automatically play it back on output as many times (**Loop**) and with as many seconds of black between each repetition (**Black**) as I want. I've used this often, and it works great.

In the days of live television and playback from tape decks, the last 10 seconds of black were replaced by a countdown. These days, with everything playing back instantly from servers, countdowns are no longer necessary. (Sigh…I miss them.)

2 | Recording Black and Timecode on Tapes

In order to use **Edit to Tape** in Exercise 3. you must first record black and timecode on your tape in a process called *striping*, or *recording black and code*.

What striping does is feed black video and silent audio, from Final Cut to your deck, so you can record it to tape. (FYI, Final Cut doesn't supply timecode to the tape; timecode signals are actually created by your deck. Final Cut simply tells your deck to generate and record timecode on the tape.)

Here's how to stripe a tape:

1 Connect your deck and be sure that Final Cut Pro can control it.

2 Put in a blank tape. Be sure the little record-lockout slider is set to **Record**.

3 Choose **File > Edit to Tape**.

NOTE:

Should You Stripe Your Tapes?

The benefits to striping your tapes are that

- You have continuous timecode from beginning to end of the tape—no timecode breaks.

- If you are recycling an old tape, all old program material is erased.

- Unlike simply recording a tape with a lens cap on the camera, you record audio black, not extraneous room noise from the camera mike.

- On high-end DV decks (you know if you have one because they cost close to $8000) and professional video tape decks, you can preset the timecode so it starts at a specific time—most often, 00:58:20:00.

Now there is a raging debate (well, OK, a few of us are kicking the idea around) that striping tapes may not be beneficial to everyone all the time.

So, here's my take on the issue:

- I stripe tapes to be shot by an inexperienced cameraperson. I will not stripe a tape being shot by a professional cameraperson.

- I stripe all tapes that I use for final output of my projects.

4 Click the small square at the top center that looks like a squashed centipede. (It's supposed to be a film frame.)

Current Settings matches the video output to the tape to the current video settings of your **Timeline**.

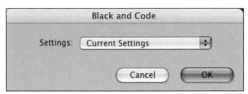

5 To send a different video format to the tape, choose it from the pop-up menu. These settings vary depending upon which deck and capture card you are using. **DV NTSC 48 kHz** is the DV standard for North America; **DV PAL 48 kHz** is the DV default for the rest of the world.

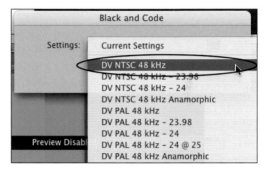

A second dialog appears if you have a deck that allows presetting timecode (which includes virtually all Beta decks and very high-end DV decks). Presetting allows you to specify the starting timecode for the tape, as well as whether you want it to be drop-frame or non-drop frame. If you can set timecode, a good number to use is 00:58:20:00. You'll understand why in the next exercise.

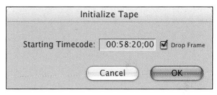

Virtually no DV camera or deck allows presetting timecode. In this case, all timecode starts at 0:00:00:00. Also, virtually all DV timecode is drop-frame.

6 This dialog appears, giving you one last warning that you are about to erase everything on your tape. When you click **OK**, the recording starts automatically.

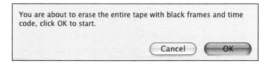

7 In the event you need to abort the recording, this dialog reminds you to press the **Esc** key. Otherwise, let the tape record completely. When it's finished, Final Cut will rewind to the beginning of the tape.

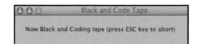

3 | Edit to Tape

In this exercise, you need to send this snowboard commercial to a broadcast station for airing. They require that your commercial start exactly at timecode 1:00:00:00 on the tape. So, here, you will learn a more advanced way to output your project: **Edit to Tape**.

The key point to keep in mind about Edit to Tape is that it *requires* you to have timecode already recorded on the tape.

NEW▶ Apple engineers told me that, although they did not change the interface for Edit to Tape in this version, they spent a great deal of time making it more accurate. So, if you had problems with Edit to Tape in FCP HD, especially with frame-accuracy, those problems should be gone in FCP 5.

One other note: you can only output up to eight audio channels using Edit to Tape. If you need more, your best method is exporting your project as a QuickTime movie. Also, DV and HDV only support two channels of audio output.

---

1 Start Final Cut and open **Chapter 13 Lesson**, if it isn't open already. Double-click **Seq – Snowboard Final** to load it to the **Timeline**.

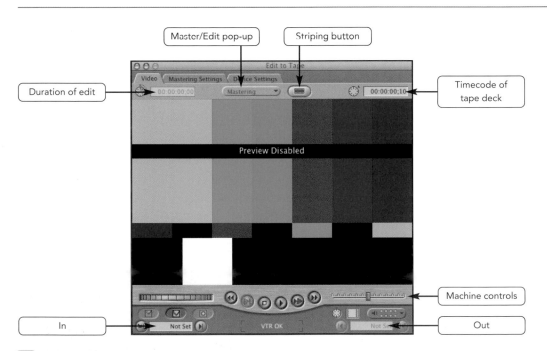

2 Using **Edit to Tape** is straightforward. Start by choosing **File > Edit to Tape**. In order to open this dialog, you must have a camera or deck attached to your computer and turned on.

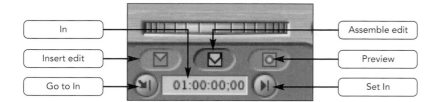

In	Assemble edit
Insert edit	Preview
Go to In	Set In

01:00:00;00

3 Enter the timecode number where you want the recording to *start* on the tape (the **In** of the tape) in the lower-left field. This process is identical to entering an **In** in the **Viewer**. In this case, the **In** is set to **1:00:00:00**. (By the way, the **J**, **K**, and **L** keys work in the **Edit to Tape** window, too.)

Important Note: If you are adding leader material, you need to subtract the time of the leader material from your **In**. For example, if you want your program to start at **1:00:00:00** and you have **1:30:00** of leader material, you need to set your **In** to **00:58:30:00**.

---

4 Select the **Mastering Settings** tab at the top of the window. Set up any pre-program material, similar to **Print to Video**—the settings are the same.

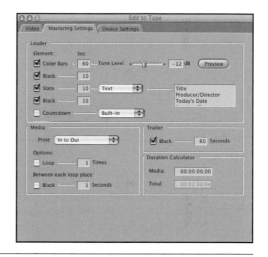

---

5 Select the sequence you want to output to tape from the **Browser** and *drag* it to the **Edit to Tape** window. Drop it on the **Assemble** overlay.

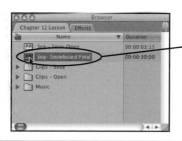

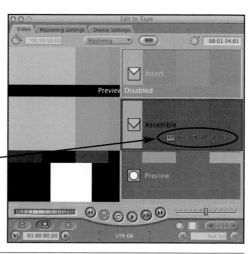

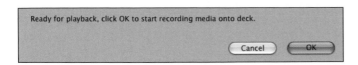

Ready for playback, click OK to start recording media onto deck.

Cancel   OK

6 Click **OK** in this dialog to start the output process. If you need to abort, press the **Esc** key.

And that's it. Your edit to tape is done.

NOTE:

Edit to Tape Options Are Limited for DV

In the world of linear editing, which means tape-to-tape, there are two types of edits: Assemble and Insert. Naturally, the word "Insert" means something different in linear editing than it does in nonlinear editing.

Why should life be easy?

Assemble edit: At the point of the edit, the deck cleanly switches into Record mode and performs a technically invisible edit. Timecode continues without a break. Audio and video edit seamlessly. At the end of the edit, however, there will be a break in timecode, along with a break in video and audio. This is sometimes referred to as a "clean In and dirty Out edit."

An Assemble edit is the only edit a DV deck or camera can make. An Assemble edit edits video, audio, and timecode simultaneously.

Insert edit: At the point of the edit, the deck cleanly switches into Record mode and performs a technically invisible edit. Timecode continues without a break. Audio and video edit seamlessly. At the end of the edit, the audio, video, and timecode switch out of the edit smoothly. This is sometimes referred to as a "clean In and clean Out edit."

A professional-grade video tape deck can make both Assemble and Insert edits. Insert edits are most often used to replace a shot within an already edited and output sequence. An Insert edit can edit any combination of video, audio, or timecode (video-only, audio-only, video and audio, and so on).

"But, Wait A Minute...!"

I hear you exclaim, "There's something wrong here."

Well, yeah. I'm playing a little fast and loose with the truth. Everything I've told you about using **Edit to Tape** is true. *Except*, on all DV decks that cost less than about $8000, you can only start timecode at 0:00:00:00. This means you can't stripe a tape to start at 1:00:00:00.

So, if you need to output a tape for broadcast, you'll need to buy a tape with the correct time-code on it from a professional video tape supply house, or make friends with the engineers at the broadcast station and have them stripe the tape for you.

And why did the broadcast station want 1:00:00:00 in the first place?

All broadcast programs start at 1:00:00:00 on tape because starting at this time makes it very easy for the broadcaster to time the length of a show just by looking at the drop-frame timecode. No calculator required. This has been true for at least the last 40 years.

Also, I mentioned earlier that most professional tapes start at timecode 00:58:20:00. This is because if your show starts at 1:00:00:00, you need to leave room before that for the pre-program leader material, such as bars and tone. Here's the timing of a "normal" broadcast tape:

00:58:20:00	Timecode and audio/video black start
00:58:30:00	Color bars and tone start
00:59:30:00	10 seconds of black starts
00:59:40:00	10 seconds of slate starts
00:59:50:00	10 seconds of black starts
01:00:00:00	Program starts.

In my programs, I sometimes build these pre-program materials into my main sequence, and other times I use the Mastering settings. Depends upon my mood.

If you are editing to a professional deck (specifically for an Insert edit), check in the Final Cut user's manual about edit settings.

Specifically, you need to set this pop-up to **Editing**.

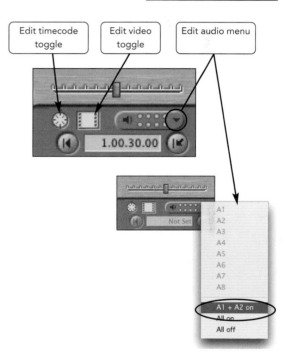

Then you need to select, using these three control points, the combination of timecode, video, and audio you want to edit.

However, as I said near the beginning, if your medium of choice is DV, most of the time you'll be just fine using **Print to Video**.

So, You Wanna Be an Export Expert?

Whether you want to export your sequence for the Web, CD, or DVD, there are a lot of options, but really only one choice: export as a QuickTime movie (**File > Export > QuickTime Movie**).

Here's the short answer to why.

Using Final Cut to create optimized, compressed files is like using a hammer to drive screws; it will work, but it's the wrong tool for the job. Final Cut does great exports, but other software does better compression.

Creating movies for the Web always involves creating multiple versions (for slow, medium, and fast connections) of multiple formats (QuickTime, Real, Windows Media, even Flash). This means exporting the same file from Final Cut over and over again.

You can do it, but life is too short.

Instead, use Final Cut to export one file, at the highest quality, then move that file into Sorenson Squeeze, Popwire's Compression Master, Apple's Compressor, or the compression program of your choice. In all cases, these do a far better job of compression than Final Cut, plus they can create all the versions you need at once through batch processing. While you are out sipping lattes at Starbuck's—or wherever world-class editors hang out in your part of the woods—your computer can be back at the office doing all the work.

Helpful Export Table

What the File Is for	What You Export	Where It Goes
Web	QuickTime movie	Your favorite compression software
CD	QuickTime movie	Your favorite compression software
iDVD	QuickTime movie	iDVD will compress it
DVD Studio Pro (<1 hour)	QuickTime movie	DVD Studio Pro will compress it
DVD Studio Pro (>1 hour)	QuickTime movie	Compressor will compress it
LiveType	LiveType export	LiveType (see Exercise 6)
Soundtrack Pro	Soundtrack export	Soundtrack Pro (see Exercise 5)
ProTools	OMF	ProTools or Deck (see Exercise 5)
Other video editing	EDL or XML	Other video editing program

When Should You Use File > Export > QuickTime Conversion?

Only when you need to quickly compress a file and don't need the highest quality or the smallest file size. Or when you need to export a still frame. Or when you need to convert a sequence into a special format, like a Targa sequence.

In other words, only in special circumstances.

Exporting a QuickTime movie always exports at the highest quality (8- or 10-bit video). Exporting as QuickTime Conversion limits your video to 8-bit. This will be noticeable if you are doing lots of compositing or gradient color work. DV, by the way, is always 8-bit video, so the effects of QuickTime Conversion will be less with DV source material.

QuickTime Conversion can be helpful, especially in a pinch. But it should not be your first choice. If you've forgotten how to export a still frame, please see Chapter 11, *"Motion Effects."*

4 | Exporting a QuickTime Movie

In this exercise, you will learn the best way to export a sequence for the Web, CD, or DVD. And, in all cases, it's the same answer: export your sequence as a QuickTime movie. This exercise explains why and how.

---

1 Start Final Cut and open **Chapter 13 Lesson**, if it isn't open already. Double-click **Seq – Snowboard Final** to load it to the **Timeline**.

---

2 There are two ways to select a sequence for export:

• Load it into the **Timeline** and select the **Timeline**.

• Choose the name of the sequence in the **Browser** and select the **Browser**.

Pick one.

---

3 Choose **File > Export > QuickTime Movie**.

---

4 Give your movie a name. (QuickTime movies use the extension **.mov**.)

Current Settings will output your movie matching the settings in your sequence.

Unless you have changed your **Render Settings**, which I do not advise or teach, you never need to **Recompress All Frames**.

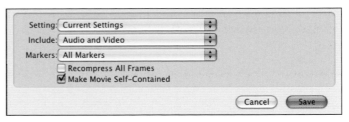

Make Movie Self-Contained is often confusing. There are two types of QuickTime movies: Self-contained and reference movies.

A self-contained movie contains all your media in a single file, which can be played, or compressed, on any system (Mac or PC) that can play a QuickTime movie. Self-contained movies are very large and can take a while to export.

When this box is *not checked*, you are creating a reference movie. This is a relatively tiny file that contains all the audio from your sequence, plus pointers that "point" to the existing media files on your hard disk. Reference movies are about one-twelfth the size of a self-contained movie. Reference movies export 10 to 15 times faster than a self-contained movie, as well. The one trick with using a reference movie is that it must reference the original media files stored on your hard disk, meaning that it will play fine on your machine, but lose the "link" to the referenced media files if you try to play the movie on a different computer.

In both cases, audio and video quality is identical. QuickTime easily plays both files. So, if you are sending the file to someone else, or need to archive the file on your system, make it self-contained. Otherwise, and this is my first choice, output your sequence as a reference movie.

By the way, both these formats work fine for compressing a video for the Web. All compressed files are always self-contained. So, whether you start with a reference movie or a self-contained movie, the end result is the same. For this reason, I almost always use reference movies when outputting for compression to the Web.

---

5 If you want to export DVD chapter markers for inclusion in iDVD or DVD Studio Pro, choose **Chapter Markers** from the **Markers** pop-up menu.

---

6 Click **Save**, and you are done. Quit Final Cut if you need a break. Otherwise, keep things open—you will use this file in the remaining exercises.

---

5 | Special Cases: Exporting Audio

In this exercise, you will learn how to export audio for special cases, such as Soundtrack Pro mixing, OMF files, and AIF files.

NEW▶ Soundtrack Pro is new and bundled with Final Cut Studio. And with the new mixing capability that Soundtrack provides, there are lots of reasons to send files back and forth between these two applications.

---

1 Start Final Cut and open **Chapter 08 Lesson 1**. (Yup, that's Chapter 08, just in case you thought this was a typo.) Select **Seq – Ready to Mix** in the **Browser**.

---

2 You can "send" a sequence to Soundtrack for mixing in two ways:

• Choose **File > Send to > Soundtrack Pro Multitrack Project.**

• **Ctrl+click** the sequence name in the **Browser** and choose **Send To > Soundtrack Pro Multitrack Project.**

The **Send To** option is new in FCP 5. What it does is export all your sequence clips as individual audio clips, generates a background video of your sequence, opens Soundtrack Pro in Multitrack mode, and loads all the sequence audio clips into the Soundtrack Timeline—ready to mix. This is great!

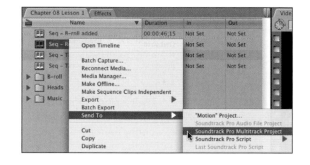

If, instead, you select **File > Export > For Soundtrack**, Final Cut will export a mixed-down stereo file, ready for import into Soundtrack Pro. Although useful in certain circumstances, this export doesn't begin to touch the power and flexibility of the **Send To** command.

Chapter 8, *"Audio—The Secret to a Great Picture,"* provides more information on the integration between Soundtrack Pro and Final Cut.

Although you will probably spend most of your export-ing time moving files between FCP and Soundtrack Pro, in some cases you need to export only the audio files. In this case you have two choices:

• Export an AIFF file.

• Export an OMF file.

An **AIF** (or AIFF) file can be played anywhere. It is the native format of the Mac, as well as all CD audio. An AIF file merges all the clips in a track into a single audio file for the entire track. The biggest advantage to AIF is that all audio programs can play them. Plus, an AIF export will include all volume changes and filters in the audio.

An **OMF** file is a special-purpose file that is used for transferring audio specifically for mixing from Final Cut into audio programs such as DigiDesign's ProTools or Bias Inc.'s Deck. The key advantage of using OMFs is that all clips remain distinct and editable, each with its own set of handles. The biggest disadvantage to OMF is that only a limited number of audio programs support them. In addition, exporting OMF files from Final Cut does not include any volume changes or filters.

---

3 To export AIFF files, choose **File > Export > Audio to AIFF(s)**. The standard export dialog box appears, except with different settings at the bottom.

The standard sample rate and sample size (or bit-depth) for DV and broadcast video is **48 kHz**, **16-bit**. So these initial two choices are fine.

If you want to export your audio as dual mono, that is with both channels linked and panned to the center, choose **Channel Grouped** from the **Files** pop-up. If you want to export your audio with all the odd-numbered channels panned to the left and all the even-numbered channels panned to the right, choose **Stereo Mix**.

Final Cut exports all audio tracks whose visibility indicator is **on**. (So, if you want to export individual tracks, turn the visibility indicator **off** for all tracks you *don't* want to export.)

---

4 To export OMF files, choose **File > Export > Audio to OMF**. The **OMF Audio Export** dialog appears. Again, the settings of **48 kHz** and **16-bit** are fine. Generally, I like working with longer handles, so I set **Handle Length** to **5:00**. This provides for more flexibility in the audio mix.

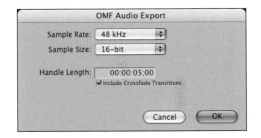

The default OMF file format is **2.0**, which appears at the bottom of the Save dialog. This, too, is fine.

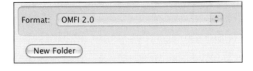

---

5 Give the export file a name, and you are done.

And that's it for this exercise. Again, you don't need to save your work in this project, because you haven't made any changes you need to keep. Quit Final Cut if you need a break. Otherwise, it's time to move on to learning about some special case video exports.

---

6 | Special Cases: Exporting Video for LiveType

In this exercise, you will learn how to export video for LiveType and Compressor, as well as some suggestions on improving your results with Compressor.

1 Start Final Cut and open **Chapter 13 Lesson**, if it isn't open already. Double-click **Seq – Snowboard Final** to load it to the **Timeline**. Leave the **Timeline** selected.

2 To export a sequence to LiveType, choose **File > Export > For LiveType**.

This dialog is just like the others you've seen earlier, except for the settings at the bottom. Notice that this time, Final Cut is including all the markers in the export. In fact, all four Final Cut marker types display in LiveType:

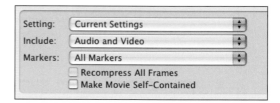

- Generic marker

- Chapter marker

- Compression marker

- Soundtrack marker

And, again, Final Cut sets the file to be a reference movie (that is, not self-contained), because you use this movie on your system simply as a reference within LiveType.

3 Give the export file a name and click **OK**.

4 To import the movie into LiveType, open **LiveType**, choose **File > Place Background Movie**, select your movie, and click **Open**. The video from your movie shows up on the **Timeline**, ready for compositing.

Chapter 10, *"Text, Titles, and Graphics,"* showed you how to use "round-tripping" to quickly switch between Final Cut and LiveType when making changes to your animation.

You only need to export your sequence to Compressor if you are going to use it in DVD Studio Pro. iDVD imports only QuickTime movies, which means you already know how to create movies for iDVD.

Let me say clearly that, in my opinion, the best way to get your video into Compressor is to export it using **File > Export > QuickTime movie**. Then, load that QuickTime movie into Compressor. This is both fast and reliable.

There are problems when you export video directly into Compressor from Final Cut using **File > Export > To Compressor**. And, according to the Apple engineers I've spoken with, these problems have not yet been resolved in Final Cut Pro 5. For this reason, if you want to get your movie out of Final Cut and into Compressor, follow the steps I indicated in Exercise 4 of this chapter.

Also, if you plan to create chapter markers for your DVD, it is best to add them into your Final Cut sequence by using markers. This is because adding markers in Final Cut is frame-accurate, whereas creating chapter markers to an MPEG-2 file in DVD Studio Pro is only accurate to plus-or-minus 15 frames.

---

1 Once you have the movie exported, open Compressor and drag your movie into it.

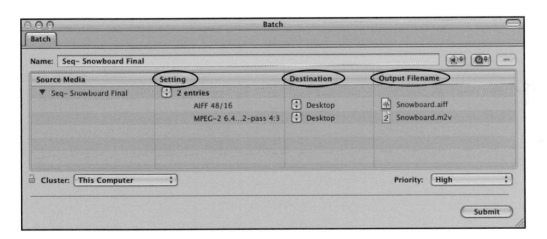

2 From the **Setting** pop-up menu, choose a compression setting. The rule is: choose the setting that is closest to, *but longer than*, the length of your sequence.

So, for a 30-second commercial, choose **DVD Best Quality 90 minutes**. For a 120-minute program, choose **DVD Best Quality 120 minutes**.

If your video is in a **4:3** aspect ratio, choose the **4:3** option. If it is in a **16:9** aspect ratio, choose **16:9**.

By the way, I always use the **Best Quality** setting. For my production clients, the length of time it takes to compress a video is never the issue; making it look as good as it can is always far more important.

3 Set the **Destination** to where you want the compressed files stored. On my production system, I created a folder on my second hard disk called **Compressed Files** and use that as the default destination for Compressor. In this example, you can use the **Desktop**.

The main reason to use Compressor is that you want to create high-quality MPEG-2 video files (which is the standard video format for DVD) to import into DVD Studio Pro. (Remember, iDVD won't read MPEG-2 files, it imports only QuickTime movies.)

---

4 One of the tricks of DVD Studio Pro is that it automatically links audio and video files that have the same file name to the left of the extension. So, I always change the **Output** file name so the audio and video file names match.

So, in this case, change the name of each file to **Snowboard** and click **Submit**.

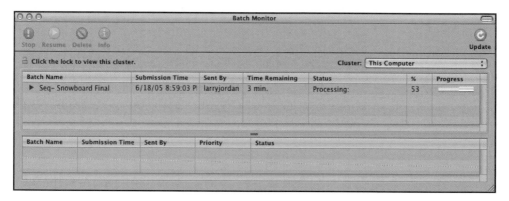

The actual compression is done by a background application. **Batch Monitor** is only there to display the status of your job.

The first 50% of the job is compressing the audio, which is very fast. The last half is compressing the video, which can take a while. The progress bar displays the amount of the job completed.

When the compression is done, look on the Desktop, and you'll see two files: an audio AIFF and video M2V. These are the files that get imported into DVD Studio Pro for your DVD. These two files get combined into one during the final stage of creating a DVD, in a process called "multiplexing."

Snowboard.m2v   Snowboard.aiff

---

5 And that's it. You've covered all the major elements of outputting and exporting out of Final Cut Pro. Don't save your work, you haven't changed anything. Quit Final Cut if you need to take a break.

Helpful Keyboard Shortcuts

Shortcut	Action
Option+R	Renders all clips in a sequence, depending upon what render elements are checked in Sequence > Render All.
Cmd+R	Renders a selected clip, series of clips, or sequence.
Ctrl+M	Opens Print to Video dialog.
Shift+N	Creates a still frame of the frame of video currently under the active playhead. The still frame appears in the Viewer.

Summary

That's it. You've completed your project from beginning to end—capture to output. All that's left is wrapping up the details and archiving your work. And that's next, in Chapter 14, *"Archiving Your Project."*

14

Archiving Your Project

Your project's done. The client's check has cleared the bank. It's time to archive your project and free up some hard disk space.

In this chapter, you will learn how to prepare a project for archiving, what to save and what to throw out, and what to do when you need to restore an old project for reediting. You'll also get an introduction to the Media Manager, along with some examples of how to use it.

Archiving Your Project

Because of the wide variations in system installation and hardware, it isn't possible to provide precise step-by-step instructions on how to archive your project. Instead, I'll show you the process and the screens, so that you can make the necessary adjustments for your system.

The goal in archiving your project is to organize your project file so that sequences are properly named, reel numbers are correct, and the file is in good condition. Then, save everything that can't be easily replaced, and trash everything else.

Here are the steps, all organized in one place:

1. Verify that all sequence names make sense, and delete all sequences not used in the final project.

2. Verify that all reel names are correct, and change those that aren't.

3. Do a **Save As** on the project file.

4. Trash all project-related render files, using **Render Manager**.

5. Back up project files and all non-timecode-based media to CD (or DVD).

6. Trash all project-related timecode-based media, using the **Finder**.

7. Remove all project files from the computer.

Now that the heat of battle has passed, take a look at all the different sequences you created. Did you use all of them? If not, delete those that are not necessary to the project. It is easier to delete them now, while they are fresh in your mind, than to spend hours trying to figure out which are the good versions when you return to this project in the future.

In a related vein, be sure your sequence names make sense. Make them less cryptic. If you gave this project to another editor, could she figure out what you did? Making sequence names easier to understand is a huge help if you need to redo this project in the future.

Once you've reviewed and corrected your sequence names, it's time to make sure all reel numbers are correct. As you will learn later in this chapter, Final Cut makes it easy to recapture material from videotape, using Batch Capture. However, in order for Batch Capture to work, your reel names must be accurate.

DVD MOVIE:

archive.mov

For tutorials on reconnecting media, the Render Manager, and the Media Manager, please view **archive.mov**, one of the QuickTime movies included on the **Final Cut Pro 5 HOT DVD**.

1 | Changing Reel Names

In this exercise, you will learn how to change reel names in the Browser.

---

1 Start **Final Cut**, if it isn't running already, and open **Chapter 14 Lesson**. It's in the **FCP Projects > FCP 5 HOT Files** folder you created at the beginning of the book. This is the same project you used in Chapter 13, *"Output Your Project."* This project file may need rendering.

---

2 Go to the **Browser** and scroll right until you find the **Reel** column. Click the **Reel** column header and drag it *left* until the **Reel** column is next to the **Name** column.

---

3 Notice that **Blue sky** has no reel name and **Down mountain** has the wrong one.

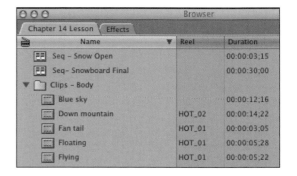

---

4 To change a reel name, double-click in the **Reel** field and enter a new name. To start, change the reel name for **Blue sky** to **HOT_01**.

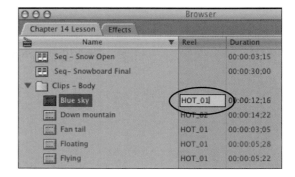

Reel names are part of the timecode data, which is stored permanently in the media file on your hard disk, along with timecode, audio, and video data. This data allows Final Cut to properly identify a media file when it is imported

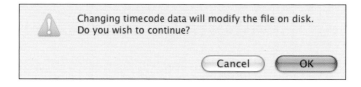

into a new project, by reading both the timecode and reel name. This dialog box appears whenever you modify a reel name, alerting you that the new reel name will be recorded in the media file. Click **OK** to allow FCP to record your change, **Cancel** if you want to leave the reel name as it is.

5 Another way to change a reel name is to **Ctrl+click** the **Reel** field and choose the correct reel name from the pop-up menu. Change the **Down Mountain** reel to **HOT_01**, as well.

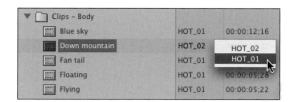

6 Verify that all other reel names are set to **HOT_01**. If not, change them. Once verification is complete, this exercise is done. Keep the lesson file open.

2 | Protecting Your Project Using Save As

In this exercise, you will learn how to use Save As to create a backup of your project files, and you'll also use it to perform final maintenance before archiving your project.

---

1 Open **Chapter 14 Lesson**, if it isn't open already. This is the same file you used in Exercise 1.

---

2 Choose **File > Save As** and save the project using a new name. (I often just use the letters **v2** or **v3**, indicating the version number of the project file.)

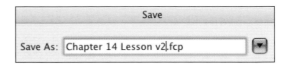

The benefit to using Save As is twofold: it provides a backup of your file in case something happens to the first one, and Final Cut uses this as an opportunity to straighten out any internal numbers or pointers that may be flaky.

Although you can easily make a backup of your file in the Finder, that just duplicates a file, it doesn't fix anything. This internal repair can only be accomplished when Final Cut does a Save As.

I find myself doing a Save As as a backup system every few days during a project, just before final output and just prior to archiving the project.

---

3 When the **Save As** is done, it's time to delete your render files. Keep everything open for the next exercise.

---

3 | Deleting Render Files

In this exercise, you will learn how to use the Render Manager. The Render Manager is a tool inside Final Cut that tracks and deletes render files. One of the benefits to using the organizational system outlined in Chapter 1, *"Get Organized,"* is that it helps the Render Manager track every render file for every project.

1 Open **Chapter 14 Lesson**, if it isn't open already. This is the same file you used in Exercise 1. (Remember, your screens and data totals will look somewhat different from mine.)

2 Choose **Tools > Render Manager**.

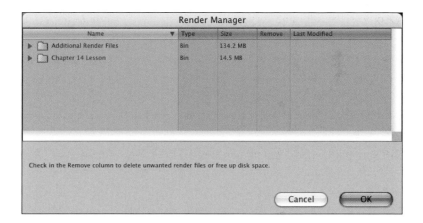

3 The current project is always listed separately, along with a folder titled **Additional Render Files**. Twirl down the **Additional Render Files** from time to time to make sure you don't have old render files taking up space.

As I was writing this chapter, I ran Render Manager to prepare the screen shots for this exercise. And I discovered

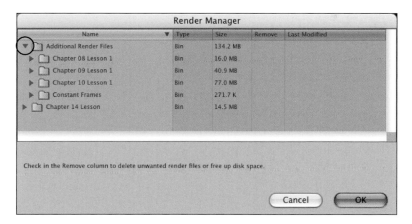

that I had gigabytes of space tied up with render files of projects that were long gone. I, um, don't check Render Manager as often as I should. Since I was using my system of keeping all my media in one folder (**Final Cut Pro Documents**), Render Manager was happily keeping track of everything, so it was simply a matter of a few mouse clicks and I got 9 GB of space back.

Sigh…it's nice when I pay attention to my own advice.

4 Clicking the **Size** column header allows you to sort files by size. Click **Size** twice to sort in descending order.

5 In this case, twirl down **Chapter 14 Lesson**. Notice that render files are grouped first by project, then by sequence, and finally by whether they are audio or video render files.

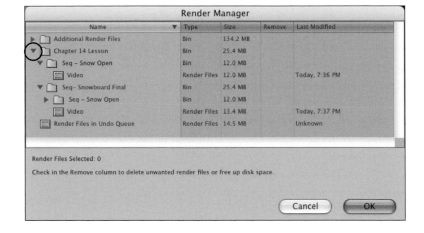

6 Because you want to get rid of *all* render files related to this project, check once in the **Remove** column on the same line as **Chapter 14 Lesson**. All render files related to that project are flagged (checked) for deletion.

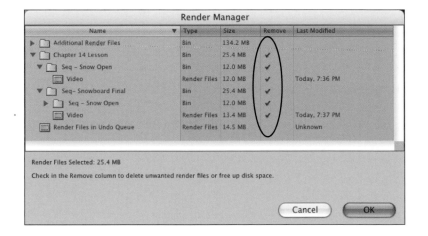

7 At the bottom of the screen is a message explaining how much disk space is involved—in this case, **25.4 MB** of space. (Your file sizes may be different.) Click **OK**, and your render files are gone.

Render Files Selected: 25.4 MB

Check in the Remove column to delete unwanted render files or free up disk space.

In the event you made a mistake and trashed the wrong render files, you won't be able to **Undo** this. However, just open your sequence, choose **Sequence > Render All**, and Final Cut will rebuild all missing render files.

By the way, for those who are curious, render files are stored in the same folder as your **Capture Scratch** folder. If you set your system up as I suggested in Chapter 1, *"Get Organized,"* the path is **[Second hard disk] > Final Cut Pro Documents > Audio Render Files**, for audio render files, and **[Second hard disk] > Final Cut Pro Documents > Render Files**, for video render files.

---

8 That's it for this exercise. Now, it's time to back up your project. To do this, quit Final Cut so all open files are closed.

---

4 | Backing Up Project Files and Trashing Media

In this exercise, you will learn which files to back up and which to trash. Rereading Chapter 1, "*Get Organized*," will be helpful in understanding how this system works.

Note: For technical reasons, I couldn't use this organization system with the DVD exercise files for this book, but this *is* the way I organize files on my production systems.

---

1 Be sure Final Cut is not running, so that all open files are closed.

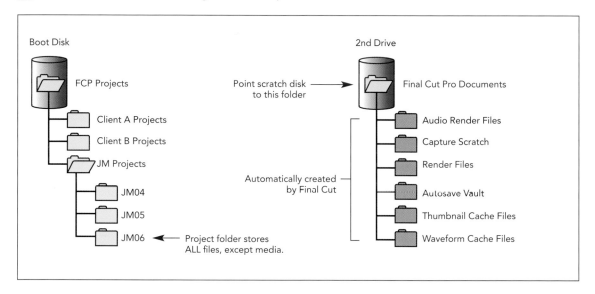

Back in Chapter 1, I described a system where you create a folder on the boot drive, called **FCP Projects**, which serves as the master folder for all your projects.

Inside this folder, I suggested you create a separate folder for each Final Cut project. Here's where that organization system pays off.

If you follow those instructions, inside that project folder you stored all your graphics, music, audio effects, animation, LiveType projects, Soundtrack Pro files...everything related to the project *except* timecode-based media. That is, everything except what is on your videotapes.

---

2 All you need to do now is copy that project folder from your computer to a CD, or DVD if there isn't enough room on a CD. Generally, these files are very small, compared to media.

Final Cut projects don't contain any media. Instead, all clips are referenced using pointers that "point" from Final Cut's Browser or Timeline to the actual media files stored on your hard disk. Each pointer keeps track of the full path and file name of each media file.

Because all your non-timecode files have been stored in this project folder throughout the project, those FCP pointers, or links, remain unbroken when you copy this project folder. This means that if you need to restore the project, everything is right where Final Cut expects it to be, without reconnecting files.

3 Finally, after all render files are trashed and all projects files safely backed up, you can trash your media files. This too, is easy, if you are using the system outlined in Chapter 1. Go to **[Second hard disk] > Final Cut Pro Documents > Capture Scratch**. Inside it you will find a folder for every project for which you captured media.

Because you set your scratch disk to **Final Cut Pro Documents** at the start of the project, and never changed it, every time you captured media it all went into the **Final Cut Pro Documents > Capture Scratch** folder, stored in a media folder with the *same name* as your project. Now, when it comes time to trash the media for this project, just select the **Final Cut Pro Documents > Capture Scratch > [project name]** folder and drag it to the **Trash**. All media clips for that project will be trashed, and you just got a lot of hard disk space back.

So, to summarize, all project files go into the project folder inside **FCP Projects**, which gets backed up to CD. All render files get trashed, because they are easily recalculated by Final Cut. All media files get trashed because Final Cut can recapture them from the original videotapes based on the reel names and timecodes stored in the project file whenever you need to reedit the project, as you will learn shortly.

A key point is to archive your media on videotape, not hard drives. Videotapes last longer. I have 20-year-old VHS tapes that I can still play; how many 10-year-old hard drives do you have that can still attach to your computer? That's my point. Tapes are for archiving, hard drives are for editing.

NOTE:

Storing Videotapes

Good quality magnetic videotapes have a shelf life of 20 to 25 years, provided you store them away from extremes of heat, light, cold, and moisture.

Tapes will last longer and play back better if they are stored on edge, rather than flat. Storing on edge decreases the effects of gravity on the tape's oxide particles and the earth's magnetic field on the magnetic signals recorded on the tape.

Even better, try to store the tape wound all the way to the head or tail of the tape. First, this assures even winding and stacking throughout the tape; second, over the long term, storing a tape wound all the way to the end offers more protection to the magnetic signals.

What Happens to Autosave Vault Files?

One of the nice features of the Autosave
Vault is that you don't need to worry about
trashing old Vault files. In Chapter 2,
"Understanding the Final Cut Pro Interface,"
you configured the Autosave Vault so that as
new projects came in, old projects got
trashed automatically. At the time, the setting I was most concerned with was **Save a
Copy Every**—and we set it to **15** minutes. This means that Final Cut makes a backup,
protection copy every 15 minutes.

☑ Autosave Vault		
Save a copy every:	15	minutes
Keep at most:	20	copies per project
Maximum of:	15	projects

Now that you are at the end of a project, the other two settings are more relevant.

Keep at Most 20 Copies means that Final Cut keeps only the 20 most recent protection copies. When it saves the 21st, the first gets trashed; the 22nd trashes the second, and so on. This means that the amount of hard disk space the Autosave Vault needs stays pretty much constant.

Maximum of 15 Projects means that Final Cut keeps only the 15 most recent projects. When the 16th project starts, all of project 1 gets trashed. (Obviously, if you are working on more than 15 projects at the same time, you should increase this suggested level.) Again, this means that the amount of hard disk space required by the Autosave Vault remains fairly constant.

So, set the Vault and don't worry about it. It pretty much takes care of itself.

5 | Restoring an Old Project

In this exercise, you will learn how to restore a project from backup, how to reconnect media, and how to use Batch Capture.

---

1 Start **Final Cut**, if it isn't running already, and open **Offline Project**. This is the same file you used earlier in Chapter 14, except all the clips are now offline.

NOTE:

Definitions: Offline vs. Online

There are *two* definitions of each of these words, depending upon context. To help you keep them straight, here they are:

Offline (1) A low-resolution version of a videotape format, used in the initial stages of editing to reduce file space requirements. For example, DV is used as the offline file format for editing a DigiBetacam master.

Online (1) A high-resolution version of a videotape format, used to create the final, high-quality version of a project for release.

Offline (2) A clip in Final Cut that is not connected to a media file on the disk, either because the media file has not been captured, or because the media file has been moved or renamed, thus breaking the link between the clip in Final Cut and the media file on disk.

Online (2) A clip in Final Cut that is connected to its media file on disk.

When a clip is offline, meaning it can't find the media file on your hard disk that it is linked to, it shows up in the Browser with a red line through the icon.

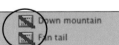

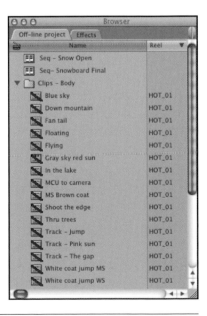

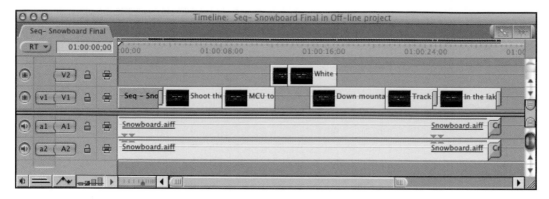

An offline clip in the Timeline shows up as white.

If the clips are offline because the media is missing—for instance, an old project where the media files no longer exist—you need to redigitize the media back into your computer in a process called **recapture**.

2 To do this, select the clips you want to recapture, and choose **File > Batch Capture**. This is where having accurate reel names and timecode makes this process dead easy.

3 The **Batch Capture** window opens. The pop-up menu is set to capture all selected clips. The default handle setting is **0:00**. I always want handles, so I set this to **3:00**. Then click **OK**.

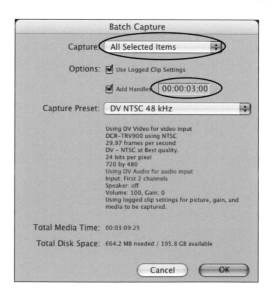

4 This dialog prompts you to put in a tape for capture. Notice that it uses the reel names you entered for each clip. Put in the correct tape and click **Continue**. Final Cut starts at the beginning of the tape and captures clips as fast as it can cue the tape.

Sigh…I love this part.

This batch capture system works great as long as your reel names are correct and there are no breaks in timecode. If you forgot to make sure your reel names are accurate (something you will only do once) or have lots of timecode breaks, you will need to recapture each of these clips manually. And that's such a painful process, I don't even want to think about it. It would be easier to just start over.

In this case, though, the media files for this project are on your hard disk, so you just need to reconnect them. Reconnection is necessary whenever Final Cut loses track of a media file. Normally, it doesn't lose track. However, if you move a media file, rename the file, rename the folder the media is stored in, or move a folder containing media files, Final Cut will need your help to find and reconnect it.

---

5 **NEW▶** Reconnecting Media has been significantly improved in FCP 5. To get started, select *all* the offline files in the Browser. This allows it to reconnect files in the Browser and Timeline in one pass. Selecting files tells FCP what to look for.

---

6 Choose **File > Reconnect Media**. The dialog lists all the selected files that are offline. (This dialog also appears when you first start a project and FCP can't find the files in it.)

The three buttons in the upper-right corner allow you to select what type of file you want to reconnect: **Offline**, **Online**, and **Render**. For the record, I only reconnect an online file when I've made changes to it outside of Final Cut, or if I mistakenly connected the wrong media file to a clip. Further, I never reconnect render files, I just re-render them. It's faster. So, that means I'm almost always reconnecting offline files.

Naturally, when I first started working with FCP 5, I figured that since the files were missing, I should **Locate** them. Wrong. Clicking the **Locate** button starts a manual search, where I need to show FCP exactly where the file is stored. This is too much work. **Search** is *much* better!

7 By checking the **Search Single Location** box, then telling FCP to look in your **Final Cut Pro Documents**

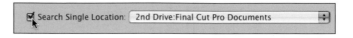

folder (or wherever your media is stored), Final Cut will look in just that one folder to find your media. This makes the process of reconnecting media *much* faster. If you don't check this box, FCP will search all connected hard disks until it either finds your media or gives up. Either way, clicking **Search** is the fastest way to find your missing media.

In all cases, FCP looks for your missing media by trying to find a media file whose name matches the clip name in the Browser. (The file name is the one you gave a clip when you first logged, or captured, the clip.) If it finds it, FCP selects it and displays the name in this dialog. If you've renamed your Browser clips, *un*check **Matched Name Only** and manually select the media file you want to reconnect to the Browser clip.

If there are other missing files stored in the same folder, checking **Reconnect All Files in Relative Path** allows Final Cut to automatically connect all the files it finds in the same folder—provided that their file names match the clip name in the Browser.

If you want to practice reconnecting media, all the missing files in this exercise are stored in the **FCP 5 HOT Files > Media > Snowboard** folder, except for the music, which is stored in **FCP 5 HOT Files > Media > Music**.

---

8 Reconnect the file by confirming that the name of the selected file (or the file you selected) in the upper portion of this dialog matches the name of the file Final Cut is displaying in the lower-left corner, then click **Choose**.

This dialog is also new with FCP 5. If you attempt to reconnect a file that doesn't precisely match the attributes of the clip in the Browser, FCP displays this dialog. I generally click **Continue** and see if the clip works. If not, then I'll go back and reconnect it. In this case, the reel number stored in the media file doesn't match the reel number of the clip in the Browser because of the exercise we did earlier in this chapter on changing reel numbers. So, in this case, an incorrect reel number is not a problem.

Because the files on the **Browser** are related to the clips in the **Timeline**, in what Final Cut calls a master – affiliate relationship, the offline **Timeline** clips should automatically relink once you finish linking clips in the **Browser**.

A **Browser** clip is automatically a *master* clip the first time it appears in the **Browser**. **Timeline** clips are *affiliate* clips. An affiliate clip is linked to the master clip via its metadata. In other words, **Timeline** clips are related to the **Browser** based on clip name, reel name, timecode, and auxiliary timecode. Changing one of these attributes in one file changes the same attribute in all related files.

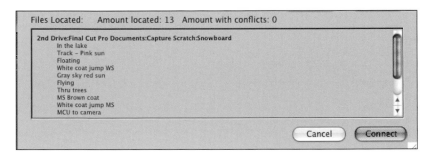

9 Once all clips are linked, this dialog appears, displaying all found clips. Click **Connect** to reconnect the media. And you are done.

Close this project, and don't save changes, since this project was designed to teach reconnection. Quit Final Cut, if you need a break. Otherwise, there's one more exercise left in this chapter.

6 | Exploring the Media Manager

The Media Manager is one of those tools that should just work. As it is, it's darn near inscrutable, with cryptic check boxes, convoluted documentation, and performance that's somewhat less than breathtaking.

The principal reasons for using Media Manager is to move media without breaking project links, delete some, but not all, of the media in a project, or to prepare a project for recapture using higher-resolution media (from "off-line" to "on-line").

In this exercise, you'll get an introduction to the Media Manager, along with an understanding of when and how to use it. But, if I could offer two words of advice, they would be "be careful."

What the Media Manager Does

Menu Choice	Action	Risk Level
Copy	Copies all selected media from wherever it is to wherever you specify. *Option:* Delete Unused Project Media.	Low
Move	Moves all selected media from wherever it is to wherever you specify. *Option:* Delete Unused Project Media.	Medium
Use Existing	Removes all project media that is not being used in whatever sequences are selected. Warning: Once this process starts, your source files are deleted. If you cancel this operation *prior* to its completion, both source and modified files may be gone. *Option:* Delete Unused Project Media.	High
Recompress	Converts existing media from its current compression format to whatever you specify. Recompress will *not* convert between NTSC and PAL.	Low
Create Offline	Converts a current project into a new project, allowing all clips to be recaptured at a different, generally higher, resolution. *Option:* Delete Unused Project Media.	Low

1 Open **Chapter 14 Lesson**, if it isn't already open. Select **Seq - Snowboard Final** in the **Browser**. Then, choose **File > Media Manager**. This is a key step, you *must* select what you want to manage before opening Media Manager.

The Final Cut manual spends 20 pages discussing the Media Manager. I've written an article, posted on my Web site, that takes seven pages just to illustrate **Create Offline**. (You'll learn more about my Web site, and other resources available to you, in the Appendix, *"Additional Resources."*) In this exercise, I want to illustrate the two most popular uses of Media Manager: Making a copy of all your project files onto a single hard disk (for example, to take to another Final Cut system), and moving all your project files from wherever they are into a single location (for example, moving from a collection of FireWire drives to a single RAID).

These two operations are very similar. The first is a **Copy**, which makes a copy of all your files in a new location, and the second is a **Move**, which moves all your files into a single location. For both of these, you'll need the Media Manager. The following table explains the relationship between what you select and what Media Manager does.

Media Manager Selection Range	
Select	**Media Manager Processes**
Everything in Browser	The entire project, all sequences, all files
One or more sequences	Only media associated with selected sequences
A section of the Timeline	Only media associated with the Timeline selection
One or more selected clips	In the Browser, Timeline, or Viewer, only the selected clip or clips

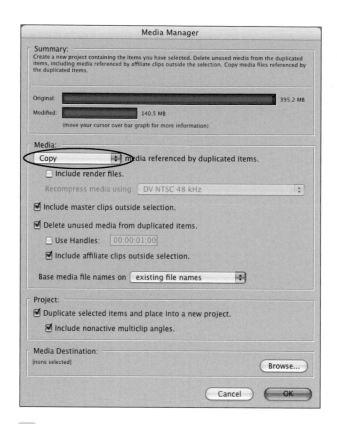

2 The top green bar illustrates how much space is used by the currently selected project. The bottom green bar illustrates how much space will be used by the project after you are done using **Media Manager**.

The pop-up menu determines what operation it will perform. If you choose **Copy**, all files will be *copied* to their new location, leaving the original project and files intact. If you choose **Move**, all files will be *moved* to their new location, with the ability to create a new project, where all links to moved media are correct.

Delete unused media from duplicated items will not copy or move media that is *not* part of the sequence you've selected. This is the principal benefit of using the Media Manager: it copies or moves only the material you want then resets the links in your project so Final Cut knows where to find the moved media. This can save a tremendous amount of space. For instance, in this example, copying **Seq – Snowboard Final** and deleting unused media saves over 200 MB of hard disk space. (The dark blue area at the end of the top bar indicates the space taken by render files, which I never move—I always re-render.)

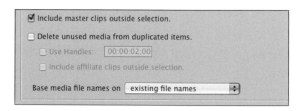

In concept, this is good. However, if you have another sequence in your project that you need but didn't include as a selected sequence, and it uses media that is also not included as a part of one of the selected sequences, the media for that nonselected sequence will be deleted (or not copied). Further, if you decide later to add a shot that you had previously digitized, it won't be there because it was not part of the original selected sequence.

If you do decide to delete unused media, be sure to provide handles; I try to use a minimum of **2:00**.

The Media Manager provides very useful media management, but it can delete media if you are not careful. Additionally, the language of the check boxes is seriously oblique. I've been using Final Cut for over six years, and I have a hard time understanding what **Include Master Clips Outside Selection** or **Include Affiliate Clips Outside Selection** mean in actual English.

If you check **Include Master Clips Outside Selection** Final Cut will include other clips in the **Browser** that have In and Out points set, in addition to the clips in the selected sequence. It is checked by default. For copying or moving, I suggest leaving this checked.

Include Affiliate Clips Outside Selection means that Final Cut will include other clips outside your selection if it has either an **In** or an **Out**, or it falls between two unconnected clips derived from the same master clip, or it appears as an affiliate clip in another sequence. For this to be active, **Include Master Clips Outside Selection** must also be checked.

NEW ▶ Duplicate selected items and place into a new project creates a duplicate of the current project, and gives you the ability to include nonactive multiclip angles. Check this if you plan to re-edit the multiclip and want

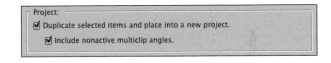

retain all the angles, Leave this unchecked if you want to "flatten" a multiclip into only the angles you are using in your edited sequence. Flattening saves space, but it makes re-editing a multiclip impossible.

---

3 Once you have the settings in place, click **Browse** to select where you want the new project and media files to be saved.

---

4 I've found it best to create a new folder; in this case, I called it **Project copy**. Final Cut will put all the files into that one folder, making them easy to find or move after this process is complete.

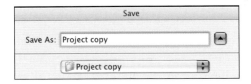

Click **OK** to begin the process.

---

5 If there is insufficient media for your handles, this dialog pops up. Generally, it is OK to click **OK**.

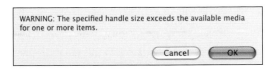

Final Cut provides an ongoing status report as it processes your files. It is really important to let it finish. Canceling in the middle can cause all kinds of problems. Because you are copying huge files, this process can take a

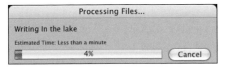

long, long time. Also, Apple warns that you should leave FCP in the foreground. Otherwise files may become unlinked.

When Final Cut is done, it has created a new project and **Media** folder. Inside the **Media** folder are all the modified clips from the selected sequence or project. Even if you stored your media in multiple folders before, all the media is now combined into this one folder.

At this point, this is just like any other Final Cut project. You can open it and start editing.

The Media Manager is surprisingly complex and difficult to master. If you plan to use it, create a small test project and practice. Make a point to read the user's manual, thoroughly, before using it. The Media Manager can do a great job of getting rid of unneeded media and recovering hard disk space, but, good golly, it's tricky.

---

6 That's it. You're done. Save what you want to save and quit Final Cut.

Helpful Keyboard Shortcuts

Shortcut	Action
Cmd+1	Selects the Viewer
Cmd+2	Selects the Canvas
Cmd+3	Selects the Timeline
Cmd+4	Selects the Browser
Shift+Cmd+S	Saves a project file, using a new name (Save As)
Ctrl+C	Opens the Batch Capture window
Cmd+8	Opens the Log and Capture window

Summary

Whew! You've taken a project from beginning to end—from planning through to archiving—and learned a ton about Final Cut along the way. In the appendix, I'll provide you with additional resources you can use to make the most of Final Cut Pro 5.

A

Appendix: Additional Resources

This appendix provides a variety of additional resources to help you get the most out of your Final Cut Pro 5 system.

Tutorial Movies on the Final Cut Pro 5 HOT DVD-ROM

Sometimes, it's a whole lot easier to understand a concept if you can see it in action. This is why I've created a series of movies illustrating key Final Cut concepts and included them on the **Final Cut Pro 5 HOT DVD**. These movies cover every major area of Final Cut from capturing video to outputting, from editing clips into a sequence to creating effects.

Best of all, these movies use the same media as the exercises in this book. This makes it easy for you to practice these techniques later on your own system.

For a complete list of all the movies and a brief description, please read **ReadMe.txt** on the **Final Cut Pro 5 HOT DVD**.

Troubleshooting Tips

Editing is stressful enough, without having to worry about troubleshooting software. Sadly, though, Final Cut is not perfect, and sometimes problems pop up. This section is designed to give you some tips on how to get things back to normal.

Assuming you don't have a hardware failure, there are three principal types of problems:

- Upgrading problems
- Operating system problems
- Final Cut problems

This section provides remedies for all three.

Upgrade Problems

More clients get into more problems due to upgrades than any other issue. Here's my basic rule: Wait *at least* 30 days after a new version of anything is released before upgrading.

Why? Because video editing is about the most taxing task you can perform with a personal computer. Unlike word processing or using a database, video editing pushes every system element to the limit: operating system, CPU, RAM, hard disks, data buses, graphics card, monitor, system I/O—everything. If even one part of your system is not running perfectly, you can't edit.

Software is software. Apple works really hard to release high-quality tools. However, until those tools get released in the real world, it's impossible to check every possible combination of hardware, software, and peripherals.

So, you need to ask yourself: is your role to test software or is your role to edit? If you like being the first one on the block with the latest version of anything, and you can afford to have your edit system down for a while because of incompatibilities, then upgrade as soon as each new version is announced.

I had a client do that when OS X 10.3 and FCP 4.0 were announced. The problem was that, although FCP worked under 10.3, the hard disk drivers for the client's RAID did not. Nor did their capture card. So this client was dead in the water for four *weeks* waiting for other, crucial, third-party vendors to update their software.

If, on the other hand, your goal is to edit, then wait a while before upgrading. This is *especially* true if your system is working fine now. Make sure that every element of your editing system is approved for the latest version of the operating system and Final Cut. When OS 10.3 came out, I made a list of everything that needed to be upgraded in order for Final Cut to work in a professional setting (items marked with an asterisk are not generally needed for DV video):

- Apple firmware
- System RAM
- Operating system

- SCSI or Fibre Channel I/O cards *

- SCSI software drivers *

- Hard disk drivers

- QuickTime

- Final Cut Pro

- Other Final Cut applications

- Third-party Final Cut plug-ins

- Capture card drivers *

- Device (machine) control drivers *

That's 12 different subsystems of your computer, not all of which are controlled by Apple, that need to work together for you to edit. By the way, this list is in the order you should upgrade your software. If you upgrade out of order, there's a good chance your system will not work properly.

So, my advice is once you've got your system operating properly, turn off Software Upgrade so it doesn't keep beeping you when new versions are announced. Be cautious about upgrading. Wait for new versions to prove themselves before you upgrade. That way when you do add the latest version, everything should go smoothly and you'll have a minimum of downtime.

Solving Operating System Problems

If you are seeing the Spinning Beach Ball of Death (SBOD) far more than you'd like, it is generally not a Final Cut problem. More often, it is a problem with the operating system. And the most common problem with the operating system is blown, or corrupted, disk directories.

Unix is a wonderful operating system. However, Apple needed to tweak it to improve its performance. And one of those tweaks was to load disk directories into memory.

A disk directory is like the card catalog in the library. The books on the shelves represent the files on your hard disk. The easiest way to find a book is to go to the card catalog and look it up. Because the cards are alphabetized, finding exactly the book you want is fast and easy.

However, there's a ghost that lives in this library and every so often it sneaks down to the card catalog, pulls out the drawers, and scatters the cards all around the floor. All the cards are still there, but they are no longer in any order. The books are still on the shelf, but with the cards all disorganized, the books are a lot harder to find.

Now, when you want to find a book, you need to go through every card, one by one, to see if it is the book you want. You can do it; it just takes longer.

This is, essentially, the problem with blown disk directories. The operating system only updates disk directories when you shut down your computer. Prior to that, whenever you create, delete, move, or rename a file, those changes are kept in memory. If your computer crashes, those changes will not be written properly to the disk.

Here's a three-step routine that can help fix this problem:

1. Restart (or start up) your computer while holding down the **Shift** key.

2. Continue holding down the **Shift** key while the gear spins on the gray screen until the blue screen appears. (It will take longer than usual for the blue screen to appear. Don't panic.) When the blue screen appears, let go of the **Shift** key. (You'll know you have done this properly when the white box in the middle of the blue screen displays the words "Safe Boot" at the bottom.)

3. Once your system fully boots up, restart it, again, this time without holding down any keys.

This process is called doing a **Safe Boot**. Make a habit to do this once a week.

When you are booting your computer in Safe Boot, you are actually doing two things: you are repairing a significant majority of disk directory problems, and you are also booting your system with a minimalist version of OS X. This limited OS is perfect for system maintenance, but you cannot run your system this way.

If you haven't run this routine, you'll be amazed at the performance benefit you get: your system will boot faster and shut down faster, and you will see the Spinning Beach Ball of Death far less frequently.

However, if your directories are really screwed up, Safe Boot won't fix them. For that you will need a more powerful utility. The best I've found, and recommend highly, is *Disk Warrior X* by Alsoft (www.alsoft.com). It is excellent. I use it constantly when maintaining my clients' systems, and encourage all of them to buy it.

The next big problem you will run into are corrupted file permissions. Every file in Unix has 12 "ownership states" that determine who has permission to read to a file, write to a file, read *and* write to a file, or who is not allowed to use the file at all.

In Unix, the operating system and applications are users, just like you and me. And, sometimes, files get confused as to who they can talk to and who they can't. With well over 100,000 files in OS X, that means there are over 1.2 million permission states that can get confused.

To straighten all this out, Apple created **Disk Utility**. I recommend you run this once a week also. Here's how:

1 With no applications running, except the **Finder**, open **Applications > Utilities** and open **Disk Utility**.

Disk Utility

2 When **Disk Utility** starts, select the *name* of the hard disk (not the line with the numbers) that contains your operating system. This is most often, but not always, called **Macintosh HD**.

3 The main **Disk Utility** window appears.

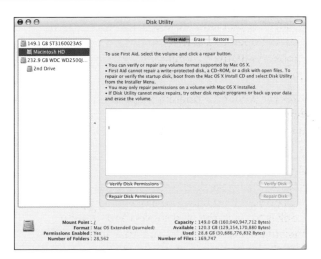

4 Be sure the **First Aid** tab is selected (colored blue).

5 Click **Repair Disk Permissions**. (There is no advantage to verifying permissions, so just go ahead and repair them.) Depending upon the size of your hard disk and the speed of your computer, this repair process will take between 2 and 10 minutes.

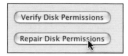

6 When the utility says **Permissions repair complete**, you may quit. The more lines of text that are displayed in this window, the more likely you were to have problems.

Repairing permissions for "Macintosh HD"
Determining correct file permissions.
The privileges have been verified or repaired on the selected volume

Permissions repair complete

I've found it easiest to run **Safe Boot** and **Repair Permissions** at the same time. That way, all my maintenance gets done together. I run them once a week, *or* when I upgrade the operating system, *or* when I upgrade any application, *or* after a crash. Since I've been running them regularly, my operating system problems have significantly diminished.

One last note. Repairing permissions is basically designed to fix problems with the operating system and Apple applications. Most other software publishers don't use this system. Although I've found this technique to be very useful in working with Final Cut, this won't help much, if at all, in solving problems with non-Apple applications.

There's one more System Preference that you need to change from it's default settings: **Energy Saver**.

Energy Saver tells your computer to shut down the display and the hard disks when there is no activity. However, the computer considers activity to be mouse movement or keyboard clicks. It does not consider what your hard disk or applications are doing to be activity.

Normally, this is not a problem. By default, after 15 minutes of non-activity, your computer turns the screen and hard disk off to save energy.

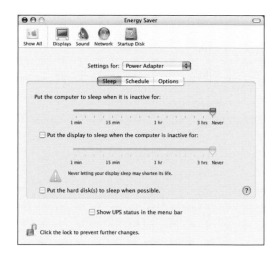

However, if you are trying to export a half-hour program, which involves no keyboard or mouse movement, half-way through your program, your computer suddenly puts everything to sleep! This leads to much gnashing of teeth and throwing of small objects.

To prevent damage to your psyche, or the surroundings, set Energy Saver to match the settings in this screen shot. Make *especially* sure to uncheck **Put the hard disk(s) to sleep when possible**.

Solving Final Cut Problems

Final Cut is a wonderful program with an Achilles heel: its preferences files. These preferences are more than the settings you create; they affect the very core of how Final Cut edits and plays media. They exist at the very deepest levels of the application, and sometimes they go south.

Once your preferences files are corrupted, for instance after a Final Cut crash, your only alternative is to trash your preferences files and let Final Cut rebuild them automatically when it restarts.

Although you should run the Safe Boot and Repair Permissions routines frequently, you should only trash Final Cut preferences when the application is not working. This is because trashing preferences actually removes elements of Final Cut and replaces them with system defaults. The following list is not exhaustive, but here's what gets lost, or reset, when you trash preferences:

- Favorite effects (deleted)
- Favorite motions (deleted)
- Favorite transitions (deleted)
- Default transitions (reset)
- Window layouts that are not saved to disk (reset)
- Browser layouts that are not saved to disk (reset)

- Timeline layouts that are not saved to disk (reset)
- Customized buttons that are not saved to disk (deleted)
- Customized keyboard layouts that are not saved to disk (deleted)
- Capture card settings (reset)
- Scratch disk settings (reset)
- Audio/video settings (reset)
- User preferences (reset)
- System settings (reset)

Trashing Final Cut preferences does not, repeat *not*, endanger any of your media files, nor affect any sequences. But it does reset Final Cut back to a known-good default state, which is what you want. However, you then need to take a few minutes after trashing preferences to reconfigure the system preferences so they meet your specific needs.

There are four (4) Final Cut Pro preference files you need to trash. Here are the steps:

1. Make sure Final Cut Pro is *not* running.

2. Open your **Boot Disk** (the one in the upper-right corner of your **Desktop** that contains the **Applications** folder).

3. Open your **User** folder.

4. Open the **Home** folder (the folder with the picture of a house on it).

5. Open the **Library** folder (note, this is *not* the **Library** folder in your boot disk).

6. Open the **Preferences** folder.

7. Locate and trash **com.apple.FinalCutPro.plist**.

8. Scroll down and open the folder **Final Cut Pro User Data**.

9. Locate and trash **Final Cut Pro 5.0 Prefs**.

10. Locate and trash **Final Cut Pro Obj Cache**.

11. Locate and trash **Final Cut Pro Prof Cache**.

12. Empty the **Trash**.

Remember to only trash files, never trash folders. Also, trash all four preference files at once, not just one or two.

Oh, one other thing. Those dropped frame warnings that you get at the most inopportune times are, most often, caused when the hard disk cannot play back video at a fast enough rate.

Running these three procedures—Safe Boot, rebuild permissions, and trash preferences—should, more often than not, solve that problem.

Other Things to Check

Here are some other things to check, from my Web site article, *Troubleshooting Your FCP System*:

- **If your video playback stutters:** You are zoomed in on the Canvas or Viewer. If you see scroll bars in the **Canvas** or **Viewer**, select the window and type **Shift+Z** (or choose **View > Level > Fit in Window**). This resizes your image for smoothest playback.

- **If you can't see video on your external NTSC monitor:** Make sure *both* the **Viewer** and **Canvas** windows are set to **Fit to Window**. Then make sure **View > External Video** is set to **All Frames**.

- **If you've imported a still image, but can't see it on the Timeline:** Make sure all imported images are RGB. CMYK images (frequently used in graphic design and printing) won't display in Final Cut.

- **If you don't have any audio:** Choose **View > Audio Playback** and set it to **Audio Follows Video.** Then, choose **View > Video Playback** and set it to **None** if you are viewing on your computer monitor, or **FireWire** if you are viewing on your deck or camera.

- **If your audio is crackly or full of pops:** You have probably imported an MP3 or AAC file. Final Cut HATES compressed audio. Re-read the audio chapter on how to convert compressed audio into an AIFF.

- **If audio and video are out of sync:** If there are red flags at the start of your clip, **Ctrl+click** the **red flag** of your video and choose **Move Into Sync** from the shortcut menu. If there are no red flags at the start of your clip, choose **View > Video Playback** and **View > Audio Playback** and make sure the video and audio playback are both set to the same point. For instance, monitoring video via **FireWire** and audio via **Built-In Audio** will automatically be out of sync by around six frames.

For the complete troubleshooting article (all 28 pages of it) go to **http://www.larryjordan.biz/ articles/lj_trouble.html**.

Helpful Software

There are lots of programs that make working with Final Cut fun—from fascinating LiveType animations and Soundtrack loops to tons and tons of special-effects plug-ins.

However, because we are in the Troubleshooting section, here are seven software packages I've found, and use, that keep my system running smoothly:

- **Disk Warrior X**, published by Alsoft (**www.alsoft.com**). If you buy only one OS X utility, this is the one to buy. It does only one thing—fix and optimize disk directories. But it does it really, really well.

- **FCP Rescue**, written by Anders Holck (**http://fcprescue.andersholck.com**). This free utility provides instant backup, restore, and removal of Final Cut Pro's preferences files. This utility helps you if Final Cut Pro crashes and corrupts its preferences files. It is also very useful if other editors use your login, and you want to be able to go back to your personal settings afterwards. It has a very simple interface.

- **TechTool Pro**, published by Micromat (**www.micromat.com**), is a great general-purpose maintenance and repair utility for the Mac. I especially like its hardware diagnostics.

- **FCP Project**, written by Brian Summa (**http://homepage.mac.com/proeditor/**). This free utility was written after Brian read my article on how to organize FCP files, which I presented in more detail in Chapter 1, "*Get Organized.*" First developed for an advertising agency, this utility provides a fast way to automatically create all the folders related to a project.

- **Macaroni**, published by Atomic Bird Software (**http://www.atomicbird.com**), is a tool that handles regular maintenance for Mac OS X, including the Mac OS X repair privileges process as well as Unix-style maintenance. Without Macaroni, some of these tasks normally run in the middle of the night, and don't get run unless you leave your Mac on all night. Others don't run automatically at all, and won't happen unless you remember when they're due.

- **MacJanitor**, written by Brian Hill (**http://personalpages.tds.net/~brian_hill/macjanitor.html**), is a freeware program, similar to Macaroni. I run Macaroni, but others are quite happy with MacJanitor. Either one can help keep your system running smoothly.

- **FCP logging template**, written by me (**http://www.larryjordan.biz/goodies.html**), is a free Excel worksheet that I use for logging tapes. For me, using this file is much faster than using the built-in logger of Final Cut. An additional benefit is that you have an Excel listing of every shot on your tape. I've been using this for years. Instructions are in the template.

Setting an External Editor

Round-tripping between FCP and other applications is an amazing timesaver—one that I discussed in chapters covering LiveType, Soundtrack Pro, Motion, and PhotoShop. To get this to work, especially with non-Apple applications, you need to set the External Editor settings in System Settings.

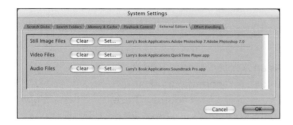

Choose **Final Cut Pro 5 > System Settings** and click the **External Editor** tab, where you set your **External Editors** preferences.

In Final Cut Pro 5, you can use external editors for three different types of files:

Still Image Files: Selects a program for editing images, both still frames and imported graphics. Popular programs you can use here include Adobe Photoshop, Macromedia Fireworks, and Graphics Converter. My personal setting is Photoshop.

Video Files: Selects a program for editing video files. Popular programs you can use for this option include Apple QuickTime Player, Discreet Combustion, Pinnacle Systems Commotion, and Adobe After Effects. I rarely do fancy video file editing, so QuickTime Player works fine.

Audio Files: Selects a program for editing audio files. Popular programs include Soundtrack Pro, QuickTime Player, and Bias Inc.'s Peak. Due to how ProTools structures a session, you can't use ProTools for this option. My personal setting is Soundtrack Pro.

Once you've tried using an external editor to quickly "round-trip" a clip, you'll be amazed at how fast you can make changes.

Online Resources

There is a wealth of online resources available to the Final Cut editor. However, here are several that I want to point out that I've found especially useful:

- **Lynda.com (www.lynda.com).** Lynda.com offers online video-based tutorials on Apple Compressor, LiveType, Soundtrack, Garage Band, OS X, previous versions of Final Cut, as well as other applications such as Adobe Photoshop, Illustrator, After Effects, Macromedia Flash, Discreet 3ds Max, and other ancillary applications that are a valuable part of your video production toolkit.

- **My Web site (www.larryjordan.biz).** I started this Web site to provide training and information on Final Cut that I couldn't find anywhere else. It has grown into a full-fledged Final Cut Pro information and support resource with dozens and dozens of free articles, techniques, and how-to tips. I also publish a free, monthly Final Cut Pro newsletter packed with tips and techniques. Visit my Web site to subscribe.

- **Apple's Final Cut Pro Web site (www.apple.com/finalcutstudio).** News and tech support on Final Cut, and all the Studio applications, from Apple itself. Need I say more?

- **L. A. Final Cut Pro User Group (www.lafcpug.org).** Everything you ever wanted to know about Final Cut. Excellent forums for getting your questions answered.

- **Ken Stone.net (www.kenstone.net).** Everything you never knew you never knew about Final Cut. Another outstanding site. An incredibly strong international viewership, with excellent forums for getting questions answered.

- **FinalCutProPlanet**
  (**www.finalcutproplanet.com**). Arguably the oldest FCP site, predating everything else listed here, started by the venerable (and esteemed) Josh Mellicker. Their forums and training programs are excellent.

- **Ripple Training** (**www.rippletraining.com**). Great training resources from one of Apple's Lead Trainers: Steve Martin.

- **Creative Cow.net** (**www.creativecow.net**). This site covers virtually every known creative tool. Worth visiting on a regular basis simply for the breadth of tools it covers.

Other Books from Lynda.com

Did you enjoy the hands-on training format of this book? There are other Hands-On Training books on many other subjects. Visit **www.lynda.com** to learn more! See the ads in the back of this book as well.

Apple-Certified Training

As an Apple-Certified Trainer, I would be remiss if I didn't recommend taking a least one Apple-Certified Training course. These hands-on training sessions, taught by an experienced Final Cut instructor, can often help you understand portions of Final Cut that are particularly hazy.

For more information, go to **www.apple.com/software/pro/training/**.

One Last Word

I've had a great deal of fun writing this book. It gave me the chance to think through how I edit and how Final Cut works, so that I could make the best possible recommendations to you.

And, although perfection may be unattainable, I've tried hard to make this book accurate. Just as Final Cut will continue to change and grow, my hope is for this book to follow suit, providing you all the latest tips and techniques to make the most of Final Cut.

Feel free to email me suggestions or questions regarding the book—especially if you find something that's wrong. I'll fix it in the next edition. You can reach me at **fcp5hot@lynda.com.** The support url for this book is **http://www.lynda.com/info/books/fcp5/**.

In the meantime, come visit my Web site— **www.larryjordan.biz**—and while you're there, sign up for my free monthly FCP newsletter. Then, be sure to send me a note when you get nominated for an Oscar…or Emmy…or Clio.

Because when you need to tell your story, Final Cut helps you bring it to life. Edit well.

Index

D

N

O

P

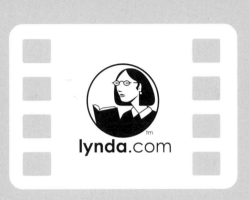

THIS SOFTWARE LICENSE AGREEMENT CONSTITUTES AN AGREEMENT BETWEEN YOU AND, LYNDA.COM, INC. YOU SHOULD CAREFULLY READ THE FOLLOWING TERMS AND CONDITIONS. COPYING THIS SOFTWARE TO YOUR MACHINE OR OTHERWISE REMOVING OR USING THE SOFTWARE INDICATES YOUR ACCEPTANCE OF THESE TERMS AND CONDITIONS. IF YOU DO NOT AGREE TO BE BOUND BY THE PROVISIONS OF THIS LICENSE AGREEMENT, YOU SHOULD PROMPTLY DELETE THE SOFTWARE FROM YOUR MACHINE.

TERMS AND CONDITIONS:

1. GRANT OF LICENSE. In consideration of payment of the License Fee, which was a part of the price you paid for this product, LICENSOR grants to you (the "Licensee") a non-exclusive right to use the Software (all parts and elements of the data contained on the accompanying DVD-ROM are hereinafter referred to as the "Software"), along with any updates or upgrade releases of the Software for which you have paid on a single computer only (i.e., with a single CPU) at a single location, all as more particularly set forth and limited below. LICENSOR reserves all rights not expressly granted to you as Licensee in this License Agreement.

2. OWNERSHIP OF SOFTWARE. The license granted herein is not a sale of the original Software or of any copy of the Software. As Licensee, you own only the rights to use the Software as described herein and the magnetic or other physical media on which the Software is originally or subsequently recorded or fixed. LICENSOR retains title and ownership of the Software recorded on the original disk(s), as well as title and ownership of any subsequent copies of the Software irrespective of the form of media on or in which the Software is recorded or fixed. This license does not grant you any intellectual or other proprietary or other rights of any nature whatsoever in the Software.

3. USE RESTRICTIONS. As Licensee, you may use the Software only as expressly authorized in this License Agreement under the terms of paragraph 4. You may physically transfer the Software from one computer to another provided that the Software is used on only a single computer at any one time. You may not: (i) electronically transfer the Software from one computer to another over a network; (ii) make the Software available through a time-sharing service, network of computers, or other multiple user arrangement; (iii) distribute copies of the Software or related written materials to any third party, whether for sale or otherwise; (iv) modify, adapt, translate, reverse engineer, decompile, disassemble, or prepare any derivative work based on the Software or any element thereof; (v) make or distribute, whether for sale or otherwise, any hard copy or printed version of any of the Software nor any portion thereof nor any work of yours containing the Software or any component thereof; (vi) use any of the Software nor any of its components in any other work.

4. THIS IS WHAT YOU CAN AND CANNOT DO WITH THE SOFTWARE. Even though in the preceding paragraph and elsewhere LICENSOR has restricted your use of the Software, the following is the only thing you can do with the Software and the various elements of the Software: THE ARTWORK CONTAINED ON THIS DVD-ROM MAY NOT BE USED IN ANY MANNER WHATSOEVER OTHER THAN TO VIEW THE SAME ON YOUR COMPUTER, OR POST TO YOUR PERSONAL, NON-COMMERCIAL WEB SITE FOR EDUCATIONAL PURPOSES ONLY. THIS MATERIAL IS SUBJECT TO ALL OF THE RESTRICTION PROVISIONS OF THIS SOFTWARE LICENSE. SPECIFICALLY BUT NOT IN LIMITATION OF THESE RESTRICTIONS, YOU MAY NOT DISTRIBUTE, RESELL OR TRANSFER THIS PART OF THE SOFTWARE NOR ANY OF YOUR DESIGN OR OTHER WORK CONTAINING ANY OF THE SOFTWARE on this DVD-ROM, ALL AS MORE PARTICULARLY RESTRICTED IN THE WITHIN SOFTWARE LICENSE.

5. COPY RESTRICTIONS. The Software and accompanying written materials are protected under United States copyright laws. Unauthorized copying and/or distribution of the Software and/or the related written materials is expressly forbidden. You may be held legally responsible for any copyright infringement that is caused, directly or indirectly, by your failure to abide by the terms of this License Agreement. Subject to the terms of this License Agreement and if the software is not otherwise copy protected, you may make one copy of the Software for backup purposes only. The copyright notice and any other proprietary notices which were included in the original Software must be reproduced and included on any such backup copy.

6. TRANSFER RESTRICTIONS. The license herein granted is personal to you, the Licensee. You must not transfer the Software nor any of its components or elements to anyone else, nor may you sell, lease, loan, sublicense, assign, or otherwise dispose of the Software nor any of its components or elements without the express written consent of LICENSOR, which consent may be granted or withheld at LICENSOR's sole discretion.

7. TERMINATION. The license herein granted hereby will remain in effect until terminated. This license will terminate automatically without further notice from LICENSOR in the event of the violation of any of the provisions hereof. As Licensee, you agree that upon such termination you will promptly destroy any and all copies of the Software which remain in your possession and, upon request, will certify to such destruction in writing to LICENSOR.

8. LIMITATION AND DISCLAIMER OF WARRANTIES. a) THE SOFTWARE AND RELATED WRITTEN MATERIALS, INCLUDING ANY INSTRUCTIONS FOR USE, ARE PROVIDED ON AN "AS IS" BASIS, WITHOUT WARRANTY OF ANY KIND, EXPRESS OR IMPLIED. THIS DISCLAIMER OF WARRANTY EXPRESSLY INCLUDES, BUT IS NOT LIMITED TO, ANY IMPLIED WARRANTIES OF MERCHANTABILITY AND/OR FITNESS FOR A PARTICULAR PURPOSE. NO WARRANTY OF ANY KIND IS MADE AS TO WHETHER OR NOT THIS SOFTWARE INFRINGES UPON ANY RIGHTS OF ANY OTHER THIRD PARTIES. NO ORAL OR WRITTEN INFORMATION GIVEN BY LICENSOR, ITS SUPPLIERS, DISTRIBUTORS, DEALERS, EMPLOYEES, OR AGENTS, SHALL CREATE OR OTHERWISE ENLARGE THE SCOPE OF ANY WARRANTY HEREUNDER. LICENSEE ASSUMES THE ENTIRE RISK AS TO THE QUALITY AND THE PERFORMANCE OF SUCH SOFTWARE.

SHOULD THE SOFTWARE PROVE DEFECTIVE, YOU, AS LICENSEE (AND NOT LICENSOR, ITS SUPPLIERS, DISTRIBUTORS, DEALERS OR AGENTS), ASSUME THE ENTIRE COST OF ALL NECESSARY CORRECTION, SERVICING, OR REPAIR. b) LICENSOR warrants the disk(s) on which this copy of the Software is recorded or fixed to be free from defects in materials and workmanship, under normal use and service, for a period of ninety (90) days from the date of delivery as evidenced by a copy of the applicable receipt. LICENSOR hereby limits the duration of any implied warranties with respect to the disk(s) to the duration of the express warranty. This limited warranty shall not apply if the disk(s) have been damaged by unreasonable use, accident, negligence, or by any other causes unrelated to defective materials or workmanship. c) LICENSOR does not warrant that the functions contained in the Software will be uninterrupted or error free and Licensee is encouraged to test the Software for Licensee's intended use prior to placing any reliance thereon. All risk of the use of the Software will be on you, as Licensee. d) THE LIMITED WARRANTY SET FORTH ABOVE GIVES YOU SPECIFIC LEGAL RIGHTS AND YOU MAY ALSO HAVE OTHER RIGHTS, WHICH VARY FROM STATE TO STATE. SOME STATES DO NOT ALLOW THE LIMITATION OR EXCLUSION OF IMPLIED WARRANTIES OR OF INCIDENTAL OR CONSEQUEN-TIAL DAMAGES, SO THE LIMITATIONS AND EXCLUSIONS CONCERNING THE SOFTWARE AND RELATED WRITTEN MATERIALS SET FORTH ABOVE MAY NOT APPLY TO YOU.

9. LIMITATION OF REMEDIES. LICENSOR's entire liability and Licensee's exclusive remedy shall be the replacement of any disk(s) not meeting the limited warranty set forth in Section 8 above which is returned to LICENSOR with a copy of the applicable receipt within the warranty period. Any replacement disk(s) will be warranted for the remainder of the original warranty period or thirty (30) days, whichever is longer.

10. LIMITATION OF LIABILITY. IN NO EVENT WILL LICENSOR, OR ANYONE ELSE INVOLVED IN THE CREATION, PRODUCTION, AND/OR DELIVERY OF THIS SOFTWARE PRODUCT BE LIABLE TO LICENSEE OR ANY OTHER PERSON OR ENTITY FOR ANY DIRECT, INDIRECT, OR OTHER DAMAGES, INCLUDING, WITHOUT LIMITATION, ANY INTERRUPTION OF SERVICES, LOST PROFITS, LOST SAVINGS, LOSS OF DATA, OR ANY OTHER CONSEQUENTIAL, INCIDENTAL, SPECIAL, OR PUNITIVE DAMAGES, ARISING OUT OF THE PURCHASE, USE, INABILITY TO USE, OR OPERATION OF THE SOFTWARE, EVEN IF LICENSOR OR ANY AUTHORIZED LICENSOR DEALER HAS BEEN ADVISED OF THE POSSIBILITY OF SUCH DAMAGES. BY YOUR USE OF THE SOFTWARE, YOU ACKNOWLEDGE THAT THE LIMITATION OF LIABILITY SET FORTH IN THIS LICENSE WAS THE BASIS UPON WHICH THE SOFTWARE WAS OFFERED BY LICENSOR AND YOU ACKNOWLEDGE THAT THE PRICE OF THE SOFTWARE LICENSE WOULD BE HIGHER IN THE ABSENCE OF SUCH LIMITATION. SOME STATES DO NOT ALLOW THE LIMITATION OR EXCLUSION OF LIABILITY FOR INCIDENTAL OR CONSEQUENTIAL DAMAGES SO THE ABOVE LIMITATIONS AND EXCLUSIONS MAY NOT APPLY TO YOU.

11. UPDATES. LICENSOR, at its sole discretion, may periodically issue updates of the Software which you may receive upon request and payment of the applicable update fee in effect from time to time and in such event, all of the provisions of the within License Agreement shall apply to such updates.

12. EXPORT RESTRICTIONS. Licensee agrees not to export or re-export the Software and accompanying documentation (or any copies thereof) in violation of any applicable U.S. laws or regulations.

13. ENTIRE AGREEMENT. YOU, AS LICENSEE, ACKNOWLEDGE THAT: (i) YOU HAVE READ THIS ENTIRE AGREEMENT AND AGREE TO BE BOUND BY ITS TERMS AND CONDITIONS; (ii) THIS AGREEMENT IS THE COMPLETE AND EXCLUSIVE STATEMENT OF THE UNDERSTANDING BETWEEN THE PARTIES AND SUPERSEDES ANY AND ALL PRIOR ORAL OR WRITTEN COMMUNICA-TIONS RELATING TO THE SUBJECT MATTER HEREOF; AND (iii) THIS AGREE-MENT MAY NOT BE MODIFIED, AMENDED, OR IN ANY WAY ALTERED EXCEPT BY A WRITING SIGNED BY BOTH YOURSELF AND AN OFFICER OR AUTHO-RIZED REPRESENTATIVE OF LICENSOR.

14. SEVERABILITY. In the event that any provision of this License Agreement is held to be illegal or otherwise unenforceable, such provision shall be deemed to have been deleted from this License Agreement while the remaining provisions of this License Agreement shall be unaffected and shall continue in full force and effect.

15. GOVERNING LAW. This License Agreement shall be governed by the laws of the State of California applicable to agreements wholly to be performed therein and of the United States of America, excluding that body of the law related to conflicts of law. This License Agreement shall not be governed by the United Nations Convention on Contracts for the International Sale of Goods, the applica-tion of which is expressly excluded. No waiver of any breach of the provisions of this License Agreement shall be deemed a waiver of any other breach of this License Agreement.

16. RESTRICTED RIGHTS LEGEND. Use, duplication, or disclosure by the Government is subject to restrictions as set forth in subparagraph (c)(1)(ii) of the Rights in Technical Data and Computer Software clause at 48 CFR § 252.227-7013 and DFARS § 252.227-7013 or subparagraphs (c) (1) and (c)(2) of the Commercial Computer Software-Restricted Rights at 48 CFR § 52.227.19, as applicable. Contractor/manufacturer: LICENSOR: LYNDA.COM, INC., c/o PEACHPIT PRESS, 1249 Eighth Street, Berkeley, CA 94710.